D1252802

CATHOLIC RECORD SOCIETY PUBLICATIONS

(MONOGRAPH SERIES) VOLUME 5

This publication has been facilitated by a grant from the Scouloudi Foundation in association with the Institute of Historical Reasearch. In addition it has received a grant from the Marc Fitch Fund.

English Catholics of Parish and Town

1558 - 1778

A JOINT RESEARCH PROJECT OF THE
CATHOLIC RECORD SOCIETY AND
WOLVERHAMPTON UNIVERSITY

EDITOR: MARIE B. ROWLANDS

CATHOLIC RECORD SOCIETY

1999

ISBN 0 902832 18 2

Published 1999

Information about the Catholic Record Society and its publications may be obtained from the Hon. Secretary, c/o 114 Mount St, London W1X 6AH

Printed in Great Britain by
Hobbs the Printers Ltd, Totton, Hampshire SO40 3WX

CONTENTS

LIST OF TABLES

LIST OF FIGURES

LIST OF PHOTOGRAPHS

(All between pp. 176 and 177)

Photographs by the late John Beswick unless otherwise stated

1 The Word: Vulgate Bible (Paris, 1560), inscribed 'George Goodwin, March 1647', 'Andrew Bromwich' (d. 1701) and R[obert] H[eydon] (d. 1718). Oscott College (= Pullen, *Bible Collections at St Mary's, Oscott, c. 1472-c. 1850*, 1971, no. 158).

2 The Sacrament: recusant chalice from Overy House, Dorchester-on-Thames, now at St Birinus, Dorchester.

3 Butcher Row, St Clement's Lane, London: the house on the right corner was that used by John Gerard from 1602 to 1605. Print by J. T. Smith, 1798. *Guildhall Library, Corporation of London.*

4 Boscobel House, Shropshire: the priest-hole in the attic chapel or Cheese Room, used by Charles II on the night of 6-7 September 1651.

5 6 Pritchatt's Road, Edgbaston, Birmingham: the Franciscan Masshouse of about 1690, used until the building of St Peter's Broad Street, Birmingham, in 1786.

6 West Grinstead, Sussex: the attic chapel of about 1755: *Timothy J. McCann.*

7 Inventory (1696) of chapel furnishings at Harvington, Worcestershire, 'for the use of the Clergy that shall assist the poor of the Parish and Neighbourhood of Chaddesley Corbett'. Birmingham Archdiocesan Archives, C.155. *Birmingham R. C. Diocesan Trustees Regd.*

8 Printed circular letter of the Bishop of Lichfield to his clergy, 1767, with the reply of the vicar of Tipton, Staffordshire. Shaw-Hellier Collection by courtesy of Mr John Phillips. *John S. Allen.*

ACKNOWLEDGEMENTS

This volume was conceived, very appropriately, in a conversation in the Via Monserrato in Rome during a Catholic Record Society study holiday. It is the fruit of a partnership between the Catholic Record Society, who undertook the cost of publication, and Wolverhampton University, who undertook responsibility for the preparation of the volume as part of its research programme. Wolverhampton has been more than generous in its provision of research facilities and costs of travel of participants to meetings. It soon became evident that the book was to be a large and lusty child, and additional money required for maps and illustrations, and further funding was obtained by the generosity of the Marc Fitch Fund and the Scouloudi Foundation. Between them these four bodies have made the volume possible, and we are very grateful to them.

Individual researchers and enthusiasts all over the country have given generously of their knowledge of local Catholic history and some have undertaken research for the project which is incorporated into Parts One and Three. These people are acknowledged below. The most substantive contributions are also acknowledged in the appropriate footnotes. The goodwill and enthusiasm of nearly sixty people all giving so freely to the project has been remarkable. Special thanks are due to those who have worked with the project throughout its life and who have done so much to raise its quality by their patient and systematic work. These include Mrs A. Brooks, Mrs Catherine Coleman, Dr Sylvia Watts and three successive research assistants provided by Wolverhampton University, Mrs Pat Andrews, M.A., Mr Christopher Bennett, M.A. and Dr Jan Broadway. Others have worked in their local record offices on our behalf, especially Mrs Margaret Panikkar, Mrs L. Adams, Mr T. McVey, Mr D. Noble and Mr S. Price. Mrs Jane Oktemgil processed the text with admirable patience and Mr Martin Pollett rescued us many times when the computer did not understand us. Mr Mat Greenwood prepared the diagrams and illustrations. Dr Jan Broadway has prepared the text for publication.

I am most grateful to the contributors who were willing to travel great distances to meet and discuss the work, so that it should become a book rather than a collection of discrete essays. I am especially grateful to Michael Gandy who produced his contribution at very short notice indeed and with little time to meet the deadline. Much of the material we accumulated in only three years remains to be analysed and some important parts of the study proved to be impossible to complete in the time.

However, it seemed appropriate to place before the Society the work that has been done, so that it may be a statement of work in progress and provide an agenda for further research.

It is impossible to list all the people on whose local knowledge we have drawn, and the many members of the Catholic Family History Society whose individual family history researches have helped us build up our overall picture of Catholics of Parish and Town. We would like to thank them all. We also acknowledge and thank the following who have assisted in the research.

Mrs Christine Ackers
Mrs Elizabeth Adams
Miss Julia Bellord
Mrs Jane Bergin
Rev. George Bradley
Mrs Angela Brooks
Mr Alexander Chatwyn
Dr E. Clavering
Mrs Catherine Coleman
Rev. Ian Dickie
Mr John Fendley
Mr Robin Gard
Miss Joan Gardner
Mrs Margaret Gosling
Sister Gregory Kirkhus
Mr C. Howarth
Mr J.A.S. Lancaster
Mr David Lloyd
Mr Leonard Lockwood
Mr Tom McVey
Mr A.J. Noble
Mrs M. Panikkar
Mr Michael Parkyn
Mrs Sylvia Pinches
Mr Stephen Price
Miss Valerie Proctor
Mr Norman Reeves
Rev. W. Sharrock
Mr J. Smith
Mr C.F.R. Tiller
Rev. F. Tranter
Miss Jo-Ann Upton
Mr Michael Walcot
Mr Peter Wasznack
Dr Sylvia Watts
Mgr. E. Wilcock
Mr R. Wilcox

ABBREVIATIONS USED THROUGHOUT

Anstruther	Godfrey Anstruther, O.P., *The Seminary Priests* (4 volumes, 1968-1977).
A.P.C.	Acts of the Privy Council
Aveling, *North*	J. Hugh Aveling, *Northern Catholics* (1966)
Aveling, *Handle*	J. Hugh Aveling, *The Handle and the Axe: the Catholic Recusants in England from the Reformation to Emancipation* (1976).
Aveling, *York*	J. Hugh Aveling, *Catholic Recusancy in the City of York* (Catholic Record Society Monograph 2, 1970).
B.A.A.	Birmingham Archdiocesan Archives
Bellenger, *Scrolls*	Dominic Aidan Bellenger, *Opening the Scrolls: Essays in Honour of Godfrey Anstruther* (Downside, 1987).
Bellenger, *Priests*	Dominic Aidan Bellenger, *English and Welsh Priests* (Bath, 1984).
B.I.H.R.	Borthwick Institute of Historical Research
Bossy, *Catholics*	John Bossy, *The English Catholic Community 1570-1850* (1975)
Bossy, *Rural*	John Bossy, 'Four Catholic Congregations in Rural Northumberland', *Recusant History* 9, no. 2 (April, 1967)
Bossy, *Northumbria*	John Bossy, 'More Northumbrian Congregations', *Recusant History* 10, no. 1 (January, 1969).
C.A.	*Catholic Ancestor*
Car. R.O.	Carlisle Record Office
C.E.	Anne Whiteman & Mary Clapinson eds., *The Critical Edition of the Compton Census* (1989).
Challoner	Richard Challoner, *Memoirs of Missionary Priests* (ed. John H. Pollen, 1924).
Ches. R.O.	Chester Record Office
Clark, *Population*	Peter Clark & J. Hosking, *Population Estimates of English Small Towns* (Centre for Urban History, University of Leicester, 2nd edition, 1993).
Corfield, *Towns*	Penelope Corfield, *The Impact of English Towns 1700-1800* (1982).
C.R.S.	Catholic Record Society
C.S.P.D.	Calendar of State Papers Domestic
Der. R.O.	Derbyshire County Record Office
Dor. R.O.	Dorset County Record Office

Duffy	Eamon Duffy ed., *Challoner and his Church: A Catholic Bishop in Georgian England* (1981).
Edgbaston Register	W.B. Phillimore, J. Whitfield & J. Bloom, The *Franciscan Register of Edgbaston, Warwickshire* (Warwickshire Parish Register Society, 1904).
Farm St.	Jesuit Archives, Farm St., London
Foley	J. H. Foley, *Records of the English Province of the Society of Jesus* (7 volumes, 1875-1883).
Gastrel	E. Raines ed., *Notitia Cestriensis: Historical notes of the Rt. Rev. Francis Gastrel* (*Chetham Society*, Old Series, 4 volumes, 1845-1850).
Holt, *Jesuits*	G. Holt, *The English Jesuits in the Age of Reason* (1993).
Holt, *Biog.*	G. Holt, *The English Jesuits 1650-1829: A Biographical Dictionary* (Catholic Record Society 70, 1984).
H.W.R.O.	Hereford and Worcester County Record Office
J.R.L.	John Rylands Library, Deansgate, Manchester
Jukes	E. Lloyd Jukes ed., *Articles of Enquiry Addressed to the Clergy of Oxford 1738 and 1761* (Oxfordshire Record Society 38, 1957).
K.R.O.	Kendal Record Office
Kinoulty	Mary Kinoulty, *A Social Study of Roman Catholicism in West Sussex in the Eighteenth Century* (M.A. University of Wales, Lampeter, 1982).
Lesourd	J.A. Lesourd, *Les Catholiques dans la Société Anglaise 1765-1865* (two volumes, Postdoctoral Thesis, University of Strasbourg, Lille, 1978).
Leys	M.D.R. Leys, *Catholics in England 1529-1829: a Social History* (1961).
L.R.O.	Lincoln Record Office
Liverpool Registers	J. Hanson ed., 'Catholic Registers of Liverpool, now St Mary's Highfield St., 1741-1773', *Miscellanea 7* (Catholic Record Society 9, 1914).
L.J.R.O.	Lichfield (Joint) Record Office

Lords R.O.	House of Lords Record Office
Magee	Brian Magee, *The English Recusants: a Study of Post-Reformation Catholic Survival* (1938).
N.C.H.	*Northern Catholic History*
N.W.C.H.	*North-West Catholic History*
P.R.O.	Public Record Office
Pres. R.O	Preston Record Office
Prothero	G.W. Prothero ed., *Select Statutes and Other Constitutional Documents Illustrative of the Reigns of Elizabeth and James I* (1913).
Rowlands	Marie Rowlands, *Roman Catholic Registers of Chillington and Wolverhampton* (Staffordshire Parish Register Society, 1958).
St. R.O.	Staffordshire Record Office
Sh. R.O.	Shropshire County Record Office
Shef. Archives	Sheffield Archives (by permission of the Director of Sheffield Libraries & Information Services)
Spufford	Margaret Spufford ed., *The World of Rural Dissenters* (Cambridge, 1995).
Staffs. C.H.	*Staffordshire Catholic History*
Statham	Sheffield Archives, MD 6853 — Autobiography of William Statham.
Steel & Samuels	David J. Steel & E.R. Samuels, *Sources of Roman Catholic and Jewish Genealogy and Family History* (Society of Genealogists, 1986).
S.W.C.H.	*South-West Catholic History*
Ushaw	Ushaw College Archives
V.C.H.	Victoria County History
W.A.A.	Westminster Archdiocesan Archives
Walsham	Alexandra Walsham, *Church Papists: Catholicism, Conformity and Confessional Polemic in Early Modern England* (1993)
Wanklyn, *Darby*	Malcolm Wanklyn, 'The Ironbridge Gorge before Abraham Darby', *West Midlands Studies* 15 (1982), pp. 3-7.
Ward	W. Ward ed., *Parson and Parish in Eighteenth Century Hampshire* (Hampshire Record Series 13, 1995).
West	J. West, *Town Records* (1983).

Williams	J. Anthony Williams, *Catholic Recusancy in Wiltshire 1660-1791* (Catholic Record Society Monograph 1, 1968).
Worrall	E.S. Worrall ed., *The Returns of Papists of 1767* (2 volumes, Catholic Record Society Occasional Publications, 1980 & 1989).
Wrigley	E.A. Wrigley, *People, Cities and Wealth* (1987).
Worcs. Rec.	*Worcestershire Recusant*

Additional abbreviations used in particular chapters are listed between the text and the notes to those chapters.

Part One:
Catholics in Society

1
INTRODUCTION

Parameters, Possibilities and Problems

Much has been written about the Catholic clergy, gentry and martyrs in the post-Reformation period, and also about recusant literature and controversy. The purpose of this volume is to examine the experiences of a group which has attracted less attention, namely the Catholics of the common sort who make up the vast majority of those named in the records of Catholics.

One of the dangers facing recusant historians is that some of the sources they traditionally use can create a false model of the relationship between Catholics and the rest of the inhabitants of early modern England. Maps and statistical tables compiled from Recusant Rolls, Quarter Sessions papers and similar sources relating to offences against the law of the realm give an impression of fragmentation. With the exception of London, Lancashire and a few other counties or parts of counties, Catholics appear to be scattered across the face of England in a random fashion, sometimes in ones and twos, sometimes in small pockets, but invariably cut off from one another by a sea of adherents of the Church of England. This picture of English Catholics as geographically dispersed implies separateness, even ghettoisation, and conjures up images of them as beleaguered and introspective, cut off from the everyday world.

Such sentiments are reinforced by what is known of the experience of the Catholic landed classes. In an age when property meant power, they were denied the right to govern at both national and local level; they married and socialised among themselves as the best means of preserving the faith; and they were fearful that any action on their own part, or on the part of others, would lead to further restrictive measures by the state and violence from mobs acting in the name of patriotism and/or Protestantism. But to what extent do studies of the upper classes give a true representation of most English Catholics ?

A different picture of the life-style of persecuted religious minorities has emerged from the study of Protestant nonconformists in post-Restoration England. This gives primacy to what happened in practice, rather than what was supposed to happen in theory, and emphasises integration rather than separation. In this volume we attempt to make use of similar techniques and to study Catholics within their parish communities.[1]

From the outset it is necessary to confront some problems of definition. Much of the considerable academic debate on the nature and significance of English Catholicism derives from differing perceptions of which individuals should be included and excluded from the group to be studied. Traditional Catholic scholarship and later Scarisbrick, Haigh and Duffy concentrated on those who 'signalled a clear and consistent refusal to participate in the worship of the established church'. Similarly Holmes emphasised that recusancy 'was a public sign of separation from heretics'.[2] Questier on the other hand has demonstrated the fluidity of the boundaries between Catholics and Anglicans, and studied those people who alternated between conformity and resistance.[3] Walsham has given central importance to the church papists who outwardly conformed, but in privacy aided the priests and rejected the new order, and considers conformity as 'an enduring phase in the evolution of early modern English Catholicism'.[4]

Those who were loyal to the Church of England called themselves and were called by others 'Protestants'. The term 'Anglican' was rarely used and then to distinguish the English Church from other national churches.

Roman Catholicism was a belief and value system; popery was a social and political construct; recusancy was a legal offence which had to be proved, and when it was proved a recusant became a recusant convict, a legal category with particular penalties and consequences. This study explores the great variety of people and circumstances comprehended in the phrase 'Catholics of the common sort' and also recognises that individuals and families changed their practice over time and that in many Catholic families there were brothers or cousins who were equally 'staunch' Protestants.

The commissioners for recusancy in Warwickshire and the churchwardens of Bishop's Tachbrooke and Tachbrooke Mallory, Warwickshire, in 1592 struggled with these problems.

> We present Michael Commander who hath come not to our church nor received communion these three years last past to our knowledge but upon the feast day of the Epiphany and the last Sabbath. We present one Palmer supposed to be a seminary and, as one Thomas Olney reporteth, the said Palmer reconciled the aforesaid Michael Commander in the Romish religion about three years last past. We present one Conway supposed to be a minister who came to Tachbrooke in Lent last and lodged at John Arrowsmiths of Tachbrooke about the space of six or eight days, which Conway showed to Thomas Court Mr. of Art a papistical book and by report of the said Arrowsmith the said Conway is now minister of Lancaster. We present Francis Flower who is now in Warwick prison. We present

Thomas Olney who cometh not to the church for fear of process, but he receiveth the communion yearly.

In the second certificate a year later it is said that Commander 'hath now promised conformity; but hath demeaned himself very lewdly in words since that promise made'.[5]

The problem of definition is especially frustrating when the question being asked is 'How many Catholics ?' B.G. Blackwood examined the distribution and importance of 'plebeian Catholics' in the 1640s and 1650s in statistical terms. He found that in Staffordshire 81% of the Catholics were 'plebeians', in Lancashire 93%, and in Sussex 83%[6]. His figures were similar to those found in Yorkshire by Aveling, in Northumberland and Lancashire by Hilton, and in the lists published in the last thirty years by local Catholic history societies and the Catholic Record Society. Most studies necessarily involve the counting of Catholics listed but it is difficult to be satisfied with the results of even simple arithmetical procedures based upon counting units which are so ill defined and so lacking in comparability. This is a problem which applies to all studies of popular religion. 'Counting the godly', as Margaret Spufford demonstrated, is a process which provides more questions than answers.[7]

Administrative units have almost inevitably influenced the way in which historians have ordered their enquiries since they were the basis on which much of the information about Catholics was collected. The many Ph.D. theses examining Catholicism in a single county are abundant evidence of this tendency.[8] Local historians have always protested that this is to compartmentalise to the point of falsification. The administrative units of parish, town, diocese, county on which the lists were based are themselves often more imprecise than at first appears. A parish may have chapelries some of which are parochial, and may contain extra-parochial and disputed territory. The county may have detached portions and contain islands of other counties. The definition of a constablewick is almost always uncertain. Parish, manor and constablewick may or may not be co-terminous.

When we explore the status of Catholics in the wider community, it is even more necessary to have an open and non-specific understanding of 'Who were the Catholics?' It is easy to formulate the questions. What was their standing in the local community? How independent were they? Were they separated from or participant in the wider society? To answer them we have to reconstruct histories of families, parishes and congregations, and bring together fragments of evidence from the widest possible range of sources, including those not primarily concerned with religion. Every reference may prove to be useful, and every aspect of their experience may prove to offer relevant insights.

The cultural history of religion in general has suffered from the continued use of stereotypes, and historians are all too familiar with the 'staunch Catholic', 'the illiterate poor', 'the Catholic family' and 'the place where Mass has been said continuously [*sic*] since the Reformation'. Stereotypes divide the English Catholics into the 'gentry' (which usually includes the nobility), and the 'plebeians'. In reality there were great differences in social degree and opportunity among those of the common sort. Street pedlars, yeomen, merchants, sea captains, labourers, servants in a great house, weavers and blacksmiths had little in common with each other and there were Catholics in all occupational groups. Female Catholics of all ranks were classified by their marital status as wives, widows and spinsters, but the wife of a butcher lived in different circumstances from the wife of a labourer.

Attribution of social status also has to be flexible and inclusive. Classification of persons according to occupation cannot be regarded as an entirely satisfactory guide to status. Persons of the common sort were usually identified by a single word in the listings (e.g. huckster, husbandman, shoemaker), whereas in reality poorer people derived their living from whatever opportunities local conditions offered and drew their income from not one but many different sources.

During the period with which we are concerned, social status was becoming more fluid with much mobility up and down. Increasingly social status depended more on wealth than upon degree and by the eighteenth century a man might be characterised as a collier, a yeoman, and a gentleman all in one lifetime, and the status of his wife and children would rise correspondingly. Furthermore, there is evidence that some papists were entered 'below their weight', as for example yeomen rather than gentry or husbandmen rather than yeomen. Whether this was on the initiative of the Catholics themselves or of the officials is not clear.

Families of the common sort were also geographically mobile. Young men went to London to settle or returned to marry. The sons and daughters of yeomen and tradesmen left home to be apprenticed or to go into domestic or farm service. In their late twenties they married and settled, not necessarily in the parish in which they had been born. Wagoners, packhorsemen, broggers and booksellers travelled the roads. Poor labourers changed their settlement again and again in search of employment. The recusants noted as 'gone out of the parish' or 'not found' were part of a much larger number, who left temporarily to evade prosecution for debt or crime. Moreover, in most communities there were several people with the same surname, Christian name and even occupation. From the beginning it needs to be accepted that there will be some lack of sharpness in our picture.

The Anglican Parish as a Unit of Government

The churchwardens, poor law overseers and constables had a key role in the administration of all the laws, not only those concerning Catholics. The parishes were increasingly important as agencies of secular government and more and more responsibilities were put upon the shoulders of the (unpaid) vestry. The landowners had no direct part in the enforcement of the criminal law at parish level. Courts baron were becoming little more than a register of changes in tenancies, and the courts leet concerned themselves with management of the open fields, nuisances and elections of local officers. The gentlemen made their contribution to maintaining law and order at county level as justices of the peace, while the more substantial householders of the common sort made their contribution to maintaining order and administration in parish and town. The interaction of vestry officers and hundred and county courts was an arrangement (system would be too precise a word), which offered great flexibility and the enforcement of the law varied both in place and over time. The parish officers had Catholic wives, kindred and neighbours and, perhaps just as important, Catholic customers, creditors and debtors.

When central government really tried to root out Catholics, they sent special commissioners of recusancy. The most important of the house searches were carried out by royal pursuivants, not by local officials whose loyalties were often ambivalent. Prosecution of the law became more vigorous when the royal Courts of High Commission became more permanent, and the most vigorous prosecution of papists in the north was carried out by the Earl of Huntingdon as president of the Council of the North.

The area over which the vestry exercised its authority might be less than 100 acres, but there were many very large parishes. Whalley, Lancashire, which covered 104,689 acres and had 15 chapels of ease, was the most extensive in the country.[9] Large parishes usually had several parochial chapelries and the chapelry or even the township rather than the parish church was the natural point of reference for the inhabitants.

Even in the smallest parish the inhabitants had to find at least eight responsible householders every year to carry out an increasingly heavy workload of statutory duties. In the day to day execution of their ever increasing responsibilities the élites of parishes and towns were accustomed to considerable autonomy, even in such matters as tax returns and certainly in the listing or otherwise of papists and the tolerance or otherwise of papist activity. Local customs and community sanctions remained profoundly influential in managing both public order and attitudes to minorities. The individual rector or vicar encouraged the new liturgy to a greater or lesser extent, while every week he had a captive audience to educate and influence. His message was re-inforced (or not in some cases) by his standing with his parishioners. A change of incumbent might produce sudden changes in the experiences of Catholics in the parish.[10]

At the same time the common people were aware of the world outside their parish; news of foreign lifestyles and foreign events came in a variety of ways — from the small books and ballads in the pedlars' pack, from the wagoners and merchants travelling regularly to the cities and ports, from hearing charity sermons encouraging people to give to 'Briefs', and through travelling companies of players.[11]

Absence from Church

The parish church was the scene of the most significant and irreversible events of the lay person's life — baptism, marriage and burial — and also the centre of local administration. It was the place where the meetings of the local vestry were held, the place where notices and information were published, and sometimes the place where the school was carried on. Attendance at parish worship every Sunday and on the Anglican 'days of obligation' was the official test of loyalty to the church as by law established and so to the State established by the law of God and man. Behind the demands of the Act of Uniformity (1 Eliz.c.2) lay three centuries of church law requiring everyone to attend Sunday Mass in their parish church. In the Middle Ages the requirement had been public worship in the parish church, but the fifteenth century had seen the proliferation of private chapels in gentry houses, chantries, schools and almshouses, and there were many exemptions. In 1517 Pope Leo X decreed that the Sunday obligation could be fulfilled in such chapels. In England by 1560 the chantries and colleges were abolished and many of the chapels were disused, but a few were occasionally used for Mass. Private chapels and chaplains in gentlemen's houses continued after the Reformation to be maintained by landowners for themselves and their servants. Catholic gentry were behaving according to their normal social role in maintaining a domestic chapel, even if what went on in those chapels was now in breach of the new laws.

The councillors of cities and towns exercised greater independence in local government than the rural vestries. Some were exempt from the county and dealt directly with central government and sat in judgement as magistrates, others controlled little more than the town hall. However great or small their power, the town councils, like the parish vestries, were a forum where stances were taken, policies established and power games played out. The attitudes and choices of local government were an important factor in shaping the experience of Catholics as they faced the pressures of the State and the State Church.

NOTES

[1] I am indebted to Dr. Wanklyn for this paragraph. The issue is developed further by him below on pp. 210-236.

[2] John J. Scarisbrick, *The Reformation and the English People* (1984); Eamon Duffy, *The Stripping of the Altars: Traditional Religion in England c.1400-c.1580* (1992); Christopher Haigh, *The Reformation and Resistance in Tudor Lancashire* (1975); Christopher Haigh, *English Reformations: Religion, Politics and Society under the Tudors* (1993); Peter J. Holmes, *Resistance and Compromise: the Political Thought of the Elizabethan Catholics* (1982).

[3] Michael C. Questier, *Conversion, Politics and Religion in England 1580-1625* (1996).

[4] Walsham, p. 95.

[5] John Tobias, 'New Light on Recusancy in Warwickshire, 1592', *Worcs. Rec.* 36 (December 1980), p. 10; Michael Hodgetts, 'A Certificate of Warwickshire Recusants 1592', *Worcs Rec. 6* (December 1965). p. 9.

[6] B.G. Blackwood, 'Plebeian Catholics in the 1640s and 1650s', *Recusant History* 18, no. 1 (1986), pp. 43-58.

[7] Margaret Spufford, 'Can we Count the 'Godly' and the 'Comformable' in the Seventeenth Century?', *Journal of Ecclesiastical History* 36, no. 3 (July 1985), pp. 414-28; Bossy, *Catholics*, p. 404.

[8] Theses by county include: Alan Davidson, *Roman Catholics in Oxfordshire from the Later Elizabethan Period to the Civil War (c. 1580-1640)* (Ph.D. Bristol, 1970); Vincent Burke, *Catholic Recusants in Elizabethan Worcestershire* (M.A. Birmingham, 1972); Roger Clark, *Anglicanism, Recusancy and Dissent in Derbyshire 1603-1730* (D. Phil. Oxford, 1979); Mary K. Kinoulty, *Roman Catholicism in West Sussex in the 18th Century* (M.A. Lampeter, 1983); Michael O. Bays, *Catholics in Essex 1558-1603* (Ph.D. Cambridge, 1995).

[9] V.C.H. *Lancashire* 6, p. 349.

[10] C. K. Kitching, 'Church and Chapelry in 16th century England' in D. Baker ed., *Studies in Church History* 16 (1979), pp. 279-91; J. Kent, *The English Constable 1580-1642* (1986); John Beckett, *Local Taxation: National Legislation and the Problem of Enforcement* (1986); Keith Wrightson, 'Two Concepts of Order: Justices, Constables and Jurymen in Seventeenth Century England' in John Brewer and John Styles eds., *An Ungovernable People: the English and their Law in the Seventeenth and Eighteenth Centuries* (1980), pp. 21-46; Susan J. Wright ed., *Parish, Church and People: Local Studies in Lay Religion 1350-1750* (1988).

[11] Tessa Watts, 'Piety in the Pedlar's Pack', in Spufford, p. 225.

2

HIDDEN PEOPLE: CATHOLIC COMMONERS, 1558-1625

Historians in the 1980s attempted to identify the character of English Catholicism. Was the post-Reformation Catholic Church in England a new Tridentine development with little in common with the mediaeval church? Or was it a development from the mediaeval church? One great virtue of this debate was to focus attention on what actually happened in the local community. More recently it has receded somewhat on the understanding that the reactions of individuals to the changes were extremely varied and the result of many different factors.[1]

Clement Norton, vicar of Faversham, told his people in 1562 not to say the *Pater Noster* in English for 'he knew not how soon the world would change'. In many parishes the first decade after the Settlement was one of procrastination. It took ten years to ensure that the parish churches were cleared of Catholic images, Mass equipment and vestments. These things belonged to the parish community and were the responsibility of the churchwardens. It is occasionally possible to trace individual 'relics of superstition' as they changed hands, and the uses to which they were subsequently put might be sacred or secular. The great majority of parish priests remained in office, setting an example to their parishioners to accept the changes.[2] Most commoners followed their lead whether they liked the new religion or not. Even when contemplating the next world in their wills, few parishioners clung to Catholic formulas expressing belief in the help of the saints and the particular intercession of the Virgin Mary. For some the latest settlement was enough, for others it was a first step towards a truly Protestant settlement and for others again it was a step too far, but for the time being the three positions could co-exist.[3]

Reluctance to list and prosecute Catholics was evident in some parishes from the beginning, but it is still not clear how far the shilling fine was enforced. In Kent the churchwardens of Wye complained that it was impossible to collect the fines because the number of recusants was too great and attempts to make habitual recusants compound with the parish were unsuccessful.[4]

In the 1560s the choices made by individuals must be regarded as provisional. It was possible both to deplore the changes and to implement them if this seemed to be the course of duty. While a small number of parish priests resigned and continued their ministry outside the law, a large majority waited upon events.

Rebellions, Plots and Executions

The settlement of religion was inescapably political, just as the political settlement had to be validated by religion. The principle *cuius regio eius religio* was axiomatic at every level not only international and national, but also in the parishes, the towns, and even in the family. Authority at any level was validated by God and secular affairs were in his hands, so that every act was of obedience or disobedience, every judgement was moral or immoral, and every conflict was about the legitimacy of authority as well as power.

Historians have all too often made unsubstantiated assumptions about the role of the common people in these conflicts. For example during the rebellion of 1569-70 large numbers of people gathered daily for Mass in Durham Cathedral, and the Book of Common Prayer and other innovations were burnt. Between 5,000 and 6,000 commoners participated in these activities. Modern historians have offered radically different interpretations of these events. On one hand the common people have been described as being driven by force to Mass, the force it is assumed being applied by the agents of the rebel leaders.[5] On the other hand more recent work has shown that only about 20% of the 5,000 or 6,000 followers were tenants of the Earls and other leaders, and this has been interpreted to suggest that the remainder joined the rising for reasons of their own and religious loyalty was one of the strongest; the event itself being described as 'an impressive display of religious enthusiasm'.[6]

All agree however that the crisis of 1569-71 was a turning point. Elizabeth had little difficulty in controlling the rebellion of the Northern Earls or the subsequent bid for power by the Duke of Norfolk and the Earl of Arundel, but for all English Catholics the effects of the crisis were serious and long lasting. The Bull of Excommunication issued in January 1570 by Pius V was of dubious legality even in Catholic terms and was never officially published in England, but this was less important than its impact on popular perceptions of popery. It became the justification for further penal legislation, and made public and explicit a conflict between loyalty to Church and to State which challenged the whole underlying theology of authority. It made the 'wait and see' position harder to maintain even for commoners. The growing conflict with Spain abroad and the pressure of Protestant activists at home, in and out of Parliament, exacerbated religious division in the seventies and eighties.[7]

The Enforcement of the Laws

Central government strove to secure the active support not only of the ruling classes but of every household at every social level. The successive initiatives of government were not only concerned to control disaffected Catholics actual and potential, but pursued a larger objective, namely to form every individual man and woman, high and low, in righteousness and true allegiance. Action against Catholics was part of a larger imperative as governors at all levels tried to impose stability on a rapidly changing society. Local government especially in towns shared the fears of central government and believed that tight controls were necessary not only to conduct the war against Spain and Roman Catholicism, but also to master the masterless, identify troublemakers, to empower them to search houses for illegal immigrants, to imprison and whip vagrants, and to fix wages.

The successive statutes, proclamations and the constant stream of orders from the Privy Council had to be administered on a case by case basis. A study of the Quarter Sessions and Assize records of recusancy in Berkshire and Oxfordshire shows how selective the county authorities were in identifying recusants for prosecution, concentrating on particular areas or social groups selected 'according to criteria we shall never fully know'.[8]

The laws as they were framed lacked precision. Churchwardens were required to present twice a year at least and this included on their going out of office at their year's end. Before presenting papists, churchwardens were required to persuade them to come to church. A churchwarden at Prescot applied for his expenses 'warning some to come to church which were suspected to be recusants'.[9] This requirement opened up the possibility of a person who had been so warned taking evasive action. In the parishes in the North where there were numerous more or less independent chapels, many of them badly staffed, it was virtually impossible to enforce church attendance.[10] Recusancy was only one element among the wide range of public behaviour which the churchwardens were expected to monitor. These included sexual offences, church levies, public defamation, sowers of discord and many more. Recently the assumption that churchwardens and constables would be unwilling to present their neighbours has been vigorously challenged, but the greater their independence of judgement, the more important was their interpretation of the relative importance of the many offences with which they were concerned.[11]

The Enemy Within

Before and during the war with Spain, England came to think of itself as an embattled island set in a silver sea protected by God from enemies on the Continent.[12] Every agent of authority was being urged into action; constables, churchwardens, parsons, archdeacons, archbishops, high commissioners, sheriffs, lord lieutenants, muster masters and assize judges were all part of a major war effort. The government mobilised armies, built ships, collected money and materials, trained musters, promoted propaganda and strained every sinew to prepare for imminent invasion, bringing home the danger from Catholic Spain to every town and village. Catholic houses were searched for arms, horses, and for evidence of Mass being said. Catholics were required to pay double levies and extra levies. The high point of the drive for national unity was the highly dramatised public execution of Catholic priests and their helpers.

County towns in particular were centres from which the authority of both the State and the State Church were impressed upon the populace, especially as many of them were also the location of the diocesan cathedral and church courts. They were the scene of the Assize courts when the visiting representatives of royal power made judgement and pronounced sentence. About half the executions of Catholics took place at various sites in London, and most of the remainder in the county towns and regional capitals. These executions were political acts, aimed at the population as a whole, rallying national unity against external threat. The Armada was sighted from Lizard Point on 19 July 1588, and it is no coincidence that the peak year for the executions of priests was 1588 and the peak month of that year was August. It was important that the priests and their helpers be seen as traitors to the Crown and the common weal. Sixty-three lay people were executed including 3 women, and in addition at least 71 men and 27 women died in prison.

The records of both London and provincial prisons provide reports of many hundreds of commoners who were repeatedly imprisoned including some, who under pressure or after conference with Anglican divines agreed to conform.[13] They might be imprisoned for repeated failure to conform, or more frequently for failure to pay fines arising from their recusancy. There were hundreds of such cases: conditions in the prison for some were appalling and disgusting while other prisoners were able to buy some degree of comfort if not freedom. Poor men and women who had no money to buy concessions were often the worst treated.[14]

The propaganda of the government was met by Catholic counter-propaganda in theological treatises and polemical pamphlets printed abroad and secretly in England. The form and tone of these accounts was similar to that of the Foxe's *Acts of the Martyrs*, which was being circulated with government support. Like Foxe's work they were promoted, especially by the Jesuits, both for polemical reasons and as an exhortation to the faithful. The 'theatre of martyrdom' was fully exploited as on the Continent and the last words on the scaffold, often taking the form of an unforgettable jest, were addressed to the populace. Portions of the bodies of executed persons became precious relics, and memorials such as handkerchiefs dipped in their blood, pieces of the rope, and fragments of clothing were treasured by relatives and friends. The lives of the martyrs were immediately presented as part of the continuum of martyrs from Roman times onward, whose blood was the seed of the church.[15] There were popular ballads describing the executions both from opponents and supporters. *The execution of four priests at Lancaster; a song of four priests that suffered death at Lancaster to the tune of Dainty come to me* celebrates those *whose lives while they did live and whose blessed deaths.....doe admonish what way we should go.* Another ballad celebrated the death of Robert Ludlam in Derbyshire. Paintings and engravings were made taking the likeness from the severed head, or in prison before execution. Engravings of the first hundred martyrs of the Jesuits were published in 1608.

The cult of these new martyrs was important precisely because they were local, well known to persons of all degrees, literate and illiterate, and remembered by relatives and friends who continued to live in the area where they had worked and died. Many of the most notable centres of Catholic commitment cultivated an association with a particular martyr.[16]

The Voice of Conscience

While the majority of parishioners conformed, the minority who refused could be clear and articulate when required by the courts to give reasons for failing to attend church. In 1576 Elizabeth, wife of William Wilkinson, miller, of York said she did not go to church because there is neither 'priest, altar nor sacrifice'; William Bowman, locksmith, said he refused because he thought 'it is not the Catholic church for there is neither priest, altar nor sacraments'; Isabel Bowman said her conscience would not serve her because 'there is not the sacrament hung up and other things'; Isabel Porter, wife of Peter Porter, tailor, because her conscience would not serve her; Gregory Wilkinson, feltmaker, said that he would remain in the faith he was baptised in; Margaret Tesimond said that she thought she should offend God and therefore her conscience would not suffer her to come.[17]

There had probably been some coaching by the priests, and anxious consultation among the accused about the right thing to say. Nevertheless there is no set formula in these statements, and the individual voices do come through. In hundreds of court cases men and women in parishes and towns showed that they understood the theological issues in debate in the Reformation, and they explicitly justified their disobedience to the State by an appeal to individual conscience. Their reasons for putting their livelihoods, their families, their local standing and their freedom at risk went far beyond simple resistance to change.

Commoners and the Harbouring of Priests

Between 1558 and 1603 815 English priests were ordained abroad and the majority returned to England, if only for a time.[18] The dangerous work of serving both Marian and seminary priests was undertaken mainly by laymen, most of whom were yeomen, servants and innkeepers. Thirty men and three women were executed; six women were condemned, but not executed; and many men and women were imprisoned for assisting the priests.[19] In this period of most acute danger to priests hiding places were built in large houses. Over 70 hiding places have been studied and verified in houses all over England. Nicholas Owen's outstanding contribution to this work and his eventual death under torture are well known, but it is less well known that his three brothers were also risking their lives. Walter died at the English College at Valladolid and John became a priest. John and Henry both suffered imprisonment.[20]

Masses were said in the houses of common people as well as in gentry houses. At Ripple on the River Severn, Catholics resorted to the house of Rhys and Thomas Moor, watermen, to hear Mass and have conference.[21] At Masham in Yorkshire the rich gentry family the Wyvills harboured 'papistical recusants', but Henry Duffield, yeoman, in the same parish also had 'Mass done in his house'.[22]

Priests' helpers were usually yeomen from those better-off families who could spare a son from the farm.[23] Harbouring was not nationally organised or financed and what was actually done varied from person to person, from the many who simply turned a blind eye to the smaller number who gave all their time and means. Some harbourers became servants of an individual priest travelling with them, leaving their work and families so to do. Others accompanied them to the next place where Mass was to be said. Priests at this period were continually on the move and needed travelling companions. In London

> One Phillips dwelling at Dr Good's, in Chancery Lane, a great dealer with priests and a sender and director of them from place to place, [and] Ingram lying at a tailor's house ... receiveth and directeth them from place to place.[24]

Innkeepers and ostlers were dealing with travellers all the time and some covered up the comings and goings of priests. William Bostock and his wife Elizabeth of Chester were suspected of harbouring priests at their inn, and were questioned about their guests.[25] The government was aware of the importance of inns in the Catholic network.

People of all social ranks were involved in hiding priests and the Jesuits in their annual letters reported many cases of very poor men, women and children demonstrating heroic commitment. Richard Jebb, a Yorkshire farmer, 'poor yet religious that he might sometime the more securely entertain priests his own house being inconvenient he built in his fields among many bushes a little house seven foot broad, ten foot long and eight foot high'.[26]

The descriptions of searches for priests repeatedly record the women of the house, the servants and even the children co-operating to outwit the searchers. Agnes Rawson of Sherburn in the West Riding of Yorkshire, innkeeper, harboured Marian clergy and in 1604 she was described as a dangerous recusant who had seminaries or Jesuits 'several times resorting to her house and that some other servants have found divers things in her barn as cope, chalice, book'. She maintained in her household Jane Hymesworth, Frances Rawson brought up by Agnes, William Middleman who was suspect in that he had been coming and going for two or three years last past and John a tailor (surname unknown) of no parish described as a 'running recusant' who had been coming and going to Agnes Rawson's house for seven years. Ann Line in London maintained three houses where priests were received for eight years before she was taken and executed.[27] The predominance of women in the sheltering of priests was to some extent a reflection of the normal division of duties between men in the public sector and women in the private sector of life. They were also slightly less at risk since the law regarding the legal responsibility of married women was unclear.[28]

Some men of low rank earned a living by supplying services to Catholics, coming and going to the Continent, carrying letters and money and escorting boys and girls sent abroad for education. Thomas Willetts was reported to the Archbishop of

Canterbury for carrying letters and escorting scholars; John Boniface aged 20 was taken at Rye with rosaries and letters. There were many other such reports.[29] Chester port with its constant movement of ships to and from Ireland, was kept under especially close supervision, the more so as it was the point of embarkation for troops to Ireland. Lists of papists include the names of Aldersley, linendraper, Primrose, tailor, and Liverpool, joiner, who like innkeeper Bostock appear regularly. From time to time the city authorities took suspect travellers prisoner. Three parties of youths were caught between April 1594 and July 1595 en route for the colleges abroad. They came from all over the country and included not only the sons of gentlemen but also of merchants, a joiner and a farmer.[30]

There was a growing trade in books among the lower orders and laymen were also active in printing and selling Catholic books. There were at least 21 presses which operated secretly in England at various times between 1575 and 1630.[31] John Oakes and his father Nicholas had been printing and selling Catholic books, including Francis de Sales' *Introduction to the Devout Life*, for 20 years when arrested in 1639. John Driffield, tailor, brought at least forty books from Antwerp including missals, breviaries and Latin primers and pictures of the persecutions in England and the executions of 'the saints as he termeth them', which he sold.[32] Henry Owen, brother of Nicholas, ran a secret printing press.[33] Some laymen were schoolmasters teaching the sons of gentry or local boys in their own homes, so avoiding the need for a public licence, or in town grammar schools which had not, as yet, all been purged of Catholic teachers.[34] Evidence about all these activities often comes from informers and busybodies who were interested in making alarmist allegations, while other statements came from the examinations of prisoners some of whom had been incarcerated for long periods and suffered torture. Even so there can be no doubt that despite the legal penalties there was a considerable network of lay families supplying the needs of Catholics with goods and services.

Catholics and their Landlords

Parishes with a strong Catholic presence in rural areas were normally those where the main landowner was a Catholic. Many of them had acquired much of their land from the dissolution of religious houses, land which often included extra-parochial places. Like their conforming peers, Catholic gentlemen built or extended their great show houses to dominate the landscape, and their kitchen doors were accessible to all classes. The great house

Table 1: Status of Convicted Recusants listed on the Recusant Rolls of the Exchequer, 1592.

County	Places	Gentry	Non-Gentry	Total
Beds.	1	11	0	11
Berks.	36	12	9	21
Bucks	8	7	0	7
Cambs.	10	3	5	8
Cheshire	20	4	12	16
Cornwall	10	7	2	9
Cumberland	2	0	0	0
Derby	24	8	57	65
Devon	6	2	0	2
Dorset	23	3	26	29
Essex	21	21	7	28
Gloucs.	13	4	5	9
Hampshire	41	26	11	37
Hereford	41	23	22	45
Hunts.	1	1	0	1
Kent	3	4	4	8
Lancs.	163	85	339	424
Leics.	4	2	2	4
Lincoln	10	8	5	13
Norfolk	52	26	27	53
Northants.	1	7	10	17
North'land	26	19	22	41
Notts.	7	1	2	3
Oxon.	25	2	5	7
Rutland	5	1	0	1
Salop	24	18	21	39
Somerset	11	5	13	18
Staffs.	52	24	32	56
Suffolk	8	1	4	5
Surrey	41	28	39	67
Warwick	31	3	65	68
West'land	12	7	2	9
Wilts.	0	5	2	7
Worcs.	48	19	73	92
Yorks.	216	147	131	278
		544	954	1498

offered employment, news, alms, patronage, and was a market for much of the produce of cottage gardens. The process usually has to be inferred rather than documented but the detailed household accounts of the East Anglian gentleman Nicholas Bacon of Stiffkey, Norfolk, show how influence worked. As a Puritan he made sure there were clergy of suitable purity in all the thirty or so parishes around his fine house. Such men depended on the gentry's patronage and not only for a home and a base of preaching but often to finance their publications, just as Catholic clergy often depended on Catholic gentry.[35]

The Privy Council constantly sought to identify and control the most dangerous of the Catholic gentry. In Sussex all the six great landowners of the county were Catholics and three of them were 'Northern Earls', 'agreeing all together and having often meetings'. They provided chaplains and Mass centres, and islands of recusancy were sustained around them at Battle, Firle, Findon, Clapham and Patching. As yet, such men of family and influence continued to hold office in the counties and still expected to participate in the networks of power, formal and informal.[36]

Nevertheless the influence of even the most Catholic of the gentry was not unlimited. The six Catholic earls of Sussex controlled most of the land but even they did not prevent the reformed religion taking hold in that county. Their influence was everywhere balanced by that of custom and law, and the relative weight of seigniorial and customary influence depended on local circumstances. On royal manors tenants had a high degree of independence, in other manors the lord might be resident or non-resident, and on some manors there were a high number of free tenancies. Yeomen in the parishes held their land not at the whim of the lord, but by tenures protected by the custom of the manor. They could and frequently did challenge their lords at the Assizes and in the prerogative courts. Long leases of three lives or 99 years were common, giving many yeomen considerable security of tenure, and in a time of inflation and land-hunger copyholds advantaged the tenant rather than the lord. The population was growing rapidly and with it the demand for food; in 1593-8 the price of grain rose to crisis levels to the advantage of farmers. Successful yeomen farmers rebuilt their houses to live in greater comfort, and they had both security and status in the parish community. They were, like their 'betters', litigious, and well understood how to play one authority off against another to their advantage.

Table 2: Occupations of Plebeian Recusants, 1592.

County	Rural	Lab.	Cloth	Miller	Wood	Skin	Metal	Retail	Build	Service	Other	Total
Berks.	9	0	0	0	0	0	0	0	0	0	0	9
Cambs.	5	0	0	0	0	0	0	0	0	0	0	5
Cheshire	2	5	0	0	0	4	1	0	0	0	0	12
Cornwall	2	0	0	0	0	0	0	0	0	0	0	2
Derby	40	16	0	0	0	0	1	0	0	0	0	57
Dorset	24	1	1	0	0	0	0	0	0	0	0	26
Essex	7	0	0	0	0	0	0	0	0	0	0	7
Gloucs.	5	0	0	0	0	0	0	0	0	0	0	5
Hants.	11	0	0	0	0	0	0	0	0	0	0	11
Hereford	15	1	2	0	4	0	0	0	0	0	0	22
Kent	3	1	0	0	0	0	0	0	0	0	0	4
Lancs.	249	22	20	7	11	6	6	4	0	6	8	339
Leics.	2	0	0	0	0	0	0	0	0	0	0	2
Lincoln	4	1	0	0	0	0	0	0	0	0	0	5
Norfolk	26	0	0	0	1	0	0	0	0	0	0	27
Northants.	8	0	0	0	0	0	0	0	1	1	0	10
North'land	22	0	0	0	0	0	0	0	0	0	0	22
Notts.	2	0	0	0	0	0	0	0	0	0	0	2
Oxon.	4	1	0	0	0	0	0	0	0	0	0	5
Salop	16	2	2	1	0	0	0	0	0	0	0	21

Somerset	12	0	0	0	0	1	0	0	0	0	0	13
Staffs.	22	5	5	0	0	0	0	0	0	0	0	32
Suffolk	4	0	0	0	0	0	0	1	0	0	0	5
Surrey	39	0	0	0	0	0	0	0	0	0	0	39
Warwick.	38	6	3	1	1	0	2	10	0	2	2	65
West'land	2	0	0	0	0	0	0	0	0	0	0	2
Wilts.	1	0	0	0	0	0	0	1	0	0	0	2
Worcs.	59	3	4	0	1	0	0	3	3	0	0	73
Yorks.	78	12	13	4	1	4	3	12	3	0	1	131
TOTALS	711	76	50	13	19	15	13	31	7	9	11	955

Rural yeoman, husbandman, warriner
Cloth weaver, shearman, clothier, dyer, draper
Wood cooper, joiner, carpenter, wheelwright
Skin glover, skinner, cordwainer, bridler, tanner, girdler
Metal smith, blacksmith, scythesmith, goldsmith, locksmith
Retail tailor, bookbinder, chandler, stationer, butcher, pedlar, shoemaker
Build mason, bricklayer
Service servant, clerk, horsekeeper, schoolmaster
Other collier, sailor.

Source: C.R.S. 18 (1916). N.B. Women omitted. None in Beds., Bucks., Cumberland, Devon or Rutland.

Catholic Commoners in the Recusant Rolls

From 1587 recusant fines were paid to the Exchequer and by 1592 separate Rolls became necessary. The first Roll of 1592 provides some guidance on the names, addresses and estates of some 4,000 Catholics, most of whom were heads of households and owners of some land and who were convicted recusants against whom processes of sequestration or compounding, or fines were outstanding. All whose names appear on the Rolls had been through the longwinded and complicated process of being prosecuted and found guilty, and were subject to penalties. The lists are in no sense complete lists of recusants, still less of Catholics, and offer only a very limited contribution to our knowledge of the Catholic body as a whole. This becomes clear when the occupations of those recorded are set out by county.[37]

The numbers of places mentioned in any county list are often quite small and some sheriffs evidently attached more importance to following up commoners than did others. Table 1 shows the variable extent of the recording of men and women below the rank of gentry in most counties. They were most numerous in the returns for Derbyshire, Lancashire, Yorkshire, Warwickshire and Worcestershire. Few were listed for Hampshire, a county which the Privy Council regarded as dangerously full of recusants. There are no figures for Cumberland. The variety of occupations included in some counties (Table 2) demonstrates the diffusion of recusancy through the social scale. As is to be expected at this date, the overwhelming majority of Catholics listed were engaged in rural occupations in rural parishes, but so were the great majority of English working people .

Where comparison of the names on these lists with the prison lists and other records has been made on a name by name basis, it is revealed that there are individuals who had been in and out of prison for years, in county gaols at first and later in London, and people who had been found at Mass or involved in clandestine marriages and baptisms, or in proselytising. Some, like Richard Jennings, husbandman of Wolverton, can be linked with young men in the colleges abroad. Some conformed under pressure of the law and the conference with divines but their conformity was not necessarily long-lasting.[38]

The Success of the Settlement

The number of Catholics by 1603 has been variously estimated at one or two per cent of the population and beyond these there was the essentially incalculable number of church papists and fellow travellers.[39] By then most people in the parishes conformed, going to church with their neighbours even if in some cases they had reservations. Some Catholic priests in writing, teaching and pastoral care took the stance that merely going into the Anglican service occasionally was permissible to save life especially for the laity, and this was the clear teaching of some of the earlier manuals of casuistry. The working man could adduce many positive reasons for conforming: loyalty to the crown, the example of superiors, the need for solidarity with respectable neighbours, good order, honesty, honour and the common weal, and it may be added common sense. During the war the anti-Catholic propaganda had been assimilated into the general collective consciousness. It was one or even two generations since Catholicism had been overt and familiar. The Elizabethan religious settlement was a success even though not every individual in the parish was a church attender, or an educated and convinced Protestant; but then, neither was every individual of godly and upright life. By the second decade of the seventeenth century most parishes were more than adequately staffed, children and servants were regularly catechised, and respectable families worshipped in an orderly manner in their new pews in the parish churches.[40]

Such weekly communal displays of Order and Degree were not a peaceful resolution of religious division, for parochial and town authorities were maintaining order and cohesion in local society only with great difficulty. The duty of doing so was not confined to the government and the gentry but was the responsibility of all 'good householders', all heads of family, all parochial officials, and all masters of workshops and of apprentices. Both Church and State by 1600 had won the active support of most responsible people in the community.

Disorder and Unrest 1592-1607

As Elizabeth's reign drew to a close there were attempts by some Catholic clergy and Catholic gentlemen to seek a *modus vivendi* both with the government of Elizabeth and with the future King James, but Catholics of the common sort had more basic problems. The last years of the century were embittered not only by the war, financial crises and religious division, but also by a series of appallingly bad harvests. Prices had been rising throughout the sixteenth century but in the last decade they peaked and there were serious outbreaks of plague in the towns. There was much local disorder, including enclosure, bread and alehouse riots. Some of these disturbances have been studied in detail and the local politics, interpersonal relationships and economic problems which lay behind them have been unravelled.

Women were prominent in riots, taking physical action, a part sanctioned by tradition.

In the last years of Elizabeth's reign and in the first few years of that of her successor there were numerous overtly Catholic riots. In 1598 in the parish of Middlesmoor, Yorkshire, Catholics invaded the parish church and put a straw figure of the parson in the pulpit.[41] In 1603 William Marshall, yeoman, and his friends at Gilling in Yorkshire, foiled an attempt by three constables to arrest John Bainbridge, son of Robert, the principal landowner in the parish, whereupon Alice Marshall felled one of the constables with her keys. At Garstang, Lancashire, the vicar was besieged in his vicarage and shot at; 77 persons were arrested. There were riots at Childwall (1598), Prescot (1598), Chipping (1601), Claughton (1601) and Poulton (1601).[42] In 1604 some recusants were buying arms and some seminary priests were rumoured to be about to revolt and to seize Chester. Royal messengers were attacked. There was an attempt to release a priest being taken to Lancaster Gaol, but the only result was that a second priest was captured.[43] There was much more serious trouble among Catholics in Herefordshire and Monmouthshire, which lasted six weeks from May to June 1605. The burial of Catholics including a priest led to a major incident on Corpus Christi day when forty or fifty men confronted the Bishop and the justices at The Darren. In June the Earl of Worcester was sent to quell the disturbances.[44] There were many other outbreaks of violence on a small scale arising from events such as arrests of Catholics, interrupted funerals and seizures of Catholic cattle or goods. These conflicts, which centred on religious issues and religious loyalties, did not operate in a void. A man angry about fines, bad harvests and inflation, frightened by rising poor rates and in dread of a Spanish invasion, might be pushed into violent action by a heavy handed attempt to arrest a relative or friend for being a Catholic.

Catholics and King James

Some Catholics expected greater tolerance from James I, who was after all a legitimate king, who was not excommunicate and had a Catholic mother and a Catholic wife. Initial gestures soon proved illusory, and the Privy Council, while issuing pardons, continued to permit executions. The Gunpowder Plot in 1605 may perhaps be called 'the last Elizabethan plot', being characterised by disaffected gentlemen conspiring in country houses for a political solution to their alienation and succeeding only in providing the ministers of the Crown with an opportunity to maximise anti-Catholic stereotypes in popular culture. Anti-

Catholic legislation after the Gunpowder Plot insisted on the responsibility of heads of households for the conformity of their wives, their families, their servants and their lodgers and also sought to clarify the problem of recusant wives. It brought the authority of the head of the family in to support that of church and state. The Oath of Allegiance 1606 (3 James I c. 4 and 5) was required of all persons of all degrees over the age of eighteen except for the nobility, and those indicted or convicted of recusancy. The Oath sought to rally loyal Catholics among persons of all degrees. The Jesuits, who were radically opposed to the Oath, reported in their annual letters that large numbers of people, rich and poor, were being summoned to take it, especially during the period when Sir Edward Coke was Lord Chief Justice.[45]

The Development of Anti-Popery

After the immediate panic caused by the Gunpowder Plot, changing political circumstances removed some of the pressure by the government to eliminate Popery, but popular anti-Catholicism remained a significant force. The propaganda of sermons, ballads, plays and polemical pamphlets constantly reinforced the stereotype of Papists as equivocators, untrustworthy, mindless and immoral. They were presented as superstitious, venerating relics and accepting false miracles. Catholics, it was believed, imposed faith by force, as the Marian martyrs and the Inquisition demonstrated. Catholics were kept in ignorance and dominated by their priests. As the years went by the various elements combined to create a popular myth, partly articulated, partly subconscious, and profoundly influential. It must be the case that those who were the victims of this myth were themselves also deeply influenced by it.[46]

There was a growing emphasis on the rational and experiential, and attitudes towards Catholics were linked with changing attitudes to the occult in a complex and subtle way which cannot be fully explored in this outline. The ‘intellectual revolution’ was not only a matter of sophisticated intellectual debates and learned treatises, but also of a slow change in popular mentality. The emphasis on the word of scripture as the sole source of truth did not denigrate the miraculous or the direct intervention of Divine Providence in human affairs, but it identified many Catholic beliefs and practices as ‘not scriptural’ and therefore dangerous to faith and morals. The Book of Revelation provided a superb repertoire of images and rhetorical phrases with which to denounce popery, a rhetoric which became more and more standardised and familiar as the Puritan impulse gathered force.

The popular press produced many pamphlets telling stories involving reputed possession by the devil, mysterious Jesuits and occult rituals. In the pamphlet of *The Boy of Bilston* a conflict between the 'superstition' of Papists and the 'rationalism' of Protestants is quite explicit. The story is presented to show, that whereas the superstitious and power-seeking Jesuits were tricked by an impostor, the reasonable and caring Anglican bishop found him out and countered superstition with reason and discipline.[47] Priests not infrequently found themselves called upon to intervene in cases of supposed possession and the Jesuits in particular were active in this work. Ambrose Barlow, O.S.B., at Myerscough, Lancashire, when called upon to perform an exorcism, was divided between recognising his priestly ministry and scepticism concerning the particular case before him.[48] Catholics believed in the miraculous and the sacramental and in the constant providential intervention of God, but were instructed to dissociate themselves from credulity and magic. The Council of Trent was adamant on this point, denouncing under pain of sin those who put trust in witchcraft, charms and omens. Nevertheless Catholics continued to be stigmatised as superstitious by their neighbours who were being taught to stress the exposition of the Word.

To make matters worse Catholics necessarily surrounded the movements of priests and their helpers with secrecy, using coded language about the Mass, and travelling abroad to unknown destinations. Any group with secrets arouses fear and suspicion but also exercises a certain horrified fascination. This was encouraged by popular literature, which preferred the sensational to the reality.

Catholic Life 1600-1625

The number of executions was fewer than in the period 1588-1597, and there were additional laws designed to make the heads of households responsible for the conformity of their dependants but there was no substantive change in the position of Catholics. Fifteen priests were executed between 1605-1625. Four of the executions were before the Gunpowder Plot and seven were associated with it. Five lay-harbourers associated with them were executed: a yeoman, a miller, a schoolmaster, a weaver, and one of unknown occupation.[49]

The concept of martyrdom was central to the spiritual formation of the Catholic laity, and even more of priests training in the colleges abroad. For both laity and priests it was an aspect of the even more fundamental concept of redemption through suffering, the triumph of the Cross. At the English College in

Rome, Circignani's frescoes showed the English martyrs as a continuation of those of the primitive and mediaeval church. Catholics in places where they had lived or worked remembered them, and cures and special favours were sought by their intercession. The relics of St Chad were kept in the bedhead of Henry Hodgetts, yeoman of Sedgley, Staffordshire, who invoked the saint on his deathbed. This is only one example of the evidence of the existence and persistence of local cults maintained by the lower orders. The relatives and friends of these martyrs are frequently found in the lists of local papists.[50]

Despite the real dangers, the number of priests in England was increasing, and they were becoming better organised. The common people could hope for a more settled ministry. The numbers of Jesuits in England reached a peak of 193 in 1639; the Benedictines established their English Congregation in 1619, the Franciscans their province in 1625. In 1623 a Vicar Apostolic was appointed for English Catholics, namely William Bishop, who set up a formal organisation of the secular clergy for the whole country. An account from 1616 distinguishes between priests who were confined to one house, priests who constantly travelled arriving in the evening and departing the next day, and those who were able to live openly.[51]

Although we know much about the danger of hearing Mass, we have little evidence of how the worshippers actually participated. The layman John Heigham of St Omer produced books of prayers to be said during Mass, translations of the Ordinary of the Mass, the Jesus Psalter, and compilations for the 'most necessary exercises' namely confession, hearing Mass, receiving (the Blessed Sacrament), vocal prayer, meditation and rules to live well, which had a great circulation and many editions. He did not offer the reader a translation of the Canon of the Mass as this was felt to be too deeply awe-inspiring. Translations of both the *Primer* and the *Manual* circulated, as did other prayer books which show that the people were expected to understand the outline of Mass with prayers which were parallel to the Mass. On the Continent participation of the laity in this way was being encouraged by the Oratorians among others, even though translations of the Mass into the vernacular were not officially permitted until 1897. The Bible in the Douai- Rheims translation was circulating from 1582 and Parson's *Directory* had a wide readership.[52]

As among the Lollards a century before, unlicensed works were circulated in manuscript as well as print. In the early seventeenth century a group of scribes in Spitalfields made their living by copying such material. In Staffordshire a priest meeting a

Catholic by chance upon the highway gave him an account of a controversial exorcism and asked him to copy it and pass it on.[53] Such casual references in the documents are few, but as historians examine local sources in depth they are beginning to accumulate.

Both the Church of England and the Catholic Church abroad and in England placed great stress on regular catechesis and question and answer methods of teaching the poor and children. Jesuits taught in this manner in their colleges on the Continent, and in the Low Countries the catechists used in addition specially written hymns. In England the secular and ecclesiastical courts provide glimpses of active lay catechists. Among them was George Swalwell of Wolverton, a papist teacher, who visited dying children and taught children to read in his own house, thus avoiding the need for a licence.[54] John Finch of Eccleston, Lancashire, a married man converted in middle life, was wholly employed as a clerk and catechist. He was executed in 1584.[55] Sister Dorothea instructed 'the vulgar sort', teaching them their Pater, Ave, Creed, Commandments etc.

> Those who in respect of the fear of persecution, loss of goods and the like I cannot at first bring to resolve to be living members of the Catholic church, I endeavour at least so to dispose them that understanding and believing the way to salvation, they seldom or willingly go to heretical churches, abhor the receiving of their profane communion, and never to offend God in any great matters.

Separation from the parish church was the most important symbol of commitment, but she understood that for many Catholics this was too much to expect.[56]

The gentry provided Mass centres, protected priests, maintained the schools and convents abroad. Their role was at its most important at this period. Some made of their homes a *hortus conclusus,* a private garden in which Catholic belief and practice, ritual, and music could flourish. To obtain a place in the Catholic Meynell household at North Kilvington in Forcett, Yorkshire, servants had to be Catholics. They were given regular instruction and pastoral care and entered into a daily round of prayers, following the liturgical cycle. These houses provided opportunities for Catholic servants to meet and occasionally secret marriages took place between them.[57]

Even the 'most Catholic' families of gentry were not always consistent in their Catholicism. Indeed it was far more usual that a Catholic gentry family would include branches and individuals who conformed or were even Puritan. Commitment fluctuated from generation to generation and Catholic gentry were not immune to failure of heirs, mismanagement of property, and financial misfortune.

The gentry Catholic centres are relatively well known but there were others. Preston, Lancashire was unusual at this date in having a chapel in Chapel Yard off Friargate serving 68 recusants in the town and 19 in the surrounding parish as early as 1609.[58] Another smaller town where there was a persistent group of Catholics and a resident priest, was Wimborne Minster, Dorset. It is possible to reconstruct something of the structure of this small group and the life in England of their priest. Some 30-40 men and women were presented to Quarter Sessions between 1598-1617 as popish recusants and five of them were excommunicated 'at the suit of the tithes', and the same names recur in other lists. About half of the Catholics lived in the borough and half in the parish. The priest was William Warmingham, who lived with his sister Elizabeth. He had had a varied experience of persecution. His father, a recusant, died in Ilchester gaol, and he himself went abroad, was ordained and returned about 1580. He was sentenced to death but returned abroad where he served Cardinal Allen until his death in 1594. On the accession of James I he returned to England and obtained one of the general pardons which were to prove illusory for others beside himself and was committed to the Clink. He took the Oath of Allegiance and published a book in its defence. He was sent to live with his brother in Wimborne, where we find him in the lists, and he probably remained there until he was again imprisoned. We can only speculate about the relations between Warmington and his flock, but what is certain is that his example and influence would encourage both resistance and accommodation.[59]

Social Standing and Relationships of Catholics

In most parishes, but especially in the South and Midlands, the most stable element among the families of the parish were the yeomen, and so correspondingly Catholic yeomen were often the most stable element in their congregations. The Catholic Greenwell family of Greenwell near Wolsingham held the same land generation after generation and most of them were Catholics. They had interests outside their own parish, and through a network of family members and marriages the Greenwells were linked with several surrounding parishes. They drew their income from many different places including Newcastle and London.[60] In Derbyshire William Parsons of Stretton was convicted eleven times between 1605 and 1638, his wife and children were also convicted recusants, and the family and their connections formed the core of recusancy in the parish.[61] In Dorset there were many members of the Budden family in Holt, Bothenwood, Long Lane and Grange. Their names appeared on recusancy lists, they suffered excommunication, and entered into clandestine marriages through many generations during the seventeenth century.[62] The Hodgson family of Biggin House, Ugthorpe near Whitby, emerge as recusant from as early as 1580. They continued as Catholics throughout the period of penal legislation. They inhabited the same central farm but branches of the family were established within a twenty mile radius from Biggin House. Most of their marriages were with Catholics and they chose the godparents of their children from a small number of Catholic kindred. They were buried in Egton churchyard and their marriages were recorded in the parish registers. By the middle of the seventeenth century sons of the family were being sent to Douai College. The influence of such a family on their kindred and neighbours remains a matter of speculation, but the continuity and sheer familiarity of the Catholic lives of these families in the parish community must have done much to encourage tolerance.[63]

Continuity and stability in the composition of the local Catholic group was far from being the whole story. There was also much change. There were some parishes where early industrialisation was already attracting immigrants, and correspondingly the number of Catholic commoners was increasing. The largest number in a single parish was at Ryton, Durham diocese, where the numbers of recusants had increased from 2 to 50 by 1642. At the time of the Civil War the majority of leading families on Teeside were popish recusants and their recusancy did not inhibit their enterprise.[64] In other areas of nascent capitalism too there were non-gentry families of Catholics, who were in the course of becoming wealthier and so more influential in the local community. At this stage such areas were few, but by the nature of their location and occupations, these Catholics escaped some at least of the legal and social pressures upon Catholics elsewhere.

Catholics, especially young people and tradesmen, moved from place to place. Even where the Catholic group appears to have remained the same in numbers, close study shows that its composition was constantly changing. At York the vigorous outspoken men and women of the urban élite who refused to conform in the first generation after the Settlement were succeeded by small retailers and tradesmen. By the early seventeenth century most of the Catholics of York were gentlemen and their servants, and the 25 citizens included widows, spinsters and labourers.[65]

Catholics and the Law Courts in the Early Seventeenth Century

The process of compounding with the government for fines continued, and those compounding included persons well down the social scale. It involved much paper work and poorer recusants were represented in groups by wealthier Catholics as their attorneys, while women were represented by male friends. Among those compounding in the North were John Allonson of Skelton, Yorkshire, yeoman, for £3 10s. a year; George Comyn of Durham City for £2; and John Pickering of Baysford, Nottinghamshire, for £3 6s. 8d. In Staffordshire out of 176 recusants who were under sequestration between 1625 and 1640, 109 had made compositions. Of these 39 had compounded for goods, three on behalf of their wives, and 66 for land. The highest individual payment in the county was £66 13s. and the lowest 2s. 2d.[66]

From 1603 churchwardens had a statutory duty to report cases of recusancy to the diocesan authorities and to the justices of the peace. Constables were also required to present Catholics for a variety of behaviour, which by the seventeenth century had been declared illegal. There were always many more presented than were indicted, and large numbers of recusants failed to appear. Unless the defendant appeared either voluntarily or under process and pleaded to the indictment, no conviction was possible. Only exceptionally were accused persons kept in custody and the law depended on a long series of writs of summons. If the defendant failed to appear for five county court sessions, a new process of outlawry became possible, but although hundreds of recusants were outlawed they did not usually suffer loss of goods or perpetual imprisonment. Married women could not be outlawed so when this point in the process was reached the case was waived.[67]

The church courts were also required to control a wide variety of Catholic activities: absence from the parish church; failure to communicate in the parish church at Easter; engaging in 'superstitious' practices; reviling the Church of England; and leaving money to 'superstitious' uses. Catholics also frequently failed to attend these courts. In the diocese of York and Norwich few Roman Catholics ever attended the parish church and they were excommunicated.

Failure to appear was commonplace in the ecclesiastical courts as in the common law courts. The only penalty the church courts could award was excommunication, which was used so frequently that it has been suggested that as many as 15% of the adult population were excommunicated at any one time.[68] In the Derbyshire village of Hathersage 81 persons were excommunicate in 1609.[69] In 1601 nearly 900 excommunications of Catholics were signified from the 12 dioceses of Chichester, Coventry and Lichfield, Ely, Gloucester, Hereford, Lincoln, Norwich, Oxford, Peterborough, Rochester, Salisbury, and part of Winchester. The largest number was 128 from Hereford diocese. The number of parishes mentioned as the place of abode of the excommunicated Catholics was small; twelve in Wiltshire, for example, and nineteen in Staffordshire.[70]

Catholics came before the courts as more than naive peasants, for all yeomen, tradesmen and craftsmen needed to have a working knowledge of the law. Normally men of this sort played an important part in the execution of the law as constables, jurors of Quarter Sessions, Coroner's and Hundred courts, and as witnesses and sureties. They engaged in law suits and property deals; tradesmen had frequent recourse to fictitious law suits for many respectable purposes, as for example the use of *pedes finium* to ensure ownership in the transfer of property. In the sixteenth and seventeenth centuries the phraseology of royal, prerogative, manor and other courts was still derived from mediaeval tenurial relationships but by then was understood to represent newer relations of tenure and forms of ownership. Catholics did not on the whole participate in local government (though there were exceptions) but they were certainly not helpless victims powerless in the face of authority. Catholic evasions and manipulations of the law were part of a more general use of legal instruments which are not always quite what they seem and where the outcome was different from the stated intention.

The law tolerated a high level of failure to convict not only in respect of Catholics, and enforcement was normally dependent on political will, local circumstances and the informer, as can be shown in cases of witchcraft and treason as well as in cases of recusancy. More often there were recognised and accepted grey areas which left room for negotiation by all parties. Most lay people of the common sort had to work out their conflicting loyalties to Church, State, family and neighbourhood without the luxury or support of separation.

NOTES

1 Rosemary O'Day, *The Debate on the English Reformation* (1986); Christopher Haigh, *English Reformations: Religion and Politics under the Tudors* (1993), pp. 242-51; Walsham, p. 190; Bossy, *Catholics*; Patrick McGrath, 'English Catholicism, a reconsideration', *Journal of Ecclesiastical History* 35, no. 3 (July 1984), pp. 414-28; E. Duffy, 'Continuity and divergence in Tudor Religion', *Studies in Church History* 32 (1996), pp. 171-205.

2 C. Buckingham, 'The movement of clergy in the diocese of Canterbury 1552-1562', *Recusant History* 14, no. 4 (October 1978), pp. 219-42. For Clement Norton see p. 229.

[3] David M. Palliser, 'Popular Reactions to the Reformation', in C. Haigh ed., *The English Reformation Revised* (1987), p. 111.

[4] John Miller, *Popery* (1973), p. 49. The enforcement of the shilling fine needs further research and this judgement may prove to be simplistic. W.P.M. Kennedy, 'Fines under the Elizabethan Act of Uniformity', *English Historical Review* 33 (1918), pp. 517-28; E. Whatmore, *Recusancy in Kent: studies and documents* (privately printed, 1973), p. 19; John E. Paul, 'Recusants in the time of Elizabeth I with special reference to Winchester', *Proceedings of the Hampshire Field Club* 21 (1958-60).

[5] Anthony Fletcher, *Tudor Rebellions* (1968), pp. 91-101; C.E. Whiting, 'The Rising of the North in 1569', *Durham University Journal* 28.

[6] Haigh, *English Reformations*, p. 257

[7] John Tanner, *Tudor Constitutional Documents 1485-1603* (1951), pp. 143-6.

[8] Margaret Gosling, 'Berkshire and Oxfordshire Catholics and the Lenten Assize of 1588', *Oxoniensia* 58 (1953), pp. 252-62.

[9] F.A. Bailey, 'The Churchwardens' accounts of Prescot, Lancs', *Lancashire and Cheshire Record Society* 104 (1953), p. 138.

[10] C.K. Kitching, 'Church and Chapelries in Sixteenth Century England' in D. Baker ed., *Studies in Church History* 16 (1979), p. 291.

[11] S.A. Peyton ed., *The Churchwardens' Presentments in the Oxford Peculiars of Dorchester, Thame and Banbury*, (Oxfordshire Records Series 10, 1928); E. Carlson, 'The Origins, Function and Status of the Office of Churchwardens' in Spufford, pp. 164-5, 170-3.

[12] Carl Z. Weiner, 'The Beleaguered Isle: a Study in Elizabethan and Jacobean Anti-Catholicism', *Past and Present* 51 (1971), pp. 27-62.

[13] Patrick McGrath & Joy Rowe, 'The Imprisonment of Catholics in the Reign of Elizabeth I', *Recusant History* 20, no. 4 (October 1991), p. 418; Claire Cross, 'The Third Earl of Huntingdon and Trials of Catholics in the North', *Recusant History* 8, no. 3 (October 1965), pp. 136-47.

[14] John H. Pollen ed., 'Official Lists of Prisoners of Religion 1562-1602', *Miscellanea* (C.R.S. 1 ibid., 'Tower Bills 1575-1589', *Miscellanea* (C.R.S. 3, 1906); Anthony G. Petti (ed.), *Recusant Documents from the Ellesmere Manuscripts 1577-1715* (C.R.S. 60, 1968), pp. 42-82; Aveling, *Handle*, pp. 63-4.

[15] Jan Rhodes, 'English Books of Martyrs', *Recusant History* 22, no. 1 (May 1994), pp. 7-26; Gillian Brennan, 'Papists and Patriotism', *Recusant History* 19 (May 1988), pp. 1-16; Claire Cross, 'An English Martyrologist and his Martyr' in David Wood ed., *Studies in Church History* 29 (1993), p. 271; Claire Cross, 'Martyrdom Preparation at Douai and Rome', ibid., pp. 276-7; C. Sullivan, *Dismembered Rhetoric: English Recusant Writing 1580-1603* (1995).

[16] Leo Warren, *Through Twenty Preston Guilds* (privately printed, Wigan, 1993), p. 11; Patrick Walsh, *Papers Relating to the Process of the Canonisations of the Forty English Martyrs*; Richard Trappes Lomax, 'The Birthplace of Robert Anderton', *Biographical Studies* [later *Recusant History*] 1, no. 3, (1951) pp. 235-7; Anon., *Portraits of the English Martyrs of the Sixteenth and Seventeenth Centuries* (New York, 1895); J.E. Bamber, 'The Secret Treasure of Chaigley', *Recusant History* 17 (October 1985), pp. 307-29.

[17] A. Raines, 'York Civic Records no. 7', *Yorkshire Archaeological Series* 1, 115 (1950), pp. 130-52.

[18] Anstruther; E.I. Watkin, *Roman Catholicism in England* (1957), pp. 42, 64, 84, 93, 96.

[19] Patrick McGrath & Joy Rowe, 'The Elizabethan Priests: their Harbourers and Helpers', *Recusant History* 19, no. 3 (May 1989), pp. 209-234.

[20] Michael Hodgetts, 'A Topographical Index of Hiding Places', *Recusant History* 16 no. 2 (October 1982), pp. 146-217; *Secret Hiding Places* (1989), p. 48; 'A Topographical Index ...II', *Recusant History* 24, no. 1 (May 1998), pp. 1-54.

[21] *C.S.P.D. Elizabeth I*, 1582, 156, p. 29.

22 John S. Hansom ed., 'Recusants of Masham, Yorks, 1589-1628', *Miscellanea 3* (C.R.S. 6, 1906), pp. 82-7.
23 McGrath & Rowe, 'The Elizabethan Priests', pp. 220, 230.
24 Foley 6, p. 721 — from *C.S.P.D. Elizabeth I*, 1583.
25 Keith Wark, *Elizabethan Recusancy in Cheshire* (Chetham Society Third Series 19, 1971), p. 6.
26 Foley, Jesuit Annual Letters, *passim*; John Morris, *Troubles of Our Catholic Forefathers* (1877), p. 18.
27 Edward Peacock ed., *A List of the Roman Catholics in the County of York in 1604* (1872); Michael O'Dwyer, *Bl. Anne Line* (Farm St. London, 1961).
28 Marie B. Rowlands, 'Recusant Women' in Mary Prior ed., *Women in English Society 1500-1800* (1985), pp. 156-8.
29 *C.S.P.D. Charles I, 1637.*
30 *C.S.P.D. Elizabeth I, 1591-4*, p. 389; *C.S.P.D. Charles I, 1639*, pp. 124, 357.
31 Tessa Watts, 'The Pedlar's Pack', in Spufford, pp. 274-534; Antony F. Allison & David M. Rogers, *The Contemporary Printed Literature of the English Counter Reformation between 1558 and 1640* (1994), p. 225.
32 P.R. Harris, 'Reports of William Udall Informer 1605-1612', Part One, *Recusant History* 8, no. 4 (January 1966), pp. 235, 238; ibid., Part Two, *Recusant History* 8 no. 5 (April 1966), p. 260; Patrick McGrath & Joy Rowe, 'Informers', *Recusant History* 20, no. 1 (October 1990), p. 420; J.S. Leatherbarrow, *The Lancashire Recusants* (Lancashire and Cheshire History Society 110, 1947); Petti, *Ellesmere Manuscripts*, p. 51.
33 Hodgetts, *Secret Hiding Places*, p. 48.
34 A.C.F. Beales, 'A Biographical Catalogue of Catholic Schoolmasters', *Recusant History* 17, no. 6 (October 1964), pp. 268-91.
35 William Hassall-Smith, 'Puritans and Neighbourhood', Conference of Regional and Local Historians paper (May 1984); William Hassall-Smith ed., *The Papers of Nathaniel Bacon of Stiffkey* (2 volumes, Norfolk Record Society, 1987-1989), *passim*.
36 P. Brandon & B. Short, *The South East from AD 1000* (1990), p. 140.
37 Mary Calthrop ed., *Recusant Roll No. 1 1592-3* (C.R.S. 18, 1916).
38 Michael Questier, *Conversion, Politics and Religion in England, 1580-1625* (1996); D.M. Clarke, 'Certificates of Conformity in the King's Bench', *Recusant History* 14, no. 1 (May 1977), pp. 53-8; *The Acts of the High Commission Court within the Diocese of Durham* (Surtees Society 34, 1858), p. 185.
39 Magee; Francis X. Walker, *The Implementation of the Elizabethan Statutes against Recusants 1581-1603* (Ph.D. London, 1951).
40 David Palliser, 'The Parish in Perspective', p. 25; Christopher Haigh, 'The Church of England, the Catholics and the People', p. 200 & *passim*; McGrath, 'Reconsideration', p. 419; J. Aveling, 'Some Aspects of Yorkshire Catholic Recusant History' in G.J. Cuming ed., *Studies in Church History* 4 (1967), pp. 110-1.
41 Christopher Haigh, *Reformation and Resistance in Tudor Lancashire* (1975), pp. 328-30.
42 *C.S.P.D. Elizabeth I, 1600*, pp. 389, 466; V.C.H. *Lancashire* 7, p. 299; J. Dottie, 'The Recusant Riots at Childwall in May 1600: a Reappraisal' in *Seventeenth Century Lancashire Essays presented to J.J. Bagley* (Lancashire and Cheshire Historical Society 132, 1983), pp. 1-29; Haigh, *Reformation and Resistance*, pp. 329, 362; Eric Clavering, 'Riot and Recusancy', *Durham Local History Society Bulletin* 49 (December, 1992), 3-23.
43 Wark, *Elizabethan Recusancy in Cheshire*, p. 19.
44 Roland Mathias, *Whitsun Riot: an Account of the Commotion among Catholics in Herefordshire and Monmouthshire in 1605* (1963).

[45] C.J. Ryan, 'The Jacobean Oath of Allegiance and England', *History Review* 28 (1942), pp. 163-4; Anne Foster, 'The Oath Tendered', *Recusant History* 20, no. 3 (May 1991), pp. 305-20. Jesuit Annual letters 1624 quoted in Philip Caraman, *The Years of Siege* (1966), p. 56.

[46] Colin Haydon, *Anti-Catholicism in the Eighteenth Century* (1993), pp. 4-6; Peter Lake, 'Anti-popery: the Structure of Prejudice' in Richard Cust & Anne Hughes, *Conflict in Early Modern England* (1989), pp. 72-107.

[47] M. W. Greenslade ed., *The Boy of Bilston* (facsimile) (*Staffordshire Catholic History* 11, 1970); Keith Thomas, *Religion and the Decline of Magic* (1971).

[48] W.E. Rhodes, *The Apostolical Life of Ambrose Barlow O.S.B. 1585-1641* (Chetham Society New Series 43, 1909), pp. 7-8.

[49] Challoner; Patrick J. Walsh, *The Martyrs of England and Wales 1535-1680* (1978), p. 30; Foley 2, pp. 231-2; ibid. 7, p. 489; *Catholic Magazine* (1833), p. 298.

[50] Foley 2, pp. 24-74, 231.

[51] Caraman, *Years of Siege*, pp. 80-1 — quoting Jesuit Archives, Rome, Angl. Hist, 1590-1618; Foley 1, p. 217.

[52] John D. Crichton, *Worship in a Hidden Church 1624-60* (1988); ibid., 'The Laity and the Liturgy 1600-1900', *Worc. Rec.* 43 (June 1984), pp. 1-19; Antony Allison, 'John Heigham of St. Omer 1568-1632', *Recusant History* 4, no. 6 (1958), pp. 226-43; Joseph Jungman, *The Mass of the Roman Rite* (1959), pp. 108, 122.

[53] Greenslade, *The Boy of Bilston*, p. 75.

[54] Ushaw, W. Smith Notes on the Records of the Court of High Commission, (TS) 10, p. 77; *C.S.P.D. James I, 1624*, 187; *C.S.P.D. Charles I, Add. 1639*, 437, p. 212. Information on catechising in the Low Countries from Fr. J. Vanden Bussche, C.P., Wezembeek-Oppem, Belgium.

[55] Foley 2, p. 144.

[56] Henriette Peters, *Mary Ward, a World in Contemplation*, trans. Helen Butterworth (1994), pp. 3-57; Rowlands, 'Recusant Women', pp. 169-75.

[57] J.Hugh Aveling ed., 'Recusancy Papers of the Meynell Family 1596-1676' , *Miscellanea* (C.R.S. 56, 1964), p. xxi; Aveling, *North*.

[58] Hilton, *Lancashire*, p. 30.

[59] Anstruther 1, p. 371; Dor. R.O. PE/WM based on unpublished work by Timothy McVey & Elizabeth Adams.

[60] Eric Clavering, 'The Dynamics of Durham Recusancy 1600-1642', *Durham Local History Society Bulletin* 48 (May 1992), pp. 3-27.

[61] Roger Clark, *Anglicanism, Recusancy and Dissent in Derbyshire 1603-1730* (D.Phil Oxford, 1979), pp. 65-71.

[62] Dor. R.O. PE/WM CP2.

[63] Information from Mrs Maureen Grieve, Cleveland Family History Society.

[64] Clavering, 'The Dynamics of Durham Recusancy', pp. 6-7.

[65] Aveling, *York*.

[66] J.J. La Rocca, 'James I and his Catholic Subjects 1606-1612: Some Financial Implications', *Recusant History* 18, no. 3 (1987), pp. 251-63; T. Smith, 'Sequestrations for Recusancy in Staffordshire in 1640', *Staffs. C.H.* 18 (1978), pp. 1-12.

[67] John A. Sharpe, *Crime in Early Modern England 1550-1750* (1984), especially chapter 3, pp. 72-93.

[68] Susan Wright ed., *Parish, Church and People: Local Studies in Lay Religion 1350-1750* (1988); Richard A. Marchant, *The Church under the Law: Justice, Administration and Discipline in the Diocese of York 1560-1640* (Cambridge, 1969), pp. 204, 208, 216; E.R. Brinkworth ed., *Archdeacons Court* (Oxfordshire Record Society), pp. vii-xxi; *Archdeaconry of Taunton Comperta and Proceedings 1623-4* (Somerset Record Society 43, 1928).

[69] L.J.R.O. B1/1/126, B1/1/103, B.C. 5/1626.

[70] Petti, *Ellesmere Manuscripts* (C.R.S. 60, 1968), pp. 102-45.

3

THE GODLY GARRET, 1560-1660

Up to her godly garret after sev'n,
There starve and pray, for that's the way to heav'n.

Alexander Pope, *Epistle to Miss Blount, On her leaving the Town after the Coronation* (1715)

Let the *Presbyterians* meet in their Halls, the *Fanaticks* in their Barns, the *Papists* in their Garrets; shall the Church of England Assembled in her Cathedrals fear the Competition of Rivals every way so inferiour to her?

Clarendon, *Second Thoughts; or the Case of a Limited Toleration* (1662)

During the last thirty years there has been an increasing interest in the liturgical and devotional life of recusants.[1] But, apart from the Embassies in London and such show-places as Wardour and Lulworth, this interest has not on the whole extended to their chapels.[2] The only full survey of the subject is Bryan Little's *Catholic Churches since 1623* (1966), and this deals only with structures built as chapels, not with rooms in houses which were adapted or fitted up for worship. The starting-date, 1623, is that of the building by Inigo Jones of Henrietta Maria's Chapel Royal at St James', by which time there had already been recusant chapels for more than fifty years; and Little takes only seventeen pages to cover the century and a half from then until 1778.[3] Pevsner and the V.C.H. are sketchy and patchy on this topic; the possibility of a recusant counterpart to the three volumes of Nonconformist chapels and meeting-houses edited by Christopher Stell for the Royal Commission on Historical Monuments has not yet even been considered.[4]

What follows is, therefore, a preliminary sketch of a large subject, which will serve its purpose if it draws attention to the gaps. For reasons of space it is confined to the century between the Elizabethan Settlement and the Restoration: the first four of the ten recusant generations and the years on which Little had least to say. Its scope can be defined by a quotation from Bossy:[5]

> Mass on Sunday, or more often, was as domestic as fish on Friday. It followed a well-marked itinerary round the house, from the halls and 'fair large chambers' where the congregations of the Elizabeth pioneers assembled, like Campion's before his arrest at Lyford; up to the less vulnerable attics, where many of the first generation of chaplain-missioners sat 'like sparrows upon the house-top' and most of the

earliest special Mass-chambers were fitted up; thence, as the seventeenth century drew to a close and houses perhaps grew larger, tentatively down to the first floor, where a suite of rooms accommodated priest, chapel and sacristy; and finally back to ground-level by the middle of the eighteenth century — though scarcely as yet to the new generation of outdoor chapels which began to go up a decade or so later.

Within this scheme, I want to ask three specific questions. First, in a gentry house where a priest was harboured, how were the requirements of security reconciled with the complex functions of the household and with access for family, servants and outsiders? Second, what evidence is there for the furnishing and decoration of the earlier domestic chapels? And third, what is known about the other liturgical setting familiar to Catholics of the common sort: the farmhouse where Mass was said ten or a dozen times a year by an itinerant or riding priest?

The Chapel and the House

Until the publication in 1978 of Mark Girouard's *Life in the English Country House,* most of what had been written about Elizabethan, Stuart and Georgian mansions had been concerned with their façades and decoration rather than with their plans and functions. The most spectacular illustration of the newer approach has been the restoration by the National Trust between 1973 and 1977 of Erddig, near Wrexham, where the estate, stable and laundry yards are as significant as the state rooms. A similar approach can be seen at Shugborough in Staffordshire and elsewhere, but within the house itself there is still a tendency to think in terms of furniture and decoration rather than of the interlocking uses of the rooms. The guidebooks to some houses omit plans, which are essential for this purpose, because they may be useful to prospective thieves. More than a century and a half ago John Kirk wrote:

> The old chapel at Moseley, like many others, while the penal laws hung over our heads, was a part of the garrets, and had no other approach to it, than through the house. Yet to this inconvenience did the family willingly submit, to accommodate their tenants, and the neighbouring Catholics.[6]

But very little has been written by recusant historians to tease out the implications of this aside.

The 'halls' and the 'fair large chambers' mentioned by Bossy are both references to single incidents in Campion's single year of missionary work. On 29 June 1580, the feast of SS. Peter and Paul, he preached his first sermon after returning to England in the hall of the London house of Lord Norreys of Rycote, which had been hired for the occasion by Lord Paget.[7] On 16 July 1581, he preached his last sermon before his arrest in 'a fair large chamber' at Lyford in Berkshire. George Eliot, the spy who brought about the arrest, had been at Mr Roper's of Orpington in Kent as a fellow-servant of the cook at Lyford, who asked him, 'Will you go up?' 'By which speech', explains Eliot, 'I knew he would bring me to a Mass'. Already, then, Mass was said upstairs and there was a set phrase which assumed that it was and which identified those who were trustworthy without giving anything away to those who were not. From the buttery, where they had drunk a mug of ale together and which would have been at the screens end of the hall, the cook led Eliot through the hall itself, through the dining parlour (which was conventionally at the upper end of the hall), past two or three other rooms, and so to the 'fair large chamber'.[8] A 'chamber' always means an upstairs room, and so, even without the cook's coded invitation, it would be certain that the pair went up a flight of stairs at the upper end of the hall. This one was probably the great chamber, which is normally off the first landing of the great staircase. But Lyford, with its two resident priests and three Bridgettine nuns from Syon, was no ordinary recusant house; and this, with Campion preaching to dons and undergraduates who had ridden or walked the twelve miles from Oxford to hear him, was no ordinary occasion. So it does not follow that Mass at Lyford was always in this chamber, still less that what happened at Lyford must have happened elsewhere.

For how long had 'go up' meant 'go to Mass'? What happened in the 1560s and 1570s in a medieval or Tudor house which already had a domestic chapel before 1559?[9] By the fifteenth century such chapels were usually on the ground floor, with access for the servants from the courtyard and with a gallery for the family reached from the solar.[10] A very grand example is the Chapel Royal at Hampton Court Palace, with its Royal Pew and flanking Holyday Closets. In Protestant houses this lay-out continued into the seventeenth and eighteenth centuries, as at Little Moreton in Cheshire with its black-letter texts painted on the walls, or Erddig with its Georgian panelling and pews. By the eighteenth century there had been a return to it in Catholic houses as well, as at Brandsby in Yorkshire or the later chapel, now the saloon, at Coughton in Warwickshire.[11] Did some of these medieval and Tudor chapels remain in use for Mass after 1559, especially where there was no village, or the house was well away from it or, as Lord Vaux claimed for Harrowden Hall in 1580, was 'a parish by itself'?[12]

There are plausible examples at Nunney Castle in Somerset, where the fourteenth-century chapel still survives on the third floor of the south-west tower;[13] at Ashbury Manor Farm in Berkshire where Campion may have said Mass in the fifteenth-century oratory over the porch;[14] at Ightham Mote in Kent, where there are two chapels, a gaunt fourteenth-century one of stone, and a sixteenth-century one with a barrel-vaulted timber roof;[15] and at Compton Wynyates in Warwickshire, the home of William Weston's friend Henry, first Lord Compton.[16] Compton Wynyates has three chapels: the little church outside the moat which replaced the medieval one destroyed in the Civil War; the ground-floor chapel of about 1510, with a screen depicting the Seven Deadly Sins and a mullioned opening to the Chapel Drawing Room; and a roof chapel with what look like the consecration crosses roughly carved on the wooden window-sill.[17] No doubt the Prayer Book was used in church, though there had been no village since 1514, when it was pulled down for a sheep-walk,[18] but what went on in the ground-floor chapel of the house (except during the Queen's visit of August 1572) is another matter; in any case, the chapel in the roof points to a greater measure of secrecy during the later 1570s or early 1580s.

Generally, it seems that by the mid-1580s Mass would normally be said above stairs. In September 1584, Ralph Miller, a former tailor at Rheims, was one of 'about eighteen persons' who heard Mass in Lord Vaux's house at Hackney.

> The said priest lieth in a chamber beyond the hall, on the left hand the stair that leadeth to the chambers, and the Mass is said in the chapel, being right over the port entering into the hall [as at Ashbury]; and the way into it is up the stair aforesaid, on the left hand, at the further end of the gallery.[19]

About the same time, William Weston landed near Norwich and his autobiography from then until his arrest on 3 August 1586 gives some relevant information which is valuable for being narrowly dated. Some of it is vague: he reconciled the Earl of Arundel (St Philip Howard) in October 1584 at a Mass said 'in a private place';[20] in April 1585, at a house about nine miles out of London, he was interrupted when about to say Mass in 'a fine room [which] had been chosen [as] well suited to it'.[21] But elsewhere a gentleman served Mass 'at the top of the house' in a surplice and with his sword handy; and a recusant wife with a conforming husband had Mass 'upstairs'.[22] At Harleyford in July 1586, Richard Bold had a properly furnished chapel, 'set apart for the celebration of the Church's offices', which seems to rule out the hall and the great chamber. But it was clearly a large room since, during the octave for which Weston, Garnet and

Southwell were there, Mass was sung with a mixed choir, conducted by William Byrd and accompanied by organ 'and other instruments'.[23] It could have been a long gallery. Weston, like most seminary priests in the 1580s, was an itinerant missioner, constantly on the move, and so we also find him hearing a gentleman's confession in the garden to avoid his prying wife and giving him communion in the best room of an inn at the nearest town on market-day.[24] He had to carry singing-cakes with him, and once left a trail of them half a mile long.[25] By contrast, in the early 1590s John Gerard found vestments and everything else necessary laid out ready in almost every house that he came to.[26] This was a consequence of the strategy worked out at Harleyford of stationing priests in gentry houses,[27] and implies, if not permanent chapels, as at Battle Abbey,[28] at least the regular use of one room with a hide for the Massing stuff close by.

The greater safety of the attics cannot have been easy to combine with privacy for the family and access for servants and outsiders. Household prayers in the hall or great chamber were a normal Elizabethan custom where there was no chapel,[29] so that the use of these rooms for Mass had posed no problems of this kind, even if they were too open to spies like Eliot. By 1668 the Long Gallery at Carlton was in use as a chapel, with elaborate permanent furnishings which are recorded in Sir Miles Stapleton's household accounts.[30] But under Elizabeth and James I it was a matter of making the best of the top floor as it was and putting up with the necessary compromises, particularly with regard to staircases. This point can be illustrated by the plans and documents at four houses: Coughton, Moseley, Ufton and Harvington.

Coughton is one of the earliest recusant houses in the country. Even in the 1530s, Sir George Throckmorton had been imprisoned for opposing Henry VIII's divorce from Catherine of Aragon[31] and his sister Elizabeth, abbess of Denney in Cambridgeshire, had returned to Coughton after its dissolution in 1537 with two of her nuns and there maintained the religious life until her death in 1547.[32] Southwell's panegyric on Edward Throckmorton, who died at the English College in Rome in 1582,[33] shows that by 1575 at latest there was a regular Mass centre at Coughton, served by a Marian priest who arrived on horseback and was therefore not the incumbent of the late-Perpendicular church forty yards away outside the moat. Although Coughton was repaired and altered by Sir Francis Throckmorton in the 1660s after extensive damage in the Civil War and was again remodelled in the 1780s by the then Sir

Robert Throckmorton,[34] the possible sites for a chapel can be reduced to four: the now-demolished east block, which was used under James II; the great hall, now the Saloon, which was the Georgian chapel; the dining-room next to it, which seems to have been the Elizabethan great chamber;[35] and the topmost room of the gatehouse, off which is a hiding-place where a Spanish-leather altar was found in 1858. It is a reasonable inference that the Tower Room, the least accessible of the four, was in use as the chapel by the time of the Throckmorton Plot in 1583; certainly by the time of the search in 1593, when 'a priest being a seminary was harboured there..., who was conveyed out of the way or lieth hid in some secret place'.[36]

A certificate of Warwickshire recusants dated 25 September 1592 includes Mrs Mary Arden (Thomas Throckmorton's sister, who was mistress of Coughton at the time of the search); John Browne, 'servant to Mrs Mary Arden'; William Mence, 'a keeper'; and Francis Bickerton, 'servant to Mr Thomas Throckmorton', and his wife.[37] Another list of 14 March 1606 names twenty-six recusants from Coughton: yeomen, husbandmen, spinsters and a tailor's wife, but no servants of Thomas Throckmorton, who had prudently gone abroad after leasing Coughton to Sir Everard Digby at the time of the Gunpowder Plot.[38] Just before that, however, both Nicholas Owen and one of Sir Everard's servants, William Handy, admitted hearing Mass 'in Coughton House' on All Saints' Day (1 November) 1605. Owen confessed that, apart from himself, there were 'some others to the number of half a dozen'; Handy said that, apart from himself, there were 'the Lady Digby and Mrs Vaux and Mrs Brooksby and some other servants', and that two Masses were said, one by Garnet and the other by John Percy, S.J.[39] But Handy's fellow-servant James Garvey 'saith he never was recusant, neither knoweth not any priest', although he, like Handy, had been one of the party that visited St Winifred's Well the previous August, when Mass had been said at each of the recusant houses on the way there and back.[40] From this it is clear, first, that servants did attend Mass with the gentry, not only at Coughton but in other houses as well and, second, that those who were not recusants could be kept from knowing what was happening. The mention of the keeper and of the recusants from the neighbourhood indicates that outsiders were also admitted, though not necessarily on the same occasions. The geography of Coughton allows a reconstruction of how this was done.

Coughton was a quadrangular building with walls rising straight out of the moat on all sides but the east. The gatehouse, with the Tower Room two storeys above it, is on the west, the family rooms on the south and the offices on the north; the east range, where the chapel was under James II, was destroyed by a mob in 1688, though the ruins were not cleared away until the 1780s. There were two bridges across the moat, one to the gatehouse and one at the north-east corner from the early-sixteenth-century kitchen outside the moat to the rest of the offices.[41] The Tower Room itself could only be reached by a newel staircase from ground to first floor in the north-east turret of the gatehouse and then by another newel staircase from first to second floor in the south-east turret. Between the two staircases it was necessary to cross what is now the Drawing Room on the first floor of the gatehouse. Both staircases are steep and narrow, and the Tower Room could easily pass, and may have been built, as a banqueting-house or a standing for watching the hunt, to which in either case only the Throckmortons and those whom they invited could expect to be admitted.[42]

Moseley Old Hall in Staffordshire is amply documented because of Charles II's stay there on Monday and Tuesday 8-9 September 1651 during his flight after the Battle of Worcester. Its date is uncertain, but it was referred to as 'Mr Pitt's new Hall at Moseley' in 1600,[43] and cannot be earlier than 1583, when Henry Pitt bought the estate.[44] It continued to be used for Mass until the 1820s.[45] It is much smaller than Coughton, with accommodation which is simpler and easier to interpret. At the north end of the hall are the brewhouse and buttery and at the south end the parlour. There was no kitchen: cooking was done in the hall. There was no great chamber either, though Thomas Whitgreave's 'parlour chamber' above the hall[46] may have served some of its functions. There are two staircases: the newel stairs next to the buttery and the main staircase, of about 1700 but built on the site of its predecessor, next to the parlour. There are three outside doors: the back door next to the newel staircase, through which the King was brought into the house; the front door with its porch into the hall; and one at the foot of the main stairs which seems to be a Georgian alteration.[47]

The newel staircase now goes only to the first floor but originally went up to the attics. Until the nineteenth century, when a corridor was inserted, Whitgreave's chamber occupied the full depth of the building on the first floor, obstructing communication between the newel staircase at the north end and the chapel, which is in the attics at the south end. Further, in 1651 the lane which runs outside the garden, a few yards from the porch and front door, was the main road from Wolverhampton to Cannock, so that a congregation admitted by that way might be observed. The Whitgreaves' chaplain, John Huddleston, had in fact said Mass in the house on Sunday 7 September[48] and on the Tuesday morning the King, from the study above the porch and off Whitgreave's chamber, watched the remnants of his army retreating northwards.[49] So it seems likely that the congregation, like the King, came in by the back door. They could then have either continued up the newel staircase and across the attics or else crossed the hall to the main staircase, which was certainly used later: even in the late eighteenth century a servant was still posted on the first landing to interrogate any stranger.[50] This second route would also have the advantage of keeping the congregation away from Huddleston's room, which was off the first landing of the newel staircase and, with its priest-hole, was that used by the King.

Ufton Court in Berkshire, the home of the Perkins family, was searched in 1586 and 1599 and still contains four priest-holes, an oratory and priest's room on the first floor and a chapel in the attics. These are all above the offices at the south end: the oratory, priest's room and chapel are over the brewhouse, which forms one stroke of the E-plan. There is direct access from outside to the brewhouse, and inside is a newel staircase, built in the middle of the wing and with no windows, which goes as far as the first floor. There it is necessary to cross two landings to another staircase, which cannot be seen from the first and leads up to the chapel. Close to the chapel, but not in it, are two priest-holes, rather as at Moseley, where the vestment hide is not in the chapel but in the gable over the porch and Whitgreave's study.[51]

Harvington has two bridges over the moat, as at Coughton, and the two chapels and three priests' rooms are above the offices, as at Ufton.[52] Of the three staircases in what survives of the house,[53] one only goes to the first floor; the great and newel staircases both ascend to opposite ends of the Nine Worthies Passage on the second floor, off which are the chapels and priests' room, and both have doors to the great chamber at the first floor landing. According to local tradition, the congregation used the newel staircase and were guided by the trefoil pattern stencilled on the underside of the treads.[54] This tradition is perhaps supported by the existence of a priest-hole under the top flight of the great staircase: if the house was raided, it would be dangerous to have the priest trying to hide under stairs which the congregation were using to disperse by. Moreover, there are remains of doorways halfway up the top flight of the newel staircase, between its top landing and the Worthies Passage, and between this Passage and the top landing of the Great Staircase.

Since almost all the timber-and-plaster partitions on this floor still have Elizabethan wall-paintings on them, we can be certain that the layout has not been altered at all during the last four hundred years, and it is therefore a survival of great rarity and importance.

On the ground floor, between the great and newel staircases, is the Elizabethan buttery. A report of 1595 on Derbyshire suggests that this point may also have a bearing on approaches to the chapels. At Yeldersley, 'four miles from Alkmonton, [was] Robert Showell, a seminary priest with a bald head, having one leg shorter than the other; and at the buttery door go up a pair of stairs to the chamber where they say Mass often'. At Roston, three miles from Yeldersley, there was 'before the parlour door a spence [buttery] where priests and church stuff are to be found'.[55] These details suggest that the constant comings and goings in and around the buttery, vividly portrayed by Charles II in his account of his experiences at Abbot's Leigh, near Bristol,[56] would make other comings and goings less noticeable; perhaps even that attempts to identify the chapel should sometimes begin two storeys below with the staircase at the lower end of the hall. Structurally as well as economically, the chapels of the recusant gentry were supported by the labours of the lower orders.

The Furnishings and Decoration of Chapels

Once a servant, yeoman or spinster had climbed the back-stairs to the attic chapel, what did he or she find there? Not choir-stalls and a pulpit, as at Battle Abbey about 1600,[57] but perhaps not either 'a gloomy garret and in no way ornamented', as at Sawston in 1757.[58] There are scattered but important remains of wall-paintings, and it is likely that systematic listing would turn up many more. At Moseley there is simulated panelling in black on grey, part original and part restoration.[59] At Todd Hall in Lancashire there is a crude mural of the Crucifixion with the two Marys in farthingales.[60] At Widmore Old Cottage, Bromley, Kent, is a plaster roundel in low relief of the pelican in her piety, framed by Ionic pilasters and an architrave.[61] At Harvington, the smaller chapel is decorated with vertical rows of red and white drops for the blood and water of the Passion,[62] and the larger one with a pattern of vines, lilies and pomegranates springing from vases.[63] Even more remarkable is the scheme at Althrey Hall Farm, Bangor-on-Dee, where the sloping sides of the gable are painted in black, grey and greenish yellow with turrets, doors, battlements and latticed windows; on the north side is a sun with face and rays and on the south side, overlooking the garden, a crescent moon, while in the apexes of the gables are the monograms IHS at the west end and INRI at the east. The design seems to represent the Heavenly Jerusalem from the Apocalypse.[64] At Ufton, the oratory is lined with clapboarding with a dark (probably black) ground divided into squares containing alternately the monograms IHS in white and MR in red and with the rails and stiles decorated with red and white stems and flowers. On the narrow panels forming a frieze at the top are the initials AP, probably for Anna Perkins, who died in 1635.[65]

The Massing stuff was sometimes remarkably elaborate, and there might be other furnishings, which were not always removed when not in use. At Sir Thomas Tresham's house at Hoxton in August 1584, the searchers, after listing all their servants and their functions, noted the discovery of 'a new-fashioned picture of Christ in a great table, and a tabernacle of sundry painted images with leaves to fold, serving, as it should seem, for a tabernacle or screen to stand upon an altar'.[66] A month later, Ralph Miller saw 'a very fair crucifix of silver' in the chapel over the hall porch in Lord Vaux's house at Hackney.[67] At Harrowden between 1600 and 1611 there were two sets of vestments in each liturgical colour, six silver candlesticks, with two more at the side for the elevation, silver cruets, lavabo bowl, bell and thurible, and a silver crucifix, except on great feasts, when it was replaced by a golden one a foot high.[68] At St Anthony's, near Newcastle, in 1624, where Compline was sung daily and all the servants attended the Litany of the Saints after dinner, the furnishings included a triangular hearse for Tenebrae in Holy Week.[69]

These chapels were in the houses of peers and gentry, but they were not exclusively private oratories for the rich. The distinction between gentry chaplaincies and riding missions should not be drawn as rigidly as it sometimes has been, and priests moved from one form of work to another. The congregation at St Anthony's included coalminers from Newcastle and foreign seamen from Catholic countries, and all were invited to mince-pies after Midnight Mass and to 'break the neck of Lent' with a joint of Paschal lamb.[70] St Henry Morse, who served there in the 1620s, became an army chaplain in Flanders in 1630 and then moved to London in 1634, where he worked among the soap-vats, pest-houses and brothels of St Giles-in-the-Fields until he was executed at Tyburn in 1645.[71] At the same time, it was the custom of St. Ambrose Barlow (executed at Lancaster in 1641) to spend three weeks of each month at Morleys Hall near Manchester and the fourth, except in Advent, 'on circuit.... sometimes to several houses in a morning'.[72] His *Apostolical Life* shows that a priest was not compelled either to 'tramp the

Yorkshire moors' or to 'relax in plush Oxfordshire manor-houses':[73]

> His solemn days of invitation were three, viz. Christmas, Easter and Whitsunday, and then he entertained all that would dine with him. Their cheer was boiled beef and pottage, minched pies, goose and groats, and to every man a grey coat at parting. He served them, and his example made some others of his richer guests to do the like. In fine, when the poor were risen, he sat down at their table and made his dinner of their leavings, and then the residue that was left was divided among the poorest to take home with them. [At Christmas] the foulest winter weather was no hindrance to them: old folks as well as young came, and those that could not well come by day came by night. Being come, they hasted to the chapel, when, the men leaving their hats upon a round table all together (representing the unity of their hearts), they passed by a fair coal-fire to the altar, which upon the Eve was ready dressed with clean linens, and a venerable old vestment laid thereon which came out but upon great days, with all other things poor and clean. The old picture before the altar was the arraignment of our blessed Saviour. Against that good time he used to prepare great wax candles, which he did help to make himself....His penitents ..., so truly united in charity, rejoiced coming, from several places, to meet one another in that holy exercise. They spent the night modestly and devoutly, sometimes in prayer before the altar, otherwhiles singing devout songs by the fireside in another room...that their singing might not disturb those that would be praying in the chapel.[74]

It may be true that the Ignatian techniques of meditation would appeal to gentry and other literate Catholics, and that the less educated would have preferred the old round of seasons and ceremonies.[75] But these instances show that recusancy had established its own traditional observances, centred on the liturgy, and therefore that we should consider three elements of spirituality, not only two.

There was another setting in which gentry and their inferiors met for Mass, one where outsiders might be present as well, and one which did not depend on the willingness of the gentry to put up with intrusions: namely the prisons. On Christmas night 1586, William Weston said three Masses in his cell in the Clink, at which all the Catholics in the prison received communion, thanks to a former gaoler among them who was also an expert lock-picker.[76] The congregation can be reconstructed from a series of prison-lists and examinations.[77] There were five or six other priests: Edward James, William Parry, John Robinson, Paul Spence, Morris Williams and probably Nicholas Smith.[78] Two of them, James and Robinson, were later martyred, and in 1590 the Privy Council was advertised that Spence, by then a prisoner in Worcester Castle, 'doth say Masses usually there, and that the under-gaoler and his wife frequent the same'.[79] There were seven gentry: Norton Greene,[80] John Lander or Landry and his wife Anne,[81] Thomas Leighton,[82] Richard Lusher (who was from Norwich and is also described as a 'scryvener');[83] Richard Randolph; and Roger Yardley alias Bruerton, who was in the service of the Earl of Northumberland.[84] Then there were two yeomen, John Bradstock of Queenhill in Worcestershire and John White of Hursley in Hampshire; Richard Dowse, a husbandman of Litchfield ('Ythfealde'), also in Hampshire; and four whose status is unrecorded.. There were also a former pursuivant from Winchester, Stephen Cheston, and the former gaoler, David Ringstead, who 'hath been an under-keeper at Winchester and, as it is suspected..., a carrier of priests from place to place by the space of three or four years'.[85] Both of these were in the Clink because it was the prison of the Bishop of Winchester.

On Good Friday 1595, again in the Clink, John Gerard conducted the complete liturgy of the day for 'all the Catholics in the prison and several others from outside' and again the congregation can be reconstructed, this time from examinations and from a list of about December 1595 which gives dates of committal.[86] It included Robert Wiseman, brother of Gerard's host at Braddocks, Thomas Wiseman; two other gentlemen, Edward Cotterington and William Cook; Robert Barwise alias Walgrave, a priest who had been with Gerard at Braddocks in 1593;[87] a weaver, John Briggs; three women, Mary Cole, Anne Glascock and Anne Byrd; Ralph Emerson, who is described as 'yeoman' but was in fact the Jesuit lay-brother; John Lilley, who was also later a Jesuit brother but was then apprentice to Thomas Pierpoint, an apothecary in St Bride's, Fleet Street;[88] and one of uncertain status, Roger Adyn. There was also David Ringstead, who by now was the longest-standing member of the community and had been joined in 1592 by his wife Christian.[89] With the outsiders, there must have been twenty or more packed into the cell above Gerard's own which was used as the chapel.[90]

Even at the height of the persecution and in prisons, it seems to have been taken for granted that Mass could not be said without the correct plate and vestments, and sometimes other ornaments as well. In 1584-5, when Gerard was in the Marshalsea, the cells were searched from time to time, not only for plate but also for Agnus Deis and relics.[91] On one such occasion the authorities took away nearly a cart-load of books and plate from hiding-places betrayed by one Thomas Dodwell, who reported: 'Now, because Sir George Carey and his servants have so often taken from them their silver chalices, they have provided a chalice of tin'.[92] In 1587 Weston had a silver chalice hidden under a brick of the hearth in his cell, and in March 1595, apart from the Massing stuff, Gerard had a reliquary in the Clink.[93] Gerard also gives a lengthy list of relics in his own possession in the early 1590s, including one of the True Cross and a thumb of the martyr Robert Sutton;[94] at Sutton Place, Guildford, part of the skull of St Cuthbert Mayne was found in the nineteenth century, enclosed in a splendid medieval reliquary;[95] and Hereford Cathedral has a late-twelfth-century chasse of oak and copper plates overlaid with Limoges enamel. This is similar to, though smaller than, the one which was sold at Sotheby's in July 1996 for £4,000,000 and is now in the Victoria and Albert Museum, and, like it, was made for a relic of St Thomas Becket. After the Reformation it was preserved by the recusant Bodenhams of Rotherwas, near Hereford, and was returned to the Cathedral in 1831. William Ely, who was ordained in Rome in 1596, worked in the neighbourhood of Hereford and had custody of the relics of St Thomas of Hereford, including the arm which is now at Stonyhurst.[96] Anstruther quotes a lengthy list of relics which were in the possession of the Vaux sisters about 1606, and some of which are also now at Stonyhurst.[97] Two of these had been 'rescued from the pillage of a monastery' and it seems that, following medieval custom, such items were exposed for veneration on high days, even during the worst of the persecution.

Space does not allow an adequate discussion of recusant vestments: three Midland examples will have to serve. The first of these is the collection worked by Helen Wintour, daughter of the Gunpowder Plotter Robert Wintour, at Badge Court, near Droitwich, and now, like the relics mentioned above, at Stonyhurst. The red chasuble and cope are decorated with parted tongues in gold thread, with the Wintour arms and the motto *Orate pro me Helena de Wintour*. Another chasuble is worked with pomegranates in silver and gold, and in two sets of vestments there are altogether four hundred and seventy-one pearls.[98] Second, there are the purple velvet cope, still at Coughton, and the dark blue chasuble, formerly at Coughton and later at Mawley in Shropshire, made up in accordance with the will of Catherine of Aragon from gowns which had belonged to her. Both of these are decorated with pomegranates (the emblem of Granada), and with floral patterns, winged figures on wheels (from Ezekiel), seraphim, fleurs-de-lys (symbols of the Trinity) and scroll shapes. The chasuble almost certainly went from Coughton to Mawley in 1722, when Sir Edward Blount married Apollonia Throckmorton.[99] Both items are therefore likely to have been in use in the Tower Room at Coughton during the

1590s and 1600s and must have made a magnificent splash of colour against the bare Tudor brickwork. Third, there is the collection at Plowden Hall in Shropshire (which, unlike Coughton and Mawley, is not open to the public). This includes an early-sixteenth-century frontal of blue cut velvet; a chalice veil with Elizabethan embroidery in gold and silver thread displaying pansies, other flowers and the monogram IHS; a chasuble with Jacobean stumpwork embroidery of pears, strawberries, grapes, and carnations and other flowers; and a seventeenth-century ivory-coloured Italian altar frontal showing the Annunciation and birds in sprays of flowers worked in silver thread and blue, red and green silks. These are worth comparing with the vestments given by the Plowdens to the convent of St Monica's in Louvain and illustrated in Hamilton.[100] Camm had good reason for his characteristic comment that

> In most striking contrast to their surroundings, the holy priests who said Mass [in such garrets] were clad in vestments exceeding magnifical, stiff with gold embroidery and covered with pearls... and, indeed, it was fitting that the 'golden priests' of that period of martyrdom should be vested in the richest sacrificial robes.[101]

Farmhouses and Cottages

The farmhouses and yeomen's houses where Mass might be said ten or a dozen times a year are not nearly so well documented as the country houses of the peers and gentry, or, for that matter, as the prisons. Some aspects of the picture are familiar enough: the portable altar-stones and, after 1615, the abbreviated Missals bound in vellum; the parti-coloured chasubles which could serve for any season or feast; the exhausting journeys on foot or on horseback, in all weathers and often at night; the risk of arrest on the highway; the code of linen spread in varied patterns on the hedges. But identifying the houses themselves, and still more the arrangements for Mass within them, is far from easy. Moreover the line between minor gentry and prosperous yeomen, and their houses, was not easy to draw, even then. As Col. George Gounter said to Charles II,

> I know divers yeomanry men where for a night we may be welcome, and here is one who married my sister, whose house stands privately and out of the way.[102]

So the royal party went to the Colonel's sister at Hambledon, rather than to the Hydes' grander, and more suspect, house at Hinton Daubnay. The 'little parlour' where she entertained them cannot have been very different from that at Moseley or from that at Tue Brook House, Liverpool, one of St Ambrose Barlow's stations, which, though a Molyneux dower-house,[103] is no larger than a substantial farmhouse. And even gentry might have reasons for 'lying private' or 'keeping secret house'[104] in more modest dwellings. There are therefore three requirements: that the house can be shown to have been lived in by 'Catholics of the common sort'; that it can be shown to have been used for Mass; and that it should have survived, if not to the present day, at least long enough to have been adequately recorded. Even in the few cases where all these requirements are satisfied, it may still not be possible to identify the room in which Mass was said, except by conjectures based on the presumed size of the congregation. All that there is room for here is a couple of pages each on the North, the West Midlands and Devon, as illustrations of the interplay of documentary and architectural evidence and of the frequent gaps in it.

In 1590 Thomas Clark gave an account of his landing at South Shields and subsequent stay at Grosmont, forty miles south and seven miles up the Esk from Whitby.[105] He also listed a dozen or so houses in the neighbourhood of Whitby at which he had said Mass. Most of these were owned by gentry, but they included 'one Poskette's near also to the parish of Egton', within which Grosmont stood. The martyr Nicholas Postgate worked hereabouts for fifty years until his execution at York in 1679, and in Egton there is a Masshouse which until its rebuilding in 1928 was a stone cottage of the sixteenth or seventeenth century. Fortunately, its original condition had been recorded by Camm in *Forgotten Shrines*, with photographs, sections and plans. About 1830 a girl was cleaning the upper part of the kitchen wall when the plaster gave way, revealing a loft under the thatch 15 ft by 10 ft and 5 ft 6 ins to the roof-beam. It was built over the southern half of the ground floor and contained an altar, vestments which are now in the Victorian church of St Hedda, and a tabernacle which took the form of a hole in the wall with an iron door bearing a crucifix.[106]

One of the priests whom Clark met at Grosmont was John Mush, who had been the confessor and biographer of St Margaret Clitherow.[107] Of her house in York, 10-11 The Shambles, there survives the 15th-century hall at right angles to the street, divided into two storeys about 1730 but still with part of its original roof. The two-storey block fronting the street was rebuilt in the first half of the 17th century and faced with brick in the early 19th century. The hiding-place was in the roof of one of the neighbouring houses (it is not known on which side)[108] and must have been entered from the original block in this position.

It is a reasonable guess that the room used for Mass was also here, as the hall would have been too open at the height of the persecution and in the heart of the city.

Across the Pennines in Lancashire, south of Preston and Blackburn, is the village of Gregson Lane, near Brindle, where there is a house used by St Edmund Arrowsmith, who was executed at Lancaster in 1628. It is a whitewashed cottage on two storeys, consisting of a single block and porch, and was originally thatched. Under the eaves to the right of the porch was a windowless attic, which could only be reached by a ladder and trap door and is reminiscent of the loft at Egton. In 1841 a gale blew down part of the attic wall, revealing a hide in which was found a box containing a chalice, two vestments and two altar-stones, one broken. One of the vestments had originally been red and the other purple. The red one was of silk, decorated with flowers and an emblem of John the Baptist, and seems to be late medieval. Elsewhere in the house there was discovered another altar-stone, broken in half and enclosed in a coarse canvas bag so that it could be folded and slipped into a pocket.[109]

For Warwickshire there are two certificates of recusants drawn up in 1592 and best known for including under Stratford-upon-Avon John Shakespeare (the poet's father) and William Fluellen and George Bardolfe, whose names may have suggested the characters in *Henry IV* and *Henry V*.[110] The second certificate is particularly rich in details of priests and other itinerant papists:

Berkswell. One Hales, a very old Massing priest, who... hath christened divers children in Warwickshire in the Popish order and resorted commonly to Mrs [Eleanor] Brooksby in Tanworth[111] and to many other places in the county of Warwick.

Tamworth. Robert Freeman, a recusant well reformed, after his conformity informed Sir Henry Goodere [of Polesworth, one of the Commissioners who drew up the certificate] that one Barlow, an old priest and a great persuader of others to Papistry, resorted much to Measham in Derbyshire and into divers places in Warwickshire, and that he useth to travel in a blue coat with the Eagle and Child on his sleeve.

Churchover. One Woorley, sometime servant to one Sampson Erdswick of Staffordshire, esq., was suspected to be a lewd and seditious Papist, and that he resorteth oft (as a wandering man, under the colour of tricking out of arms in churches) to the houses of many gentlemen known to be ill-affected in religion, both in Warwickshire and in other shires near adjoining. He is suspected also to be a carrier of letters privily between Papist and Papist...

Rowington. One Sir John Appletree, presented there for a seminary priest and fugitive, and resorteth sometimes thither; and is suspected that he was within three years last past at the house of one Thomas Oldnall, their neighbour.[112]

Here is one house that can be identified and is still standing. The Oldnalls' house in Rowington was Whitley Elm at Mousley End, 1100 yards ENE of the church. It is a two-storey building of close-studded timber-framing, now mostly encased in brickwork, and consists of hall and cross-wings. In 1665 it was assessed at four hearths, and the original interior can be reconstructed from the probate inventory (1559) of Thomas Oldnall's father Roger.[113] In the south-west corner of the same parish is South Rookery Farm, the home of the Greswolds or Grissolds, one of whom, John, was Garnet's servant and was racked almost to death in the Tower, and another of whom, Robert, was executed with John Sugar at Warwick in July 1604. According to an account quoted by Challoner, Sugar 'travelled afoot very much in Warwickshire, Staffordshire and Worcestershire to serve, help and comfort the meaner and poorer sort of Catholics', and it is a reasonable conjecture that one of the places where he did so was South Rookery Farm. Though much pulled about, this also retains some close-studded timberwork: in 1606 it had six bays and there were five and a half bays of barns and stables.[114] The unavailing pardons which they obtained while in prison described Sugar as of Claines (near Hindlip) in Worcestershire and Grissold as of Beeley (perhaps Bearley near Stratford), which may indicate two other villages which they had visited together.[115]

Still in Warwickshire and Staffordshire, but at the end of the period, we have the the register kept by the Franciscan Leo Randolph from 1657 onwards.[116] This seems to have been begun at the Randolph family home, Wood Bevington Manor, near Alcester, a house which also still stands, though much altered in 1821 and now divided into two holiday cottages.[117] Mass here was probably said in the great parlour, which still has its Tudor panelling and in 1578 was furnished with a table, forms, crewel-work cushions, three old pieces of carpet and 'one pair of playing tables'. In Mrs Ferrers' chamber there was also 'one picture of Mary Magdalen', worth twelvepence.[118] In 1660 Leo Randolph reconciled his cousin Edward Ferrers of Baddesley Clinton, so beginning the long Franciscan association with Baddesley which still continues with the Poor Clares' convent in the village. There are frequent references in the register to Tanworth-in-Arden, Solihull (where there was another branch of the Greswolds), Birmingham (where Randolph built a Masshouse dedicated to St Mary Magdalen in 1687-8) and Edgbaston, three miles away (where he retired after 1688 to what is now 6 Pritchatt's Road). Less often, there are references to Yardley, Bickenhill (now the site of the airport and the National Exhibition Centre), Upton Warren (near Bromsgrove), King's Norton, 'Barr' (which may be either Great Barr or Perry Barr) and Willenhall, between Walsall and Wolverhampton. Of these, King's Norton probably means the Middlemores; Barr, the Stanfords at Perry Hall; Upton Warren, the Adyses at Durrance; and Willenhall, the Levesons. Robert Stanford of Perry Hall was rector of the English College in Rome when Randolph's fellow-Franciscan St John Wall was a student there;[119] Edmund Adys of Durrance obtained leave for Wall's burial after his execution at Worcester in 1679;[120] Willenhall was the home of two other Franciscans: Francis Leveson, who died in prison at Worcester in 1680, and his brother William, who took refuge at Willenhall during the Oates Plot.[121]

For Devon, there is an illuminating account from 1621, when John Sweet, S.J., was arrested in the house of Alexander and Alice Snelgrove of St Lawrence's in Exeter.[122]

> At the time of his apprehension [the officers] found in his chamber a bag, wherein were divers Popish books, a chalice with a crucifix on the foot thereof, a silver plate parcel-gilt to carry the wafer-cakes, a casket of silver wherein are three little silver boxes of oil, and other superstitious things tending to Popery; and in his pocket we found a Mass-book and a box of wafer-cakes.[123]

From the examinations it is clear that Sweet was a travelling missioner whose work extended across Devon from coast to coast, along the roads through Crediton to Barnstaple and Bideford. At the time of his arrest he was bound for Babeleigh at Parkham, between Bideford and Clovelly, the home of the Risdons, which was Mrs Snelgrove's maiden name.[124] There he was succeeded by Philip Powell, O.S.B., who was executed at Tyburn on 30 June 1646.[125] The magistrates also 'discovered [his] often saying of Mass and the having of great store of Popish books' at the house of Mr George Drew at Morchard Bishop, six miles north-west of Crediton and close to the junction of the roads from Bideford along the valley of the Torridge and from Barnstaple along that of the Taw.[126] In Exeter itself they searched several other houses to which Sweet had resorted, where they found 'many crucifixes, Popish books, Agnus Deis, grayves, beads and such other superstitious relics'. Among these were

> the house of Risdon, a tailor dwelling in one of Sir Amos Bampfield's new houses; the house of the old Podger and of one Northerst who dwells where Crapp, the tailor without Eastgate, dwelleth; the house of young Hellier in Key Lane; the house of one Bendon, a recusant; and the old Brogomes his house within Eastgate; ... also Sampson's house by St Martin's church, a retainer to Mrs Boxe; and John Lugg's house.[127]

Many Elizabethan and medieval houses still survive in Exeter, and the Subsidy Rolls of 1602 and 1629 allow some used by Sweet to be plotted, at least roughly.[128] 'Nicholas Hellier, recusant, in goods £3' is recorded in 1629 in Holy Trinity parish, and Key or Quay Lane ran just outside the walls on the south-east side from the Water Gate to South Gate, where Holy Trinity church was.[129] In June 1625 a priest was 'taken at Mass in Mr Giffard's house near South Gate in Exon.'.[130] In 1602, John Podger was living in St Sidwell, a large parish of nearly 400 acres outside East Gate.[131] St Martin's, now with furnishings of about 1700, is on the north side of the Cathedral; next to it (No.1 Cathedral Close) is what has been known since the seventeenth century as Mol's Coffee House, and a few doors away, at No. 7, was the town-house of the Courtenays.[132] In such houses, the usual long narrow plot would dictate a recurring plan, with the tailor's shop or whatever fronting the street, the owner's chamber above it, and the hall and other buildings further back, either at right angles to the street or parallel to it. This was the plan of the Clitherows' house at York, and the same layout is implied at Newcastle-upon-Tyne in 1615, where William Southern worked from a house on Sandhill. Downstairs there was a shop where a widow in a four-cornered cap sold ropes, salt fish and red herrings; upstairs was Southern and, at the left side of the chamber, a red chest containing books, rosaries and hosts in a painted box.[133] There were regional differences (in Devon, for example, houses had communicating galleries at first-floor level)[134] and individual differences caused by awkward-shaped sites or by building on former courtyards and gardens. But in all the houses used for Mass account had to be taken, not only of security and access but also of the mundane requirements of cleaning, cooking, eating, sleeping, bringing up the children and earning a living.

Mr George Drew's house at Morchard Bishop was probably Easton Barton, half a mile south-west of the village. This was built about 1500, with a first-floor chapel, and has been little altered since.[135] Babeleigh (Bableigh) Barton at Parkham has been rebuilt, but Halsbury Barton in the same parish, the birth-place of Thomas Risdon's wife Willmot Giffard, is still a mid-16th-century house with panelled rooms.[136] Not far from Morchard Bishop, in Cheriton Fitzpaine, is Upcott Barton, a 15th-century building behind an Elizabethan façade: inside there are two Elizabethan staircases and a parlour with an elaborate plaster ceiling of about 1620. By 1592 James Courtenay of Cheriton Fitzpaine already owed £1,360 for sixty-eight months' recusancy:[137] it is likely that priests were harboured here, as they certainly were in the senior Courtenay house of Powderham Castle, a few miles south-west of Exeter.[138] Even this sketchy exploration of a single episode suggests that fieldwork might throw much light on recusancy in Devon; perhaps even that the evidence of buildings, which for this county is astonishingly rich, might be used to make up for the loss of the Western Vicariate archives in the riots of 1780.

When the Catholic Record Society was founded in 1904, with the motto *Colligite fragmenta ne pereant,* it was reasonable to suppose that paper and parchment were more perishable than brick and timber, but that is no longer the case. In the last forty years much rewarding work has been done on the built environment. Yet there is still a lack of appreciation of houses as evidence for recusancy. Such interest as there is has concentrated on those where Mass was said over a prolonged period. It will never be possible to make a complete list of all the houses which were used for Mass, especially as many of them were used only occasionally: one of John Gerard's in London, for example, seems to have lasted for only six weeks, from the beginning to the end of Lent 1605.[139] Such a listing should nevertheless be attempted. For those who take the Incarnation as their standpoint the significance of such houses does not lie in how long they were used but in the fact that they were used at all; any account of recusancy which disregards the information they provide is incomplete and lopsided.

ABBREVIATIONS

Camm	Bede Camm, O.S.B., *Forgotten Shrines* (1910).
Devon	Cherry & Pevsner, *The Buildings of England: Devon* (1989).
Fea 1904	Allan Fea ed., *After Worcester Fight* (1904).
Gerard	P. Caraman ed., *John Gerard: the Autobiography of an Elizabethan* (2nd edition, 1956)
Girouard	Mark Girouard, *Life in the English Country House* (1978).
Hoskins	W.G. Hoskins ed., *Exeter in the Seventeenth Century: Tax and Rate Assessments, 1602-1699* (Devon and Cornwall Record Society New Series 2, 1957).
Troubles	J. Morris, *The Troubles of Our Catholic Forefathers* (I-III, 1872-1877).
Vaux	Godfrey Anstruther, *Vaux of Harrowden* (1953).

Weston P. Caraman ed., *William Weston: the Autobiography of an Elizabethan* (1955).

NOTES

[1] As in Marie Rowlands, 'The Education and Piety of Catholics in Staffordshire in the Eighteenth Century', *Recusant History* 10 (1969-70), pp. 67-78; Sr Marion Norman, IBVM, 'John Gother and the English Way of Spirituality', *Recusant History* 11 (1971-2), pp. 306-19; Michael Hodgetts, 'Recusant Liturgical Music', *Clergy Review* 61 (1976), pp. 151-7, repr. in Christopher Francis and Martin Lynch eds., *A Voice for All Time* (Association for Latin Liturgy, 1994), pp. 168-82; J.M. Blom, *The Post-Tridentine English Primer* (C.R.S. Monograph 3, 1982); J.D. Crichton, *Worship in a Hidden Church* (Columba Press, Dublin, 1988).

[2] But see Roderick O'Donnell, 'The Architectural Setting of Challoner's Episcopate' in Duffy, pp. 55-70.

[3] Bryan Little, *Catholic Churches since 1623* (1966), pp. 19-35.

[4] *An Inventory of Nonconformist Chapels and Meeting-Houses in Central England* (R.C.H.M., 1986); *An Inventory... in South-West England* (R.C.H.M., 1991); *An Inventory... in Northern England* (R.C.H.M., 1994).

[5] Bossy, *Catholics*, p. 127.

[6] Kirk, 'Catholic Chapels in Staffordshire', *The Catholic Magazine and Review* 5 (1834), p. 394, repr. with original pagination in *Staffs. C.H.* 14 (1974).

[7] Richard Simpson, *Edmund Campion* (1896), p. 178; Evelyn Waugh, *Edmund Campion* (1961), p. 107.

[8] Waugh, *Edmund Campion,* pp. 145-6; from Eliot, *A True Report of the Taking of Edmund Campion*, in A.F. Pollard ed., *Tudor Tracts* (1903), pp. 451-74.

[9] The Act of 1581 imposing the £20 fine required attendance at the parish church only four times a year for those who had divine service in their own houses. Text in G.R. Elton, *The Tudor Constitution* (1960), pp. 423-4.

[10] Girouard, p. 56 & plates 28, 29 on p. 57 (with the correction in note 17 below).

[11] The texts at Little Moreton are from the Coverdale and Tyndale versions and seem to be contemporary (c. 1580) with the wall paintings of 'Susannah and the Elders' in the parlour: Christopher Rowell, *Little Moreton Hall* (The National Trust, 1979), pp. 14-18; Brandsby: *Country Life* 145 (1969), pp. 18, 69; Coughton: Vincent Hemingway & Jeffrey Haworth, *Coughton Court and the Throckmortons* (1993), pp. 19-21, 25-7.

[12] *Vaux*, p. 113.

[13] S.E. Rigold, *Nunney Castle* (Her Majesty's Stationery Office, 1957), p. 14.

[14] *Country Life* 140 (1966), p. 974, 1084; Margaret Wood, *The English Medieval House* (1964), index under 'Ashbury Manor'.

[15] P.R.O. SP 12/182/26/i-v, 182/34, 182/34/i, in Woodruff, *Archaeologia Cantiana* 24 (1900), pp. 198-9; Nigel Nicolson & Edward Fawcett, *Ightham Mote* (The National Trust, 1988), pp. 9, 23-6.

[16] *Vaux*, p. 121; *Troubles* 2, pp. 157, 408; M. Hodgetts, 'Elizabethan Priest Holes 2', *Recusant History* 12, no. 3 (October 1973), p. 116. Also Foley 2, p. 587 (from a report by George Eliot dated 10 August 1581).

[17] *Compton Wynyates* (guidebook, *c.* 1950), pp. 16-17, 18, 20. Plate 29 in Girouard (note 10 above) shows the supposed secret chapel, not the 'Chapel Drawing Room' overlooking the chapel of *c.* 1510.

[18] M.W. Beresford, 'The Deserted Villages of Warwickshire', *Birmingham Archaeological Society Transactions* 66 (1950), p. 90.

[19] P.R.O. SP 12/173/64.

[20] *Weston*, pp. 12-13.

[21] Ibid., p. 23.

22 Ibid., pp. 33-4.
23 Ibid., p. 71.
24 Ibid., p. 62-5.
25 Ibid., pp. 65-6.
26 *Gerard*, p. 40.
27 *Weston,* pp. 72, 77-8, nn. 15, 16; Michael Hodgetts, *Secret Hiding Places* (1989), pp. 5-17.
28 A.C. Southern ed., *An Elizabethan Recusant House* (1954), p. 57.
29 Girouard, p. 88.
30 J. Charles Cox, 'The Household Books of Sir Miles Stapleton, Bart', *The Ancestor* 2 (July 1902), pp. 17-39, esp. pp. 20-7.
31 *Letters and Papers of Henry VIII* vol. 11 (1536), nos. 1405-6; vol. 12/1 (1537), no. 86; vol. 12/2 (1537), nos. 951-3.
32 David Knowles, *The Religious Orders in England: III — The Tudor Age* (1959), p. 124; Coughton parish register.
33 Foley 4, pp. 291, 294, 297-8.
34 *Country Life* 189 (1995), no. 12, pp. 76-9; no. 13, pp. 680-1.
35 Hemingway & Haworth, *Coughton Court and the Throckmortons* , p. 21; cf. V.C.H. *Warwickshire* 3, pp. 75-8.
36 *Acts of the Privy Council* 24 (1592-3), p. 148.
37 P.R.O. SP 12/243/76, printed in *Worcs. Rec.* 5 (June 1965), p. 30; ibid. 6 (December 1965), p. 13.
38 *Worcs. Rec.* 18 (December 1971), pp. 31-2.
39 P.R.O. SP 14/215/121/ii, in *Worcs. Rec.* 47 (June 1986), pp. 27-8; Foley 4, p. 259.
40 P.R.O. SP 14/216/153/ii, in *Worcs. Rec.* 47 (June 1986), pp. 30-1.
41 *Country Life* 189 (1995), no. 12, p. 78.
42 Hemingway & Haworth, *Coughton Court and the Throckmortons,* p. 19.
43 Roy Chand *et al.*, *Moseley Old Hall* (The National Trust, 1993), pp. 5-6.
44 Ibid., pp. 5, 23.
45 Kirk, 'Catholic Chapels in Staffordshire', *The Catholic Magazine and Review* 5 (1834), p. 394, repr. with original pagination in *Staffs. C.H.* 14 (1974).
46 Fea 1904, p. 166; William Matthews, *Charles II's Escape from Worcester* (1967), p. 121 (both transcribe Whitgreave's *Account of Charles the Second's Preservation.*)
47 The present staircase of about 1700 replaces an original in the same position, which was probably destroyed by fire: Chand, p. 16. The door at the bottom may have been put in to allow the Georgian congregation to go straight up to the chapel without crossing the house.
48 Allan Fea ed., *The Flight of the King* (1908), p. 60.
49 Fea 1904, pp. 159, 165.
50 Granville Squiers, *Moseley Old Hall* (Bloxwich, 1950), p. 26.
51 Michael Hodgetts, 'Elizabethan Priest Holes 2', *Recusant History* 12, no. 3 (October 1973), pp. 100-13; Hodgetts, *Secret Hiding Places*, pp. 23-33.
52 Ibid.
53 Michael Hodgetts, 'Elizabethan Priest Holes 4', *Recusant History* 13, no. 1 (April 1975), pp. 18-55, esp. 18-29; Hodgetts, pp. 82-99.
54 First recorded by George K. Stanton, *Historical Account of the Old Manor House at Harvington* (1884), p. 10, for which see *Recusant History* 8 (1965-6), pp. 131-2, n. 11.
55 P.R.O. SP 12/251/13-14, printed in Foley 4, pp. 470-1, and *Vaux*, pp. 253-5.
56 Fea 1904, pp. 24-6.
57 A.C. Southern, *An Elizabethan Recusant House* (1954), p. 57.
58 T. Geoffrey Holt, 'An Eighteenth Century Chaplain', *Recusant History* 17 (1984-5), p. 184.
59 On a light grey background the panels are drawn in black, dark grey and white lines. The scheme was found in 1984 under two layers of whitewash and one

of emulsion. I am grateful to the Perry-Lithgow Partnership of Chipping Norton, Oxfordshire, for a copy of their report on the conservation work.

60 Photograph in *Liverpool Daily Post*, 20 May 1938.

61 Photograph in *The Sunday Telegraph*, 27 May 1990.

62 Illustrated in *Country Life* 96 (1944), p. 291, and in Michael Hodgetts, *Harvington Hall* (Archdiocese of Birmingham Historical Commission, 1998), p. 15.

63 Illustrated in *Archaeologia* 88 (1940), p. 247, and in H.R. Hodgkinson, *Birmingham Archaeological Society Transactions* 62 (1938), Plate XIII, Fig. 2, opp. p. 25.

64 Briefly mentioned in Hubbard, *The Buildings of Wales: Clwyd* (1986), p. 321; fuller description in Michael Hodgetts, *Recusant History* 24 (1998-9), p. 52. The decoration is reminiscent of the work of the 1660's in Compton Wynyates church and at Bromfield, near Ludlow, Shropshire.

65 A. Mary Sharp, *History of Ufton Court* (1892), p. 153; V.C.H. *Berkshire* 3, p. 439.

66 *Vaux*, p. 150.

67 Ibid., p. 153.

68 *Gerard*, p. 195.

69 William Palmes. *The Life of Mrs Dorothy Lawson* (ed. Richardson, 1855) p. 43.

70 Ibid pp. 31, 44.

71 Philip Caraman, *Henry Morse: Priest of the Plague* (1957).

72 'The Apostolicall Life of Ambrose Barlow', *Downside Review* 44 (1926), p. 240.

73 Christopher Haigh, 'From Monopoly to Minority', *Royal Historical Society Transactions* Fifth Series 31 (1981), pp. 145-6.

74 'Apostolicall Life', pp. 143-6.

75 Bossy, *Catholics*, pp. 108 ff.

76 *Weston*, p. 117.

77 *Miscellanea* (C.R.S. 2, 1906), pp. 246, 258, 260, 262, 268, 271; St George Kieran Hyland, *A Century of Persecution* (1920), pp. 394-6 (two lists of 7 March 1585/6 and June 1586 made by Sir William More of Loseley, who as a Surrey magistrate was concerned with prisoners in the Clink).

78 Anstruther 1, pp. 188-9, 269-70, 293-4, 328, 382, 320-1; also J.H. Pollen ed., *Unpublished Documents relating to the Martyrs 1584-1603* (C.R.S. 5, 1908), pp. 155, 157, 159, 162, 290, 395.

79 *Acts of the Privy Council* 19, p. 304.

80 H. Bowler ed., *Recusants in the Exchequer Pipe Rolls 1581-1592* (C.R.S. 71, 1986), pp. 70-1 and n. 101. His manor-farm, Frognall in Teynham, Kent, is still standing. But Sir William More (Hyland, *A Century of Persecution*, pp. 395-6) gives 'Mrs Katherine Greene of Newby in the co. of Yorkshire'; cf. C.R.S. 18, p. 82.

81 *Miscellanea* (C.R.S. 22, 1921), p. 14 and n. 3. Anne Lander died in the Clink in 1589. Cf Foley 3, pp. 253-7.

82 Bowler, *Recusants in the Exchequer Pipe Rolls*, p. 109.

83 Ibid., p. 115.

84 Ibid., p. 198.

85 *Miscellanea* (C.R.S. 2), pp. 246-7.

86 *Gerard*, p. 100; C.R.S. 2, p. 285.

87 Anstruther 1, pp. 25-6.

88 Anthony G. Petti, *Recusant Documents from the Ellesmere Manuscripts* (C.R.S. 60, 1968), pp. 64, 87.

89 Ibid., pp. 64-5.

90 *Gerard*, p. 100.

91 Ibid., p. 5.

92 Ibid., p. 217.

93 Ibid., p. 103.

94 Ibid., pp. 49-50.

95 Bede Camm, O.S.B., *Lives of the English Martyrs* 2 (1905), p. 222; cf. Foley 1, pp. 297-8.

[96] Foley 4, pp. 452, 454, 456-7.
[97] *Vaux*, pp. 386-7.
[98] Foley 5, p. 848; Camm, pp. 275-6; W. Sterry-Cooper, *Worcestershire Archaeological Society Transactions* New Series 28 (1951), pp. 23-33 and plates VII and VIII between pp. 28 & 29.
[99] Paul Sidoli, 'The Catherine of Aragon Chasuble from Mawley Hall', *Cleobury Chronicles* 4 (Cleobury Mortimer History Society, 1996), pp. 35-44.
[100] Adam Hamilton, OSB, ed., *The Chronicle of the English Augustinian Canonesses of Louvain, 1548-1625* (1904), illustration opp. p. 255.
[101] Camm, p. 275.
[102] Fea, *The Flight of the King*, pp. 280-1.
[103] 'Apostolicall Life', p. 240; identified as Tue Brook by Robert Julian Stonor, OSB, *Liverpool's Hidden Story* (1957), pp. 99-101.
[104] Girouard, pp. 76, 106; cf. *Troubles* 3, p. 194; P.R.O. SP 12/173/64; V.C.H. *Lancashire* 3, pp. 85-91.
[105] P.R.O. SP 12/244/5.
[106] Camm, pp. 281-303.
[107] *Troubles* 3, pp. 360-440.
[108] R.C.H.M. *York* 5 (1981), p. 214, with plan of nos. 7-12; Katherine M. Longley, 'Three Sites in the City of York', *Recusant History* 12 (1973-4), pp. 3-4.
[109] Camm, pp. 188-97, with photographs and illustrations, p. 189.
[110] Warwick R.O. 1886/BL 2662 (March or April 1592), printed in *Worcs. Rec.* 30 (December 1980), pp. 8-27; P.R.O. SP 12/243/76 (dated 25 September 1592), printed in *Worcs. Rec.* 5 (May 1965), pp. 18-31; *ibid.* 6 (December 1965), pp. 7 -20.
[111] See Michael Hodgetts, 'Elizabethan Priest Holes 3', *Recusant History* 12, no. 4 (January 1974), pp. 182-4.
[112] For Appletree, see Anstruther 1, p. 10.
[113] Joy Woodall, *From Hroca to Anne: A Thousand Years in ... Rowington* (Shirley, West Midlands, 1974), pp. 24, 92-4, 115, 119, 121, 122, 126, 147, 164.
[114] Ibid., pp. 85, 114, 162, 166-7 (John Greswold's probate inventory, 1582).
[115] Anstruther 1, pp. 341-2.
[116] B.A.A., C.88.
[117] V.C.H. *Warwickshire* 3, pp. 157-8.
[118] H.S. Gunn, *History of the Old Manor House of Wood Bevington* (1911), Appendix, pp. v, viii. There was also a 'chapel chamber' (pp. v-vi).
[119] Anstruther 2, p. 308.
[120] Bede Camm, O.S.B., *Life of Blessed John Wall* (1932, 1947, 1972), p. 77.
[121] B.A.A., Alban Butler Collection (bound vol.), printed in *Worcs. Rec.* 2 (December 1963), pp. 23-5. For other itinerant priests in the Midlands and the houses they frequented, see the examinations of George Snape, 1592 (P.R.O. SP 12/229/78), Anthony Sherlock, 1606 (P.R.O. SP 14/18/51, summarised in Anstruther 1, p. 309) and Richard Bubb of Siefton, Shropshire, 1607 (P.R.O. SP 14/28/122/i, published in *Worcs. Rec.* 47 (June 1986), pp. 31-5).
[122] George Oliver, *Collections Illustrating the History of the Catholic Religion in... Cornwall, Devon, Dorset, Somerset, Wilts and Gloucester* (1857), pp. 5-8; Foley 4, pp. 647-52 (P.R.O. SP 14/123/115-6, 124/30).
[123] Foley 4, p. 648; cf. Oliver, *Collections Illustrating the History of the Catholic Religion*, p. 6.
[124] Foley 4, p. 647; Oliver, *Collections Illustrating the History of the Catholic Religion*, p. 5.
[125] Challoner, pp. 474-5.
[126] Foley 4, p. 652.
[127] Foley 4, p. 649.
[128] Hoskins; *Devon*, pp. 362, 391, 410-9, 423-4.
[129] Hoskins, p. 9 and map inside back cover.
[130] *The Diary of Walter Yonge, 1604-8* (Camden Society First Series 41, 1847), p.18.

131 Hoskins, pp. xi, 2.

132 *Devon*, pp. 391, 413; Hoskins, p. 16.

133 Anstruther 1, p. 325.

134 Michael Laithwaite, 'Town-Houses: Medieval to Mid-Seventeenth Century' in *Devon*, pp. 78-82, with plans p. 71.

135 *Devon*, pp. 574-5; W.G. Hoskins, *Devon* (New Survey of England, 1954), pp. 439-40; Richard Polwhele, *History of Devonshire* 2 (1793, repr. 1977), p. 41; Tristram Risdon, *The Chorographical Description or Survey of the County of Devon* (1811, repr. Barnstaple, 1970), pp. 43-4. Cf Foley 3, pp. 432-3.

136 *Devon*, p. 624; Hoskins, *Devon*, pp. 450-1; Risdon, *Chorographicall Description*, pp. 242-3; *Visitation of* Devonshire (Harleian Society 6), pp. 241-2; Oliver, *Collections Illustrating the History of the Catholic Religion*, p. 20. Thomas Risdon's son Giles died in 1632: *Parkham Registers* (Devon and Cornwall Record Society 1, 1905-6), p. 136.

137 Mary Calthrop ed., *Recusant Roll 1, 1592-3* (C.R.S. 18, 1916), p. 36; W.G. Hoskins, 'Some Old Devon Bartons', *Devonshire Studies* (1952), reprinted in *Old Devon* (1967, 1972), pp. 38-43.

138 Anthony Kenny ed., *Responsa Scholarum of the English College, Rome, Part 2 1622-1685* (C.R.S. 55, 1963), no. 718; Anstruther 2, p. 13; Ezra Cleaveland, *A Genealogical History of the Noble and Illustrious Family of Courtenay* (Exeter, 1735), p. 298.

139 *Gerard*, pp. 205-7.

4

SURVIVING THE TIMES, 1625–90

Catholics and Puritans

The reign of Charles I offered easement and opportunities for advancement to some Catholic gentlemen and peers, but not for Catholic yeomen, tradesmen and townsmen. The activities of Henrietta Maria, the visits of Papal diplomats and the freedom which some Catholic nobility at court enjoyed were not advantageous to Catholics at parish level, for they raised anxiety about court religion and fuelled the fears of local Puritans. In many towns and villages the godly were rising up to rebuke sin. The persistence of covert Catholicism and practical accommodations between popery and the parish were to them an affront to decent moral order, against which they must bear witness. To defeat such evils they needed to ensure that local office and leadership were in godly hands. Catholics and crypto-Catholics who had hitherto been tolerated in office were removed. William Jenkinson, alderman and boothman, was asked to resign by the common council of Newcastle-upon-Tyne, but was awarded a pension of £40 a year in compensation, an event which illustrates the pragmatic balance between persecution and toleration. At Handsworth, Staffordshire, in 1626 Katherine Edwards 'a wilful, obstinate popish recusant' was regularly denounced from the pulpit on Sundays, and when she died she was buried by night in the church without the minister being present or the Prayer Book ritual being observed. Francis Norris was reported at the Visitation for assisting. He knew who to blame. 'A Puritan', he said of a neighbour, 'is one who hawks about to other churches with a book under his arm but the devil in his heart and studies how to do his neighbours an ill turn'.[1]

Puritan ministers were determined to eradicate the remnant of Catholic traditions. Thomas Draxe in 1613 took up his post of vicar of Colwich, Staffordshire, and was dismayed to find that popish burials in the parish were carried out with processions, prayers for the dead and a 'popish bagpiper'. In response to his 'no popery' sermons and manner of arranging the liturgy, the gentleman in the front pew walked out with his family and many of the congregation followed. The lord of the manor was a Catholic and harboured in his house a man thought to be a priest. Draxe succeeded in suppressing the bagpiper, but Colwich remained a recusant centre. Puritan enthusiasm was not confined to the clergy. At Terling, Essex, the village officers were supported by an especially godly group of the principal inhabitants, who worked zealously to bring the behaviour of their neighbours under control.[2]

By the late 1620s the Puritans were faced not only with the moral failings of their neighbours, but also with clergy of new Arminian and Laudian tendencies who were introducing more elaborate liturgy into some parish churches. Altars at the East end replaced communion tables, communion rails were installed, and during the services there were genuflections and even signs of the cross. Puritans denounced the new altars, the organs and the elaborate rituals of Laud and of the Arminians as dangerous flirtation with the devil of Popery. Some were dismissed for their zeal, and continued the battle for righteousness with even greater vigour.

The Puritan tendency was particularly marked in towns. To some extent town governors defined their independence by conflict with the lords and landowners of the neighbouring parishes. The process is well illustrated by the case of the small market town of Alcester, Warwickshire. Coughton Court, three miles away, was the home of an influential Catholic family, the Throckmortons, who owned much land in neighbouring parishes. Most (though not all) of this family had been conspicuously Catholic for over 100 years. The rector of Alcester and most of the townspeople had already by 1561 accepted the new order, as their wills demonstrated, but even at the end of Elizabeth's reign there were still 22 Catholic adults in a parish of 511 ratepayers and 108 cottagers. In the seventeenth century the Puritan influence came uppermost. By 1633 the patron of the living and chief landowner was Lord Brooke of Warwick Castle, an ardent Protestant. The majority of the town followed their patron's lead albeit on their own terms; the new rector in 1633 was not instituted until he had preached and been accepted by the townsfolk.[3]

Even in York there was Puritan preaching in at least 11 out of the 25 city churches and the cathedral. At Dorchester, Dorset, the Puritans sought to control all the offices of influence to reform the people. On the eve of the Civil War in many parish churches, respectable inhabitants pulled down the new altars and altar rails, women refused to wear a veil in church, and slogans were written on the walls.[4] In many places local Puritans secured the replacement of grammar school masters (by definition clergy), some of whom had connived at recusants' children not going to church or had shown undue deference to Catholic parents. This closed an important opportunity of education for the sons of Catholic yeomen and townsmen.

The court of High Commission was busy in prosecuting Puritans, but from time to time continued to prosecute Catholics, particularly in cases where it was alleged the defendant had been seducing others to popery.[5] By 1641, Pym and other politicians were stirring up anti-Catholicism in their struggle with the Crown. Then in November came news of the Irish Rebellion and anti-Catholic pamphlets began to circulate in the provinces as well as London. People were encouraged to believe that hordes of papists and Jesuits assisted by the savage Irish were about to subvert the realm. There were demonstrations in London and some Catholics suffered attacks from soldiers.[6] Men over the age of 18 were required to take an Oath of Allegiance and make a Protestation, that they accepted the true Protestant religion expressed in the doctrine of the Church of England and that they stood firm against all popery. The Protestation was in a form intended to exclude Catholics, but only 1,375 persons are recorded as refusing as against 11,800 who made the Protestation and took the oath.[7] Local authorities carried out the procedure to some extent as they saw fit; in some places women were included for example. The detail in particular places shows yet again the way in which Catholics even in a time of crisis could be eased through a difficulty by the local administrators. Many of the returns say explicitly that all the adult male inhabitants over 18 made the Protestation; others that certain named individuals are away in pursuit of their trades, but that 'if longer time were allowed they would have taken it'; others, who were away, were 'outside warning'. In the South and Midlands only a few persons were listed as refusing the oath even in places where we know from other listings that there were many Catholics. At Easebourne, Sussex, fourteen took the oath in a modified form. In Midhurst, Sussex, 210 took the oath and 54 recusant papists refused. This took place on the estate of one of the most active Catholic lords, Lord Montague. Here and in Midhurst town both patronage and pressure were exercised to maintain the Catholicism of the tenants.[8]

In the North of England much greater numbers of Catholics refused the oath. In Durham county 452 persons refused out of 16,142 named, comprising 56 gentlemen, 4 squires, 5 knights and 471 plebeians. In a few small parishes such as Esh and Tanfield the numbers refusing were as much as one in four of the total listed, but in the majority of parishes, especially the larger ones, the proportion was much smaller. In Lancashire, the number of refusers was so great that the exercise as a declaration of loyalty was scarcely valid. In Brindle, Mawdesley and Bispham more than half the adults refused to take the oath.[9]

On the outbreak of the Civil War some adult Catholic men were drawn into active service, often by the local Catholic royalist gentry. At least 250 Catholics were officers in the royal armies, and they were assisted by other ranks who included some Catholics. In addition there were the unknown but considerable number of Catholic gentry who established their own troops. Catholics were required, in some cases compelled, to assist in the defence of local Catholic houses and castles. Sir Richard Fleetwood and his brother Thomas barricaded Wootton Lodge, Staffordshire, and made it 'one of the strongest places in the county', manning it with 'such a company of obstinate Papists and resolute rogues as the like was hardly to be found in the whole kingdom'.[10] Such 'soldiers' rarely went far from home and spent much time strengthening fortifications, making shot and moving artillery field pieces. They came under fire only intermittently.

Catholics of the lower orders in both towns and countryside suffered like their neighbours from the effects of the Civil War. They all endured forced billeting, requisition of food, animals and money, vandalism by soldiers and disease. They were subject to heavy taxation, trade and agriculture were interrupted, and parish churches and private property were damaged. The Parliamentary army increasingly identified with the Independent sects, and both perceived papists as particularly malignant and dangerous to the Commonwealth. Mobs of weavers in Essex plundered Catholic houses.

Bitterness increased as Catholics were again involved in the 'Second Civil War' and in the renewal of hostilities after the execution of Charles I. Some, including the yeomen Pendrell family, were famously concerned in the escape of Charles II after the Battle of Worcester.[11] The national and the county committees, which became the key agencies of government during the Interregnum, had no sympathy for papists, but the demands being made upon their time and energies were such that they had little time for a drive against them. The committees specifically concerned with compounding and sequestration engaged in the elaborate and complicated processes of transferring the estates of papists and delinquents, involving far more persons than those who had been active in the fighting. In Warwickshire 61 estates were sequestered, only 8 of them owned by papists in arms. The process of sequestration was mainly concerned with the estates of the gentry, but also included those of yeomen with land worth as little as £20 and commoners had their goods sequestered. The Cavalier gentry, including the Catholics, suffered severely and in many cases papist gentry fled abroad, or were forced out of their houses. Traditional centres where Mass was said were not available. In most cases this was a temporary disruption but in some cases the loss was permanent.[12]

The change in government changed the circumstances of Catholics only to a limited extent. During the Interregnum participation in parish worship and communion ceased to be the test of loyalty. The Book of Common Prayer and the Thirty-Nine Articles were abolished as were episcopacy and the church courts. Civil marriages were introduced in 1650. In about one third of the parishes the incumbent was replaced by a Presbyterian minister, and the radical preachers of the new Independent sects lambasted Popery with fervour. The collection of recusancy fines was in abeyance and the gaols were empty of Catholic lay prisoners. During the period from the execution of the King to the Restoration of his son (1649-1660) only two priests were executed. Otherwise there was no real change in the pressure on Catholics. An Oath of Allegiance was introduced which required a rejection of Catholic doctrine including transubstantiation. Catholics paid additional tax, and taxes were probably more systematically collected.

Catholics and the Restoration

By 1656 power in the counties, parishes and towns was gradually falling back into traditional hands and the country as a whole began to reconstruct step by step the forms of social order. The Act of 1657 put recusancy on a new basis, requiring constables to report papists and those popishly affected, so that listings arising from this Act are not confined to those who did not attend Sunday worship.

After the death of Cromwell and a period of uncertainty the Monarchy, the Church of England, the traditional Parliament and the gentry in the counties once again led society. Most of the Catholic gentry had already managed to claw back their estates though often at great cost. There were exceptions such as the Tichbornes of Tichborne, Hampshire, and the Middlemores of Edgbaston, Warwickshire, but their disappearance did not lead to extinction of Catholic activity on their estates. Attendance at the Book of Common Prayer service again became compulsory, but prosecutions for recusancy were in abeyance until 1673. Charles II surrounded himself with Catholics and made no secret of his dependence on Catholics in his escape from the Battle of Worcester. Mass was said in the Queen's Chapels of Somerset House and at St James'.[13]

Despite the euphoria of May 1660, it was a different not a restored society which emerged in the sixties, profoundly influenced by the events of the previous twenty years. Although it was to be many years before official tolerance of diversity was accepted and legitimated, in reality national unity in religion and authority could not be restored. The *de facto* existence in many parishes of dissenting groups, often consisting of respectable householders of recognisable piety, was already weakening unanimity of religion in the parish. The Presbyterian clergy ousted from the parishes became the focal points of organised Protestant dissent and the hard core sects such as the Quakers were still unreconciled.[14] Catholic commoners in the parish found that they were not the only ones refusing to attend Sunday worship for conscientious reasons, nor the only ones maintaining their own worship and subculture.

Protestant dissenters were treated with deep suspicion by the restored gentry and Quakers in particular suffered severely. Many were prosecuted for recusancy during this period, became recusants convict and some appeared on the Recusant Rolls. Anthony Williams showed that lists of recusants in Wiltshire at this period often included Quakers and the same has been found elsewhere. In contrast Peter Challinor has shown that this was not the case in Cheshire, as has Malcolm Wanklyn for Shropshire.[15] Roger Clark compared the indictments of papists and of dissenters under the recusant laws in detail for Derbyshire and showed how the ratio of indictments between the two groups shifted from year to year before, during and after the Oates Plot, with a great preponderance of Catholics in 1678, and a majority at all times.[16] Like all lists of recusants, these were the result of the attitudes and decisions of the responsible official. In 1678 the Lord Lieutenant of Staffordshire made a composite return of the Staffordshire constables' lists numbering 1,411 persons, and remarked that he had been at some pains to eliminate non-Catholic recusants from the list, 'but 9 or 10 Quakers may have slipped in'.[17]

Catholics at the Restoration appeared to be in a strong position. Their clergy were numerous in terms of the numbers of Catholics and were both systematically trained abroad and well organised in England. The great array of legislation did not prevent Catholics from maintaining close association with the Continental Church. Despite listings, fines and harassment they normally worked and lived in security and travelled freely, despite the repeated proclamations confining them to within five miles of their homes or excluding them from London. They accepted the recognised limits on their participation in local life, and they had routines for the avoidance of legal difficulties. There even appeared to be a lull in the hostility towards them. The earnest young farmer, Roger Lowe of Winwick, Lancashire, described in his diary in 1665 how he made a visit to neighbouring Sankey Hall to meet a young man, a papist named Roger Kenyon, and they 'discoursed long together about papistry and after our discourse we was very loving'.[18]

Religious bitterness could be covered by apparently normal relations and particular individuals could form personal friendships, but there was no real reconcilation and violence could erupt with astonishing speed. The mid-sixties were distressed by war, trade depression and plague. The Great Fire of London was blamed on papists and there were anti-Catholic riots around Warwick and Coventry. There was suspicion of a rising in Lancashire and Catholic houses were searched for arms and horses in 1666. The conversion to Catholicism of the heir apparent of the Crown became known about 1668 and from then until the accession of William of Orange in 1689 the Catholic religion was a critical political issue and the corresponding campaign inside and outside Parliament was both anti-Court and anti-Catholic. The first phase (1673-1680) was the attempt to exclude James Duke of York from the succession and to control Charles II's relations with France. These public affairs were reflected in the local community by an outburst of local accusations and rumours. Pope-burning processions were revived in London and on a smaller scale in the towns of Oxford, Salisbury, Taunton and Abergavenny. As in 1641, there was a tension between local parish governors, who dreaded popular disorder, and London politicians and informers, who were stimulating unrest for their own wider political objectives.[19]

Although the excitement died down as quickly as it had blown up, the furore surrounding the Popish Plot was profoundly disturbing while it lasted. Sixteen priests, nine of them Jesuits, were executed: eight for complicity in the Plot, eight for their priesthood. Twelve more died in prison under sentence, while others escaped abroad. Four laymen were executed for complicity in the Plot: Edward Coleman, secretary to the Duke of York; Viscount Stafford; John Groves, servant; and Richard Langhorn, barrister. Hundreds of common people were committed to prison in London and into the county gaols. In Cheshire in 1679 there were many arrests not only of the Catholic gentlemen of the Wirral but also of two carpenters, a weaver, a miller and a watchmaker, all resident in Chester.[20] The reports of searches and the accounts of the trials of priests throw light on priests and Catholics, who had been keeping out of sight. Catholics brought to Hereford, Stafford, Worcester and London to give evidence had to be bullied by Chief Justice Scroggs, until they reluctantly admitted to some knowledge of small groups of Catholics who were in the habit of going to certain houses on Sundays, where they were ushered upstairs, and the curious heard a man dressed as a priest say words in a foreign tongue, and saw him give the wafers, and hear confessions. In Wolverhampton, Staffordshire, it transpired that Mass had been said in several houses, that there was one Jesuit priest who had been resident for fifty years, and others visited regularly and met for retreats. Some witnesses pleaded ignorance, others failed to appear, some were apprehended and bound over to witness against the priest on trial.

In this crisis Catholic witnesses were aware that they were on oath and incriminating themselves as well as the prisoner and they made use of standardised methods of evasion and damage limitation. Sympathetic lawyers advised defendants that the onus of proof was on the court to show that the man was a priest, that the witness knew he was a priest, that he had been ordained abroad, and that what he had said was Mass. The witnesses tried to follow this advice. Charles Kerne defended himself successfully on the grounds that it was not unusual for Catholics in the absence of a priest to read prayers together and distribute bread which was not the transubstantiated host. He said that it was this that the witnesses had seen, not Mass. Witnesses asserted that they did not know Latin, that they did not know what the accused was doing, that they did not know whether the man was ordained, that they had not heard properly, that they had only 'gone up' out of curiosity Their sullen silences contrast with the naive outspoken replies of Catholics under examination a hundred years before. The survival of Catholicism by that time depended rather upon keeping as invisible as possible than on bold outbursts.[21]

During the last four years of the reign of Charles II the succession of James Duke of York was assured, but pressures on Catholics in parish and town continued. Robert Kenyon, receiver general of fines and forfeitures of popish estates in Lancashire, had a great deal of business in organising the forfeitures of land. Of 217 estates sequestered, 125 were worth between £10 and £99. Poor Catholics included Ellen Worral and Thomas Rothwell both of Little Crosby, who paid ten shillings each. It was not uncommon for the goods and chattels of commoners to be seized. Entering houses and taking away furniture was always an emotive matter and Catholics attacked the bailiffs in the Wigan area in 1681 on more than one occasion.[22] The Exclusion Crisis in political terms lasted only three years, but its effects on Catholics in some parts of England lasted longer. Several priests and many common people were imprisoned and remained in gaol some of them for four to five years until the accession of James II.

In the Welsh Marches the Catholic Church never really recovered.

> Up to that time Catholicism had survived in considerable strength and there is evidence of growth and increasingly public practice following the restoration. Some 40 priests are known to have been serving in [the Wye Valley]. but following the executions of 1679 we can trace only 8 priests surviving... The Lord Worcester of Raglan, though he died a Catholic himself, introduced an Anglican clergyman to educate his son and heir. There were others who did likewise and the number of those who held on in any public way was greatly reduced.[23]

When James II came to the throne his precipitate efforts to transform the religious complexion of England by royal prerogative increased the fear and suspicion in which Catholics were held. To the Protestant mythology of the Inquisition, the immoral and power-mad Papacy, and the outrageous Guy Fawkes Plot was now added the spectacle of a bigoted and fanatical King, plotting with his Jesuit chaplains and his Italian wife, intruding Catholics into every place of power, influence and profit, reneging on his coronation oath and destroying the liberties of the Protestant subject. Modern historians have been at pains to qualify this picture of the King in the interests of a sober evaluation of the evidence, but in popular culture the imagined tyrant was as much a historical factor as the more moderate King. For a little more than two years Catholics and crypto-Catholics suddenly appeared in office in parishes, towns, school and charity boards and every position of local authority, interventions which directly affected Catholics in the local communities.

The towns were the main objective of James' interventions, especially the 215 parliamentary boroughs. The opposition which might have been expected from the corporations was not forthcoming since the town councils had been remodelled by *quo warranto* proceedings and by the intrusion of aldermen by royal appointment, and dispensed by royal perogative from all oaths under the Test Act. At Gloucester John Hill who 'declared himself a papist in James' reign' served two terms, and was then succeeded by a Catholic landowner, Anselm Fowler, elected by command of the King.[24]

In twenty-four provincial towns public Mass houses were opened and eighteen more in London. Only five years before Catholics had been prosecuted for hearing Mass in small groups in private homes and priests had been executed. There were new chapels at the pilgrimage centres of Fernyhalgh and Holywell, three chapels were opened in Oxford Colleges, and garrison chaplains at Bristol, Chester and Plymouth. The cost of building these new chapels came from subscriptions from the clergy and the Catholic gentry and in most cases there was a contribution from the King. The common people made small contributions, but in general the chapels were provided for them rather than by them. The chapels were decorated and furnished in a manner corresponding to Continental chapels and must have been exciting for the many Catholics, who were used to Mass on temporary altars in private houses and cottages. In addition to the city and town chapels the gentry subscribed to chapels and schools in rural centres including Hathersage, Goosnargh and Ugbrooke.[25]

The opening of town chapels was given the greatest possible encouragement by the King and was a political statement. At York six public chapels were opened even though there were probably about less than 100 Catholic citizens living in the city.[26] In Bath a chapel was opened and the King ordered that the chapel and priest be protected. When the King visited the city to touch the King's Evil, Mass was said in Bath Abbey and a sermon preached. Francis Carne, a Catholic was appointed Master of the grammar school.[27] At Worcester the King attended Mass in the popish chapel although the corporation refused to go with him.[28] He visited Gloucester and part of the meeting room of the City Council known as the Tolsey House was converted into a chapel for him to hear Mass. He was received with the utmost pomp and lavish entertainment.[29] Efforts were also made to restore the chapel of St Winifred at Holywell with the help of those who 'have HM's favourable ear'.[30]

Among the chapels opened in London was that by James Stanford of Lime Street. Although English by birth, he held the position of the Resident of the Elector Palatine of the Rhine. He appears to have been the figurehead for an influential group of Catholics. James contributed to its building, and made an official visit at Easter 1688. The chapel was elaborately furnished and the rules for its chaplains and services are extant.[31]

For some people the accession of James II meant actual release from prison, among them some who had been in prison since 1679. Many more were relieved of prosecution as recusants. In the course of 1686 commissions were sent under royal warrant to stay process in the cases of thousands of named recusants of all degrees including many tradesmen. The orders applied to people living in Lincolnshire, Gloucestershire and North Warwickshire among other places. The lists included Quakers under process, as well as Roman Catholics.[32]

It has often and rightly been said that the most important change in the conditions of Catholics was the appointment of the four Vicars Apostolic. The appointment of John Leyburn on 5 August 1685 and of three more bishops in January 1688 set up a structure of organisation which, despite opposition expressed before the event, was readily accepted by both Catholic clergy and laity.[33]

The immediate result was to make it possible for Catholics to be confirmed in England. According to the rubric confirmation should have preceded Communion but in practice in England this had been unrealistic. In 1687, Bishop Leyburn made a journey of 1,260 miles in 14 weeks and confirmed 18,955 persons. He travelled through the north and east of England but this confirmation tour did not include London. He started at Weston Underwood in Buckinghamshire in July 1687 and ended at Peterley in October. Large numbers of people were confirmed in Lancashire, the largest group being 1,132 at Wigan. Over a thousand were also confirmed at Euxton, at Fernyhalgh and at Preston. Bishop Leyburn visited York in July 1687 and confirmed 315 and another 98 in the Franciscan chapel at Jubbergate, in the Bar Convent and elsewhere. The new Bishop (Smith) of the Northern District conducted a second confirmation at York in August 1688 at the secular priests' chapel in Minster Yard, and again at the Franciscan chapel at Jubbergate.

The lists give evidence of the confirmation not only of the town Catholics, but also of school boarders and the servants of the country gentry, and there was an attempt before Smith's arrival to gather in the lapsed.[34] Analysis of the list of confirmations at Stafford shows that some of those confirmed probably came from known Catholic centres to the north and north-west of Stafford. The next confirmation was at Wolverhampton, which included the Catholics of Sedgley. No ages were given, but the lists often took the form of a man's name, a woman of the same name, followed by three or four more individuals of the same surname, which suggests family groups coming for confirmation after the long interval when there had been no opportunity for the sacrament in England.[35]

Catholics and the Revolution

With the collapse of James II's government his attempt to reconstruct the government of local communities was quickly overturned and the 'old' local governors replaced those intruded. In view of the provocative nature of the building of the town chapels it is not surprising that almost all of them became the target of the soldiers and the mobs on the arrival of William in

Places of Residence for those cases for which it can be established.

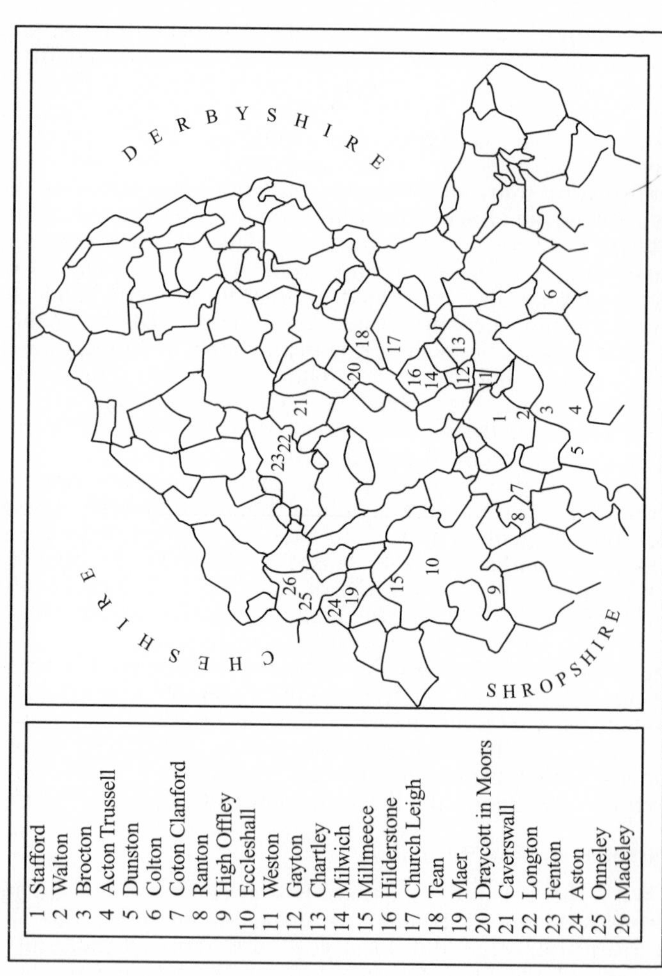

Figure 1: Stafford, Residence of Confirmandi, 1688

November 1688. There were minor riots in towns all over the country, as the populace attacked the chapels, drove out the priests and destroyed the church fittings. Hull, Yorkshire, was one of the few towns which had resisted James, but even it had been forced to accept Lord Langdale as mayor. When James fled, Catholic houses were ransacked and the shops closed.[36] From Cheshire Lord Delamere marched south to join William, and along the route the chapels were burnt by troops and finished off later by the rabble. In Birmingham the chapel was completely destroyed, 'the townsmen of the better sort not resisting the rabble but quietly permitting, if not prompting, them to do it'. The chapel of James Stanford was only partly damaged and the altar-piece painting is now in a domestic chapel in the north of England.[37] In Wolverhampton the house where the Jesuits had their chapel and school belonged to the Earl of Plymouth and was respected but the contents were destroyed and a man was accidentally killed in the excitement.[38] At least twelve other town chapels were attacked in a similar manner and there were also attacks on some Catholic houses and chapels in the countryside. Three of the Vicars Apostolic were imprisoned for short periods in the Tower, as were a number of prominent Catholic gentlemen.

Catholics in the Jacobite Era

Catholic affairs in the last years of the century were dominated by the perceived danger of Jacobitism to the Succession and to the country. Catholics were most at risk when the government felt itself most threatened by the Stuarts in alliance with France: in 1696 on the death of Queen Mary; in 1701 on the death of William III; in 1705 when there were fears of an invasion; and in 1714 on the transfer to the Hanoverian monarchy. On each of these occasions there were new laws, many proclamations, renewed listing, and confiscations of the property and goods of people of the common sort.[39]

From time to time Catholics were still required by proclamation to leave London and to remain within five miles of their dwellings. On November 12th 1696 Nathaniel Piggot a London lawyer who did much business for Catholics wrote that

> We had here last Tuesday an alarm of about 400 and 500 horse guard were continually about the town [i.e. London] all night and no one knows to this hour the meaning of it. It had the effect that all the Catholics in England are ordered to surrender their arms,. Most Catholics here are summoned according to the new Act.[40]

In 1696 the adult men of every village and town were again asked to step forward and swear to protect the King against the detestable conspiracy carried on by papists. Some lay people were again imprisoned in 1696 and there were a number of 'treason trials' including that of John Felton. Much use was made of the common informer and there was a constant ferment of discoveries of land left for 'superstitious' uses, especially in Lancashire.[41]

Nevertheless, there was a growing sense of security. English Catholics began to plan for a future as well to survive the moment. Both lay people and clergy left money for long-term Mass foundations, and for the financing of a priest to work in a particular area. In 1698 Daniel Fitter left a fund for a priest

> who was to have no servant, nor depend on any family, but was to reside in the county of Stafford, and was to assist any poor body in the county, and within four or five miles of it, who might want help, either by reason of their own ghostly father being absent, or by reason of the want of one in those parts where such poor may live.[42]

The Howden riding mission in the East Riding was endowed by a group of gentlemen so that a priest could visit 69 places once every five weeks in favourable weather. The first record of an incumbent of this fund was dated 1672.[43] In 1701 Thomas Purcell made a foundation for a monthly Mass at Yieldfields Hall, Bloxwich, Staffordshire. His family were of modest gentry status and had interests both in Madeley, Shropshire, and in Bloxwich. The priest receiving the Yieldfields endowment was to say Mass, and also to instruct the people, catechising, visiting the dying and giving money to the poor. For this, five shillings per journey was, Thomas thought, 'sufficient'. His will throws considerable light on the expectations of Catholics in 1700 as they peered into the future. Thomas anticipated that 'for reasons of State' the priest might not always be able to come to Yieldfields, that he might not be able to travel on horseback, but 'by difficulty of the times' should have to travel on foot. If times are so bad that he cannot come at all he is to say the foundation Masses wherever he can, or if persecution gets even worse the Bishop is to send the money overseas. Thomas is concerned about the danger of informers and more mundanely about the interest rates and the document itself suffering from rats and mice. Thomas was obviously a worrier, but essentially he does believe that a regular ministry will be possible, and hopes that Philip Hicken (a neighbour's son) will be appointed to be the first incumbent, 'if alive and in these parts'. In the event Philip Hicken went to Oscott. Yieldfields became part of the Wolverhampton circuit and was served by Chetwyn Purcell, Thomas's nephew.[44]

Some foundations provided for both a domestic chaplain and a riding priest. In the East Riding of Yorkshire Lord Dunbar kept two priests one as a chaplain and one to help at Marton, Newton and Marsham. From 1655 until his death in 1692 the priest on this fund lived with Mr Beckwith at Marton, serving about 80 souls in a wide area. The endowment was needed as the three or four other priests in the area were confined to the service of the family only.[45]

The legislation against Catholics had been designed to enforce unity of belief in Church and State, in the family and in the parish. By 1700 religion and politics were drifting apart and increasingly God and his laws were separated in people's minds from the need of the State for political unity. Protestant bishops preached a 'broad church' and minimised doctrine. Protestant parish clergy in many rural parishes were becoming 'squarsons', identified with the ruling families, with status and learning rather than evangelical zeal. High Tory defenders of Church and State were in opposition to prevailing government. The licensing laws relating to books were dropped and in both town and country Protestant chapels demonstrated the legitimacy of dissent. New legislation against Catholics related mainly to their land holding rather than their beliefs, notably the double land tax. The penalty for priesthood was reduced to life imprisonment, and as early as 1692 a list of the residences and work of 81 priests (probably less than half of all the priests in England) could be made and filed by the Old Chapter.[46] The end of the seventeenth century marked the end of the resistance phase of the Catholic experience, and the beginning of the long road to normalisation and growth.

NOTES

1 Pauline Howells, *Newcastle-on-Tyne and the Puritan Revolution* (1967); Lichfield R.O. B/C/5/1629 Latham v. Norris.

2 S.A. Burne, 'Three letters of Thomas Draxe concerning the Recusants at Colwich, 1613', *S.H.C.* (1933); Keith Wrightson & David Levine, *Poverty and Piety in an English Village 1525-1700* (1979), pp. 155-62.

3 G. Edward Saville ed., *Alcester, a History* (1958).

4 David Underdown, *Fire from Heaven: Life in an English Town in the Seventeenth Century* (1992); David Rollison, *The Local Origins of Modern Society: Gloucestershire 1500-1800* (1992); Aveling, *York*; Brian Manning, *Aristocrats, Plebeians and Revolution in England 1640-1660* (1996), pp. 30-2; D. A. Johnson & D. G. Vaisey eds., *Staffordshire and the Great Rebellion* (Staffordshire R.O., 1965), p. 20.

5 Ushaw, William Smith, *Notes on the Records of the Court of High Commission 1626-1642* (T.S.), pp. 182, 193.

6 Robin Clifton, 'Popular Fear of Catholics during the English Revolution', *Past and Present* 52 (August 1971), pp. 23-55; Bromhead Collection, Douai Abbey: various pamphlets, especially *A Relation of the Rare Exploits of the London Soldiers*, Bromhead X/19.490691-3; W. Palmer, 'Catholic Plots and the English

Reformation', *Catholic History Review* 73, no. 1 (January 1987), pp. 81-6; A. Fletcher, *The Outbreak of the English Civil War* (1981), pp. 86-90.

[7] House of Lords Main Papers Protestation Returns (I am grateful to Dr. Whiteman for the loan of her photocopies of the returns); Anne Whiteman, 'The Protestation 1641-1642', *Local Population Studies* 55 (Autumn 1995), p. 14; ibid., Part Two (Spring 1996); P.R. Newman, 'Roman Catholics in Pre-Civil War England', *Recusant History* 15, no. 2 (October 1979), pp. 148-51; D.S. Reid, 'P.R. Newman and the Durham Protestations', *Recusant History* 15, no. 5 (May 1981), pp. 370-2; David Underdown, *Revel, Riot and Rebellion* (1985), pp. 144-5.

[8] Timothy J. McCann, 'Midhurst Catholics and the Protestation Returns of 1642', *Recusant History* 16, no. 3 (May 1983), pp. 319-24; J. Gibson ed., *Oxfordshire and Berkshire Protestation Returns and Tax Assessments* (Oxfordshire Record Society 59, 1957).

[9] Eric Clavering, 'The Dynamics of Durham Recusancy', *Durham Local History Society Bulletin* 48 (May 1992), pp. 3-27; John Hilton, *Catholic Lancashire: from Reformation to Renewal 1559-1991* (1995), pp. 34-5.

[10] P.R. Newman, 'Catholic Royalist Activities in the North, 1642-1646', *Recusant History* 15, no. 6 (October 1981), pp. 396-406; P. Newman, 'Catholics in Arms: the Regiment of Sir Robert Clavering of Callaly', *N.C.H.* 9 (Spring 1979), p. 101; David F. Mosler, 'Warwickshire Catholics in the Civil War', *Recusant History* 15, no. 4 (October 1980), p. 262; Brian Manning, *Religion and Society in Elizabethan Sussex* (Leicester, 1979), pp. 166-9; Thomas Cliffe, *The Yorkshire Gentry from the Reformation to the Civil War* (1969); John S. Morrill, *Cheshire 1630-1660: County Government and Society during the English Revolution* (Oxford, 1974); Johnson & Vaisey, *Staffordshire and the Great Rebellion*; B.G. Blackwood, *The Lancashire Gentry and the Great Rebellion 1640-1660* (Manchester, 1978); W. Hunt, *The Puritan Moment: the Coming of the Revolution in an English County* (Cambridge, Mass., 1983), p. 293.

[11] J. Hughes ed., *The Boscobel Tracts relating to the Escape of Charles the Second* (1857), pp. 151-5.

[12] *Calendar of the Proceedings of the Committee for Compounding with Delinquents 1643-1660* (5 volumes H.M.S.O.); John H. Pollen, 'Sequestration of Papists' Estates 1647-1651' in Challoner, pp. 491-99.

[13] John Miller, *Popery and Politics in England 1660-1680* (Cambridge, 1973), pp. 27, 84, 86.

[14] Trevor Watts, *The Dissenters* (1978), p. 24.

[15] J. Anthony Williams, 'English Catholicism under Charles II: the Legal Position', *Recusant History* 7, no. 3 (1964), pp. 134-6; Peter J. Challinor, *The Structure of Politics in Cheshire 1660-1715* (Ph.D. Wolverhampton Polytechnic, 1983), p. 246; Malcolm Wanklyn, 'Recusancy in Seventeenth Century Shropshire, with particular reference to the Parish of Madeley', *Worc. Rec.* 43 (June 1984), pp. 22-31.

[16] Roger Clark, *Anglicanism, Recusancy and Dissent in Derbyshire 1603-1730* (D.Phil Oxford, 1979).

[17] Dudley Fowkes & M. W. Greenslade, 'A List of Staffordshire Recusants 1678-1680', *Staffs. C.H.* 24 (1990), pp. 1-27.

[18] D. Lucy, *Diary of Roger Lowe* (1965), p. 30.

[19] *C.S.P.D. Charles II, 1663,* p. 278; *C.S.P.D. Charles II, 1665-6*, p. 107; Colin Haydon, *Anti-Catholicism in Eighteenth Century England c.1714-80: a Political and Social Survey* (1993), pp. 3-4.

[20] Brian Coward, *The Stuart Age* (1980), pp. 271-4, 282-341; John Miller, *Popery and Politics in England 1660-1688* (1973), pp. 152-4; John P. Kenyon, *The Popish Plot* (1972).

[21] William Cobbett, *Cobbetts' Complete Collection of State Trials*, vol. 7 (1810), pp. 715-63.

[22] B. Foley, *Some Other People of Penal Times* (privately printed, 1991), pp. 133-43.

23 David Mullins, 'Catholicism in the Wye Valley', *Gloucestershire and North Avon Catholic History Society* 16 (Winter 1990), pp. 11-2. For a different interpretation see Philip Jenkins, 'A Welsh Lancashire ? Monmouthshire Catholics in the Eighteenth Century', *Recusant History* 15 (1981), pp. 176-87.
24 John A. Hilton, 'Gloucester and its Catholics during the reign of James II', *Gloucester and North Avon Catholic History Society* 13 (Spring 1990), pp. 16-33.
25 Sources for chapel-building in the reign of James II are innumerable. Those used here are principally: J. Anthony Williams in *The New Catholic Encyclopaedia*, Foley, Anstruther and an extended series of articles by John Hilton entitled 'The Catholic Ascendancy in ...' published in the journals of regional history. For full details, see Michael Gandy, *Bibliography.*
26 Aveling, *York*, p. 103.
27 J. Anthony Williams, *Post-Reformation Catholicism in Bath I* (C.R.S. 65, 1975), pp. 37-9.
28 J. Noake, *Worcester Sects* (1861), p. 64; T.G. Holt, 'The Residence of St George: Jesuits in Warwickshire and Worcestershire in Penal Times', *Worc. Rec.* 20 (December, 1972), pp. 45-78.
29 John Hilton, 'Gloucester and its Catholics, pp. 16-33.
30 Basil Hemphill, *The Early Vicars Apostolic 1685-1750* (1953), p. 124.
31 Margaret Panikkar is engaged on a substantive study of the Stanford chapel in London. I am grateful for her contribution. Detailed accounts of the building and furnishing of Birmingham chapel preface the *Edgbaston Register*, introduction — original at B.A.A.; Judith F. Champ, 'The Franciscan Mission in Birmingham 1657-1824', *Recusant History* 21, no. 1 (May 1992), pp. 40-50.
32 *C.S.P.D. James II*, vol. 2 (1964), pp. 6, 138, 571 and other references as indexed.
33 Hemphill, *The Early Vicars Apostolic*, p. 4.
34 Thomas B. Trappes-Lomax, 'Leyburn's Visitation of 1686', *C.R.S. Newsletter* 4 (1962), pp. 16-21; John A. Hilton ed., 'The Leyburn Visitation of 1686', *Transactions of the North-West Catholic History Society* (October 1996), pp. 3-14; Aveling, *York*, p. 105.
35 Michael Greenslade, 'Bishop Leyburn at Stafford and Wolverhampton', *Staffs.C.H.* 2 (Spring 1962), pp. 19-26. I am grateful to Mrs Catherine Coleman for the analysis.
36 J. Sheihan, *History of the Town and Port of Kingston upon Hull* (1866), pp. 186-8.
37 *Edgbaston Register*, introduction.
38 John S. Roper, *Transcript of Wolverhampton Constables Accounts* (T.S., 1974), p. 4.
39 John C.D. Clark, *Revolution and Rebellion* (1986); Leo Gooch, *The Desperate Faction* (1995); E. Cruickshanks & J. Black, *The Jacobite Challenge* (1988); Proclamations June 17 1690, May 6, 1689.
40 W.A.A. C13/3/20.
41 W. Gandy, *Lancashire Association Oath Rolls* (Society of Genealogists, 1985), pp. v-xix.
42 B.A.A. A 550.
43 Aveling, *North,* p. 343.
44 B.A.A. A 416, A 417.
45 Aveling, *North,* p. 54.
46 Raymond Stansfield ed., 'Particulars of Priests in England and Wales 1692', C.R.S. 9, pp. 106-114.

5

THE CATHOLICS OF 1676 AS RECORDED IN THE COMPTON CENSUS

The Census of 1676 offers an exceptional opportunity to place the Catholics in the context of their parish and at the same time to consider individual returns against a national background, but the individual figures must be regarded as indications rather than statistics. The Census ought to have provided the numbers of persons who were papists and Dissenters in the parishes of England and Wales in 1676. However, this did not happen for various reasons which are explained in the general and diocesan introductions in the critical edition published in 1986 by A. Whiteman with the assistance of Mary Clapinson (referred to below as C.E.).[1] If the complexities discussed there are not understood, a valid analysis of the national distribution of papists cannot be undertaken.

Introduction to the Returns of Papists and their Context

The information in the Census derives from the answers which the incumbents of the Church of England parishes provided to three specific questions. A detailed study of all the evidence reveals that they were not worded in the same way in all the dioceses and were moreover imprecisely drafted. Although the organisers wanted a return of adult men and women over the age to communicate (sixteen), not all incumbents gave the required answer when asked what number of persons 'inhabit your parish'. Others replied in terms of men over 16 only, households or the whole population including children. Whether they answered the questions about the numbers of papists or Dissenters with the same variety of interpretations is not known. Moreover, a return of papists may include 'suspected' or church papists, and one for Dissenters (called Nonconformists in the original MS.) may or may not include 'partial conformists', who attended church but also went to their own conventicles. There is a good deal of evidence to suggest that the number of papists is underestimated in the Census. For example, Rowington, Warwickshire, reported 26 papists, presumably men over 16 only; seven years later, 70 men and women in the parish were presented for recusancy at the Trinity term Quarter Sessions.[2]

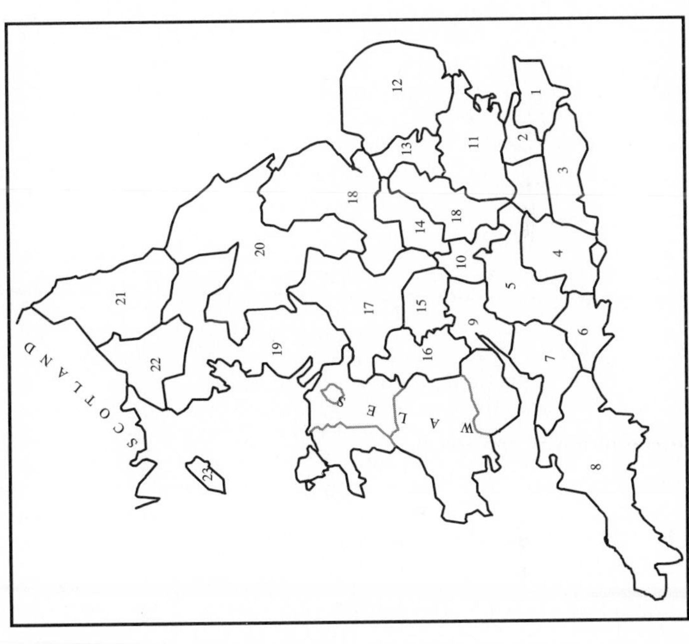

Figure 2: Map of the English Dioceses

1 Canterbury
2 Rochester
3 Chichester
4 Winchester
5 Salisbury
6 Bristol
7 Bath & Wells
8 Exeter
9 Gloucester
10 Oxford
11 London
12 Norwich
13 Ely
14 Peterborough
15 Worcester
16 Hereford
17 Lichfield
18 Lincoln
19 Chester
20 York
21 Durham
22 Carlisle
23 Sodor & Man

The MS. in the William Salt Library at Stafford is a fair copy of the figures for the greater part of England and the sole surviving source for most of them. The figures were set out in three columns headed Conformists, Papists and Nonconformists. In the case of Lincoln diocese the heading Conformists is almost certainly correct, meaning those of age to communicate in the Church of England, excluding papists and Dissenters. In three other dioceses (Canterbury, Salisbury and Chichester) and perhaps part of London and Hereford a 'persons total' was adapted to give one for 'conformists'. Almost all the other figures, however, are 'persons' and not 'conformists'. Figures for both 'persons' and 'conformists' are given below; one or the other is calculated by addition or subtraction as necessary. In the tables P or C is used to indicate what the return reported or is thought to have reported.

About two thirds of the returns appear to have enumerated adult men and women (i.e. men and women over 16 and of an age to communicate in current seventeenth-century usage), so the validity of many of the figures is probably reasonably high. The returns throw light on the distribution of Catholics and their context in particular places, revealing some unexpected correlations and some pointers to further research. However, they cannot be used on their own to provide statistics or systematic comparison. But with all the Census' shortcomings and complexities, no other source can provide so much information.

The Distribution of Catholics in 1676 based on the Evidence of the Census

Although returns are known for nearly 7,500 parishes and chapelries in England, the coverage is very uneven with many omissions and a number of entries of names without figures (see Tables 3-4, pp. 82-83). Consequently, the number of Catholics in England is impossible to establish, though the census may be used to arrive at a *tentative and incomplete* total of at least 11,500.

Surviving original returns as sent in by the incumbents, and compilations of them in diocesan records, throw light on how the incumbents understood or misunderstood the three questions asked and how their answers were processed. These include six illuminating returns for parishes in Lancashire of particular interest to historians of seventeenth-century Catholicism[3].

T. B. Trappes-Lomax regarded the returns as seriously underestimating the number of Catholics, basing his judgement on his study of Norfolk, but J. A. Williams regarded them as reasonably correct for Wiltshire,[4] two counties for both of which the returns are remarkably complete; even greater problems of evaluation arise for the counties where large numbers of returns are missing. For example, there are no papists returned for Ingatestone, Writtle and Brentwood, Essex, the homes of various branches of the Petre family and three other associated Catholic gentry families. For Buttsbury, Essex, only 90 conformists are given despite the regular appearance of Catholic villagers and servants in the churchwardens' and constables' returns and in the parish register. The national maps which have been published on the basis of these returns by diocese or by county, and which will be familiar to most readers, are clearly unsatisfactory. They grossly oversimplify the picture, whether the maps are by diocese or by county, for they do not show in sufficient detail the parishes omitted. The C.E. of the Census on the other hand does provides a list of such parishes in each section and the disparities become very evident when the returns are mapped.[5]

Catholics and their Neighbours

Despite the irregular coverage, some tentative conclusions can be drawn from considering the Census as a whole. Although attempts at national totals are bound to be imperfect, a calculation based on available figures gives a total of 2,108,913 persons, of whom 88,923 were Dissenters, and 11,482 papists. The Census provides a basis, albeit flawed, for relating Catholics to Conformists and to Dissenters. It shows that Catholics lived in just over one fifth of the parishes for which there are returns, and that in two thirds of those parishes they lived alongside Protestant Dissenters: whether Presbyterians, Baptists or Quakers the return does not tell us. Papists alone were reported in just over 6% only of the total number of parishes and chapelries. All but one of the parishes reported a majority of 'conformists' and two thirds had 'conformists' only. What is particularly noteworthy is that some parishes with a relatively high number of Catholics also had a considerable number of Dissenters; for example Hampstead Norris, Berkshire, with 21 papists and 61 Dissenters and Kilmeston, Hampshire, with 19 papists and 13 Dissenters.[6] It is evident that Catholic landlords in almost every case had conforming tenants, and in many cases, Dissenting tenants as well. People of the common sort might be influenced by their landlords but were not necessarily controlled by them, and the same social and economic circumstances might support both Catholic and Dissenting families.

Confessional history has considered the Dissenters and the papists separately, and this separation has been reinforced by a general assumption that papists and Dissenters represent opposite ends of a spectrum of belief with Conformists in the centre.

Table 3: The Coverage of Parishes in the Compton Census

Diocese	Returns	Omissions	
Bath and Wells	0	All	
Bristol	0	All	
Canterbury	259	3	
Carlisle	86	0	Figures missing for 26 parishes
Chester	0	All	
Chichester	288	20	
Durham	0	All	
Ely	143	8	No returns for University Colleges
Exeter	636	21	
Gloucester	288	9	
Hereford	327	12	
Lichfield	442	100	
Lincoln	1,259	93	
London	400	121	And figures missing for 141 parishes
Norwich	933	12	Suffolk Archdeaconry omitted
Oxford	218	7	No returns for University Colleges
Peterborough	309	12	
Rochester	90	38	
Salisbury	352	43	
Winchester	432	11	Considerable areas extra-parochial
Worcester	255	4	
York	596	136	
Total	7313		

A high proportion of the missing parishes were Peculiar Jurisdictions.
All dioceses included extra-parochial places for which there was no return.
Based on Ann Whiteman, *The Compton Census 1676: A Critical Edition* (1986), p. ciii.

Table 4: Religious allegiance by parish as reported in the Census, 1676

	Returns	Reporting Papists	Reporting Papists Conformists Dissenters	Reporting Conformists Papists
Bath and Wells	No Returns			
Bristol	No Returns*			
Canterbury	259	31	26	5
Carlisle	86	24	22	2
Chester	No Returns			
Chichester	288	44	26	18
Durham	No Returns			
Ely	143	13	9	4
Exeter	636	61	37	24
Gloucester	288	41	32	9
Hereford	327	117	57	60
Lichfield	442	177	128	49
Lincoln	1,259	185	118	67
London	400	79	66	13
Norwich	933	160	101	59
Oxford	218	68	41	27
Peterborough	309	30	19	11
Rochester	90	18	15	3
Salisbury	352	91	74	17
Winchester	432	144	104	40
Worcester	255	94	71	23
York	596	220	165	55
Total	7313	1,597	1,111	486

Source: C.E., passim
*But see C.E., pp. 547-8.

Whether or not this is the case in respect of theology, it would seem that in their social setting and experience they may have had some things in common. Both groups struggled with the consequences of rejecting the State as the prime arbiter of religion.

The Parish Returns

As explained above, it is essential to treat the Census as a large collection of local records of particular places, but they were made by the incumbents and parish officers, who routinely carried responsibility for listing communicants, papists and Dissenters. They were not carrying out a novel and discrete administrative exercise. Every year the incumbent and churchwardens compiled what was known as the Easter Book, listing parishioners with sums due as Easter Offerings. Parish officials kept lists of the men, women and children in receipt of poor rate. They also had to produce lists of persons chargeable and non-chargeable for Hearth Tax. The incumbent and the parish clerk had to register baptisms, marriages and burials. Occasionally the vestry also had to collect money from house to house for charitable briefs, and list persons contributing to the maintenance of the highways. When there was an Episcopal Visitation there will have been demands for information not only about the number of families, papists and Dissenters in the parish, but also about the church fabric and the effectiveness of the incumbent. In 1662 Bishop Cosin of Durham had conducted a very thorough visitation, which was particularly concerned with the identification of religious nonconformity. Work done on the returns of Protestant Dissenters for Cambridgeshire shows that there was a 'close correspondence between the Census and the church court records'.[7]

The discussion which follows considers the returns from rural areas, from urban parishes and ports and from parishes where agriculture was combined with manufacture. This is, of course, a very arbitrary proceeding, since some towns and cities were also ports and some small market towns had functions so vestigial that it is difficult to distinguish them as urban. Many single parishes comprised a small town and a wide rural area, and the many parishes of the great cities comprehended surrounding rural territory. Nevertheless, as will emerge, there were real differences between the distribution of Catholics in different environments.

CATHOLICS IN THE COUNTRYSIDE

The great majority of rural parishes reported no Catholics at all. Only about 43 reported more than 20. Three reported more than 100, more than any town or city outside London, always with the proviso that many important areas are missing. The rank order of rural parishes returning 40 or more papists is given in Table 5 (p. 86).

The significance of groups of Catholics in their parishes changes when we consider the number of Catholics in relation to the total number of persons reported in the Census.

In only one parish in the return (not necessarily in the country) were Catholics in a majority. This was at Weston Underwood, Buckinghamshire, a small parish in which the manor was held by the Catholic Throckmorton family, who had a chapel and priest in the house. Weston Underwood was five miles from Newport Pagnell and a mile from Olney, and the surrounding parishes contained many Dissenters but no papists. In Weston itself there were seven Dissenters as well as 52 conformists and 67 papists.[8] Many of the parishes where there were more than 20% papists were also very small in the aggregate. These included Gaudby, Irnham, Clixby and Northorpe, Lincolnshire; Norbury, Derbyshire; Gothurst, Buckinghamshire; Brandsby, Yorkshire; and Llanrothall, Herefordshire. The total return for Ewhurst, Hampshire, was only 17, of which 8 were Catholics.[9] These were often parishes where a Catholic was the principal or only landowner and with few or no Dissenters; classic centres of Catholic tradition. However, only a small proportion of the known Catholic body lived in such circumstances, even in 1676, and some well-known Catholic families are shown to have had less than complete dominance in their locality.

The numbers of conformists, Catholics and Dissenters also need to be related to the geographical area of the parishes. The experience of Catholics in small compact parishes was qualitatively different from that of Catholics living in large parishes where settlement was scattered and families isolated by large areas of forest, mountain, moorland and water. Contrast, for example, the life of the 65 papists reported in the 41,000 acres of Bakewell, Derbyshire, with that of the 54 reported as living in the 1,412 acres of Otterbourne, Hampshire.

The Grouping of Catholics

Whiteman commented on the frequency with which only one or two recusants or Dissenters are reported in a parish. The impression that these Catholics were isolated and eccentric

Table 5: The Largest Returns of Papists, 1676

The 22 rural parishes reporting the most papists in the Census, arranged in descending order.

Parish	County		Persons	Conform.	Papists	Dissenters
Egton	Yorkshire	p	610	388	217	5
Hathersage	Derbyshire	c	580	440	140	0
Handsworth	Staffordshire	p	500	398	101	1
Arrow	Warwickshire	p	302	222	75	5
Garway	Herefordshire	p	176	105	71	0
Twyford	Hampshire	p	430	360	70	0
Weston Underwood	Buckinghamshire	c	126	52	67	7
Coughton	Warwickshire	p	331	264	67	0
Norbury	Derbys	c	139	74	65	0
Gt. Mitton	Warwickshire	p	1,139	1,074	64	1
Bidford	Warwickshire	p	526	462	61	3
Brandsby	Yorkshire	p	157	97	60	0
Irnham	Lincolnshire	c	137	81	56	0
Otterbourne	Hampshire	p	135	81	54	0
Hoveringham	Norfolk	p	430	372	53	5
Stourton	Wiltshire	c	250	196	51	1
Somerton	Oxfordshire	p	191	140	51	0
Swine	Yorkshire	p	400	345	47	8
West Firle	Sussex	c	152	107	43	2
Easebourne	Sussex	c	160	120	40	0
Barwick in Elmet	Yorkshire	p	795	750	40	5
West Hallam	Derbyshire	c	150	107	40	0
Shipley	Sussex	c	600	540	40	20

individuals is, however, illusory. When the returns are mapped parish by parish, it becomes evident that in very many cases the one or two mentioned were part of a small congregation. The lone Catholic reported at Mongewell, Oxfordshire, and the two at Goring were within walking distance of Mapledurham. When put together, the returns record a small congregation of 30 adult Catholics scattered over half a dozen contiguous parishes centring on the house of the Catholic Blount family at Mapledurham. In the Thames valley there were almost 200 Catholics within an eight-mile radius of Woolhampton, who included 28 at Ufton Court, where Perkins influence was strong; 21 at Hampstead Norrys, Berkshire, where the Dancastle family were influential; 32, the most in any single parish in Berkshire, at Buckland, where Dame Mary Yate had endowed a chaplaincy.[10]

To understand the distribution of papists, we need to think in terms of congregations and to combine the returns from contiguous parishes, disregarding county boundaries but taking features such as hills, rivers and roads into account in so far as they affected short-distance travel. Although these groups of Catholics have been mapped for the whole of England, a few examples must suffice here. Swaffham, Oxborough and Cockley Cley in Norfolk formed one such group. Between them they returned 865 persons, made up of 792 conformists, 27 papists and 46 Dissenters.[11] In Devon, Arlington, Berrynarbor and Barnstaple between them returned 3,474 persons, comprising 3,322 conformists and 29 Catholics and 100 Dissenters.[12] The area around Winchester had been notoriously Catholic since Elizabeth's reign. The Census reports 70 adult Catholics in Twyford, Hampshire, among a population of 430 adults, and exceptionally, no Dissenters. In the nearby parishes of Morestead, Owslebury, Otterbourne and Bishopstoke there were 100 more Catholics, all within ten miles of Twyford. This group of parishes together had 1,255 'persons', 1,065 'Conformists', 170 Catholics, and 20 Dissenters.[13]

Groupings might comprise adjacent parishes in different counties. In the Forest of Dean, partly non-parochial at this date, an important, if small, group of Catholics centred on Lydney in Gloucestershire and overlapped into Monmouthshire. Lydney, Woollaston, Tidenham, and St Briavels together reported 1,573 communicants, 36 Catholics and 59 Dissenters[14]. Other cross-county boundary groups included the parishes in Shropshire east of Severn and the adjoining parishes in mid-Staffordshire, while Catholics in north-west Shropshire were linked with Catholics in Flintshire and Denbighshire and those of south Herefordshire with Monmouthshire. In Yorkshire,

Table 6: The Largest Proportionate Returns of Papists, 1676

Parishes with the highest proportion of Catholics relative to reported persons in the Census, arranged in descending order.

			Persons	Conform.	Papists	Dissenters	%
Weston Underwood	Bucks	c	126	52	67	7	53
Ewehurst	Hants	p	17	9	8	0	47
Norbury	Derbys/Staffs	c	139	74	65	0	47
Clixby	Lincs	c	47	27	20	0	43
Irnham	Lincs	c	137	81	56	0	41
Garway	Herefords	p	176	105	71	0	40
Otterbourne	Hants	p	135	81	54	0	40
Bransby	Yorks	p	157	97	60	0	38
Gothurst	Lincs	p	65	41	24	0	37
Egton	Yorks	p	610	188	217	5	36
Everingham	Yorks.	p	210	176	34	0	32
Llanrothall	Heref	p	38	25	13	0	32
Brampton	Norfolk	p	59	33	18	8	31
Tichborne	Hants	p	79	55	24	0	30
Buckland	Berks	c	700	666	32	2	30
West Firle	Sussex	c	152	107	43	2	29
West Hallam	Derbys	p	150	107	40	3	27
Bedhampton	Hants	c	45	31	12	2	27

Middleton cum Hilton	Yorks	p	111	81	30	1	27
Wootton Wawen	Warw	p	62	44	17	1	27
Arrow	Warw	p	302	222	75	5	25
Somerton	Oxon.	p	191	140	51	0	25
Easebourne	Sussex	c	160	120	40	0	25
Hathersage	Derbys	c	580	440	140	0	24
Leigh	Staffs	p	500	465	35	0	23
Barwick in Elmet	Yorks	p	795	750	40	5	23
Bodney	Norfolk			20	6	0	23
Gaudby	Lincs	c	45	35	10	0	22
Ufton Nervett	Berks	c	126	98	28	0	22
Arlington	Devon	p	158	124	34	0	22
Calton	Staffs	p	140	80	30	30	22
Northorpe	Lincs	c	61	48	13	0	21
Stourton	Wilts	c	250	196	51	1	20
Burton and Coates	Sussex	c	30	24	6	0	20
Coughton	Warw	p	331	264	67	0	20
Bodecton	Sussex			24	6	0	20

C.E., passim. It must be again emphasized that these percentages are based on the figures as given by each return and are offered at best as a rough guide.

Northumberland, Worcestershire and Herefordshire the groups overlapped and Catholics were diffused through much of the county. Whether in the North or South of England the returns show very few Catholics living more than seven to ten miles from a larger grouping of Catholics. These groupings usually cover an area of some ten miles radius, which, it can be assumed, represents the distance over which Catholics travelled to Mass, or priests were in close touch with their people. A Catholic not in touch with a congregation probably ceased to be regarded as a papist, or slipped into conformity.

Catholics and their Priests

While it is practicable, though time-consuming, to locate and even to map clusters of Catholics in the return, it is much more difficult to correlate the grouping of Catholics in the Census with known resident and active priests. Secrecy was still necessary and they were still liable to the death penalty simply for being priests ordained abroad and living as priests in England. The records of the Old Chapter, which organised the work of the secular clergy, provide names and deaneries of priests but rarely places. The Jesuit records provide lists of priests by College but information about the precise residence of priests is erratic and the same applies to the Franciscans and Benedictines. One group of records which seems to throw light on the matter is the documentation concerning the collection of money by Catholics for Charles I in 1639. The lists from Lancashire give names of both priests and the gentlemen with whom they were associated, arranged by Church of England parishes. Up to four priests are found in some parishes, and members of different religious orders as well as seculars. It is difficult to know whether these represent regular pastoral care or rather the contacts the priest could make for the collection. The one return giving a list of names from whom the priest has collected shows persons from seventeen parishes.[15]

While it is broadly the case that both secular and regular priests lived in the houses of wealthy laymen, there were others who lived with relatives, or in lodgings at their own expense. The large number of Catholics at Garway relates to the Jesuit centre at The Cwm in Llanrothall parish in the south of Herefordshire. Two houses here were leased to the Jesuits by the Earl of Worcester from at least 1637. When The Cwm was raided in 1679, accommodation for six priests and their servants was discovered and although the priests had fled, there were found the remains of a chapel with altar-stone, vestments, pictures, crucifixes, a bell, an incense-pot, wafers and holy oils. Among the books were 'many small popish catechisms printed and tied up in a bundle and some Welsh popish books lately printed'.[16]

There is one mission register contemporary with the Census to enable us to relate papists to priests and to landlords. It is known as the Edgbaston register as the mission settled in that parish in 1689, but the entries commence in 1657. Franciscans were administering the sacraments to families from Solihull, Tanworth-in-Arden, Edgbaston, and Birmingham, Warwickshire, and Harborne, Staffordshire; it seems possible that the priests were based at Baddesley Clinton, Warwickshire, and that Catholics were being visited rather than coming to a centre. Almost all the baptisms and marriages recorded were of common people living in farms, cottages and in small towns. The Census clearly reflects this grouping, even though there is no return for Edgbaston itself, and Harborne was one of the many peculiars in Staffordshire, for none of which is there an extant return. However, there are figures for the parishes of Birmingham, Rowington, Solihull and Tanworth-in-Arden as follows.[17]

Table 7: Return of Papists in Birmingham and District, 1676

			Conforming	Papists	Dissenters
Birmingham	p	2,582	2,541	11	30
Solihull	p	733	634	73	26
Knowle belonging to Solihull	p	239	226	239	13
Rowington	p	171	141	26	4
Tanworth-in-Arden	p	400	354	30	16

Source: C.E., pp. 452, 453.

The Catholic register confirms the implication of the Census showing that the Franciscan missionaries worked over a radius of about 10 to 15 miles. This mission included two towns, two rural villages and two industrial villages in its scope. In some of these places there was an active Catholic landowner, while in others in the same mission the manor was in other hands or not subject to manorial control.

The Congregations of Papists

Even without registers, disjointed scraps of evidence gathered from many sources make it possible to build 'mission histories' for some of the groupings of papists revealed by mapping the Census parish by parish.[18] The three largest returns were from Egton, Yorkshire; Hathersage, Derbyshire; and Handsworth, Staffordshire. By examining what is known of these missions it may be possible to discover whether there were factors in common.

Egton, Yorkshire

As we have seen, Egton provided the largest aggregate return from a rural parish, and was among those with the highest percentages. The surrounding parishes also had large numbers of papists.

Table 8: Return of Papists in Egton and District, 1676

			Persons	Conforming	Papists	Dissenters
Egton	Yorks.	p	610	388	217	5
Stokesley	Yorks.	p	826	676	105	45
Lythe	Yorks.	p	291	256	20	15

Source: C.E., p. 599

Egton chapelry was four miles inland from the port of Whitby and a part of the parish of Lythe, Yorkshire, and it covered 18,378 acres. The Smiths owned two of the three farms and the Salvins had the small manor of Newbiggin. Ugbrooke in the same parish was also a regular Mass centre. Stokesley parish to the west included a market town. Returns from the reign of Elizabeth and throughout the early seventeenth centuries show a group of families whose names recur, but also many whose names appear only once. Even the most well-defined Catholic families included many who conformed, and there were probably many families with a mixture of faiths. In the years immediately preceding the Census, the priest Nicholas Postgate was active in making converts, and another priest, Andrew Jowsey, was arrested in Egton in 1678. Correlation with the Hearth Tax has proved possible for 183 occupied houses in the chapelry and shows that three of the four largest houses were occupied by Catholics. The other Catholics were distributed through the middle and lower socio-economic groups. Listings for Quarter Sessions indicate that the Catholics followed the occupational profile as well as the social profile of the parish as whole. They followed thirteen different occupations and there were 17 yeomen, 8 cordwainers, 7 weavers and 17 labourers.[19]

Hathersage, Derbyshire

Hathersage lay in the Peak District and with other nearby parishes made the second largest return of papists in the Census from a rural area.

Table 9: Return of Papists in Hathersage and District, 1676

			Persons	Conforming	Papists	Dissenters
Hathersage	Derbs.	c	580	440	140	0
Eyam	Derbs.	c	532	526	3	3
Ecclesfield	Yorks.	p	3,267	3,246	9	2
Bakewell	Derbs.	c	4,500	4,235	65	200

Source: C.E. pp.443, 446, 595

These Catholics lived in an upland region of valley and moorland, where most of the people were farmers, but they were not isolated. They were only about nine miles from Sheffield, in an area of not only of pastoral farming but also of lead-mining, and the millstone grit of the mountains was worked to produce mill-stones, which were transported many miles for sale. Coal and lime was regularly transported from Tideswell to Sheffield, and malt and other commodities came in the returning wagons.

The mission can be traced from the reign of Elizabeth, and in 1592 36% of all the recusants on the Recusant Roll for Derbyshire had lived in Hathersage. The leading Catholic then was Thomas Barrow of Nether Hirst, a second son of a family of very minor gentry who married Matilda, daughter of John Fitzherbert. He was one of the people arrested in 1588 at a house at Padley at Mass together with the priests Robert Ludlam and Nicholas Garlick, both local men. Sir Thomas Fitzherbert, uncle of Thomas Barrow's spouse, had spent thirty years in gaol for recusancy, and many members of the family including Matilda had also been imprisoned. The Barrows' farmhouse became the Mass centre for Hathersage and the surrounding area, and in 1592 Mr Barrow of Hirst and his relative Thomas Eyre were reported for harbouring priests. It is not clear how far there followed a regular succession of priests, though Richard Arnold, alias Wheatley a secular priest may have been living in Hathersage in 1660. Both the Fitzherberts and the Barrows ceased to be influential in Hathersage. The Fitzherberts had lost much of their property in Derbyshire, and the Barrows also ceased to be recorded in Hathersage. However, this did not prevent the continuance of a Catholic group which now centred on the Eyre family, and a large Catholic population was reported in 1676. This family were not related to the Eyres of Hassop, but were yeomen farmers.[20]

Handsworth, Staffordshire

There had been strong Catholic gentry influence in this part of south Staffordshire in the sixteenth and early seventeenth century, but by 1667 the Comberfords of Wednesbury and the Stanfords of Perry Barr had sold their estates, and the influential Rider family of yeomen of West Bromwich were in financial decline. The Mountfords maintained a priest at Bescot Hall in the Foreign of Walsall not far from Handsworth, and the recusant Purcell family were residents at Yieldfields Hall. About the time of the Census the mission came to centre on the farmhouse of Oscott, which was in the manor of the Protestant Wyrley family and was the home of William Bromwich, yeoman. This family was linked to the Catholic Fitter family of Wolverhampton, two of whom were priests. In the year after the Census, William's son Andrew was ordained at the English College at Lisbon.

Table 10: Return of Papists in Handsworth and District, 1676

				Conforming	Papists	Dissenters
Handsworth	Staffs	p	500	398	101	1
Walsall	Staffs	p	1,360	1,120	40	200
West Bromwich	Staffs	p	621	604	2	15
Wednesbury	Staffs	p	854	808	1	45

Source: C.E., pp.488, 499

The part of Handsworth in which Oscott lay was rural and off the main lines of communication, but the main Holyhead road ran through the south of the parish, and West Bromwich, Walsall and Wednesbury were already distinctively industrial parishes where coal, ironstone and lime were exploited, and the power of the River Tame, which ran through all four parishes, was used for industrial purposes. West Bromwich, Wednesbury and Walsall all had strong groups of Protestant Dissenters, some of whom were influential in local government. The industrial and commercial leaders of this group of parishes included conformists and Dissenters but no papists.[21]

Hathersage, Egton and Handsworth provide examples of 'large' congregations in populous 'open' parishes, where manorial control was weak or non-existent. They were very different from Weston Underwood, Buckinghamshire, and Irnham, Lincolnshire, where the total number was small and centred on the 'Great House'. They were also very different in landownership, economy and social composition from each other, suggesting that many diverse elements led to the perpetuation of a rural mission, not

Figure 3: Catholics along the Derbyshire — Yorkshire border, 1676

Derbyshire

1	Bakewell	65
2	Barlborough	23
3	Beighton	2
4	Castleton	2
5	Chapel-en-le-Frith	3
6	Chesterfield	6
7	Dronfield	4
8	Eckington	32
9	Eyam	3
10	Glossop	4
11	Hathersage	143
12	Hope	10
13	Killamarsh	23
14	Norton	7
15	Staverly	6
16	Sutton-cum-Duckmanton	12
17	Tideswell	30
18	Whitwell	2
19	Wingerworth	4

West Riding

20	Doncaster	8
21	Ecclesfield	9
22	Rotherham	8
23	Sheffield	7

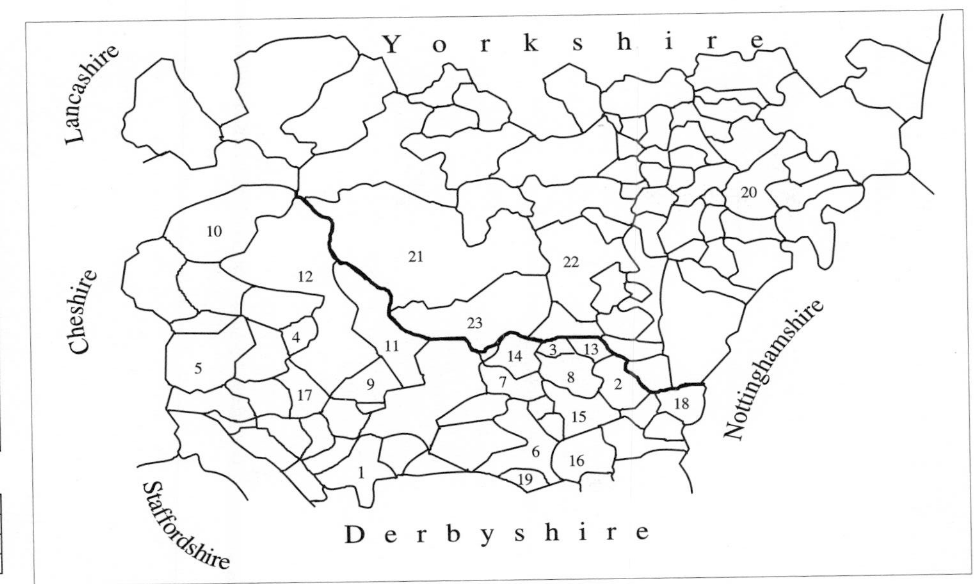

This map should be compared with Fig. 14, p. 299.

least the influence of example and tradition, as appears in the case of Sarnesfield.

Sarnesfield, Herefordshire was a congregation which drew its strength both from gentry influence and from the vigour of commitment of both clergy and yeomen, and, as in so many cases, from the cult of a local martyr.

Table 11: Return of Papists in Sarnesfield and District, 1676

				Conforming	Papists	Dissenters
Sarnesfield	Herefs	p	70	61	9	0
Eardisland	Herefs	p	283	261	5	17
Pembridge	Herefs	p	684	678	3	3
Almeley	Herefs	p	150	46	4	100
Weobley	Herefs	p	602	584	16	2

Source: C.E., pp. 253, 254, 256.

Nine Catholics were reported in Sarnesfield with 28 more in contiguous parishes: 37 in all. What the Census does not tell us is that the priest John Kemble (alias Holland) lived in the area, having been first mentioned there in 1643. He lived with his uncle George Kemble at Pembridge Castle and served Catholics at Llyn Craig, Hilston, Lye and Weobley. There were four Catholic gentlemen's houses nearby, namely Ley (Bridges), Kinnersley (Vaughan), Winsley (Berington) and Gattertop (Street). Evidence given at the time of the Oates Plot concerning Charles Kerne reported that Mass was said at several houses including that of Mr Somerset, where 'several people used come thither and go upstairs into the Chamber' and also that he led prayers at Bollingham where 'several people came out of the town and country'. The altars were, it was said, richly adorned in white, and there was a 'fine crucifix on the altar'. The gentlemen and their servants must have made up the greater part of the congregation, but there were also the Abel family, carpenters. John Abel had been employed on the Royal works and market halls in several towns in Herefordshire. He serves as a reminder that some commoners had considerable autonomy and an experience wider than their own village. Henry Weobley, yeoman of the parish, had been executed for harbouring priests, and three years after 1676 John Kemble was to be executed at the age of eighty years for being a popish priest. Such 'mission histories' could be multiplied for the Catholic clusters in the C.E. demonstrating that each had its particular profile of size, cohesion, and balance of gentry and commoners. However, many important Catholic missions are missing from the return, most significantly those for Lancashire.[22]

The Compton Census for Lancashire

In the absence of the return for the diocese of Chester, special interest attaches to some documents believed to be original returns for six parishes in Lancashire, all giving names and some personal details. These all relate to the south-west of Lancashire, namely Bispham, Broughton, Chipping, Kirkham, Woodplumpton and Lytham. They do not give ages, but appear to relate to adults.

The incumbent and churchwardens of Bispham listed 383 persons (182 men and 201 women) including seven papists (all women and two of them servants) and two Dissenters. The Kirkham document is incomplete. The list for Lytham gives 205 persons and 63 papists (29 men and 34 women) but no Dissenters. Woodplumpton summary gives 646 persons: only 46 papist recusants and 3 Dissenters. Kirkham parish and Woodplumpton were strong centres of recusancy, as is evident from Quarter Sessions prosecutions. The Chipping document has not been found, but a reference to it was made about 1900 and summarises it as showing 564 persons, of which 84 were recusants. Of these lists, four have been published, and the most illuminating is that for Broughton. This chapelry near Preston included the pilgrimage shrine of Fernyhalgh. The main landowners, the Langton family of Broughton Tower, were resident at that time in Bispham, and were not convicted recusants. The most prestigious Catholic in Broughton was Nicholas Wadsworth, esquire. The return was made with the utmost thoroughness and care, and a good deal of additional information was provided. The summary figures would have been 787 persons (587 Conformists), 200 papists (88 men and 112 women), and no Dissenters. Catholics formed perhaps a third of the adult population and in numbers were comparable with Egton, Yorkshire, Hathersage, Derbyshire, and Handsworth, Staffordshire. Occupations were not given, but three Catholics were described as servants in non-Catholic households and many Catholic heads of households have servants not described as papists. In a region where Catholics were so numerous, these middle income yeomen and tradesmen could have obtained Catholic servants, had this been their main priority. It also shows that some non-Catholics had no objection to taking a post with a Catholic master.[23]

Where rural missions were located in groups the priests enjoyed mutual support and the lay families had opportunities to find

Catholic marriage partners, servants and apprentices. A relatively small number of rural missions had only a single local centre, and examples of this are mainly to be found in East Anglia, Northamptonshire and Cornwall. These missions tended to be small in numbers and limited in geographical range. There were wide stretches of rural England where there were no Catholics, especially in the Eastern counties. Nevertheless the rural missions did not exist separately from each other but were connected with missions in other areas through the network of family ties and property holding of the landowners; the Throckmortons, for example, in south-west Warwickshire at Coughton and at Weston Underwood, Berkshire. Different houses or different branches of the family provided the main focus of the mission over time. Rural missions were also linked by the priests who had by the second half of the seventeenth century well-established organisations and funds; the Jesuit priests through organised Colleges and Residences, the seculars through the Chapter with its Archdeaneries. There was a pattern of missions emerging with endowed funding. The clustering of missions, the pattern of landholding, the growing stability and security of the clergy all contributed to the continuity of locations of rural missions over long periods of time. The extent to which these continuous locations correlate with continuity in the composition of the Catholic group is one of the themes of Part Two of this volume. Meanwhile, it is appropriate to consider the situation in towns as it appears in C.E.

CATHOLICS IN TOWNS AND PORTS

In the period 1650 — 1750 only about 10% of the population of England as a whole lived in towns and half of those who did so were in London, so that to characterise seventeenth-century Catholics as predominantly rural says no more than that they followed the general pattern.[24] The Census is not particularly helpful in tracing Catholics living in towns. About 250 towns, large and small, are missing from the Census. There are no returns from Lancashire, Cheshire, Somerset, and Dorset. Among the missing returns are those for some towns with known groups of papists, such as Wolverhampton, Staffordshire; Holywell, Flint; and Preston and Wigan, Lancashire. A recent study of Catholics in Devon shows that in that highly urbanised county Catholics were poorly represented in towns and cities. The priests who occasionally appeared in Exeter served the scattered Catholics of the surrounding parishes and there were only five in the town itself. The studies of Wiltshire and Yorkshire carry the same implications.[25] With this important caveat, it is still the case that we can gain some insight by examining the evidence we have and correlating this with other sources.

London

London was radically different as a place in which to live from anywhere else in England in point of its size, organisation and the composition of its residents. Mr. Gandy, on pp. 153-78 below, has explored its complexity and that of the Catholic groups who lived there. In summarising the Census return we consider the amorphous social unit called 'London' of which the City was only a part. North of the River Thames, it comprised the City of London, the City of Westminster, and the parishes between the two cities, even though they were were part of the county of Middlesex. Similarly, on the south side of the river, seven populous parishes were also part of the capital in social and economic terms, joined to it by the River Thames and London Bridge, though in a different diocese and county. Within the area were many peculiar jurisdictions and extra-parochial places. This complexity makes it difficult to correlate estimates and figures based on the parish returns since it is often far from clear what is included and what is excluded. The total population at this date has been estimated as 400,000; a figure which implies that one in every ten Englishmen at this date lived in London.[26] Many men and women lived in London for only part of their lives, but

London's population was maintained by a steady flow of immigrants from all over Britain, and there were many foreigners.

The returns for Bishop Compton's own diocese of London, as we have them, are the 'least satisfactory of the answers sent in', but they are virtually complete for the City of London itself. There are returns for the peculiar jurisdiction of the Archbishop of Canterbury, and three out of six parishes in that of the Dean and Chapter of St Paul's. London parishes were extremely diverse in size of population, ranging from fifty persons in Honey Lane and St Benedict Sherehog, to 17,000 in St Martin in the Fields.

No parish in the City of London returned more than twenty papists. The archdeaconry of London returned only 131 papists from 31 parishes, and 56 parishes made no return of papists. The City parish with the highest return of papists was St Peter le Poer with 20. Throughout the City, Protestant Dissenters were far more numerous than Catholics, with twenty-five parishes returning over 20 Dissenters and St Giles Cripplegate returning 8,140, about one half of the total return of the parish. There were 55 parishes with Protestant Dissenters, compared with 31 parishes returning Catholics. This is to be expected given the great strength of Puritanism and later Presbyterianism in the City of London. Their control of the Corporation of London at this date was uncertain, but papists had few friends there.

Westminster and Whitechapel are missing from the return, while the five parishes south of the Thames closely linked with London reported 24,000 persons: 23,358 conformists, 1,130 Dissenters, but a mere 12 papists .

These very low figures are difficult to accept, as other sources show (cf pp. 172-5 below). The London population was even more unstable in 1676 in the aftermath of the Plague of 1665 and the Great Fire of 1666, when 132,000 houses had been destroyed. From time to time Catholics were ordered to leave the capital. In difficult times they might go into the country without waiting to be ordered to do so. The bitterness of anti-Popery in the capital may also have affected the count, making Catholics more secretive, or the neighbours more anxious to avert their gaze.

There must have been many persons in London who had no continuous links with any church. In the capital, houses were divided and let and sublet in multi-occupancy and there was a huge floating population of lodgers, apprentices, casual labourers and people without a fixed home, despite the efforts of the authorities to control overcrowding and vagrancy. There was constant movement in and out of London of carriers of manufactured goods and foodstuffs by road and river. Huge numbers of people were involved in the great traffic overseas from the Port of London, including merchants and their agents and the crews of merchant vessels. Soldiers and sailors and government agents and officials were all constantly travelling through.

The hazards of Catholic life in the capital are demonstrated by the account of the priest Thomas Churchill, who described how when he came to England he was advised that in London he must 'play the coney and make [his] own burrow'. This he proceeded to do, having a chapel in his lodgings and accumulating chalices and other church stuff at his own expense. He suffered a fire at his lodging, and during the plague travelled among the farmers in Kent, Sussex, Surrey and Middlesex, saying Mass in different places but enabling his people to communicate once in every five weeks. He returned only to be caught up in the hysteria of the Oates Plot. On four different occasions he was forced to withdraw to the Continent. His experience probably gives a good impression of the problems for the laity of Catholic practice in the capital, where to an even greater extent than elsewhere short periods of relative security were interrupted by violent disturbances. The low figures of the Census for London may reflect the difficulties in maintaining any settled pastoral care in the capital, as well as the problems of the authorities in counting the papists in their midst, but must neverthless remain deeply suspect.[27]

Catholics in the County Towns

The figures for the county towns correlate somewhat better with what is known from other sources. Maidstone, Okehampton, Launceston, Northampton, Bedford and Gloucester were county towns of over 1,000 inhabitants which reported no papists or only one. These towns had a long-standing pride in their Protestant purity. In the reign of Charles II towns were often in conflict with the Court and with the Tory county gentry, and disputes were embittered and perpetuated by confrontation between rural conformists and urban Dissenters, with Catholics aligned with the rural conformists rather than the Dissenters. Even county towns with an established Catholic tradition reported only modest numbers of Catholics, and not even the county towns and provincial capitals made returns as large as the largest rural returns. In no case were Catholics more than a very small group in the numerical total.

The county towns with the most substantial Catholic groups were York, Norwich and Winchester, all towns whose economic importance was stagnating and which were slipping down the league tables of urban population.

York, which had been such an active Catholic centre a hundred years before, had a significant Catholic congregation, which, though large in comparison with other Catholic groups, was a very small minority of the whole population of the city. By 1676 it was the fifth largest town outside London with a population of about 12,000. Aveling, correlating all available records, believed that there were about 100 adult Catholic recusants in the city at this time, rather more than the 86 returned. These included 40 of the county gentry and resident professional people, and the rest were families of tradesmen and service trades. The Palmes family living just outside the city walls at Naburn were the most notable Catholics. Priests appeared intermittently at York, when the families with whom they were resident were staying in the city and the secular clergy held meetings. It is not clear whether there was a regular Catholic Masshouse and priest in the city at this time, although Samuel Banks, a writing master, was accused of having assemblies at his house. Few of the middling and lower orders were linked with the families of the period before the Civil War, though some may have been linked in the female line. Until 1678 the Catholics of York were left in comparative peace, and even during the Popish Plot period the main pressure fell upon the gentry families there.[28]

In **Norwich** the Duke of Norfolk had a town house of 60 hearths and his influence might be expected to have created a strong Catholic presence in the city, but this was far from being the case. Norwich was the second largest town outside London with a population of about 21,000, and although Foley called it 'a very ancient mission' and Jesuits were recorded there from time to time, only 49 Catholics were reported. Although it had the second largest return of papists among the county towns, they cannot have exercised much influence in the city or been very noticable except in times of acute anti-Popery.[29]

Winchester is the third largest return we have for a county town and the city was surrounded, especially to the east, by parishes which also made exceptionally high returns and had their own focus in gentry houses and maintained chaplaincies. In the city itself, the Catholics were numerous only in the parish of St.Thomas, where there were 30 Catholics and a further seven in the parish of St Maurice. A priest, Bonaventure Codrington, is recorded in Compton near Winchester. Catholics in the town were greatly exceeded by Dissenters. Winchester at this date was dependent on its county and diocesan status, and the occupations of the townspeople comprised mainly innkeepers, tailors, hosiers and retailers.[30]

Table 12: The Number of Catholics Reported from the County Towns, 1676

County	County Towns	No. of Returns / No. of Parishes		Persons	Con-form.	Papists	Dissent.
Yorks	York	18/18	p	3,806	3,559	86	161
Norfolk	Norwich	31/31	p	10,796	10,188	49	546
Hants	Winchester	11/11	p	1,198	1,815	48	135
Oxfords	Oxford	13/13	p	4,180	4,075	34	71
Lincoln	Lincoln	12/12	c	2,,014	1,862	30	122
Nottingham	Nottingham	3/3	p	2,912	2,496	27	389
Worcester	Worcester	11/11	p	2,641	2,476	24	141
Hereford	Hereford	6/6	p	1,677	1,596	23	58
Staffs	Stafford	1/2	p	1,100	932	13	155
Warwick	Warwick	2/2	p	1,860	1,710	11	139
Buckingham	Buckingham	1/1	c	1,403	1,377	9	17
Shropshire	Shrewsbury	4/7	p	3,110	3,030	8	72
Wilts	Salisbury	3/3	c	3,400	3,336	8	56
Devon	Exeter	20/20	p	7,710	7,583	5	122
Derby	Derby	4/4	c	2,119	2,014	4	101
Leicester	Leicester	6/7	c	2,071	2,024	4	43
Berkshire	Reading	2/23	c	3,000	2,857	3	140
Surrey	Guildford	3/3	p	991	882	3	106
Cambridge	Cambridge	14/14	p	3,168	3,088	3	77
Westmorland	Appleby	2/2	p	810	802	3	5
Cumberland	Carlisle	2/2	p	909	866	2	41
Sussex	Lewes	6/6	c	1,130	940	1	189
Bedford	Bedford	5/5	c	1,239	1,117	1	121
Gloucs.	Gloucester	10/11	p	3,183	3,072	1	110

(The figures from the several parishes of each city have been combined. Insufficient returns or no returns for Cheshire, Dorset, Durham, Lancashire, Northumberland, Somerset. Hertfordshire, Kent, Cornwall, Northamptonshire, Rutland, Huntingdonshire and Essex reported no Catholics in the county town.)

Worcester also had a strong, if smaller, Catholic group, but in contrast with York, Norwich and Winchester it was a town of many sources of prosperity, sustaining its economic postion. In addition to its county and diocesan status, it was a port on one of the most commercially important rivers in the country, and was a centre of the textile trade. This may have been an underestimate, as only four years before, in 1672, Worcester had reported 84 Catholics from its 14 parishes, mainly tradesmen and shopkeepers, at a time when the city had a population of about 2,301 households, or about 11,000 persons. The surrounding parishes all reported two or three families of Catholics.[31]

Only seven other county towns reported more than ten papists. The existence of a continuous mission is uncertain at this date. It cannot even be certain that the few Catholics returned actually lived in the city. In most cities the parish boundaries included large areas of agrarian land outside the built-up urban area occupied by yeomen, husbandmen and labourers, and some of the population of a 'town' were actually 'country people'.

Catholics in Market Towns

This problem is even greater when we consider Catholics in the small market towns, where the little town itself was often part of a much larger parish and no distinction between the two was made in the returns. The returns in the Census relating to market towns are very defective. About 100 of the 700 market towns made no return at all, and in the great majority which did so the numbers were small.

The largest aggregate returns for parishes which included a market town are as follows:

Table 13: Market Towns with more than 50 Papists, 1676

Town	County		Persons	Conform.	Papists	Dissent.
Stokesley	Yorks	p	826	676	105	45
Solihull	Warwicks	p	733	634	86	26
Bakewell	Derbys	c	4,500	4.235	65	00
Tamworth	Staffs/War.	p	2,895	2,773	63	62
Christchurch	Hants	p	1,104	931	57	06
Midhurst	Sussex	c		341	56	50

Source: C.E., pp. 90, 143, 420, 446, 448, 452, 599. Tamworth was partly in Staffordshire and partly in Warwickshire.

Stokesley, Yorkshire, made the largest return of papists among the market towns. It was a town of 2,947 acres set in a parish of 8,365 acres, a centre of pewter-making and linen manufacture and a market centre in this arable region of flat, dry farmland. It was associated with the townships of Guisborough, Crathorne, Skinnington, Lythe and the parish of Egton, which, as we have seen, had one of the largest rural congregations of Catholics. High numbers of recusants had been consistently returned from Stokesley since the sixteenth century. There were a cluster of Mass centres nearby, at Lythe, Ugthorpe and Danby. It was in the sphere of influence of the Foster and Meynell families. Most of the Dissenters in the area were Quakers with whom Catholics seem to have lived without hostility.[32]

Solihull, Warwickshire, was a small market and post town between Birmingham and Coventry, but the parish area was over 11,000 acres. The manor belonged to the Throckmortons until about 1620 and then passed to the non-Catholic Archer family. The leading family in the town were the Greswolds, who were related to the Catholic Greswolds of Rowington but were themselves Protestants. The yeoman families of Field and Averill were conspicuous in the lists of papists. By 1676 it was the home of several gentry families, none of them Catholics. Solihull Catholics appear in the Franciscan mission registers.[33]

Bakewell was a town founded in Roman times and in the seventeenth century was a market town. There was no Catholic influence within the immediate area and it remains unclear why this town should have been so marked a Catholic centre.[34] But **Tamworth**, Warwickshire/Staffordshire, had a long Catholic tradition. The Catholic Comberford family had lived at Moat House in Lichfield Street, Tamworth, in 1600 and there were also Catholics in the neighbouring villages of Hopwas, Bolehall, Shustoke, and Wilnecote. The town was a focus of routes, had a good market and was a parliamentary borough.[35]

The market town of **Christchurch**, Hampshire, was also a seaport but accessible only to small ships. It was in the area of influence of the Arundell family, and later of the Webb family. The town was a seigneurial borough with two M.P.s and it may well be that here as elsewhere Catholics were mainly in the parish rather than the town.[36] With the exception of Bakewell it seems evident that the few market towns with a strong Catholic presence were part of a cluster of Catholic centres in an area where the landlords were Catholic. This is less evident in the case of some of the smaller groups of Catholics in towns.

Three market towns returned between forty and fifty papists: Baldock, Walsall and Bury St Edmunds.

Table 14: Market Towns with between 40 and 50 Papists, 1676

			Persons	Conformists	Papists	Dissenters
Baldock	Herts.	c	495	495	45	00
Walsall	Staffs	p	1,360	1,120	200	200
Bury St Edmunds	Suffolk	p	3,496	2,496	40	67

Source: C.E., pp. 237, 322, 448

These three towns could hardly have been more different from each other. **Baldock** was a small and decaying country town at the intersection of the Great North Road and Icknield Street; barley and malt were the main business of the district. **Walsall** was already by this date a populous industrial town which had parted company with the gentry in the Middle Ages. In this case, however, it is possible to distinguish between the inhabitants of the town and the Foreign. The papists lived in the rural Foreign which contained Yieldfields, a very modest house without grounds. From the Restoration this house was occupied by members of the Catholic Purcell family and the priest Walter Giffard S.J., a relative. The Foreign was also associated with another Catholic centre, Oscott in Handsworth, Staffordshire.[37] **Bury St Edmunds** was a market town of middling size dependent on its rural hinterland. Protestant dissent was much stronger than recusancy here, but there had always been a small Catholic group in the town itself.[38] Such diversity makes simplistic generalisations about social and economic contexts seem naive.

For some of the towns which are omitted from the Census, a Catholic presence can be established from other sources. In the small market town of **Wimborne Minster**, Dorset, with a population of perhaps about 1,500 there were at least 43 Catholics. It seems probable that such numbers would merit a visit from the Jesuits at Stapehill or Cranborne, both less than three miles from the town. Most followed urban trades as fullers, clothiers and draper, apothecary and tanner in Wimborne borough and town, but others lived outside the town itself in the tithings, mainly as husbandmen. The group included persons of a range of social status from poor labourer to apothecary, paying tax upon houses of up to seven hearths.[39]

Quarter Sessions and other records show that there were strong groups of Catholics in the towns of Preston, Warrington, Wigan, Ormskirk and even in Manchester, none of which appear in the C.E. We also know of priests residing independently in Preston and Wigan at this time.[40]

It is difficult to identify any common features between towns with papists to provide an 'explanation' of persistent Catholicism. They are located all over England, and their predominant economies were diverse. The extent to which they managed their own affairs as independent boroughs also varied; while some, like Stokesley and Midhurst, lay in the sphere of influence of a Catholic family, others, like Solihull, did not. Some were very small and declining; others, like Bury St. Edmunds and Tamworth, were of a respectable size for the period and of commercial importance. Others which lay in the sphere of influence of Catholic gentry returned no papists, Worksop, Nottinghamshire, being a case in point.[41] No evidence has been found of Catholics taking part in public affairs in the towns at this date, although some at least were of the appropriate social status.

Catholics in the Ports

Catholics were even more poorly represented in the sea and river ports than in the market towns, although it is possible that there was a greater degree of under-registration in these places, since populations in such places were particularly mobile. There is only the scantiest evidence of papists even in the largest of the ports outside London. Hundreds of small coastal and river ports were growing in importance, busy centres for the distribution of goods all over England, to London and overseas, with a constant movement of men, money and materials. In the sixteenth century the smaller ports, as for example along the Hampshire coast, had been the favoured places for secret landings of priests, but in the post-Civil War period priests were watched less and used the growing network of public transport and inns.

Bristol was England's most important port outside London and, according to Foley, was 'believed to be a very ancient mission', but it is not clear on what he based this judgement. The fourteen parishes reported 7,200 persons over the age of 16, and 600 Dissenters. Only four papists were returned, in the parish of St Stephen. However, the returns for Bristol are deficient: and it may be that there were more who went unrecorded.[42]

Among the handful of small ports which reported Catholics, the most notable were **Whitby**, Yorkshire, which reported 1,640 persons, 24 Catholics and 97 Dissenters[43] and the small Yorkshire river port of **Yarm**, which reported 375 'persons', of whom 345 were conformists, 15 'popish recusants' and 15 'other Dissenters'. From the Reformation the Sayer family had occupied a house in Yarm called The Friarage, which contained a chapel. At the time of the Census it was in the hands of Nicholas Mayes, a merchant who had two sons abroad in Douai College.[44] The

Dissenters outnumbered the Catholics in all these ports. Even allowing for the deficiencies of the C.E., it seems clear that there were very few Catholics in the coastal ports.

Catholics as Visitors to Towns

The provision of leisure services was gradually being commercialised and at Bath there was a regular influx of visitors taking the waters. Catholics were more at liberty to travel without licence than formerly. There is no return for Bath, but the few Catholic residents were reported by the churchwardens. These included Mrs Winfred Sloper, wife of Simon Sloper, who ran an imposing lodging-house overlooking the King's Bath. The town area of Bathwick covered 353 acres and the wider area an additional 1,023 acres; there were three parishes, but no return of papists. There seems to have been some regular gathering of Catholics in Bath described by a contemporary as 'a dozen simple women and three or four inconsiderable men who were at their beads', and a Benedictine priest was living in Bath and receiving a stipend of £20 a year from his order.[45]

Another form of Catholic presence in cities and towns would not necessarily be taken into account by the Census returns, but was of significance for Catholics. Towns had formerly been the forum of the middling sort, but in many English cities and towns at this date the gentry were seeking to extend their influence and subject the government of towns to their influence. Concurrently with the political 'invasion' of the towns by the gentry, there was a social 'invasion'. The county and diocesan towns and the regional capitals became more than ever a focus for the leisure activities of the gentry. Listings of this period show Catholic gentry with town houses in York, Durham, Lichfield, Norwich and many other provincial capitals. They visited the towns from time to time, taking their family chaplains with them, and Catholic widows often resided there. Twelve years later, revelations at the time of the Oates Plot showed that Mass was often said in the town house of a gentlewoman or gentleman, rather than in the homes of those tradesmen and professionals who had been notable in earlier times.

By the 1670's the number of Catholics in cities, towns and ports was probably at its lowest since the Reformation. The few who did live there were much less conspicuous than they had been under Elizabeth. Even where the numbers of Catholics returned appear to be similar at different dates, the actual composition of the group had changed and the wealth and influence of Catholic townsmen had declined in relation both to the rest of the Catholic community and to their fellow townsmen.

CATHOLICS IN INDUSTRIALISING PARISHES

Much manufacture was carried on not only in London and in provincial towns, but also increasingly in the countryside by families who combined farming and manufacture. Catholics in such localities were already a significant part of the Catholic body and, as the growth of population in such areas continued after 1650 when it slowed down elsewhere, so correspondingly did the growth of that sector of the Catholic population.

The Census as we have it gives no indication of names or occupations. Information about occupation and social status has to be derived from court proceedings, especially those of Quarter Sessions. B.G. Blackwood in his study of the Recusant Roll and the Subsidy List for 1641 for Lancashire found that 15% of his list consisted of trademen and craftsmen and that professional people were almost non-existent. Only 4% were described as yeomen, fewer than might have been expected, but this may be due to the terminology of land holding in Lancashire. However, by their very nature, listings to Quarter Sessions relate to particular counties at particular times and are influenced both by local and political circumstances.[46]

The most widespread and the longest established manufactures were the textile trades in Gloucestershire, Wiltshire and Somerset, East Anglia, Yorkshire and Devon, where weavers, fullers and shearmen produced cloth for national and international markets. The weavers were supplied by their womenfolk with yarn of wool, linen and hemp. A detailed study of Devon suggests that Catholics were on the whole under-represented in the larger weaving communities and relatively stronger in the agricultural communities in that county. No Catholics were reported in the deanery of Honiton, for example, except for one at Axminster and one at Membury. No Catholics were reported in the deanery of Tiverton, except for one at Collompton, where there were 3,000 persons and 60 Dissenters, and another at Rewe. Individual Catholic weavers and spinners are to be found in many villages, but Catholics were not numerous in parishes in the weaving districts of Norfolk and Yorkshire.[47]

Small numbers of Catholics are found working in the mineral industries. Some Catholic landlords exploited the mineral assets of their estates, mining coal, iron and lead, and making use of waterpower for furnaces, forges and slitting mills. Sir Basil Brooke at Madeley, Shropshire, and Sir Thomas Preston of

Barrow-in-Furness are cases in point, but there is no evidence of any preponderance of Catholics on their estates.[48]

In Durham county, in contrast, there was a marked difference in the strength of the numbers of Catholics on the estates of Catholic landlords in comparison with parishes in other hands. In the early seventeenth century the large production of coal in Durham county from Ryton to Hebburn was largely on the estates of the Catholic Lawson, Riddell and Tempest families. The tenant farmers of the region provided horses and drivers, and large numbers of colliers and labourers were employed in the coal-works, many of them Catholics. However, during and after the Civil War, when these estates were sequestered, the mines were badly managed and were in decline. The mines in the parish of Whickham, in contrast, were leased by a partnership called the Grand Lease, and the parish provides a very striking example of conformity, both then and after the advent of the Quaker Crowley firm.[49]

Throughout England, wherever there was a suitable site, waterpower was being used to drive the hammer mills producing iron and lead. The forgemen, being highly skilled and highly paid specialists, are easier to trace than some other workers, and they are equally likely to be found employed by non-Catholic entrepreneurs, including the Quakers. The manufacture of iron into nails, locks and cutlery was well established in several regions of England by 1667, notably in Sheffield and Hallamshire and in the West Midlands but also in Prescot, while Southwell, Wigan and Walsall were important for the manufacture of pewter. The Quarter Sessions and probate records show Catholic families engaged in all these trades, often in the employment of Dissenters.[50]

The Catholics of the industrialising parish of Madeley, Shropshire are studied in detail by Malcolm Wanklyn below. Sedgley parish, Staffordshire, provides an example of an industrialising parish where Catholicism was strong despite the even greater strength of Dissent. The parish returned 690 Conformists, 55 papists and 200 Dissenters. There were Quakers, Baptists, and Independents, among them some of the wealthiest families. The manor was never in Catholic hands but was part of the estate of the Earls of Dudley, and the leading Catholics were yeomen families on the edge of gentility. There were also several families of Catholic lockmakers and bucklemakers and a family of tailors. There were Catholic labourers and colliers. The surrounding parishes included a number of Mass centres, and the Sedgley Catholics were closely associated with those of the town and out-hamlets of Wolverhampton, where there were resident priests.[51] There were innumerable such centres of small manufactures, and they put up no barriers to the entry of Catholics.

Conclusion

This examination of the Census has not dramatically altered our understanding of English Catholic commoners in 1676, but it has enabled us to be more secure in recognising the main features of Catholic life and to place the individual missions in a national framework. Catholic practice was a matter of choice, though one influenced by family, local leadership and opportunity. Even where a Catholic landlord had great economic control, people followed the Church of England, the vestry still had to be appointed, and the routines of the state church were usually carried out. The location of Catholics had changed remarkably little since the reign of Elizabeth, surviving great changes in society, including the Civil War and the Restoration Settlement. The great majority of Catholics lived in rural areas and, although a presence was maintained by the clergy in and about London and in cities of administrative importance most of them also lived in the countryside. The influence of Puritanism and the Interregnum had reduced urban Catholicism to a very small element indeed.

The individual congregations very rarely exceeded a hundred souls and were usually far smaller. They were almost always drawn from several Church of England parishes, and such groups themselves often overlapped with other groups of Catholics. Although our evidence is presented by parish, it is important to think of Catholics as belonging to clusters of parishes, and although the word 'missions' is technically anachronistic at this date, it would seem to suit the circumstances. The distribution of these clusters or missions does not correlate to any great extent with geographical regions; parts of Hampshire were as 'Catholic' as parts of Yorkshire. Neither does the distribution offer support to theories of survival at the periphery of society, even if indeed any part of England in the late seventeenth century can properly be described as peripheral. These clusters were not Catholic ghettos or even Catholic districts. Catholics lived among conformists and Dissenters and in a constant tension between belonging to their local community and being separate from it.

Catholics were not numerous in the textile towns and regions, but neither were they excluded from them, and the omission of the diocese of Chester from the return as we have it certainly conceals not only large numbers of Catholics but also an important sector of the Catholic body who were engaging in manufacture. The notable presence of Catholics in the emergent metalworking districts of Lancashire, Staffordshire and Shropshire and some of the coalmining parishes of the north east is a portent of things to come.

The examples we have examined of rural and urban congregations do not provide us with convenient academic generalisations, quite the reverse. The most striking aspect is precisely the great diversity of congregations and the extent to which they are part of the particular economic and social context. Their wide diffusion and their minority status, the lack of a unified system of pastoral provision and the relative freedom and openness of English society all make it inappropriate to see the Catholics of England as a minority with recognisable collective social and economic characteristics.

The special ties that bound Catholics lay in the practice and transmission of their religion, their daily experience of anti-Popery and in many cases the experience of the deaths or imprisonments of members of their families in the recent past. These experiences were to be renewed in an acute form only three years after the Census was taken. Intolerance and religious bitterness can lie under the surface covered by apparently normal relations for years and then be triggered off into violence. The orderly columns of data in the Census contrast with the violent diatribes written everywhere only three years later at the time of the Oates Plot. In this respect, as in so much else, the similarities with the Protestant Dissenters and the Quakers are very evident.

NOTES

1 Anne Whiteman ed., *The Compton Census of 1676: a Critical Edition* (1996), referred to below as C.E. Dr. Whiteman has revised and corrected this chapter throughout.

2 V.T.J. Arkell, 'An Enquiry into the Frequency of Parochial Registration of Catholics in a 17th Century Warwickshire Parish', *Parish Local Population Studies* 9 (1972), pp. 23-32, esp. pp. 29-30.

3 J.H. Adamson, 'Popish Recusants at Broughton Lancs. 1676', *Recusant History* 15, no. 3 (May 1980), pp. 168-75; Margaret Panikkar ed., *The Compton Census of 1676: the Lancashire Returns* (N.W.C.H. Society, 1995).

4 Thomas B. Trappes-Lomax, 'Roman Catholicism in Norfolk 1559-1780', *Norfolk Archaeology* 32 (1961), pp. 27-46; J.A. Williams, *Catholic Recusancy in Wiltshire* (C.R.S. Monograph Series 1, 1968), pp. 253-60.

5 Andrew Browning, *English Historical Documents 1660-1714* (1953), pp. 413-5; Magee, p. 7.

6 C.E., pp. 94, 131.

7 Keith Wrightson, *The Making of an Industrial Society* (1991), p. 166; E. Coulson, 'The Origins, Functions and Status of Churchwardens' in Spufford, pp. 178-9.

8 C.E., p. 369.

9 C.E., p. 83.

10 Anthony Hadland, *Thames Valley Papists* (1991), pp. 97-106.

11 C.E. pp. 209, 210.

[12] C.E. pp. 291, 292.
[13] C.E., p. 93.
[14] C.E., p. 544.
[15] WAA. OB 111 (2), 174-93; Godfrey Anstruther, 'The Lancashire Clergy in 1639: A Recently Discovered List among the Towneley Papers', *Recusant History* 4, no. 1 (January 1975), pp. 38-46; Caroline Hibberd, 'The Contribution of 1639: Court and Country Catholicism', *Recusant History* 16 (1982-3), pp. 42-62; Richard Dottie, 'John Crosse of Liverpool and Recusancy in the Early 17th Century', *Recusant History* 20, no. 1 (May 1990), pp. 31-48.
[16] Foley 4, pp. 466-7.
[17] *Edgbaston Register*; J. Burman, *The Story of Tanworth-in-Arden* (1930). The first superior of the Franciscans was Leo Randolph, son of Randolph Ferrers, lord of the manor of Wood Bevington between Evesham and Stratford. It is possible the priests were based at Coughton: Sir Francis Throckmorton's will of 1676 has a bequest 'to my cousin Mr Francis Levison in case he be living with me at my decease'; and Coughton is mentioned in the 'True Honorer's' life of St John Wall: Michael Hodgetts, 'The Yates of Harvington 1631-1696', *Recusant History* 22 (1994–5), p. 167.
[18] Mapping of all available Returns has been undertaken as part of this project by Mrs C. Coleman, Mrs A. Brookes & Mr M. Parkyn.
[19] V.C.H. *North Riding* 2, p. 324. I am grateful to Dr. W.J. Sheils for permission to use material from his forthcoming article on Egton. His work is based on a detailed analysis of church and civil court records.
[20] For the 1592 calculations, see John A. Hilton, 'Post-Reformation Catholicism in Derbyshire', *Derbyshire Miscellany* (Spring 1987), p. 55; Rosemary Meredith, *Farms and Families of Hathersage Outseats, Derbyshire, from the 13th to the 19th Centuries,* Part 2 (privately published, n.d.).
[21] C.E., p. 448; Beth Penny, *Maryvale* (1985), pp. 1-3; V.C.H. *Staffordshire* 17, pp. 60-1, 239-40, 282-4; John Ede, *History of Wednesbury* (Wednesbury, 1962), pp. 95-153.
[22] Norman C. Reeves, 'Saint John Kemble, Priest and Martyr', *Worcs. Rec.* 34 (December 1979), pp. 22-4; *idem*, 'The Church and Parish of St. Thomas of Hereford at Weobley', *Worcs. Rec.* 47 (June 1986), pp. 1-11; William S. Cobbett, *State Trials VIII*, pp. 707-15. Kerne was acquitted, because he successfully claimed that 'in times of straitness persons that are not priests may read prayers and give out blessed bread'; cf p. 68 above.
[23] J.H. Adamson, 'Popish Recusants at Broughton, Lancs. 1676', *Recusant History* 15, no. 3 (May 1980), pp. 168-75; M. Panikkar ed., *The Compton Census of 1676: the Lancashire Returns* (Wigan, 1995); J. Burgess, 'A Cumbrian Religious Census', *Recusant History* 15, (1980-81), p. 372.
[24] E. A. Wrigley, *People, Cities and Wealth* (1987), Table 7.9, p. 184. The term 'town' is applied following the conventions of the Cambridge Univeristy Centre for Population Studies and the Urban History Centre, Leicester University. Alan Everitt, 'The Market Town', in J. Thirsk (ed.), *The Agrarian History of England and Wales* IV (CUP, 1967), pp. 467–506; Clark, *Population.*
[25] Richard Hole, 'Devonshire Catholics 1676-1688', *Southern History* 16 (1994), p. 89; Williams, *Catholic Recusancy in Wiltshire*, pp. 69-95; Aveling, *North*; J. Hugh Aveling, *Post-Reformation Catholicism in East Yorkshire* (East Yorkshire Local History Society, York, 1960); *idem*, 'The Catholics in the West Riding of Yorkshire', *Proceedings of the Leeds Philosophical Literary Society* 10, part 6 (1963). The county studies cited in chapter 1 (note 8) show the same pattern in general terms.
[26] A.L. Beir & Roger Finlay eds., *London 1500-1700* (1986).
[27] C.E., pp. 57-60; Anstruther 2; John McMaster, *St Martin in the Fields, London* (1916); Gary de Krey, *A Fractured Society: the City of London 1688-1715* (1985).
[28] Aveling, *York*, pp. 90-107.

[29] C.E., pp. 198-9, 216, 217, 218; P. Corfield, 'A Provincial Capital in the Late-Seventeenth Century: the Case of Norwich' in Peter Clark & Paul Slack eds., *Crisis and Order in English Towns 1500-1700* (1972), p. 263; Foley 4, p. 592; John Pound, *Tudor and Stuart Norwich* (1988), pp. 26, 89.
[30] C.E., pp. 92; V.C.H. *Hampshire* 5, pp. 1-81; Anstruther 3, p. 37.
[31] C.E. pp. 170-8; V.C.H. *Worcestershire* 2, p.77-8.
[32] V.C.H. *Yorkshire* 3, p. 518; Aveling, *North*, pp. 342, 344, 422.
[33] C.E., p. 452; R. Pemberton, *Solihull and its Church* (1905), pp. 27-48, 132.
[34] C.E., p. 446.
[35] C.E., p. 448; A.H. Banks, *A History of St John's, Tamworth* (privately published, n.d.), pp. 1-3.
[36] C.E., p. 90; V.C.H. *Hampshire* 5, pp. 83-110.
[37] C.E., p. 448; Ernest J. Homeshaw, *The Story of Bloxwich: a South Staffordshire Village* (Bloxwich, 1995), p. 102; *idem*, *The Borough and Corporation of Walsall* (Walsall, 1960), pp. 59-82; cf p. 94 above.
[38] Foley, 5, p. 237; J. Rowe, *Catholic Bury St Edmunds* (n.d.)
[39] Dor. R.O. PE/WM Dorset Hearth Tax Returns 1662.; unpublished work by Tom McVey and Mrs Liz Adams for a detailed study of Dorset recusancy.
[40] Lancs. R.O. ED/V 1678 and 1681. I am indebted to Mr John Hilton for the photocopies of this material.
[41] C.E., p. 614.
[42] C.E., pp. 547-51; Foley 4, p. 449.
[43] C.E., pp. 214, 600.
[44] C.E., p. 600; J.W. Wardell, 'The Recusants of The Friarage, Yarm, Yorkshire', *Recusant History* 8, no. 3 (October 1965), pp. 158-68.
[45] J. Anthony Williams, *Post-Reformation Catholicism in Bath* I (C.R.S. 65, 1975), pp. 36. 60.
[46] B.G. Blackwood, 'Plebeian Catholics in the 1640s and 1650s', *Recusant History* 18, no. 1 (May 1986), p. 48-9.
[47] Richard Hole, 'Devonshire Catholics 1676-1688', *Southern History* 16 (1995), p. 87.
[48] C.E., p. 286-9; Wanklyn, *Darby*; M.D.G. Wanklyn, 'John Weld of Willey: Estate Management 1631-1660', *West Midlands Studies* 4 (1970-1), pp. 63-71; M.J. Galgano, 'Iron-mining in Restoration Furness: the Case of Sir Thomas Preston', *Recusant History* 13, no. 3 (April, 1976), pp. 212-9.
[49] Eric J. Clavering. 'Catholics and the Rise of the Durham Coal Trade', *N.C.H.* 16 (Autumn 1982), pp. 16-25; Keith Wrightson, *Whickham: the Making of an Industrial Society* (1989), p. 368.
[50] Lancs. R.O. ED/V/1678.
[51] C.E., pp. 259, 448; Dudley R.O. Dudley MSS., Manor Court Rolls of Sedgley; Foley 2, pp. 231-2; H.R. Thomas ed., *Sedgley Register 1558-1684* (Staffordshire Parish Register Society, 1940); T. Underhill, *The Ancient Manor of Sedgley* (privately printed, Sedgley, 1941); John S. Roper, *History of Coseley* (privately printed, 1941).

6

THE CATHOLIC POOR: PAUPERS AND VAGABONDS 1580 - 1780

This chapter examines the condition, extent, and character of the Catholic poor, more precisely paupers and vagrants, under the penal laws. In both respects, as Catholics and as poor, they were subject to legislation enacted under Elizabeth I, which, with various subsequent modifications, remained law until the end of the eighteenth century and beyond.[1]

The Legal Framework

The Act of Uniformity of 1559 imposed a fine of one shilling for failure to attend the church on Sunday, at a time when one shilling was a good day's wage, and the fine was to be used for the relief of the poor. The penalty of £20 per month, imposed by the Act of 1581 and designed to secure the conformity of the gentry, was beyond the capacity to pay of the common people, and one-third of this fine was devoted to the relief of the poor.[2]

The Elizabethan Poor Law was almost as harsh as the recusancy laws. The Act of 1572 recognised the duty of the local community, the parish, to provide for its poor, especially the aged, impotent, and decayed, but 'vagabonds', the able-bodied who wandered about begging, were to be whipped and bored through the ear with a hot iron for the first offence, to suffer as felons (that is, to be imprisoned) for the second offence, and to be condemned to death for the third. The Acts of 1598 and 1601 re-enacted these provisions, and established the machinery of parochial overseers of the poor, under the supervision of the magistrates, by whom they were applied.[3]

Both the recusancy laws and the Poor Laws aimed at preventing offenders from wandering about and keeping them in their native parishes. The Act against Popish Recusants of 1593 confined convicted recusants to within five miles of their own home, and ordered those 'not having any certain place of abode' to take up residence with their parents or in their place of birth, and to remain within five miles of it. Similarly the Act for Punishment of Rogues, Vagabonds and Sturdy Beggars of 1598 ordered them to be returned to their native parish or the parish where they had last spent a whole year or to the parish through which they had last passed without punishment, there to remain.[4]

Indeed, both the recusancy laws and Poor Laws were motivated by an overlapping fear of dissidents, whether religious or social, whether they were according to the Recusancy Act of 1593

> sundry wicked and seditious persons, who terming themselves Catholics...hiding their most detestable and devilish purposes...do secretly wander and shift from place to place

or according to the Poor Law of 1572

> rogues, vagabonds and sturdy beggars...by means whereof daily happeneth horrible murders, thefts and other great outrages'.[5]

The hostility to religious dissent and the fear of the vagrant poor were spread across Europe, as Christendom clashed with Islam and the nation-states fought each other and turned in on themselves to uproot heresy and to put down social upheaval. The English identification of Catholicism with poverty was at its most explicit during the Northern Rising of 1569, when vagrants were looked upon as potential recruits for the rebel army. In response, the Privy Council launched a campaign of whipping for vagrants that lasted from 1569 to 1572 and resulted in a temporary suppression of vagrancy.[6]

Despite the Elizabethan government's identification of rebellion, Catholicism, and vagabondage, Catholic paupers and vagrants have been almost invisible to historians of Catholicism. For Aveling, 'plebeian Catholicism was a small and amorphous thing'.[7] This invisibility is partly the result of the absence or opacity of the sources. The application of the penal laws seems to have been confined to the land-holding classes, to those who could afford to pay the fines, to those whose status or skills made a positive contribution to society and whose religious dissidence could least be tolerated. The Recusant Rolls concentrate on the land-holders, and even Quarter Sessions records tend to ignore anyone below the admittedly lowly rank of labourer. The Poor Law records seem to be religion-blind, making no distinction between Catholic and Protestant paupers. The men who made and kept the records were themselves land-holders. Paupers and vagrants did not make and keep records. Accordingly the history of Catholicism has tended to concentrate on the priest and gentleman. As Hoskins puts it, 'the dead hand of the seventeenth-century squire still guided, until recently, the hand of the living antiquary'.[8] Fortunately, a few general surveys of Catholics provide us with some details.[9]

Poverty is a relative and vague term, requiring definition. Gibbon remarks that

> The ancients were destitute of many of the conveniences of life, which have been invented or improved by the progress of industry; and the plenty of glass and linen has diffused more real comforts among the

> modern nations of Europe, than the senators of Rome could derive from all the refinements of pompous or sensual luxury.[10]

Contemporaries defined poverty as the inability to support oneself and, therefore, the need to receive poor relief, that is, to become a 'pauper'. The landowning classes, the nobility, gentry and yeomanry, obviously fell outside this definition, as did merchants and shopkeepers, but under-employment meant that poverty in this sense was endemic in the rest of society, especially for wage-earners, and it was aggravated by a rising population, enclosures, and occasional slumps in trade or bad harvests. Fifty to sixty per cent of the total population could be described as 'the poor'. Gregory King reckoned that in 1688 over half the population could be described as 'decreasing the wealth of the Kingdom'. In addition to the permanently under-employed, there were the permanently unemployed, such as the old, the sick, the injured, the widowed, and orphaned children. King's largest group of families was made up of both 'Cottagers and Paupers': 400,000 out of 1,350,000 families, or 1,300,000 people out of a total population of 5,500,000. In addition, there were the vagrants, who included, according to King, 'Gypsies, Thieves, Beggars, &c', amounting to 30,000 people.[11]

Pre-industrial English society was socially and, despite the legislation, geographically mobile. There were, of course, the upwardly mobile, the yeomen who became gentlemen and the shopkeepers who became merchants, but this essay is concerned with the downwardly mobile, the artisans and labourers, their widows and orphans, who were reduced to paupers. Similarly the wealthy were geographically mobile, the nobility and gentry moving between their estates and to and from the capital and the universities, but this essay is concerned with the vagabonds who wandered between the ditch and the whipping-post. Somewhere between the Catholic underground of priests and spies and the criminal underworld of rogues and vagabonds lay the Catholic under-church of paupers and vagrants.[12]

The Recusant Poor

In 1595 the clergy and the churchwardens of the province of York made a return to the Privy Council of

> the number of all popish recusants, of their station, degree, and value of livelihood, how many be residing in their country or fugitives, and how many be indicted etc.

Although the return is the product of the concerns and prejudices of its clerical and land-holding authors, it provides a detailed picture of Northern Catholic recusancy in general towards the end of the sixteenth century and of the recusant poor in particular.[13]

The recusant poor were scattered widely throughout the North. They were thin on the ground in conformist Cheshire, a mere eleven poor Catholics out of a total of some 120 recusants. There were not many more in sparsely populated Cumbria: five in the diocese of Carlisle and fourteen more in the parts of Cumberland and Westmorland covered by the diocese of Chester. There were rather more in the North-East, a total of 74 poor Catholics in the diocese of Durham, including 41 in County Durham and 33 in Northumberland. There were even more, 95, in Lancashire. They were concentrated in Yorkshire: 223 in the diocese of York and another 202 in the archdeaconry of Richmond (part of the diocese of Chester). In other word, not unexpectedly, where there were few recusants there were few poor recusants, but where there were plenty of recusants there were plenty of poor recusants.

In some places, poor Catholic recusants were at the bottom of a seigneurial community. In Pemberton township in Wigan parish, Lancashire, the list of recusants ranged from Joanne Laithwaite, widow, 'a gentlewoman of good wealth', through James Molenex, 'husbandman of good ability', down to Joan, the wife of Wilfrid Harvie, a poor labourer. In other places, the only Catholic recusant was a solitary poor person. In Kippax, Yorkshire, the only recusant was Isabel Bullayne, a widow worth nothing. In other places a number of poor people formed the local recusant community to the exclusion of others of higher rank. The largest such group was at Pateley Bridge chapelry in Ripon parish, Yorkshire, where there were eighteen 'people of mean wealth, yet very obstinate recusants'.

Varying Conditions

The conditions in which these poor recusants found themselves varied considerably. Some were resident in their own parish, like Peter Witham and Elizabeth Cowpeland, both described as 'very poor', at Ledsham in Yorkshire. Others were vagrants, like Robert Croft, also 'very poor', of Rothwell in Yorkshire, 'wandering we know not where'. Some were old, like John Grais at Braworth in Hutton Rudby, Yorkshire, who was aged eighty. A few were blind, like Ellen Robinson, one of seven vagrants at Whorlton, Yorkshire, all of whom were 'very poor, for the most part of them have no relief but by the help of their neighbours, so that they live very miserably'. Some were married couples like Thomas and Ellen Wilson, and others were widows like Jane Stockton, also at Worlton. Isobel Thornborrow of Withnell,

Westmorland, was the wife of a gentleman but apparently poor. Robert Cuthbert, yeoman, was 'late schoolmaster of Manfield [Yorkshire], a vagrant person, poor'. Richard Taylor at Carlisle, Cumberland, was a scholar and a vagrant. Robert Young of Wycliffe, Yorkshire, was a vagrant, 'a conveyor of seminaries from place to place and a persuader to popery'. John Arye of Whinside, Grayrigg, Westmorland, and his wife Margaret were poor, but four poor vagrants were listed as sometimes resorting to their house. Anthony Lightfoot, a vagrant, was relieved by Clement Ogle, gentleman, of South Dissington, Newburne, Northumberland. Mary Pool, widow of Hale, Lancashire, had been indicted for possessing an Agnus Dei, and become a fugitive. Maud Kelsall, the wife of a poor man at Earsburne, Cheshire, had appeared before the High Commission and imprisoned in Chester Castle 'yet remaineth obstinate'. Thomas Hickson of Aycliffe, Durham, in prison at Sedbergh, was 'a simple fellow, half frantic'. Beale Harrison at Crossthwaite, Cumberland, had come there from London. Robert Simpson, cordwainer, of Egton, Yorkshire, worth £3, was 'a player of interludes' and lived with Jane 'his wife, as he saith, but not by any known marriage, for they live and beget children and condemn the discipline of our holy church both in matrimony and baptising their children'.

The condition of the poor at the beginning of the seventeenth century is illuminated by the Jesuit John Gerard's account of his adventures. On landing in Norfolk he found that:

> Every track we took led up to a house as we knew at once when the dogs started to bark...... Afraid we might wake the people inside, we decided to go off into a nearby wood and rest till the morning. It was about the end of October, raining and wet, and we passed a sleepless night.[14]

He realised that 'people travelling on foot are often taken for vagrants and liable to arrest, even in quiet times'.[15]

Catholic Practice

Recusancy was defined negatively by failure to attend the services of the Church of England for example, in 1595, Thomas Wiggan of Bury, Lancashire, 'absenteth himself thereof for want of clothes being a poor man' but Catholicism involved distinctive beliefs and practices. Attendance at Mass and confession in the seigneurial households of the gentry was possible for the poor. As the case of Robert Simpson, the player of interludes, indicates, the administration of matrimony and baptism was also possible (especially as they did not necessarily require a priest). Extreme unction might be available from a priest, but Catholic burial was more difficult as graveyards were under the control of the Church of England. Keeping feasts might be difficult, and fasts were probably only too frequent for the poor, though they might be reluctant to forego food when it was available.[16]

While many clergy became chaplains to the gentry, there were also priests who ministered to the poor. About 1600, according to Gerard, Fr. Edward Oldcorne, S.J., *en route* to Holywell,

> stopped at the dwelling of two maiden sisters. They were poor people, but rich in other ways, for they feared God, living and serving Him together, and keeping in the house a priest whom they looked up to as their father.[17]

In 1625 the Jesuits in Durham and Northumberland found that the nature of the country and the habits of the people necessitated long journeys on foot and a very plain diet. Perhaps as a result, they won converts by instructing the poor. In 1632 the clergy in Northumberland included three priests described as 'footmen', that is they went about on foot like the poor rather than on horseback like the landed classes; they were a secular priest, George Douglas, and, appropriately since they belonged to the poorest of the mendicant orders with a special mission to the poor, two Friars Minor, Thomas Brown and A. Seaton.[18] In the years before the Civil War the Benedictine Ambrose Barlow lived in a house called Morleys (still in use as a farm-house) in Leigh, Lancashire, as the lodger of a poor man and his wife and also took in poor Catholic lodgers. He would tell the gentry: 'You must not be offended with our clownishness, for we are all clowns'. He kept open house for the poor, and at Christmas, Easter, and Whitsun he served them a dinner of 'boiled beef, pottage, mince pies, goose and groates', giving a grey coat to each guest. One week in four he would set out to walk the twenty miles to the house of a widow in Sefton, administering the sacraments as he went.[19]

The ignorance and superstition of the poor was emphasised by contemporary observers, especially in 'the uttermost skirts of the North, where', according to the one M.P. in 1628, 'the prayers of the common people are more like spell and charms than devotions'.[20] An outstanding example, cited by historians such as Christopher Hill, is an old man of Cartmel in Furness, Lancashire who had apparently never heard of Jesus Christ, but the story is slightly more complicated. The Puritan John Shaw recounted:

> I told him that the way to salvation was by Jesus Christ God-man, who as He was man shed His blood for us on the cross etc. Oh sir,

> said he, I think I heard of that you speak of, once in a play at Kendal called Corpus Christi play, where there was a man on a tree and blood ran down, &c. And after he professed that though he was a good Churchman that is, he constantly went to Common Prayer at their chapel yet he could not remember that ever he heard of salvation by Jesus Christ but in that play... I then judged that Common Prayer would not serve.[21]

Shaw was concerned to demonstrate the inadequacy of the Church of England. The old man may have been more baffled by Shaw's Puritan expression 'Jesus Christ God-man', a rather condensed expression which does not find a place in the Book of Common Prayer, rather than truly ignorant. Then again, he may have been responding ironically. Ignorance is sometimes a pose assumed by the poor in the face of the condescension of the learned.

However, the Catholic clergy won converts by their success in carrying out exorcisms. In 1638 and 1639 the Jesuits of Durham reported increasing numbers of converts and the extension of their mission into Westmorland, partly as a result of several instances of miraculous exorcism. The Dominican Robert Armstrong, who lived in a cottage at Hexham, Northumberland, working among the poor until his death in 1663, won fame as an exorcist.[22]

Sister Dorothea, a member of Mary Ward's Institute of the Blessed Virgin Mary, also worked amongst the poor in Suffolk. She lived in a poor woman's house, pretending to be her kinswoman. She taught children and 'the simple and vulgar sort', and looked after 'poor people in their sicknesses'. She noted the difficulties the poor faced in receiving the sacraments, partly because of a shortage of priests and partly because of the fear of the penal laws, but she was able to get priests to reconcile poor people, even in the poor-house.[23]

Priests for the Poor

Throughout the seventeenth century increasing provision was made by lay and clerical donors for the clerical mission to the poor. Ambrose Barlow was maintained by a fund of £8 per annum left by Sir Thomas Tyldesley's grandmother 'to a priest that would take charge of these poor neighbouring Catholics' in Leigh.[24] In 1678 John Birket, a priest imprisoned at Lancaster and probably a Jesuit, left £200, together with his house and other property

> to maintain a pastor to help and comfort our Lord's poorer lambs (which amount nearer to the number of a thousand than half thereof) in Brindle, Walton[-le-Dale], Hoghton lordship, Samlesbury, etc in cir-

cuit round about, which pastor I will to be one of the Society of Jesus.... the Society shall see that he perform his care to the people (sparing the purse of the poor)....[25]

A list of clergy compiled about 1705 and mainly concerned with the chaplains of the nobility and gentry notes that:

In several parts of England, where the Catholics of the low rank are numerous and are taken care of by the [secular] clergy

At Bely [Bearley?] and Tanworth in Warwickshire....

At Edgbaston....

At Wolverhampton...

At Durham ...

At York ...

At Blackimore in the North of Yorkshire where there are great numbers of poor Catholics not able to maintain a priest....

In Northumberland: there are funds established by the priests, who have died there, to help the poor that cannot contribute towards a priest's maintenance. The same is done in many parts of Lancashire ...

In Yorkshire upon Tees Water....[26]

The Poor in the 1705 Returns

The poor made up a significant proportion of the Catholic population of Lancashire according to the return of papists of 1705.[27] In the parish of Wigan, poverty amongst Catholics was a rural rather than an urban phenomenon. In the borough of Wigan, there was only one poor Catholic out of total of seventy-three named in the return. In the rural townships, the poor often formed the majority of Catholics and sometimes the entire Catholic community. Thus there were 46 poor Catholics out of 69 in Pemberton, six out of eight in Dalton, 11 out of 14 in Upholland, and eight out of 13 in Woodhouse. All 11 Catholics in Hindley were poor, and all five in Winstanley. Most other townships contained some poor Catholics: Orrell seven out of 40,

Haigh one out of eight, and Abram six out of twelve. Only Billinge, with its gentry, yeomen, and labourers, contained no Catholics listed as poor. As for the parish of Sefton with its 500 Catholics, the return noted that:

> Very few of these in the said parish of Sefton exceed £30 or £40 per annum. Many have much to do to live and pay taxes and their dues, and not a few are so poor that they live by their neighbours' charity.

Such surveys as that of 1705 present problems of interpretation, as the prejudice or inefficiency of the authors could result in inaccuracy. Thus for the parish of Dean, Lancashire, for which returns of 1705 and 1706, have survived, although 41 recusants are listed in 1705 and 34 in 1706, only 20 persons can be identified in both returns. Nevertheless, given the small size of the total population the authors were in a position to know the facts, and in 1706 the Vicar of Dean insisted that:

> I have taken such particular care to inform myself of all the particulars enjoined that I verily believe there is not one papist more in all the parish ....[28]

In 1705 there were three poor popish families in the parish of Deane: Roger, John, and Adam Hulton; Thomas Gregory and wife; and Henry Norris and child. In 1706 Roger Hilton (Hulton?) and his son were still there; so were Thomas Gregory, his wife and two children; and Henry Norris (Morris?) and his wife. There was in addition in 1706 'poor Mary Smith'.

Mobility

Early modern society was geographically mobile, and localities saw 'an astonishing rate of turnover in individuals'.[29] Between 1676 and 1688, 244 people disappeared from the village of Clayworth, Nottinghamshire, with fewer than 100 being buried there, and there were over 250 newcomers to the village. That patient and shrewd observer W.H. Hudson came to a similar conclusion about the discontinuities of rural life. Mobility on a massive scale during the earlier phases of the Industrial and Agrarian Revolutions is evident from the Return of Papists of 1767 which gives the age and length of residence of local Catholics.[30]

The 1767 Return

There were extreme examples of such mobility. As the return for St Paul's, Deptford, Kent, in 1767 pointed out:

N.B. Returned that there must be in St Paul's, Deptford, many more; but as they are inmates living in cellars and garrets, perpetually coming and going, their names and other circumstances are unknown.

In 1767 the Catholic poor were scattered in small numbers in parishes ranging from the North through the Midlands into the South, with 58 in Wiltshire, including a concentration of 49 out of 188 Catholics in the parish of Tisbury, a community dominated by the household of Lord Arundell of Wardour at Wardour Castle. There were, however, significant concentrations in and around the cities of London (59) and Bristol (69).

Usually described not just as poor, but as paupers, that is in receipt of poor relief, they were mainly old and/or widowed and overwhelmingly female. Some were in the workhouse, like the nine men, 23 women, and two children in the parish of St George's, Hanover Square, Westminster. At Cartington in Rothbury, Northumberland, there were four living in an almshouse founded by Sir Nicholas Shireburn. In the poor house at Dickleburgh, Norfolk, there was a fifty-year old woman, converted to Catholicism about three years previously, but described as 'almost an idiot'.

There were also the exotic, though gypsies were conspicuous by their absence. There were the first harbingers of the Irish poor who were later almost to overwhelm the English Catholic Church: a poor spinner at Berry Pomeroy, Devon, and a poor labourer at West Winch, Norfolk. There was Aeneas McDonald, presumably from the Scottish Highlands or Islands, a former servant become a pauper at Tormoham, Devonshire. There were also two black servants, who may well have been slaves: a man at Stoke Newington, Middlesex, and another normally resident at Chelsea but then at sea with his master, a sea-captain.[31]

Life remained hard for the Catholic poor, especially if they were pregnant women. Alice Mitchelson was born about 1760, the daughter of a weaver in Wigan. On 1 April 1786, as a single woman of twenty-six, she gave birth to an illegitimate son, who became chargeable to the borough of Wigan. She appeared before the magistrates, and declared that the father of the child was William Grimes. He was ordered to pay £1.14s. to the expenses of her delivery and one shilling a week towards the maintenance of the child. She was also ordered to pay one shilling a week if she failed to take care of the child herself. The child was baptised a Catholic on 25 April 1786 and named Thomas, but he died and was buried as a 'base pauper' in All Saints (Anglican) churchyard. In 1786 a poor woman, leaving her husband in Liverpool, arrived at Kirkham in the Fylde of Lancashire, 'very sick and far gone in her pregnancy'. She was lodged by the overseer of the poor, who 'was very rough and harsh', in a room of four beds in the poor cottage of a Protestant family. She died, and, despite the efforts of the Catholic priest to have it saved, her unborn child died with her.[32]

Nevertheless, there were 'counterfeit Catholics and penitents'. In 1787 a woman claiming to be a Catholic and apparently in danger of death was found at Weeton near Kirkham. She mentioned that she had been at Holywell in North Wales, but, when enquiries were made there, it transpired that she had feigned illness there and received a guinea and clothing from Lady Mostyn, and her stories in Holywell and Weeton did not match .[33]

The Catholic gentry considered provision for the poor to be one of their obligations. Sir Nicholas Shireburn recorded in his account books that he had 'paid to Catholics in necessity for these years ended Michaelmas 1700 £140', and he completed the Shireburn almshouses in 1706. In 1710 Apollonia Yate of Harvington left a fund of £10 per annum for the poor of the Shrewsbury district. The clergy were also active on behalf of the poor. Chetwyn Purcell (priest of a lesser gentry family) left various legacies to provide money, clothes, medicines, books, and apprenticeships for the poor. Milner recorded that Bishop Challoner of the London vicariate 'considered himself as particularly commissioned to preach to the poor, whose cellars, garrets, hospitals, workhouses and prisons were much more agreeable, as well as familiar, to him, than the splendid habitations of the great and opulent'. In 1722 Thomas Berington made a bequest to the Staffordshire clergy for the relief of orphans. At Oscott, doles were given to the poor at Easter and Christmas. The Rev. Robert Banister, the priest at Kirkham in the late eighteenth century, employed 'a charity girl' as a servant. From 1753 the clergy in Lancaster were arranging apprenticeships for Catholic boys. The Rev. John Barrow, the priest at Claughton in Lancashire from 1766 to 1811, served as both surveyor of the highways and overseer of the poor, employing the poor to build the roads. Catholic workers made provision against poverty for themselves, forming clubs in such places as Kirkham 'for the relief of members when sick'. There were also clubs to relieve the poor, such as the Broughton Catholic Charitable Society formed in 1787 by small farmers to assist widows and orphans.[34]

Catholicism remained a régime of feast and fast, and in the Fylde 'even our day-labourers will not grudge to pinch their morning and evening meals in Lent at least'.[35] Meanwhile, an increasing emphasis was placed by the clergy on education as a means of evangelisation. As early as 1678 Fr. John Birket had insisted that the priest who was maintained by his fund in Brindle should 'teach children the Christian catechism and evidence of credibility for the holy Catholic faith'.[36] In County Durham by 1736 Francis Liddell had left '£5 to put poor Catholic children of Sunderland [Bridge] to school', and Brian Salvin of Croxdale also made provision for the education of the poor. In 1736 the vicar of Gainford complained that Francis Jakes, a poor man, had become a Catholic and 'sends two of his children to be brought up Papists in consideration (as the report is) of their being taught to read and write gratis'.[37]

The transition from conversion by exorcism to evangelisation by education marks the shift to the age of the Enlightenment. Once the poor were taught to read, they had to be provided with suitable reading matter. Copies of the Catechism and of the Scriptures were made available to the poor in Staffordshire. In 1792, the Rev. Robert Banister wrote to his nephew, the Rev. Henry Rutter, the priest at Minsteracres, Northumberland:

> I vehemently wish to see a proper collection of the saints' lives calculated for the reading and intellects of common people. I am sure Mr Butler's *Lives* are far above this capacity... Above all, I wish you could find the life of some holy woman, or women, married to an idle husband, having seven or eight shirtless children, herself too almost naked, neither servant maid to assist her, nor anyone to comfort her... In short, I wish to see the lives of those saints who, living in a laical state, or in marriage, have by those virtues which, as St Francis of Sales says, grow at the foot of the cross, made their way safe and secure to eternal glory.[38]

The English Catholic martyrs are celebrated, but the Catholic poor under the penal laws and the Poor Law, lived obscure and penitential lives and some went to paupers' graves. Meanwhile a different attitude to poverty prevailed elsewhere. In Rome in April 1783 crowds flocked to Santa Maria del Monte to pray at the grave of a recently interred beggar, Benedict Joseph Labre, who in 1883 was canonised.[39]

NOTES

1 I am grateful to Dr. M. Rowlands and to Dr. A.J. Mitchinson for their help in the preparation of this paper.

2 G.W. Prothero ed., *Select Statutes and other Constitutional Documents illustrative of the Reigns of Elizabeth and James I* (Oxford, 1913), pp. 13-20, 74-6.

3 Prothero, *Select Statutes*, pp. 67-72, 100-5; John Pound, *Poverty and Vagrancy in Tudor England* (1971), pp. 53-7.

4 Prothero, *Select Statutes*, p. 92-3, 100-2.

5 Prothero, *Select Statutes*, p. 67.

[6] F. Braudel, *The Mediterranean and the Mediterranean World in the Age of Philip II* (2 volumes, 1975) vol. 2, pp. 739-42, 954-57, 1205-16; Pound, *Poverty and Vagrancy*, pp. 46-7.
[7] Aveling, *Handle*, p. 162.
[8] W.G. Hoskins, *Local History in England* (1972), p. 26.
[9] John A. Hilton, 'The Recusant Commons in the North-East, 1570-1642', *N.C.H.* 12 (1980), pp. 3-13.
[10] Edward Gibbon, *The Decline and Fall of the Roman Empire* (1776-1788), chapter 21.
[11] Peter Laslett, *The World We Have Lost* (1979), pp. 32-3, 36-8, 47; Pound, *Poverty and Vagrancy*, 79-85.
[12] Michael Reed, *The Age of Exuberance* (1987), p. 300.
[13] Clare Talbot & J. Hugh Aveling eds., *Miscellanea: Recusant Records* (C.R.S. 53, 1960), pp. 15-107.
[14] John Gerard, *The Autobiography of an Elizabethan* (1951), p. 9.
[15] Gerard, *Autobiography*, p. 11.
[16] Talbot & Aveling, *Miscellanea: Recusant Records*, p. 71.
[17] Gerard, *Autobiography*, p. 47.
[18] Foley, vol. 3, p. 2, vol. 7 (2), p. 1112.
[19] W.E. Rhodes ed., 'The Apostolical Life of Ambrose Barlow', *Chetham Society Miscellanies* (Chetham Society New Series 2, 1909), pp. 3-6.
[20] Christopher Hill, *Change and Continuity in Seventeenth Century England* (1974), pp. 19-20; Christopher Hill, *Society and Puritanism in Pre-Revolutionary England* (Harmondsworth, 1986), p. 242.
[21] V.C.H. *Lancashire* 8, p. 255.
[22] Foley, vol. 3, p. 122; *Dominicana* (C.R.S. 25, 1925), pp. 107-8, 126; Keith Thomas, *Religion and the Decline of Magic* (Harmondsworth, 1978), pp. 60-2, 528-88; Mervyn James, *Family, Lineage and Civil Society: A Study of Society, Politics and Mentality in the Durham Region 1500-1640* (Oxford, 1974), pp. 125-6.
[23] Mary Chambers, *Life of Mary Ward*, 2 volumes (1885), vol. 2, pp. 27-8.
[24] Rhodes, *Chetham Miscellanies*, p. 3.
[25] *Miscellanea 4* (C.R.S. 4, 1907), pp. 431-6.
[26] J. Anthony Williams, 'The Distribution of Catholic Chaplaincies in the Early Eighteenth Century', *Recusant History* 12, no. 1 (1973), p. 47.
[27] Alan J. Mitchinson ed., *The Return of Papists for the Diocese of Chester, 1705* (Wigan, 1986).
[28] J.A. Lancaster ed., 'Returns of Papists for the Parishes of Bolton and Deane in the Diocese of Chester, October 1706', *N.W.C.H.* 18 (1991), pp. 1-6.
[29] Reed, *Age of Exuberance*, p. 300.
[30] W.H. Hudson, *A Shepherd's Life* (1910), chapter 4; Edward S. Worrall, *Return of the Papists 1767* 2 volumes (C.R.S., 1980-1989).
[31] M. Whitehead, *Peter Newby* (Lancaster, 1980); T. Burke, *Catholic History of Liverpool* (Liverpool, 1910), pp. 14-5.
[32] Worrall, *Return of Papists 1767*, vol. 1, p. 54; Lancashire Record Office, Preston, Quarter Sessions Papers 2217/16; P.S. Fairclough ed., *The Catholic Registers of St. John's Wigan 1732 to 1786* (Wakefield, no date), p. 79; Wigan Record Office, Leigh, All Saints, Wigan, Funeral Register, p. 123; Leo Gooch ed., *The Revival of English Catholicism: The Banister-Rutter Correspondence 17777-1807* (Wigan, 1996), p. 86.
[33] Gooch, *Banister-Rutter Correspondence*, p. 110.
[34] F.O. Blundell, *Old Catholic Lancashire*, 3 volumes (1915-1939), vol. 1, pp. 92-118; vol. 2, p. 118; Michael Hodgetts, 'The Yates of Harvington 1631-1696', *Recusant History* 22, no. 2 (1994), p. 164; B.A.A. C 245, C255; Gooch, *Banister-Rutter Correspondence*, pp. 124, 191; C. Willoughby ed., *Transcriptions of Documents Concerning Land Ownership and Apprenticeship in the Fylde Community* (Lancaster, 1994), pp. 167-223; 'The Rev. John Barrow of Claughton 1766-1811', *N.W.C.H.* 3 (1971), pp. 31-3.

[35] Gooch, *Banister-Rutter Correspondence*, p. 74.
[36] *Miscellanea 4*, p. 436.
[37] William V. Smith, '18th Century Catholic Education in Co. Durham', *Ushaw Magazine* 217 (1963), pp. 20-7.
[38] Gooch, *Banister-Rutter Correspondence*, pp. 189-91.
[39] B. Plumb, 'Catholicism in the Workhouse', *N.W.C.H.* 20 (1993), pp. 1-11; H. Daniel-Rops, *The Church in the Eighteenth Century* (1964), pp. 269-72.

Part Two:
Studies of Particular Places

7

HOUSEHOLD, AGE AND GENDER AMONG JACOBEAN YORKSHIRE RECUSANTS

The debate about the nature of the early Catholic community has concentrated on the role of the clergy in transmitting beliefs to the laity. There are, however, suggestions on both sides that consideration of the non-gentle laity is also of importance. Christopher Haigh points to the widespread survival of traditional beliefs among the people of Lancashire, from which many of the missionary priests were recruited, to argue that concentration on evangelisation of gentry households at the expense of this popular audience represented a fundamental misdirection of missionary activity and led inevitably to a

Figure 4: Places discussed in Part Two within Modern Counties

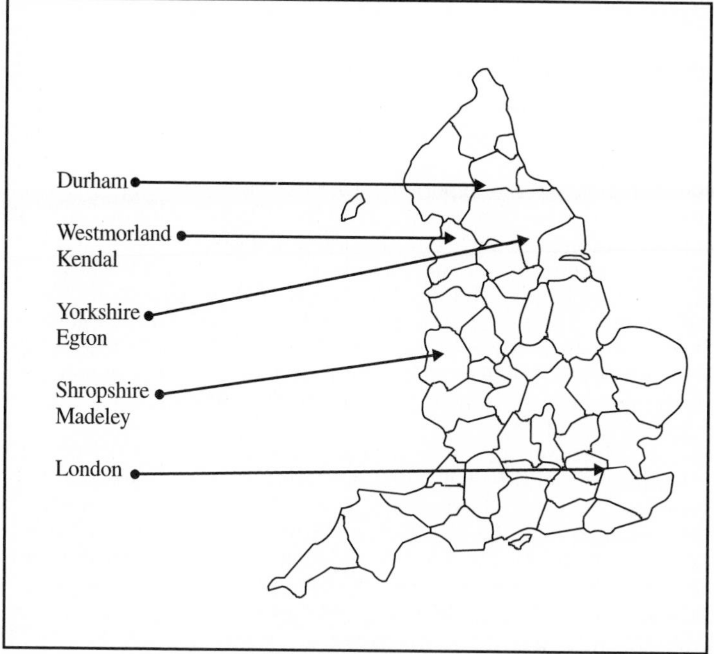

Catholic community which he characterised as a 'seigneurial sect'.[1] John Bossy argues that the geographical distribution of Catholics in the early seventeenth century raises questions of religious geography. He notes the importance of the upland regions and of remoteness in the formation of Catholic congregations, which had 'habitual use' of the services of the missionaries.[2] In addition to these general remarks about the contexts in which non-gentry Catholicism was likely to prosper, Bossy goes on to discuss the role which women played in the transmission of religion within gentry households, arguing that they played a significant part in the fostering of vocations in particular, and his emphasis on the importance of gentlewomen has been taken up by other writers.[3] These challenging interpretations have been subjected to little detailed regional study. Our present state of knowledge about Catholics from the lower strata of society is not much greater than that of Hugh Aveling in 1966 when, within an exhaustive account of gentry Catholicism in the North Riding, he concluded that the 'mind of the Catholic of the lower classes has to be judged from actions rather than reported words' and that the 'Jacobean and Caroline Catholic laity in the Riding have left us few indications of their outlook'.[4]

The Sources: The Visitation of 1615

The problem, of course, is one of sources, and even the most recent historian of church papists, in the absence of detailed local studies, has had to rely largely on literary evidence of clerical origin to uncover the experience of this important element within Catholic history.[5] We cannot recover direct testimony of non-gentry Catholics in any but the most fleeting of ways, and the recusant community did not, as far as we know, produce its own version of Nehemiah Wallington to provide insight on its mental world,[6] but traditional sources can be re-visited to explore the context in which lower-class Catholics, to use Aveling's phrase, lived out their religion. The main source for this paper is a traditional one, the return for Archbishop Matthew's Visitation of the diocese of York in 1615.[7]

Tobie Matthew was a convinced Calvinist and firm opponent of Catholics, and revived the activities of the Northern High Commission against recusants.[8] Assisted in the secular courts by Puritan gentlemen like Sir Thomas Hoby, whose determination to use the full force of the law against recusants led him into conflict with some of his gentry neighbours,[9] Matthew's Visitation records provide detailed listings of recusants, non-communicants and those described as 'rarely coming to church' at regular intervals throughout his episcopate.[10] The Visitation of 1615 is particularly useful, however, as it gives details of the age of about two-fifths of the recusants presented and information about how long they had remained recusant. This was a new departure, but the intention behind the initiative remains obscure as Matthew's Visitation articles have not survived.[11] The dating is significant, however, for it is clear from the Quarter Sessions records, the High Commission Act Book and the Exchequer returns at London that the middle years of the decade were ones of heightened activity in the detection and harassment of recusants, particularly those in the North Riding.[12] The detailed nature of the Visitation is surely another reflection of that tension, and it is noteworthy that the fullest returns come from the North Riding. Analysis of the data provides a more contextualised understanding of the social circumstances in which Catholics in this region led their lives than that derived from the straightforward numerical and geographical analysis of previous studies, but numbers and geography must remain our starting point.

The Distribution of Recusants

Aveling's work on Elizabethan Catholicism led him to the conclusion that non-gentry households, which he numbered about 100, comprised roughly one-third of the Catholics in Yorkshire between 1580 and 1603.[13] By 1615 that number had grown, both among the gentry and their peasant neighbours. The Visitation gave names of 1,237 individuals presented for recusancy in the three archdeaconries of Yorkshire, two-thirds of whom were below gentry status.[14] As Table 15 shows, recusants were not distributed evenly throughout the county. The quality of detail increased with the density of numbers, suggesting that the authorities were particularly concerned with what they saw as the most intransigent concentrations of recusancy.

Table 15: Distribution of Recusants in Yorkshire, 1615

	West Riding	East Riding	North Riding	Total
Males	122	88	216	426
Females	230	197	384	811
Total	352	285	600	1,237
Ages given	32	97	382	511

In the Archdeaconry of York, which covered the city and the West Riding recusants were identified in 66 parishes or chapelries, in the East Riding they were presented in 37, and in Cleveland archdeaconry in 70. These figures obscure clusters of recusants in parishes in the Ainsty near Aberford, in the Ripon area, in Howdenshire and Holderness in the East Riding, on the moors and in Allertonshire in Cleveland. What is striking about this distribution is the fact that there were concentrations of recusants in three areas outside the normal diocesan jurisdiction, the archiepiscopal peculiar of Ripon and the Durham peculiars of Howdenshire and Allertonshire, and that two other clusters, in Holderness and on the moors, were to be found near the coastal extremities of the diocese at some considerable distance from the cathedral city and separated from it by difficult terrain.[15] It is hard to escape the conclusion suggested in Bossy's book that, in addition to geography, administrative boundaries or what might be termed 'jurisdictional remoteness' was an important factor in the sustenance of popular recusancy, as it had been in heresy earlier.[16]

This remoteness could be said to support the argument for continuity and survivalism, for parishes in peculiar jurisdictions were not only able to evade close scrutiny from diocesan officers but were also poorly provided for pastorally, bedevilled as they were with impropriations. In such places the academic quality of the parochial clergy was generally low, and able preaching ministers of a Protestant persuasion were unlikely to be placed in such livings.[17] Thus traditional patterns of piety went unchallenged, as at Studley in the peculiar of Ripon where presentments were made as late as 1615 for 'burning candles suspiciously' and for 'laying a cross at a burial'.[18] Continuity can also be found on the North York moors where ex-monks from the houses of Grosmont, Whitby and Guisborough appear to have sustained their monastic contacts and, in the early years of Elizabeth's reign, served cures in future strongholds of recusancy such as Egton, Loftus and Danby.[19] The distribution of recusancy in early seventeenth century Yorkshire suggests that where a recusant peasantry was found in some numbers it was rooted in a tradition of conservatism often going back to the early years of Elizabeth's reign and sometimes recorded in subsequent Visitation records.[20]

That distribution also informs us that recusants of below gentry status cannot be considered independently of their social superiors. All of the clusterings mentioned above existed in close proximity to gentry presence and, in the case of the parishes in the Ainsty they owed their presence very directly to the gentry, mostly being employed in their households or as tenants on their farms. Most of the non-gentry recusants of Barwick in Elmet, for example, who numbered nine in 1615, were probably introduced to Catholicism or sustained in their beliefs by association with the households of the Gascoignes and of Mistress Ellis,[21] but the relationship between gentry Catholics and their social inferiors was not always so direct. In the scattered hamlets of the moors the presence of minor gentry households such as that of the Smiths of Egton Bridge was important in providing resting places for the missionary priests and thus ensuring the 'habitual use' of their services to the peasantry, which Bossy sees as a defining characteristic of recusancy at this time, but within the chapelry there had also emerged a core of senior non-gentry figures such as the farmer John Hodgson, members of the Simpson family of cordwainers, and the widow Barton. The recusancy of these people went back to the 1590's and they played a leading role in the life of a confident community, whose troupe of players fostered links with gentry households throughout the county and made activities at Egton the particular concern of Puritan magistrates like Sir Thomas Hoby.[22] Non-gentry recusancy co-existed with gentry households, but the relationship was not always a dependent one and in some cases, as at Egton, the peasantry were just as important, if not more so, in defining the recusant experience.

Defining the Catholic Experience

The Catholic experience remains largely undefined in the case of those below the rank of gentry, but there is no reason to suppose that it followed meekly the directives of the clergy or the patterns established by other scholars for the gentry. In the absence of direct internal evidence from recusants themselves, the material from the 1615 Visitation provides the opportunity to explore that experience in a variety of contexts: mention has already been made of the notion of 'remoteness', but further consideration of the prevailing religious temper of those areas of known recusant activity may also clarify the relationship between Catholicism and the Established Church. Within the recusant community itself the role of the household, so central to the gentry, can be assessed, as can the extent to which women, also important within the gentry experience, were identified with recusancy.[23] Finally, analysis of the information given about the ages of recusants and the length of time for which individuals had been identified as such will open questions about the status of individuals within their own localities and the broader community in a period when age and stability of residence were important attributes in the exercise of trust and authority within the parochial context.[24]

Catholics and Others who did not attend Public Worship

By 1615 the presentments at Visitation suggest that recusancy did not generally co-exist alongside other recorded forms of disaffection born of dissatisfaction with the established religion.[25] One or two examples of conservative practice have been noted in parishes with large numbers of recusants but it is only in the archdeaconry of Cleveland that we get much more information. At Brandsby at the foot of the Hambledon Hills there were several presentments for not attending church or receiving communion, and also for rush bearing and playing Robin Hood, but no recusants were recorded there although neighbouring parishes contained small numbers. At Felixkirk, a little further north, a man accused of harbouring recusants, though not of being one himself, was also presented for 'taking the bread and not eating it', and at nearby Thirsk, where one female recusant was presented, there were several 'negligent comers to church', who were said to have been encouraged in that by Thomas Brande, a recusant. Traditional burial practices were also noted there when on three occasions individuals were presented for going out of their way to ensure that the corpse they were carrying passed the cross on its way to burial and for 'putting the metwande in to the winding sheet'. On the moors at Brotton, where 48 recusants were presented, similar burial practices were recorded and a number of parishioners refused to pay the church rate; at Guisborough the recusant community existed alongside others who were irregular in church attendance and at nearby Thornaby the clearly frustrated curate was reduced to abusing his parishioners 'and in his drunkenness hath called his honest neighbours traitors, and charged them with the Gunpowder Treason'.[26] The material collected by the Visitors in 1615 gives little support to the view that recusancy was at one end of a spectrum of conservative religious survivals, but this may be more a question of definition than of practice. What is clear is that the evidence from this date contrasts greatly with that from earlier Visitations. In 1595-6 there were 38 parishes in which recusants were recorded alongside others described as non-communicants or non-attenders, whose non-participation did not seem to be attributed to sexual or moral misdemeanours. These figures suggest that, at the end of the sixteenth century, there existed in the county a penumbra of conservative beliefs and practices of which recusancy formed one strand, a view supported by the fact that a number of the parishes affected, such as Ripon, Spofforth and Drax in the West Riding. Nunkeeling in Holderness, and Hovingham and Whitby in Cleveland had become strong centres of recusancy by 1615.[27] This suggests that, under the changing criteria of the recusancy laws and in response to the loyalty born of a practice developed over time, the boundaries between the recusant community and the rest of the population had become more clearly defined, at least in the legal sense, by 1615.[28] Whether that legal sense reflected social reality remains to be tested.

Recusant Households and Families

Given the stress on the role of the household on religion in general and on recusancy in particular at this period,[29] it is surprising to find that less than half the recusants listed in 1615 can be identified as members of a distinctly recusant household. Of those listed there were approximately 550 individuals living in 219 households of various sorts. By far the most common were those headed by a married couple, but there were others where a parent lived with at least one child also described as a recusant and where servants lived as members of a gentry household or perhaps as a companion to a co-religionist.[30] Even at this basic definition of households it is clear that it was only a minority who shared their households with fellow recusants, and that among this sector of society the more common experience was that of John Poole of Wheldrake or Ursula Bovell of North Cave, whose religious loyalties were not shared by other members of their families or many of their neighbours.[31] Indeed, of the parishes with recusants recorded, less than half contained a household as defined above, and if the gentry are excluded this figure reduces to little more than a third. On this evidence, opportunities for household religion among these people were very limited, and consideration of the distribution of these households reinforces the impression.

Very few parishes contained three or more recusant households: 11 in the West Riding, 7 in the East Riding, and 12 in the North Riding, and their distribution is worth noting. In the West Riding, where recusants were most thinly represented among the population, it is clear that the presence of gentry households in parishes to the west of York and towards Ripon was critical to the growth of small communities of peasant families,[32] and the same was true of the East Riding. At Swine, the gentry households of the Langdales and Constables no doubt provided support for the other families in the parish, and at Howden the four recusant households which were reported among twenty individuals must have emerged under the influence of the Metham and Saltmarsh families, though neither of these gentry recusants were presented.[33] Only in parts of the North Riding is it possible to discern a recusancy which was only marginally touched by gentle influence. This was especially true of parishes on the moors such as Brotton, with 19 households, or Egton with 29, where the importance of the modest gentry presence in those places has to be weighed alongside the substantial peasant support for recusancy. These places were the exception, however, and in so far as the Visitation was successful in uncovering recusancy it revealed a scattered flock of households and individuals with very few opportunities for regular communal practice of religion.[34] In so far as these people could have 'habitual use', or even occasional use, of the services of the mission it had to be found beyond their parochial boundary and much depended on access to a gentry household. In so far as they were able to sustain a communal life it depended, not on the household devotion characteristic of the gentry or of the Puritan godly, but on the friendship of like minded neighbours, the support of non-recusants members of their families, and the fellowship involved in gadding to and from those occasions when a priest might be present in the neighbourhood. The last of these activities remains elusive, but the Visitation throws light on the first two aspects of recusancy.

As has already been suggested, the majority of recusants did not appear to share their level of commitment with other members of their families, and the most common experience was that of comprising a small, or even isolated number of individuals within a parish. In almost half the parishes of the West and East Ridings in which recusants were recorded they were counted in ones or twos, and even in the North Riding this was the case in 25 of the 70 parishes with recusants. Adherence to Catholicism in these circumstances depended on those wider neighbourhood contacts provided by a peripatetic mission or a gentry household, but such contacts were far from regular and continuity of tradition among such people was difficult to sustain. There is hardly any evidence to suggest that recusants living in these parishes were withdrawing from them for marriage, as was the case in some of those parishes with greater concentrations of Catholics. Furthermore the fitful survival of presentments of particular individuals or family names of those below gentry status at earlier and subsequent Visitations and Quarter Sessions indicates that the pressures of living within the parochial community were of greater significance than the support of the wider recusant community in influencing the behaviour of such people in the long term.[35] It is not common to find a surviving recusant tradition within a non-gentle family living in these circumstances, and the extent to which such people, who made up a considerable proportion of those presented, may have felt themselves to be part of something which could be called a Catholic community is open to question.

Questions of Gender

Notwithstanding these difficulties, there is evidence to suggest that, whether in recusant households or not, there were a number of parishes in which the possibility of some form of mutual support was possible. At Atwick in Holderness female members of the Caley family had recently joined the recusant community with Margaret Fenwicke, and a tradition was established among these yeoman families which was to last into the next century; at nearby Beeford we have an example of an enduring loyalty in a parish where only one recusant, a member of the Fussy family, was returned. In both these parishes the presence of nearby gentry and of other non-communicant families within the parish no doubt provided a supportive environment.[36]

Other parishes with modest numbers of recusants were also able to establish traditions of recusancy, and what is striking about the presentments from such parishes is the preponderance of women. The situation at Drax, where all nine recusants were women, was exceptional, but at Aughton in the East Riding there were four recusants returned, two widows and two married women.[37] Even in parishes where recusants were numerous, women predominated: at Eastrington in Howdenshire there were 27 women named among the 32 recusants recorded, and in the North Riding 21 of the 24 recusants presented at Hovingham were women.[38] For the county as a whole the proportion of females to males was roughly two to one, as Table 15 shows. The significance of women within the recusant community, however, is even greater if we consider those individuals who were not members of households. Of the 'unattached' recusants noted in Visitation approximately 510 were women and 175 men, a ratio close to 3 to 1. This distribution tends to support the argument of Bossy, based largely on his study of the gentry, that women were disproportionately represented in the community, and that their role was particularly significant in the transmission of the tradition, especially as most of them were in fact attached, domestically if not religiously, through marriage to a non-recusant husband.[39] Relatively few single women not living as servants or daughters in recusant households were recorded, and of the remaining about 80 per cent were described as 'wife of' in the returns. This leaves about another 100 women either described as widows by the churchwardens or whose status is not known. Many of the latter were, like Grace Simpson of Londesborough or Jane Butler and Barbara West of Seaton Ross, already in their fifties or sixties and were probably widows at this time, though we cannot be sure of this.[40]

The experience of the gentry, whose wives were often known as recusants while their husbands conformed in order to avoid the financial and civil penalties of recusancy, is well known and, despite a hardening of attitudes on both sides, can still be discerned in the presentments at this date.[41] At Woolley near Doncaster, Frances, the wife of Michael Wentworth, esquire, was returned as a recusant, and her husband was described as a 'negligent comer to church' and was presented for being a harbourer of recusants, including 'one Anne Apicer, a roamer to and fro'. This gentry house was a known resort of Catholics, providing hospitality to a woman who apparently travelled in the locality conveying news and maintaining contacts within the community.[42] Similar evidence of church-papist activity can be found elsewhere among non-gentry families; the husband of Jane Emyson of Holme on Spalding Moor, a woman in her fifties who had been recusant since the beginning of James' reign, was presented for negligently coming to church, and at Beeford Margaret Fussy's husband was presented for failure to receive the communion.[43] What is surprising about the evidence in the Visitation, however, is the rarity of such presentments, suggesting that the pattern observed for the gentry was not commonly found among the peasantry. But, as is suggested below, this may be due to the limitations of the evidence.

Other forms of dissociation from the Church are found in the case of the Appleby family of Thornaby on Tees: Margaret Appleby, a widow and a recusant of long standing, was presented to the court, and a kinsman, James, was also presented for not paying the church rate. Another member of the family, Anne, had contracted a clandestine marriage with William Duck, a course of action no doubt demanded by the committed recusancy of his bride's family, but, as a letter from the curate indicates, prosecution for this offence was fraught with risks:

> Though the crime be very grievous and heinous in the sight of God and all honest men, yet I beseech you to be favourable unto him in the way of pity and compassion, for the marriage hath made his wife of a obstinate popish recusant a godly Christian woman, of a non-communicant a godly receiver of the blessed sacrament, and if her husband and she be driven from the church, God knows whether they will be reclaimed or no.[44]

Whatever lay behind the writing of the letter, it is clear that its author considered marriage to be of crucial importance in the matter of religious affiliation and, anticipating Bossy's judgement that 'by definition recusant Catholicism could not be a vehicle for community', he argued that every effort should be made to keep such people within the parochial community as far as possible.[45] If marriage and involvement in the local community were so important, what can we make of these apparently divided households with recusant wives and conforming husbands?

Among the gentry, and probably also among the more substantial Catholics in London and other major towns, recusancy was defined by the community itself, either in the terms set out in the polemical writings of the missioners or by the pious scruples and observances undertaken by the laity and recorded by Bossy, whose book takes as its premise the view that the Catholic community is properly defined by limiting it to those who were actively in touch with the mission and who could be said, to some degree at least, to share in its priorities as set out by the clergy. Thus the records provide us with a variety of ways in which to judge the recusancy of these people. For the peasantry the problems are greater. The decision to separate from the communal religious life of the parish was clearly one taken by the individual or household and in that respect recusants defined themselves, but the decision to record that separation was often made externally, by neighbours serving as churchwardens or constables and sometimes acting under pressure from diocesan officials or magistrates. Thus our knowledge of recusancy at this level of society is often determined by the attitudes of those outside the Catholic community and, at this date, can rarely be tested against evidence from within the community itself.[46] It is against this background that questions of gender and age need to be considered.

Drax and Aughton were not the only communities where those presented for recusancy were exclusively women. There were also the widows of Thornaby and the two female households at Osmotherley.[47] Among parishes with modest numbers of recusants, however, these were the exception and it was more usual in such communities to find a more even distribution of males and females, as at Brotherton in the West Riding, Thornton-upon-Spalding-Moor in the East Riding, and Whorlton in Cleveland.[48] Thus, except in those few places mentioned above, the preponderance of women is not to be explained by small pockets of female recusants standing aside from the parochial community whilst their husbands participated in its activities. Apart from the West Riding, where it has been suggested that gentry influence was most important, it is in those parishes with larger numbers of recusants that the proportion of women is most marked: we have already mentioned Eastrington and Hovingham in the East and North Ridings and to these we can add Howden, with four men among twenty recusants, Great Ayton, with a solitary male in a community of seventeen, and Fylingdales, whose nineteen recusants included only three men.[49]

Catholics and Parochial Life

In these places, and others like them, recusancy had penetrated a significant sector of society, and in such circumstances the motives of those making the presentments have also to be considered. Even more than presentments for Protestant nonconformity, which could and did put practical difficulties in the way of those convicted, a presentment for recusancy placed individuals clearly outside the formal structures of parochial life. In such circumstances the motives for church papistry, despised as it was by some of the clergy in their public writings, are obvious enough and have been well chronicled.[50] What has not been considered, however, is the effect which recusancy might have on the smooth running of parochial institutions in those communities where it had become established among a sizeable sector of the peasant community. The pattern of presentments from Yorkshire suggests that in some places at least the maintenance of the institutions of the parish and the need to sustain the charitable community required that the more substantial male householders were not returned as recusants. That is to say that, in addition to the well known personal motive for church papistry there was, in some places, a strong communal imperative for the same practice or, if not that, then the concealment of the recusancy of certain individuals.

The Catholics of Egton

This possibility is given further support from consideration of the situation at Egton on the North York Moors, the chapelry which contained the largest and most notorious recusant community in the diocese at this time. In 1595 the then Archbishop reported the existence of 23 recusants at Egton and by 1607 their number had grown to 61, though this had included a significant turnover in personnel. The effect of the more stringent definition of recusancy after 1606 meant that 139 individuals scattered throughout the chapelry were reported to the Quarter Sessions in 1611 and 96 names were presented in the Visitation of 1615.[51] Nine of these were survivors from the return made in 1595, suggesting that a group of committed senior figures had emerged within the recusant community to provide leadership and to contribute to its self-confidence. Among the recusants there were 27 married couples, and six households contained adult children who were also named as recusants. The community also comprised five apparently unattached men, including the prosperous farmer George Hodgson, whose recusancy dated from 1595 and who was the most senior figure within the community.[52] The others were all young men still in their twenties, and two at least may have been members of other recusant families. As a group, these men hardly represented a significant element within the community. Of more significance were the 29 women listed: of these, 13 were wives, one was identified as a widow, and 15 had nothing other than their names recorded. This last group differ from the unattached men not only in numbers but in age, twelve of them being in their forties or older and therefore almost certainly widows. As a group, they probably represented a well established sector of the community, as did many of the wives listed, seven of whom were also over forty. Unfortunately there are no parochial or manorial records surviving of sufficient quality to locate these people within the chapelry more accurately. Their surnames, however, are suggestive in that many of them came from families which figured among the parochial office holding class in the later seventeenth century.[53] Furthermore the Quarter Session return of recusants in 1641 gave details of occupations and revealed the strength of recusancy among the prosperous yeomanry. In this context it is noteworthy that in five cases it was the wives of these yeomen and not the yeomen themselves who were presented, whilst other yeoman family names occurred among the substantial number of widows, 21, listed in the return.[54] Among these substantial peasant families one of the most prolific was the Pearsons, whose early commitment to recusancy was noted at the 1607 Visitation, when members of five branches of the family were presented: one entry concerned a married couple, another a Pearson female who was reputed to have married a Francis Harrison, and three were of women married to Pearsons, none of whom were presented themselves. Given the choice of marriage partners available in a populous chapelry, the fact that three of their wives were recusants suggests that the Pearson males were sympathetic to Catholicism, if not Catholic themselves. A similar pattern emerges from the 1615 Visitation, when five branches of the family were again presented. Anne and Elizabeth, each married to a William Pearson, were survivors from 1607, but the others were more recent recruits to recusancy: Francis and his wife Ellen, and Elizabeth, the wife of another Francis, were all in their mid-thirties and had apparently been reconciled about 1610, shortly after Ann Pearson, who was aged 60 in 1615, was said to have become a recusant.[55] Female members of the family continued to be presented at subsequent Visitations[56] and one is drawn to the conclusion that the importance of this family to the running of parochial affairs meant that its menfolk were not presented at Visitation by the churchwardens. In this respect they enjoyed the same sort of immunity as godly yeomen and tradesmen were granted in Puritan parishes elsewhere.[57] In such places, therefore, recusancy can be viewed as representing one end of a spectrum of essentially conservative views, among which church papistry had a central and respectable place, and the preponderance of women presented at Visitation reflects in part at least the way in which such communities accommodated to the pressures from authority. Among the peasantry, women no doubt played an important part within the recusant community, but analysis based on simple numbers which does not take into consideration the administrative and social contexts from which our information is derived is likely to inflate that importance. The Visitation not only revealed that there was indeed some gender bias within the recusant community, but also that in some important centres of peasant Catholicism recusancy was itself a gendered category. The Egton material suggests that the boundaries between recusancy and other shades of religious opinion were perhaps more fluid and permeable than the language of the presentments, or that employed by clerical polemicists on both sides of the argument, would have us believe.

Recusancy and the Life-Cycle

Despite this fluidity, protagonists on both sides of the historical debate about survival or revival tend to agree that in the early seventeenth century the recusant community had begun to establish a distinct identity during a period of steady if unspectacular growth in the generation following 1610. We have already seen that some of the Egton recusants of 1615 could trace their allegiance back to the 1590s and it is worth considering the details of age and conversion given in the Visitation to try and test the character of Yorkshire recusancy more generally. Did it represent survivalism in a notoriously conservative part of the country, or was it the product of a new and revitalising mission?

The Visitation provides age data for 511 of the 1,237 named individuals, predominantly drawn from what were thought to be the greatest centres of recusancy. Detail is much greater for the North Riding than for the West, and in the East Riding it is fullest for Howdenshire and Holderness, where recusants numbers were greatest. The age information for individuals is also variable, with quite specific details given of the ages of those under forty, but for those of that age and upwards figures are usually rounded to a multiple of ten.

Table 16: Age and Gender of Yorkshire Recusants

Ages		60+	50+	40+	30+	40+	>20	Total	(Pars.)
West Riding		**6**	**10**	**9**	**2**	**2**	**3**	**32**	**(8)**
	Male	2	3	5	-	2	1	13	
	Female	4	7	4	2	-	2	19	
East Riding		**13**	**21**	**26**	**22**	**10**	**5**	**97**	**(23)**
	Male	3	6	11	6	2	1	29	
	Female	10	15	15	16	8	4	68	
Cleveland		**65**	**85**	**79**	**92**	**50**	**11**	**382**	**(33)**
	Male	26	29	24	33	23	6	141	
	Female	39	56	55	59	27	5	241	
Total		**84**	**116**	**114**	**116**	**62**	**19**	**511**	**(64)**
	Male	31	38	40	39	27	8	183	
	Female	53	78	74	77	35	11	328	

In the cases of married couples, both partners are usually given the same age, especially among the older members of the population, but there are enough exceptions (as in the case of Robert Hodgson, aged 50, and his wife Isobel, aged 36, of Egton, or, more pertinently William and Marjorie Bates of Guisborough, who were said to be 51 and 49 respectively) to assume that age differences thought to be significant were recorded, and that where a figure is applied to both partners it is a reasonable approximation to reality.

Given the approximate nature of the evidence, it should not be forced to say too much, but some tentative conclusions can be drawn. As Table 16 indicates, over 60% of those adults with ages recorded were in their forties or older and, perhaps more surprisingly, 40% were over fifty. It is dangerous to compare these figures too literally with the age structure of the population as a whole, but the fact that 12.4% of the recusant population were 60 or over, compared to 8.06% nationally, does suggest that recusancy in this region was most likely to be found among the older members of the community. The national figures are derived from the work of the Cambridge Group for the History of Population and Social Structure; the recusant figure has been worked out by adding the proportion of under 25s in the Cambridge computation to those over 25 in the Visitation so that a figure for the whole population, including children, can be derived. The percentage figure is striking, though other local factors may have been as important as recusancy; it is very rare to find one with such a high proportion of the elderly.[58]

This was not due to any particular gender bias, despite the literary evidence for the propensity of widows to recusancy, as the age distributions for males and females follow each other closely. The explanation may rather be found in the nature of the evidence, for the Visitation may have concentrated on identifying recusants within households rather than as individuals in their own right. Thus younger adults within households, except perhaps where they were servants in gentry households, may be under represented in the presentments.[59] Even so the figures suggest that there was a disproportionate number of the elderly, those over fifty, among recusants, but that is not to say that they were an ageing conservative community. There were some whose recusancy went back well into Elizabeth's reign, but the Visitation reveals a number of individuals (like Margaret Jackson of Eastrington, who was in her fifties, or Ann Chappell, a widow in her sixties from Howden, who had both been identified as recusants within the previous five years), as well as the occasional community, such as that at Northallerton where the six recusants identified were all said to be over fifty years of age and to have been converted seven years previously.[60] There was no strong correlation between age and the length of time an individual had been noted as a recusant, which suggests that conversion was as important as tradition and that the mission was consistently making new converts among the adult population. It may also suggest that recusancy was, in some cases, linked to life-cycle, so that as individuals grew old and perhaps (through widowhood in the case of women or as younger branches of the family took on social responsibilities in the case of the men and married couples) withdrew from full participation in the parochial community, so their Catholicism became recorded as recusancy.[61] Whether this was because their own religious stance became more determined, or whether it meant that the parochial officers were more disposed to present such people as their role in the local community diminished, can only be tested by the most detailed parochial analysis. However, the statistics from the Visitation open up the possibility that the public presentment of recusancy might, in some communities, reflect the social and domestic status of individual Catholics as much as their level of commitment.[62]

Where the information provided by the Visitation is quite specific is in the length of time for which individuals had been known to be recusant.

Table 17: Length of Time as Recusant

	West Riding			East Riding			Cleveland		
Years	M	F	C	M	F	C	M	F	C
>1	1			1		2		3	2
1	1			7	10	1	6	7	2
2	1	2		1	12	2	6	17	4
3	2	8	1	1	5	2	5	13	6
4	1			3	12	3	6	11	2
5				1	2		2	7	4
6	1				6	1		6	7
7					4	3	2	9	1
8					3	2	1	6	4
9							5	6	4
10					4		3	14	10
11		1					1	2	2
12				1	1		3	9	8
13							3	4	4
14							2	2	3
15							2	3	1
16					3	3	1	2	4
17								1	
18						1	1	1	1
19									1
20+		2	1	1			4	12	5

M = male, F = female, C = couple.

This information survives individually for 76 men, 210 women, and 98 married couples, and there are also a few general comments about whole communities as at Barwick in Elmet where, centred on the gentry Gascoigne household, the recusants were said to be of long standing. In Cleveland long-standing peasant communities were noted at Skelton, Loftus and Ayton, whilst in Allertonshire recent converts had been made at Deighton, Osmotherley and Leeke.[63]

The Impact of the Egton Mission

It is possible from these data to trace in rudimentary fashion the effect of successive stages of the mission on particular communities, and the Visitation reveals the differing character of recusancy in the East Riding, where it appears to be a relatively recent phenomenon among the people, with that of the North

Riding, which seems to be of longer standing, especially in Cleveland. At Howden none of the twenty-one presented had been recusant for more than eight years, and at Eastrington nearby there were two female recusants of ten years standing among a community which had almost entirely been noted as recusants for less than five years. These patterns can be repeated throughout the East Riding, with those recusants of long standing generally being found among the gentry or in parishes with gentry influence. In North Yorkshire the pattern is very different, both in terms of the duration of recusancy and the pattern of conversions. At Hovingham recusants of over twenty years standing are found alongside recent converts and there is no clustering of converts in particular years, and the same can be said for the large communities at Egton, Lythe and Brotton where individuals were first recorded as recusants at intervals throughout the period between 1590 and 1615.[64] At Appleton Wiske, also on the moors, there were a few surviving recusants of twenty years' standing but the community seems to have been revived by a number of conversions in the years after 1610, if the Visitation is to be believed, and at Stokesley the continuing vitality of the community was attributed to George and Jane Harrison, a long-standing recusant couple in their sixties who, in the words of the Visitors, were 'suspected to have done much harm'.[65] Recusancy among the peasantry demonstrated widely varying responses to the mission in these years, but in general supports arguments for vitality and conversion rather than survivalism.

The Visitation of 1615 has shown that, while Aveling's view that we can know little of individual recusants of below gentry status except from their behaviour remains broadly true, the detail provided at this date, and consideration of the contexts from which that information emerged, considerably advances our understanding. Firstly it must be said that in both the West and East Ridings it is impossible to understand peasant recusancy without consideration of the distribution of Catholicism among the gentry. The evidence from the West Riding is too sparse to do much with but in the East Riding, in contrast to Haigh's analysis, it looks as if the mission built on gentry support in the later sixteenth century began to make some inroads among the people in the early seventeenth century. The story was not so much of withdrawal into a seigneurial sect as one of outreach from secure bases. In the North Riding a similar pattern emerges in the Vale of York, but among the peasant communities of the moors, where tradition provided a fertile field for missionary endeavour, there is strong support for the argument from continuity. Even here, however, conversion was important. Not only was it the case that most recusants presented did not appear to be members of a recognisably recusant household, but the considerable turnover in names between Visitations reflected both the mobility of the recusant population and the dynamism of the mission as much as the deficiency of the reporting. Whilst it was true that in the majority of parishes recusants existed in very small numbers, there was a significant minority of places where Catholics were not confined to a backward looking and socially marginalised sector of their local communities, excluded from local participation in secular affairs and ignored by the clergy in favour of the gentry. Where they existed in some numbers, most of them first appeared in the record as recusants when already well into their adult life, a fact which testifies to the vigour of the mission but which also, when considered alongside the gender bias noted among those communities, might also be taken to indicate some level of complicity about the reporting of these recusants by their conforming neighbours. The evidence from Egton is suggestive and some of these people may have played a vigorous part in the lives of their localities, but that hypothesis can only be tested by the sort of detailed community studies which have been undertaken for other nonconformist congregations.[66] This study of one Visitation has shown that the experiences of those recusants of below gentry status were varied, and has offered some tentative explanations for that variety. It has also demonstrated that the contexts in which Catholics lived their lives required compromises not only on their part but also on the part of their neighbours. In this situation recusancy was not the defining boundary between the Catholic community and its environment, despite the impression gained from the implementation of the law. No doubt for many Catholics, and possibly for most, recusancy was indeed a strongly-held position based on personal conviction, but it could also be an externally determined categorization in which, at the level of the local community, those questions of status which centred around household, age and gender also played their parts.

ABBREVIATION

Aveling, *West*	J. Hugh Aveling, 'The Catholic Recusants of the West Riding of Yorkshire, 1558-1790', *Proceedings of the Leeds Philosophical and Literary Society* 10, part 6 (1963).

NOTES

[1] C. Haigh, 'The Continuity of Catholicism in the English Reformation', *Past and Present* 93 (1981), pp. 37-67, and the introduction and conclusion to his *The English Reformation Revised* (Cambridge, 1987), esp. p. 214.
[2] Bossy, *Catholics*, pp. 78-107.
[3] *Ibid.*, pp. 157-8; M. Rowlands, 'Recusant Women 1560-1640' in M. Prior ed., *Women in English Society 1500-1800* (1985), pp. 149-80, esp. pp. 160-6; Claire Cross, 'The Religious Life of Women in 16th-Century Yorkshire' in W. J. Sheills & D. Wood eds., *Women in the Church* (Studies in Church History 27, 1990), pp. 307-24.
[4] Aveling, *North*, pp. 192, 286.
[5] A. Walsham, *Church Papists: Catholicism, Conformity and Confessional Polemic in Early Modern England* (Woodbridge, 1993).
[6] P. Seaver, *Wallington's World: a Puritan Artisan in 17th-century London* (1985).
[7] B.I.H.R. V.1615/CB.
[8] K. Fincham, *Prelate as Pastor: the Episcopate of James I* (Oxford, 1990), pp. 167-8.
[9] G.C.F. Forster, 'Faction and County Government in early Stuart Yorkshire', *Northern History* 11 (1976), pp. 70-86; for Hoby see pp. 74-84.
[10] Visitations were held in 1607, 1611, 1615, 1619, 1622-3 and 1627: Fincham, *Prelate as Pastor*, p. 322.
[11] Those for 1607 and 1622-3 are published in K. Fincham, *Visitation Articles and Injunctions of the Early Stuart Church, Vol. 1, 1603-25* (Church of England Record Society 1, 1994), pp. 55-61, 66-7.
[12] Aveling, *North*, pp. 214-6; P.R.O. E368/538 mem. 97. I am grateful to Dr M. Questier for this reference.
[13] J. Aveling, 'Catholic Households in Yorkshire, 1580-1603', *Northern History* 16 (1980), pp. 85-101, esp. p. 85.
[14] B.I.H.R. V.1615/CB. These figures include those noted as gentry or listed as such by Aveling in his volumes.
[15] Bossy, *Catholics*, p. 85, notes the jurisdictional point also. The coastal areas were natural receiving points for priests; for Whitby and the moors see Aveling, *North*, pp. 161-2, and for Holderness his *Post-Reformation Catholicism in East Yorkshire* (East Yorkshire Local History Society 11, 1960), pp. 21-2.
[16] A. Hudson, *The Premature Reformation: Wycliffite Texts and Lollard History* (Oxford, 1988), pp. 121-5, shows the importance of jurisdictional boundaries in Lollard growth; pp. 136-7 also points to the importance of the household and of women within heresy.
[17] W.J. Sheils, 'Profit, Patronage or Pastoral Care: the Rectories of the Archbishopric of York 1540-1640' in Felicity Heal & Rosemary O'Day eds., *Princes and Paupers in the English Church, 1500-1800* (Leicester, 1981), pp. 91-109.
[18] B.I.H.R. V.1615/CB, f. 161v.
[19] C. Cross & N. Vickers eds., *Monks, Friars and Nuns in Sixteenth-Century Yorkshire* (Yorkshire Archaeological Society Record Series 150, 1995), pp. 55, 238-9, 272.
[20] Aveling, *North*, pp. 406-40; Aveling, *West*, pp. 275-304; J. Hugh Aveling, *Catholicism in East Yorkshire*, pp. 58-68, contains listings of places where Catholics were identified from 1558.
[21] Aveling, *West*, pp. 222, 225, 287; B.I.H.R. V.1615/CB, f. 34v.
[22] Aveling, *North*, pp. 288-91; Forster, *East Riding Justices,* pp. 37-9; J.T. Cliffe, *The Yorkshire Gentry from the Reformation to the Civil War* (1969), pp. 273-6.
[23] Bossy, *Catholics*, pp. 155-9, talks of a 'matriarchal era' ending in about 1620; Aveling, 'Catholic Households', pp. 85-101. Of the 300 households identified by Aveling he categorized 200 as 'matriarchal' (p. 88).
[24] K. Thomas, 'Age and Authority in Early Modern England', *Proceedings of the British Academy* 62 (1976), pp. 205-48; M. McIntosh, *A Community Transformed:*

the Manor and Liberty of Havering, 1500-1620 (Cambridge, 1991), pp. 235-6 and table 3.6, suggests that the principal parochial offices were held by men in their 40s or 50s.

25 B.I.H.R. V1615/CB, ff. 31-2 gives the entry for Bilton, where a number of parishioners were presented for not attending church and other conservative practices.

26 B.I.H.R. V.1615/CB, ff. 255-v, 264v, 282-v, 315-v, 337v. Metwande = a measuring rod.

27 See map; B.I.H.R. V.1595-6/CB 1, passim.

28 3 & 4 James I, cap. 4.

29 The most famous Yorkshire example is the Puritan Hoby household: see Cross, 'The Religious Life of Women', pp. 307-24; for recusants the best surviving Yorkshire evidence is that of the Meynells of North Kilvington: Aveling, *North*, pp. 74-5, 286-7, 297, 313-5.

30 Household is defined here as that which contained more than one recusant; they mostly comprised a married couple, but a few also included children and some servants. On the margin are those where a recusant has been listed with another member of the family who was not their husband or wife; these have been included as households.

31 B.I.H.R. V.1615/CB, ff. 204, 286v.

32 These were Aberford, Barwick in Elmet, Kirkby Overblow, Spofforth, Ilkley, Mitton, Featherstone, Ripon, Pateley Bridge, Bondgate and Bishop Thornton in the West Riding; Bubwith, Bewholme, Marton, Swine, Skeckling, Howden and Hemingbrough in the East Riding; Aislaby, Brotton, Egton, Eskdaleside, Guisborough, Kirklavington, Loftus, Lythe, Stokesley, Whitby, Deighton, and Thornton le Street in the North Riding; compare with Aveling's listings cited above for gentry locations.

33 B.I.H.R. V.1615/CB, f. 233; Aveling, *East Yorkshire*, p. 26 for their church papistry.

34 B.I.H.R. V.1615/CB, ff. 314-5, 320-1; I have made a more detailed study of Egton in my forthcoming article, 'Catholics and their Neighbours in a Rural Community: Egton Chapelry 1590-1780', *Northern History* 35.

35 In such a context it is necessary to consider the degree to which such people considered themselves to be part of a 'Catholic community' and the extent to which that community touched their lives.

36 B.I.H.R. V.1615/CB, ff. 216, 219v.

37 B.I.H.R. V.1615/CB, ff. 57, 188.

38 B.I.H.R. V.1615/CB, ff. 242v, 296.

39 Bossy, *Catholics*, p. 156; M. Questier, 'Clerical Recruitment, Conversion and Rome, *c.* 1580-1625' in M.C. Cross ed., *Patronage and Recruitment in the Tudor and Early Stuart Church* (Borthwick Studies in History 2, 1996), pp. 76-94, esp. p. 86.

40 B.I.H.R. V.1615/CB, ff. 198, 209.

41 Aveling, *Handle*, pp. 47-8, 157-8.

42 B.I.H.R. V.1615/CB, f. 153-v and see Aveling, *West,* p. 303.

43 B.I.H.R. V.1615/CB, ff. 196, 219v.

44 B.I.H.R. V.1615/CB, looseleaf at ff. 337-8.

45 John Bossy, 'The Map of Christianity in Early Modern England' in E. Royle ed., *Regional Studies in the History of Religion in Britain since the Later Middle Ages* (Hull, 1986), p. 16.

46 Contrast with studies of non-conformity at this date, e.g. R.C. Richardson, *Puritanism in North-West England: a Regional Study of the Diocese of Chester 1602-42* (Manchester, 1972), pp. 74-144.

47 B.I.H.R. V.1615/CB, ff. 281v, 368.

48 B.I.H.R. V.1615/CB, ff. 88v, 210, 342v.

49 B.I.H.R. V.1615/CB, ff. 243, 312, 322v.

50 Walsham, *Church Papists*, pp. 22-49.

51 B.I.H.R. V.1607/CB, ff. 203-4; V.1615/CB, ff. 320-1; J.C. Atkinson ed., *North Riding Quarter Sessions Records* (North Riding Record Society, 9 volumes, 1884-1892), 3, pp. 70-1.

52 'A Return of Recusants made in 1595 by the Archbishop of York to the Privy Council' in C. Talbot ed., *Miscellaneous Catholic Records* (C.R.S. 53, 1960), pp. 32-3.

53 B.I.H.R. V.1615/CB, ff. 320-1; Parish Register transcripts, Egton 1660-1700, for names of churchwardens.

54 North Yorkshire County Record Office, Northallerton, QSC, return of recusants 1641, ff. 55-6.

55 B.I.H.R. V.1615/CB, ff. 320-1.

56 B.I.H.R. V.1627/CB, ff. 155v-8; V.1633/CB 1, ff. 395-8.

57 P. Collinson, *The Religion of Protestants: the Church in English Society 1558-1625* (Oxford, 1982), pp. 210-20; W.J. Sheils, *The Puritans in the Diocese of Peterborough 1558-1610* (Northants Record Society 30, 1979), pp. 79-88, 131-42.

58 I am grateful to Dr. Roger Schofield of the Cambridge Group for communicating the national figures for the proportion of elderly; see table 5.3 in P. Laslett, *Family Life and Illicit Love in Earlier Generations* (Cambridge, 1977), p. 188.

59 Aveling, 'Catholic Households', p. 90, notes that younger members of families were rarely presented before 1622-3.

60 B.I.H.R. V.1615/CB, ff. 242v, 366.

61 M. Spufford, 'Peasant Inheritance Customs and Land Distribution in Cambridgeshire from the 16th to the 18th Centuries' in J. Goody, J. Thirsk & E.P. Thompson eds., *Family and Inheritance: Rural Society in Western Europe 1200-1800* (Cambridge, 1976), pp. 173-6, gives examples of retirement with age in rural society.

62 The issue of the way in which both Catholics and their nonconforming neighbours may have had reasons for not removing themselves from the local charitable community has been discussed by John Bossy in his recent Birkbeck Lectures at Cambridge, *The Counter-Reformation and the Moral Tradition.*.

63 B.I.H.R. V.1615/CB, ff. 34v, 312, 330v, 340, 367A-v, 368.

64 For example at Hovingham recusants were noted as having remained so for 21, 20, 15, 13, 12, 10, 8, 6, 5, 4 and 3 years respectively and at Brotton for 20, 14, 13, 12, 10, 9, 8, 6, 4, 3, 2 and six months: B.I.H.R. V.1615/CB, ff. 296, 314. One of the earliest missionaries, Richard Holtby, came from a family with Hovingham connections: Bossy, *Catholics*, p. 89.

65 B.I.H.R. V.1615/CB, ff. 312v, 336v-7.

66 See for example the four essays by D. Plumb and W. Stevenson in Spufford, pp. 203-63, 332-86.

8

ORDINARY CATHOLICS IN MID-SEVENTEENTH CENTURY LONDON

Since long before the Reformation, London had been the capital city of England, the centre of both royal and parliamentary government, the most important trading centre, the most attractive city for anyone with a career to make or a dream to realise and, since it was always vastly bigger than most provincial cities, the best place in England for anyone who needed to hide. In the seventeenth century the ordinary Catholics in London lived in a way which had no equivalent anywhere else in the kingdom. The problems of discovering who they were, and how many of them there were, are at once much easier and much more difficult than for any other part of the country.

Which London ?

In 1558 London was still centred on the old City. Southwark lay at the southern end of London Bridge and, otherwise, there was just one long road leading to Westminster. By 1603 the population of the whole metropolis had grown by at least a quarter. No figures are reliable but, in general terms the population of the metropolis was about 200,000 in 1600, between 350,000 and 400,000 in 1650 and between 575,000 and 600,000 in 1700; in 1631 the population of the City alone was estimated at 131,000. Throughout the seventeenth century London continued to expand westwards and, despite the Plague, by 1700 it contained 10% of the nation's population and 20 times more inhabitants than the next largest town in England.[1] Within a hundred years London quadrupled in area. First, Lincoln's Inn and Holborn were built up, then Covent Garden, St Giles, Soho and Piccadilly, which began to be developed in 1635. Along the riverside to the east the population grew from 20,000 in 1600 to 90,000 in 1700 and there was equal growth in the northern suburbs. Moreover, a simple comparison of numbers camouflages the fact that London was so unhealthy, and mortality rates so high, that a steady flow of immigration was always needed just to maintain the population.

London has always consisted of both the City and Westminster. In the seventeenth century there were a number of separate Londons which overlapped but had nothing in common. Almost all of them had a Catholic aspect.

Political London

The risk of a Catholic take-over, whether by invasion, infiltration or inheritance, was a feature of political life from Elizabeth's reign to the accession of James II in 1685, when the nightmare came true. Political events, which were just distant rumours in the countryside, had an immediate effect on Catholics in the streets outside the Palaces of Westminster and Whitehall. Events at home, the Armada, the Gunpowder Plot, the Spanish Marriage, the French and Dutch Wars, the Plague and the Fire, the Titus Oates Plot and the Exclusion Crisis all had immediate repercussions on Catholics. So did English reactions to political events abroad such as the assassination of William of Orange, the Siege of La Rochelle, the Thirty Years War and Cromwell's support of the Vaudois, and the Revocation of the Edict of Nantes. 'No Popery' was a rallying cry used throughout the century by politicians and Puritans for their own ends. The unhealthy excitement of seeing priests hung, drawn and quartered was increasingly replaced by the officially sanctioned Gunpowder Plot celebrations and the enormous, stage-managed Pope-burning processions.[2] All of them boded ill for Catholics; it only needed a little tub-thumping to rouse the London mob.

Royal London

To a substantial extent this overlapped with political London and the populace had a perennial interest in the Royal Family. There were always powerful Catholic influences at Court. Every monarch had a Catholic wife and a Catholic mother; the marriage settlements of each foreign Queen protected the practice of their religion and their chapels deliberately encouraged conversions. Aveling's *The Handle and the Axe* gives a detailed account of just how many Catholic gentry there were swarming around the court.[3]

The Catholicism of some members of the Royal Family was in fact a disgrace to Catholics rather than an asset. Anne of Denmark's stolidity had made a decent if uninspiring contrast to the boorish drunkenness of her own relatives and the vanity and wastefulness of her husband. Henrietta Maria of France by her loyalty to her husband and her active support of his policies was disastrous. Her Frenchified chapel with its Jesuits and Capuchins, confessors and papal agents fed the fears of ordinary Englishmen that the independence and the religion of England were under threat. In the 1630s Protestant Englishmen felt very isolated. All over Europe, Catholicism was expanding and Protestantism was retreating. Poland, Hungary and Bohemia had been lost; the

French Protestants no longer had the security of their fortified towns; after the death of Gustavus Vasa the North Germans were failing to hold off the Imperial armies. Only England could defend true religion and there was, they feared, a Trojan horse already inside the seat of government.[4] In London the deep distaste of all decent people for things they could see every day with their own eyes was heightened by the arrival of Marie de Medici, the Italian Dowager Queen of France, who came to live with her daughter in 1637.

Gentry London

It is a commonplace that in much of rural England Catholicism survived where it was protected by the local gentry, and indeed in many rural areas the Catholics were mostly from the better classes. Almost all the gentry had occasion to visit London from time to time: to keep up their connections at Court, to prosecute their law suits, or simply for amusement. The West End of London was a very aristocratic quarter and ladies and gentlemen who were very important in their home parish cut no great dash. Although the very great had their own town houses, most of the gentry took lodgings and were at the mercy of strangers. There was no such thing as an 'old retainer' when you took rooms short-term. Servants were independent, had to be paid well and could not be trusted. Catholic gentry might manage to get Catholic servants, but they could not guarantee Catholic neighbours. There was no privacy in London, where even the upper classes lived cheek by jowl with their servants and neighbours.

Moreover there was an endless coming and going. When Parliament was sitting there were hundreds of MPs and their connections; during Charles I's personal rule there was an even more amorphous mass of clients and hangers-on, all elbowing each other for some preferment at Court. Catholicism was not the obvious way to power and privilege (although there were periods, as for example during the 1630s, when Catholics obtained preferment), but, despite the dictates of conscience, it was the way chosen by some. Plenty of other gentlemen tried to balance being Catholic enough to get into Heaven (eventually) with being little enough Catholic for a public position and preferment.

Embassy London

In the seventeenth century almost everyone looked on religion as a matter of group loyalty. The English Protestants identified the chief bone of contention as Royal as opposed to Papal Supremacy. French and Spanish subjects (in England or at home) were entitled to be Catholic since that was the religion of their rulers. The laws against recusancy were not concerned with the details of personal belief; they were aimed at those English who betrayed their sovereign by not following him in religion.

The Catholic countries of Europe all maintained embassies and some of them purposely maintained chapels and staffs large enough to provide Mass for all-comers. This was a point of contention when the authorities, from time to time, attempted to stop English Catholics from attending the embassy services, and the ambassadors themselves complained of harassment.[5]

Unfortunately there is little indication how many attended the embassy services. Robert Baxter, gentleman, examined in 1614, said there were 'sundry [English] ladyes and gentlewomen... as also English men' at one of a number of Masses for Palm Sunday at the Spanish Embassy. Robert Wise, weaver at a Mass on the same occasion, said that there were 'at least 200 persons the one half thereof being no Spaniards' and Henry Wise, also a weaver, said that, at the Mass he was at, there were 'forty people many of them English'. On the other hand the examinations are endorsed: 'Catching the Catholiques armed men 200. Pilgrimes 1500. 600 in procession with Palmes'.[6]

The Spanish Embassy had been closed for many years towards the end of Queen Elizabeth's reign. It first came into prominence in the late 1610s as courtiers prepared for the religious accommodation which they expected to follow the Prince of Wales's intended marriage to a Spanish Princess. In 1621 John Chamberlain commented that the Spanish Ambassador had 'almost as many come to his Mass' at Ely House as there were attending 'the sermon at St Andrew's [Holborn] over against him'. In fact the chapel was closed again from 1622 to 1627. It was attended by 'scores' of Londoners in the 1630s and became even more of a symbol after 1642 when the Queen's chapels at Somerset House and St James' Palace were closed. It remained open until 1655.[7]

No doubt many people in the congregation at both the embassy chapels and the Queens' chapels were merely spectators. This is certainly true of the Henrietta Maria's chapel after the Restoration and Samuel Pepys visited it with pleasure a number of times, as for example when on the 15 April 1666 he 'walked into the Park to the Queen's chapel, and there heard a good deal of their Mass and some of their musique, which is not so contemptible, I think, as our people would make it, it pleasing me very well...'[8]

Foreign London

There were of course a great many foreigners in London. The largest group were the Dutch and French-speaking Protestants who had fled to London from the Spanish Netherlands after 1567. England was very involved, and very partisan, in the war between King of Spain and his rebellious subjects. Sometimes the 'strangers' were suspected of taking work away from the locals, but for the most part they brought valuable skills and taught them to their English apprentices. From the religious point of view they flew the flag for the Reformation and brought eye-witness horror stories of Catholic atrocity and persecution. In fact most of them settled on the east side of the City but their full-blown Calvinist Presbyterianism confirmed the Puritanism of the City and put in at loggerheads even with the Anglicans at Court, let alone with the Catholics.

The 1593 'Return of Strangers' had listed 7,113 foreigners, of whom 5,545 (77.95%) lived in the City. In the 1635 Return (in the State Papers Domestic) the figure for the whole metropolis had fallen to 3,622, of whom 888 lived in Westminster and Middlesex. The membership of the (Protestant) French/Walloon and Dutch churches totalled 2240.

Many of the foreign immigrants had simply come to work. They brought French and Italian skills and fashions in clothes, hair, food, etiquette, furniture, art and music, and settled in Westminster where their customers would be found. They were largely Catholic in principle and the English luxury tradesmen in Westminster were out of sympathy for what they stood for, even as they tried to compete in the same market.

In the 1630s the number of French in Westminster was growing. In 1627 they were 23% of the foreign population; in 1635 they were 46% and in 1639 76.5%. In that year 23 tailors in Westminster out of 27 were French as well as a French embroiderer, a cap-maker and a 'maker of French flowers for ladies'. In addition both perfumers were French, eight out of 19 jewellers, four out of 12 shoemakers and 13 out of 15 people working with food. Charles I had five French servants, the Queen had 18 and the Duchesse de Cheveryes 22. The Queen Dowager, Marie de Medici, had 45. Many of the English nobility also had French servants. Endymion Porter had five, the Earl of Bedford four, Sir Kenelm Digby three, Lord Villiers three, the Earl of Salisbury two. The religion of these servants is not recorded but it is probably safe to assume that they were Catholic.[9]

Later, in the 1650s and 1660s there were a series of wars with the Dutch and French which confused religious demarcations of good and bad nations; however, the growing aggression of Louis

XIV and support for William of Orange meant that in the 1670s people could settle down into their classic prejudices again.

One group of foreigners preferred to be known as Catholic. It had been illegal for centuries to be a Jew in England and a community of fifty or sixty Sephardic Jews masqueraded as Catholics and attended services at the Spanish Embassy until its closure in 1655. Cromwell then gave them unofficial toleration, and in 1656 a house was rented as a synagogue.[10]

A few foreigners were explicitly aiming at conversions. Luisa de Carvajal was a Spanish lady with a very conscious mission and worked tirelessly in London from 1605 until her death in 1614.[11] Others were not above drawing a moral from public events. One Spanish correspondent, writing home to Valencia in 1666, had observed that the Great Fire stopped before the Queen's Catholic chapel in Somerset House: 'It is clear and certain that in this way the Almighty... wished to rebuke the blindness of the heretics. A hundred and forty churches of the heretics...were destroyed in the flames but at the sight of a Catholic temple the fire acknowledged itself to be conquered...'[12]

Irish London

It was a moot point whether the Irish were foreigners or not. Were they outside the Law or beneath contempt? After the union of the English and Scottish Crowns in 1603 there was something of a crisis of identity which was solved in theory by James' personal decision in 1611 to be called King of 'Great Britain'. The Irish certainly did not feel 'English' and some of them were listed in the Returns of Strangers, yet they were clearly subject to King James (or, at least, not subject to any other ruler, the test of nationality in the seventeenth century). In the early 1600s there were Irish sailors along the riverside, Irish lawyers studying at the Inns of Court and Irish literary drifters in Whitefriars, but then, as later, the majority of the Irish made a poor living by casual work. There were a number of edicts and proclamations from the 1590s to the 1630s commanding the masterless ones to go home but these were quite ineffective and, indeed, the plantation of Ulster by Protestants brought over a great many more. The poor Irish, who swarmed chiefly in St Giles in the Fields, were largely Catholic and a number of Irish priests ministered to them. This did nothing to bring their religion into good odour with decent citizens.

Legal London

All the groups so far referred to gave native Londoners a negative view of Catholicism; gave it, moreover, consistently and over a long period. They were all centred on Westminster. Further to the east, the Inns of Court had been very conservative in the early reign of Elizabeth. By the seventeenth century there were still lawyers from Catholic or church papist families and lawyers were equally willing to help prosecute the laws or avoid them, to argue loop-holes into or out of existence. It was in practice impossible for a committed Catholic to conduct a career in the law but there were a number of lawyers whose sympathies meant that they could be relied on as trustees or conveyancers to mitigate the penalties of the law when Catholics were unlucky enough to get enmeshed.[13]

Merchant London

The merchants of London were solidly Protestant, indeed Puritan. During the reign of Elizabeth there was a certain amount of residual Catholicism amongst the older generation, but from the 1570s there was never a whisper of Catholic influence, however slight, in either the Corporation or the great City Companies. This complete homogeneity saved London from the dismal fate of Paris in the same period. The square mile of the old City had a dense patchwork of parish boundaries and, as long as religious discipline was exercised through the parishes, the Protestantism of the City could be closely policed.[14]

On the other hand, however far and fast London grew, the Lord Mayor and Corporation made no attempt to extend their authority beyond its established boundaries. Shoreditch, St Sepulchre and Clerkenwell to the north were all outside its jurisdiction. So were Holborn, St Clement Danes, St Giles in the Fields, the Strand and Covent Garden to the west, all densely populated and a vibrant, thriving mixture of rich and poor. All these areas continued to govern themselves by the parish system which had been set up when they were still mostly fields; even the great destruction brought about by the Great Fire gave the City authorities no wish to extend their area of authority.

Prison London

There is a whole literature of 'rack and rope' concerning Catholics in the London prisons. All but the Tower of London and the Gatehouse (by Westminster Abbey) were to the west of the City (namely Bridewell, the Fleet, Newgate and the Counters in Wood Street and the Poultry) and in Southwark (King's

Bench, the Marshalsea, White Lion Prison, the Counter by St Margaret's and the Clink). Prisoners who had money seem to have been free to go out and about during the day provided they met the curfew restrictions, and even those who could not go out could receive guests and wine and dine them. Many of the imprisoned Catholic priests maintained that they were able to ply their trade pretty freely, and indeed they seem to have networked with Catholics more effectively when they were in prison than while they were technically free but in fact having to hide and skulk round corners. Both in court and on the scaffold most priests made their point bravely, but in fact, once the furore of the Gunpowder Plot had died down, the heroic age of Catholic martyrdom was over, though Catholics could not know that and there were occasional flare-ups.[15]

The Artistic Underworld

A good case has been made for Shakespeare's Catholic connections and that of other actors but, however God-given their talent, life on the South Bank was decidedly louche. No-one ever accused actors of Puritanism and, to the extent that any of these people were Catholic, it was just another nail in the coffin of their reputation.[16]

At a slightly more respectable level, a whole group of painters, musicians, and architects depended on the Westminster Court and the gentry for their living. Some were foreign, some were Catholic, and to the Puritans who dominated the London pulpits where decent public opinion was formed, artists were deeply suspect. Puritans were not going to be won over to Catholicism by these role-models.

Catholic London

All the overlapping groups catalogued above, with the important exception of the City merchants, contained numbers, possibly large numbers, of Catholics, crypto-Catholics or Catholic sympathisers: the definition of degrees of commitment is an important part of the problem.[17] However, the gentry were just visitors, the foreigners do not count, the prisoners, actors and even the priests were disreputable fly-by-nights, and certainly not 'citizens'. To what extent was there was a body of respectable, committed, indigenous, plebeian Catholics equivalent to the tenant-farmers of the Lancashire Fylde and the North Yorkshire moors?

Sources

There is a great deal of anecdotal material on the Catholics of London. Much of it was hysterical and written by their enemies; much of it was hagiographic and written by their friends. We have to be equally suspicious of both categories.

The Puritans were loud in denouncing Popery but in fact their venom was mostly aimed at the ceremonial element within the Established Church, and they threw the dirty word 'Popery' at a great deal of what such men were trying to do. They went on exploiting the Smithfield Fires, the Gunpowder Plot and 4,000 (later 30,000) Jesuits hiding in the sewers of Southwark (as if there were any sewers in Southwark), but they never confused Catholics with the widespread witchcraft scare, nor did they accuse them of daubing for the plagues. It was a 'well-known fact' that the Catholics had burnt London down in 1666, as well as trying to blow Parliament up in 1605. Even when there was some truth in their accusations, there was very little that was reliable in their information. For example, the Frenchman who confessed to starting the Great Fire was both a Protestant Huguenot and clearly mad, while the Catholic supervisor (named Grant), who was 'known' to have turned off the stop-cocks at the New River Company so that there would be no water for the fire-fighters, had not started work for the Company until three weeks after the Fire.[18]

On the other hand the Catholic material is equally one-sided. We still rely in many cases on a single account for our knowledge of the martyrs, of their treatment in prison, the treachery of informers and the behaviour of pursuivants, the sufferings of the faithful. Many of these accounts were written years later in the safety of continental retirement; others were written closer in time to the events they describe but were always intended as propaganda, either to horrify or to encourage. They dwell on the appalling behaviour of the heretics and the bravery of the Catholics.

The problem is compounded by the fact that many of these accounts were edited and published in the late nineteenth century by converts who clearly had a axe of their own to grind. They had the defensiveness of Englishmen who had converted to a foreign religion and were very consciously concerned to show that it was possible to be both English and Catholic. The argument was that the English had been forced to be Protestant by a reign of merciless terror but that the bravest and best had always held on to the True Faith.

Both the seventeenth- and nineteenth-century writers had a further prejudice, which makes our search for plebeian Catholics more difficult: their eyes were on the cream of society. They were interested in the spiritual lives of ladies and gentlemen. Occasionally they could make good copy out of a faithful servant or a very special case like Nicholas Owen. They could write up the northern yeomen because they were northerners themselves; they could describe devout peasant heads bowed in adoration, provided the peasants kept to their role and did not say anything; but they could not understand Cockneys. In the seventeenth or the nineteenth centuries, in real life or in history, Catholic writers had no grip on the mentality of the London working class.

Sixteenth- and seventeenth-century Catholic letters are larded with estimates of how many Englishmen were secretly Catholic, how the numbers varied from region to region or were going up and down but these are usually just pious assertion or wishful thinking. They had no evidence, nor any means of getting any, and, once their fanciful figures have been put aside, their accounts usually come down to another gentleman reconciled or a lady who was so keen she actually walked a mile to Mass.

Most accounts of Catholics' sufferings are written from the point of view of a gentleman. They resented it fiercely if priests or lay Catholics were not treated with courtesy and deference, despite the fact that they were breaking the laws of their country, laws which were acceptable to the vast majority. They were horrified at prison conditions whenever they were treated like common criminals (i.e. like everyone else). They complained bitterly about their trials when, whatever their justification, they were all guilty. They expected their consciences to be respected and to quibble over proof about their priesthood but they were priests, they knew the law and they intended to go on breaking it. They expected to play a star role on the scaffold and to harangue the crowd about religion because they saw every difference between themselves and the common criminals who were turned off the ladder at every hanging without much ceremony.

This is not to underplay their sufferings, or the value of their work, but Londoners were connoisseurs of a good hanging. They got a good laugh out of a coward and they gave a brave priest the same due that they gave a brave highwayman — they swung on his legs to speed his death while the running patterers worked the crowd with his last words (printed in advance to make the best of the sales opportunity). Those who wrote up the deaths afterwards for Catholic consumption may or may not have been there, but they knew what 'must' have happened and recorded the last words of testimony, the cruelty or consideration of the executioner and the pious handkerchiefs dipped in blood. Neither their accounts nor those who published them have anything reliable to tell us about the crowd who watched the martyrs die or how many of them were actually Catholics.

Some of the Catholic material is more objective, but the records of the various recusant colleges, convents and seminaries abroad serve almost wholly to document the gentry and the 'middle sort'. Of the students who filled out questionnaires when they entered the English College, Rome, very few were from artisan backgrounds.[19] The letters, diaries and account books of many great Catholic families have survived and often throw incidental light on their own Catholicism. By a hundred and fifty years later they were making very interesting entries about ordinary Catholic provision in London, Bath and elsewhere, but in the seventeenth century their position was far too precarious. Perhaps material has not yet come to light but the well-known printed histories, such as those on the Stonors, the Timperleys, Francis Throckmorton or William Blundell, have nothing original to say about the position in London.[20]

By the later seventeenth century some of the Carmelite biographers give useful indications. Fr. Bede of St Simon Stock says that the year of the Great Plague (1665) was very fruitful in conversions, but even he was based at the Spanish Embassy where, he says, he did not wish to lose the chapel 'which proved so beneficial to the poor Catholics'. He asserts, when discussing the situation throughout England, that 'the majority of Catholics live in London'.[21]

Throughout the century there was an unknown number of Irish priests working in London. Some were attached to the embassies, some haunted the slums to serve their fellow countrymen, and many others came to London from time to time, as anyone might visit the capital city and seat of the government of their country. Occasionally they come into prominence, as when Fr. Peter Walsh proposed an oath of allegiance to the restored King Charles, or when the Archbishop of Armagh was brought over to London to be tried for treason in 1681. Beyond this the references to them are casual and the records of the Irish religious orders, in which they may figure, have not yet been researched by historians of English recusancy.

In 1632 it was estimated by John Southcote (himself a priest) that there were 29 priests in London jails and 36 priests at liberty in London; with the eight Capuchins who served the Queen this makes a total of 73.[22] It should go without saying, that at this period there are none of the standard sacramental records which any parish priest of the time in France, Spain or Italy was keeping. Registers of baptisms or marriages, lists of confirmandi or communicants would have brought death to the priest who kept them and financial ruin, if not worse, to all the people mentioned in them.

After the Restoration a register of baptisms and marriages was begun in the safe haven of the Chapel Royal.[23] There were, for example, 15 marriages recorded in the year 1664 (Old Style). For the most part no indication of status is given, implying that they were 'ordinary' people. We have only anecdotal evidence as to how many other marriages Catholic priests may have performed in London in that year and how many of the couples also had an Anglican marriage to ensure legality.

Some Catholics were clearly not only marrying but separating. In a case heard before the High Court of Delegates in 1663, Colonel William Hawley deposed that Dr John Collupp, and his wife had been married in the Tower of London 'by a Romish priest' but Mary Newhouse, who 'believes they were accounted papists', had also heard Dr Collupp say, 'Madam, it is long ago since I disowned her... We gave each other release in the presence of Colonel Hawley'.[24]

Later in the century Fr. Gaspar of the Annunciation appears to have kept at least a statistical register during his years at the Spanish Embassy where he arrived in 1680. Fr. Lucian says of him: 'I fully believe he hears as many as ten thousand confessions a year, and on his register I find a large number of baptisms and marriages, as well as the following figures concerning conversions: in 1681 he received into the Church twelve persons; in 1682 thirteen; in 1683 thirty-one; in 1684 sixty-seven, and until 5th May 1685, twenty-one'.[25]

In fact, such slight information from the 1680s merely highlights the fact that for the early to middle seventeenth century there is simply no reliable Catholic information about numbers.

Public Records

In one form and another there are extensive records of Catholics compiled by the public authorities, whether secular or religious, at national or local level. The State Papers, in fact, contain as much rumour and hysteria as the Puritan broadsheets. Anglican propaganda was often convinced that Catholics and Puritans were working together for the overthrow of the religion by law established, and indeed they had a lot in common in their attitude towards it. When Quakers first began to preach widely in the 1650s many people were confident that the whole movement was simply another Jesuit plot.

However, among the State Papers Domestic is a printed volume, containing the names of recusants convicted in London and Middlesex between 1625 and 1642 and estimated to contain about 3,750 entries.[26] The book is of 67 pages, giving the names and surnames of Catholics (arranged by first letter), their place of habitation and when and where they were indicted, and often their class or occupation. Unfortunately the first two pages are missing so that we do not have the letter 'A' nor any explanation as to how or why the book was compiled.

Almost all the Catholics listed are of various parishes in London and Westminster: only 155 are from the provinces and those mostly from Lancashire, Staffordshire and Somerset. Taking five pages at random, of the 207 people whose 'condition' is described, 71 are gentry and above, 48 yeomen, 10 tailors, 4 labourers, 2 carpenters, a goldsmith, a silversmith, a merchant, a Doctor in Physick, an apothecary, a 'six clerks clerk' (i.e. a clerk in Chancery), a cutler, a chandler, a tobacco seller, a brush seller and a weaver, many of whom have wives. However, any attempt to produce class statistics is spoilt by the presence of 38 widows and 23 spinsters whose social level cannot be determined. Although this list is, in principle, only a secondary source derived from the Sessions material discussed below, it purports to be a complete list for its period, whereas the surviving Sessions records now have substantial gaps.

A number of other record sources for the seventeenth century are fairly objective and, after understanding their limitations, we may be able to draw some conclusions from them.

Pipe Rolls, Recusant Rolls and Sessions Records

From 1559 Catholics are simply another form of criminal and may be cited before the Quarter Sessions. After 1581 they may be enrolled in the Pipe Rolls[27] or, after 1592, in the Recusant Rolls.[28] Of the London recusants recorded in the Exchequer Pipe Rolls 1581-1592 the vast majority are either priests or gentry, a few are 'yeomen'. Clearly this is the class of person we are looking for, but it is difficult to be sure what 'yeoman' means in an urban context and many of those who have been cited before the courts in London may not actually be Londoners . In the first Recusant Roll (1592-1593) only about a dozen of those listed are not gentry and some of them may be servants (not all servants were working class) to the people after whom they appear. In the roll for 1593-4, between yeomen, widows and spinsters (whose class cannot be determined) there are less than a dozen who are not gentry; in 1595-6 slightly more but certainly not two dozen. In fact the size of the fines involved would rule out most ordinary people. The Recusant Rolls for London and Middlesex of the reign of James I show the widest variation of social status from lords and ladies to actors and servants. The majority listed were women.[29]

At local level the first stage in convicting recusants was to present them to Quarter Sessions. At every Sessions throughout the country and for most of the century a list of names would be presented 'for refusing to come to church for three months' or some such phrase, and the people named would then be 'proclaimed according to statute'. Many of the same names come up time and time again but it is still by no means clear why certain Catholics are often cited, and others never; why the numbers fluctuate and why lists in the same period contain quite different names.

In London there were two separate Sessions, one for the City of London and one for Middlesex and their geographical jurisdiction was quite clear in principle, though not always so clear in practice. We are fortunate that every reference to Catholics in the surviving Middlesex Sessions from 1558 to 1689 was published by J.C. Jeaffreson between 1886 and 1892[30] and that Dom Hugh Bowler went through the surviving London Sessions records equally thoroughly.[31] There are big gaps in both series, due, apart from other causes, to destruction in the Great Fire of London in 1666. Nevertheless, as the following examples show they are revealing.

The Newgate Gaol delivery (to the London Sessions) for January 1605/6 (the first after the Gunpowder Conspiracy) contains the indictment for recusancy of twenty people: two goldsmiths, a carpenter, a tailor, a weaver, two yeomen, a musician, a mercer's wife, a doctor, a knight, the wife of another knight and eight gentlemen. Five were from Holborn, two from Blackfriars, three from Aldersgate, one each from St Sepulchre and Christ Church, Newgate Street, and the rest from various parishes within the City. The total figures for the next few Sessions are as follows:

April 1606	39	32 *armiger*, *miles* or *generosus*
July 1606	55	28 *armiger*, *miles* or *generosus*
February 1606/7	Two priests	
May 1607	4 bills ignored	3 *armiger* and 1 *vidua*
Sept 1607	6	2 *armiger*, 2 *generosus* and 2 *vidua*

In October 1607 Oswald Needham was presented for saying Mass in the parish of Christ Church, Newgate Street (actually, in Newgate prison), and thirty other persons for being present. They were three clerks, two tailors and two wives of tailors, a clothworker, a widow, nine yeomen, eight spinsters and four gentlemen. Unfortunately they are all just given as 'of London'. This is a particularly interesting reference, as it gives the make-up of a specific congregation on a specific occasion. Moreover people who actually went into prison to hear Mass must have been pretty committed, making a personal choice and risking consequences.

References continued, but usually to small numbers of persons:

February 1607/8	16	Seven gentlemen, seven knights and two widows
June 1608	1	No description
September 1608	8	Seven gentlemen and a knight
December 1608	99	
January 1608/9	4	Two gentlemen, a knight and a mercer
February 1608/9	3	A widow, a gentleman and a knight

The 99 presentments for December 1608 do not include many plebeians. Of the 42 people presented from St Andrew, Holborn, 15 of the men are described as gentlemen and, of the 14 people presented from St Dunstan in the West, every one of the men is either a gentleman or a knight. Evidently the small fry are escaping, or they are being ignored, or there are no small fry.

There is a fairly complete run of London Sessions records for the reign of James I but only one Session has survived for the whole reign of Charles I, so no information is available for the vital years of the Personal Rule and the Civil War. During the Commonwealth period the London Sessions records include three lists of 'reputed Catholics in London'. One for 13 January 1657/8 contains 78 names, quite a number referring to people in the same family or household. Of these only two are English gentlemen. Five are Italians (including the Ambassador of the Duke of Tuscany), five are French, one Portuguese and a number Dutch. Many of the others may also be foreign: John Baptist Guyatt, Barnard Dargavell and Peter Le Adore, for example, or Adrian Henricks, with a wife and three children. Nine people were actually indicted. The lists for April 1658 and January 1658/9 are of about the same length and composition. For November 1678 the Sessions records contain a list of 'Reputed Catholics in London who took the oaths 21 November 1678'. The list contains 49 names, all of ordinary people, and three more names were added on 10 December.

The figures for the Middlesex Sessions show more variation, but the Sessions' jurisdiction covered the part of London where the general growth in population was most dramatic throughout the century. In the reign of James I the surviving sessions give us the names of some hundreds of recusants — not more, though many of them are presented many times. It is not very significant to say that they are mainly from Holborn with large contingents from St Giles and Clerkenwell, since those were the most populous parishes within the jurisdiction. However, the lists include a large number of the well-known gentry.

For part of the reign of Charles I we are lucky to have a separate 'Process Book of Indictments'[32] running from October 1631 to December 1640. This brings all the presentments for recusancy together and from it some further statistics can be compiled. In October 1631, 85 people were presented, of whom 45 were from St Andrew, Holborn. Of those, 20 were yeomen, many with wives, while only two were gentlemen. Of the 17 from Clerkenwell, five were yeomen; there were two tailors, a butcher and a stationer, four widows, a spinster, a knight, a gentleman and an esquire.

The indictments for April and October 1632 are of about the same length and contain many of the same names, but the indictments for December 1632 contain over a hundred names. Almost all are gentry from the northern counties (with their home parish cited) but also described as 'late of St Margaret, Westminster'. In February 1632/3 about another fifty were indicted from St Margaret's, six from St Giles and five from Holborn, but, again, they are all gentry with their country addresses also given. Not a Londoner and certainly not a plebeian Londoner amongst them.

The presentments continue in the same vein. In April 1636 eighty seven people were indicted for recusancy, of whom about a dozen are gentry. The figures for the following sessions are as follows:

April, 1637	259	October, 1639	81
October, 1637	90	April, 1640	244
April, 1638	96	May, 1640	128
October, 1638	96	October, 1640	58
April, 1639	90	December, 1640	1,430

The last list began with Thomas Cope, tailor, and ran through the entire social scale from Margaret, Lady Manners and the Dowager Countess of Portland, through Philip Roper, gentleman, Robert Flood MD, 'Signior Franciso', John Dunnington, fan-maker, and William Richardson, apothecary, to Teague Corpen and John Walsh, both chimney sweeps, late of Wapping. All these lists contain a great many gentry and may contain a great many repetitions, but they clearly constitute the starting point for any census of the English Catholic community in London in the reign of Charles I.

It has often been suggested that, by the end of the reign of James I, poor people were not being fined for recusancy as the authorities were aware that fining them would have forced them to apply for poor relief. No list which includes chimney sweeps from Wapping can be accused of omitting all the poor.

It seems at first sight a serious gap that we have no Sessions records relating to Catholics for the middle and late 1640s. However on August 17 1640 a document in the State Papers (16/464/15) declares:

> Whereas Pulford and others have caused divers of our subjects living in remote parts of this our realm of England and dominion of Wales to be indicted for recusancy at the Sessions of Peace and Gaol Delivery held for London and Middlesex, some of them being not recusants but comformable, others beyond the seas, some dead and many not able to travel to London, and few or none of them had notice of the indictment so that they could not possibly yield their bodies to the sheriff of the county before the next sessions, accordingly..... these are therefore to declare that none shall hereafter indict or cause to be indicted any for recusancy forth of the counties where they live.

These assertions, if true, throw doubt on any conclusions drawn from the sessions records!

As the difficulties between the King and Parliament drew to a head, recusants were commanded to leave London. Whether they did so immediately or not is not known. There was, of course, no Court in London after 1642 and we may suppose that the number of Catholics in the capital fell dramatically. It would be interesting to know what happened to the twenty-three French tailors.

The figures from later in the century are more problematic. Until the Civil War the majority of Puritans remained within the Church of England and during the Commonwealth period the Established Church lost its primacy. After the Restoration Government was much more concerned about 'fanaticks' than Catholics and therefore, when reading the presentments at Quarter Sessions, we have a much greater problem of recognition. Quakers in particular were often convicted as recusants by their refusal to swear the Oaths of Allegiance and Supremacy, through they had no objection to the content. Sometimes names are helpfully annotated: 'Quaker', 'Sectary', 'Popish Recusant' but often not. Even the long lists of recusants from *c.*1673 clearly contain a very large number of non-Catholics.[33] The very short lists for London and Middlesex in that volume are useless for any Catholic purpose.

The Protestation, Lay Subsidy and Poll Tax Records of 1641

The election in 1640 of a Parliament very concerned about the growth of Catholicism led to a spate of records which may help in the search.

The Protestation Returns are widely used for assessing recusancy, because they were specifically intended to establish who was in support of Protestantism. On the other hand, work on the published returns, such as those for Oxfordshire and North Berkshire shows clearly that many known Catholics were in practice willing to sign and in London Fr. Gervasius, the Carmelite, recorded on 19 July 1641: 'Many Catholics take the oath acknowledging the Royal Supremacy, and conform to the Protestant Church in order to avoid punishment'.[34]

The records of the City of London have unfortunately not survived, but those for the Hundred of Ossulstone have been printed[35] and they cover all the eastern suburbs. No recusants were reported in Limehouse, Poplar, Blackwall, Ratcliff, Stratford, Old Ford or Bethnal Green. In Spitalfields 'for recusants we have all by one, whose name is Simon Smith, a silk weaver by trade'. In Shoreditch no-one is stated to have refused, but in Clerkenwell 1,077 people signed the Protestation and 87 refused. In that parish the list is divided. Under the heading: 'These persons hereafter named, being known popish recusants, have not taken the Protestation', 12 men are listed including a pewterer, a labourer, a distiller, a collarmaker and four gentlemen. The second heading simply says : 'The persons hereafter named have not taken the Protestation', but the list begins with Patrick Graddey and includes Teague Silke, so it seems probable that many, if not all, of the people are to some degree Catholic but have not technically been convicted. Further out, four people in Islington refused and two in Stoke Newington, but no-one in Highgate or Hornsey.

The records of the Poll Tax of 1641 have survived for a great deal of the City and those for the Aldersgate, Bassishaw, Billingsgate, Dowgate, Farringdon, Langbourne and Lime Street Wards (and some other parishes) have been transcribed.[36] They are arranged in family units and foreigners pay double, as do Catholics. Money is involved here, rather than 'mere' religion, so we may expect the assessors to take some trouble. Yet in Bassishaw Ward 'There are no popish recusants residing in the said ward that are known' nor were any listed in Billingsgate, Lime Street or Walbrook Wards. The only Catholic household in the parish of St Olave, Old Jewry, was that of Lady Weld, and in Aldersgate Ward there were eleven recusants, of whom four were in the household of Lord Petre. Apart from foreigners there was only one recusant in Langbourne Ward and none in Dowgate Ward. In Farringdon Ward, covering the Precincts of Smithfield, Holborn Cross, St Sepulchre's Church and Old Bailey, there were only eight recusants, though we might have expected more. There is no reason to suppose that the wards which have not been transcribed would produce many more. In the previous subsidy of 1629[37], which was limited to fairly prosperous people, the records for Langbourne Ward specifically notice that there is 'a special tax on aliens and popish recusants', yet not one recusant is listed.

The records of the 1641 Poll Tax also include returns for twenty seven City Companies with approximately 7,000 names.[38] In principle these should not include Catholics and it seems highly unlikely that anyone will be explicitly stated to be a Catholic. It is evident from the Sessions records that an unknown number of Catholics were in practice trading without molestation, but mostly in Westminster to which the City Companies never extended their jurisdiction. John Gee listed 'Popish Physicians in and about the City of London' in 1624. There were 17, including 'Monsieur, a French Doctor, lurking about the Strand', together with five apothecaries and three surgeons.[39]

Unfortunately there are no records of the Freemen of the City before 1681 and the many thousands of seventeenth-century records of apprenticeship recorded by individual Companies give no information about the religion. Catholics could not be admitted to the Freedom of the City, but there was no religious stipulation for apprenticeship.

The Lay Subsidy records for 1641 for London[40] are unfortunately rather poor. Only two membranes (approximately 100 names) survive for the whole Hundred of Ossulstone. For the Assessment of 1642, about 8,000 - 10,000 names are recorded, out of an estimated population of perhaps 350,000 including the rural parishes north to the Hertfordshire border.[41] Here again, the records of the parishes we should be most interested in have not survived and there is nothing west of the City at all except some lists of defaulters in Westminster.

Lesser State Records of Catholic Interest

The Civil War and its aftermath produced many records of recusant interest, especially those of the 'Committee for Compounding with Delinquents',[42] but these relate almost wholly to the gentry, and those who had property in London often lived in the country. The many court records also relate primarily to gentry and, even where Catholics are involved, their Catholicism is not the point at issue. These records may help to document the lives of known Catholics but they will not help to identify them as Catholics.

Church of England Records

Whether convicted recusants or not, Catholics of all degrees of commitment in fact had something to do with their parish church. At the very least they buried their infant children there and in due course were buried themselves with their wives. They may or may not have been married or taken their children to baptism there. As Catholics they were not supposed to, of course, but in fact Catholics at all levels seem to have compromised with the Church of England to a very great extent. There has never been any suggestion that Catholics refused to pay tithes or other rates administered through the parish, as Quakers consistently did. Catholics were not in a ghetto and, as recusant historians frequently need reminding, Catholics of all levels were fully integrated into every aspect of ordinary life except the religious one.

In many rural parishes the rites of passage of the Catholics (and other nonconformists) are annotated in the register. The notes may be pejorative or neutral, but they show that their Catholicism is known. In London I can find no such notes. None of the City burial registers[43] that I have checked for the 1630s have any recusants noted, though this might be because there were none. On the other hand, there are none noted either in parishes such as Holborn and Blackfriars, where we should certainly expect there to be some. Being French is noted, however.

In 1623 a number of people were gathered at a sermon in Blackfriars when the floor collapsed and about a hundred people were killed. They are themselves an interesting cross-section of the London Catholics, from Lady Webb and Lady Blackstone's daughter to 'Davie, an Irishman'. This disaster was the talk of the town[44] and was widely used as propaganda by Puritan preachers but the burial register of Blackfriars[45] makes no attempt to score points: 'Oct. 28 1623, Dorothy, wife of Mathew Somers. She was slain at a priest's sermon. Mary Clement, waiting woman to the said Dorothy. Slain with her mistress'. The register of Holborn contains the names of 23 of the dead and they are listed under one heading where the incumbent seems more concerned that they went out of the parish than outside the Church of England: 'The names of those persons that went out of the parish of St Andrew, Holborn, to Blackfriars, near Ludgate, the 26 of October 1623, being the Sabbath Day, and weare slaine there by the fall of an house as they were hearing of a sermon. Not buried here but registered'.

As before, it seems that the parish registers will document the lives or at least the deaths, of many Catholics, but they will not help us to identify them.

The same applies to the enormous collections of wills, administrations and inventories for probate. Until the Civil War London wills were most likely to be proved in the Archdeaconry or Commissary Courts of London, the Archdeaconry Court of Middlesex or the Prerogative Court of Canterbury (which, despite its title, was London-based); there were some other courts with very limited jurisdiction. During the Commonwealth period all wills were proved in the P.C.C.

Wills have been used to prove family, business and religious connections; however, by the early seventeenth century the common religious introduction was in standard form and no conclusions can be drawn from its wording. Wills show the links between people whose interests are already known, but those who had temporised over religion all their lives were hardly likely to risk their wives' or children's inheritance by a deathbed confession in a document which was actually intended for formal public scrutiny.

In many counties the records of the Bishop's Visitations are a prime source but unfortunately in London there is almost no material before the Restoration. A national diocesan Return of 1603[46] gives a figure of 318 recusants for the diocese of London and a total of 146,857 communicants. The later returns are by parish with no diocesan totals.

A return of the 'names of the Popish recusants in the parish of St Dunstan in the West'[47] (undated: 1630s) gives eleven men and eight women: an apothecary with his wife and two servants, two gentlemen, one with a wife, two Doctors of Physick, one with a wife, a goldsmith with a wife and servant, a yeomen, a pewterer, a fruiterer, another servant, a widow and a wife. We have no way of knowing if such a list is complete, but no evidence for asserting that it is not.

At the Visitation of 1664 the churchwardens of St Paul's, Covent Garden, presented six Catholics and three Quakers. The Catholics included Lady Mary Clanricarde, Sir Kenelm Digby and the Hon. Lady Abergavenny, with three others who sound foreign. On the other hand, St Giles in the Fields presented about 200 people, many of whom are marked as Quakers and Anabaptists. The churchwardens of Kensington, which was still a couple of miles outside London, stated: 'There is a maid known by the name of Papist Nan, who is a papist, and one Dr Richardson reputed to be so.'[48]

The figures in the later surviving Visitations seem equally unreliable. In 1669 Holborn declared: 'Concerning parishioners, all well', implying that everyone attended church, which seems unlikely. In 1677 St Giles reported 18 people, but these were 'for refusing to pay the respective sums assessed upon them towards the repair of the parish church', which implies that they were Quakers witnessing against 'steeple houses'; on the other hand at the Sessions in March 1679 they indicted 153 persons (of whom only three were gentleman) for recusancy and a very large number of other presentments followed over the next three months as the Titus Oates Plot thickened. Yet in 1680 the churchwardens of Holborn presented only five people 'for not coming to church'.[49] Likewise in 1677 St Martin's in the Fields presented chiefly various schoolmasters for not bringing their children to church; these do not seem likely to be Catholics.[50] Yet the 'Return of Lodgers of the Suffolk Street Ward in the parish of St Martin's in the Fields of 8 Nov. 1680'[51] lists more than 40 Catholics in one part of the parish, 21 of whom were English.

Throughout the various Visitations, the vast majority of the City parishes report no Catholics at all. For those who had been formally convicted as recusants, there was a complicated procedure for conformity. This procedure has been described in detail[52] and the names of those who conformed in the years 1590-1625 have been published.[53] In that period only forty people conformed in London and Middlesex and, 25 men out of 33 are gentry and above. Of the others, one is from Islington but also from Oakham in Rutlandshire, and the others are from Aldgate (two), St. Mildred and St Olave's in the City, Norton Folgate, Whitechapel and Holborn (two).

At parish level some parishes have records of communicants. In the returns of 1603 for the diocese of London there were stated to be 318 recusants[54] but 1572 'noe communicants'. In St Saviour's, Southwark, (south of the River Thames) in 1603 there were 4,232 persons of age to communicate. Of these 32 were recusants most of whom were in Montague Close, owned by the aristocratic Sussex Catholic family of Montague, and 300 men and 200 women were non-communicants.[55] Magee considers that these were all Catholics who were prepared to compromise so far as going to church but not so far as taking communion. This seems unlikely and reminds us that our own concentration on Catholicism may make us forget that for many incumbents the problem of non-attendance was with the Puritans.

Summary

London had a large Catholic population and numbers fluctuated enormously, especially between the 1630s, when numbers in Westminster were large and may have been increasing, and the 1640s, when the Court left the metropolis, leading to a severe depression in the luxury trades. There were almost no Catholics in the City itself and those in Westminster included a high proportion of foreigners, Irish and gentry, who were not permanent residents and had their roots elsewhere. Catholics were less isolated than in many parts of the country but even more affected by politics, Puritan propaganda and the mob. In Catholic circles it was thought that there were more priests than were needed.

Numbers were objectively quite large and there were probably more Catholics in London than anywhere in England except possibly the Hundreds of West Derby and Amounderness in Lancashire. Nevertheless they were a very small percentage of the population and it is inconceivable that they ever amounted to 1%. Although every one was very conscious of the Catholic threat that they thought existed, in fact no working-class presence ever made itself felt in London throughout the seventeenth century and none of the many anti-Catholic riots or processions was ever resisted by an equivalent mob of Catholics in the way that the Irish banded together to defend their chapels in the eighteenth century.

The names, occupations and residences of many English London Catholics can certainly be reconstituted from the surviving Sessions records and the list of convicted recusants 1625-1642. A good deal of standard genealogical detective work would enable us to find out a great deal more about this group. A high proportion of the London working class in every generation had actually come in from the country, but the counties immediately around London were already a Catholic desert in the seventeenth century. Once we are looking at specific individuals, it will be interesting to see what proportion of the London plebeian Catholics were actually immigrants from the Catholic northern counties.

NOTES

1 B. Weinreb & C. Hibbert eds., *The London Encyclopaedia* (1983).

2 Tim Harris, *London Crowds in the Reign of Charles II* (1987); David Cressy, *Bonfires and Bells: National Memory and the Protestant Calendar in Elizabethan and Stuart England* (1989); O.W. Furley, 'The Pope-burning Processions of the Late Seventeenth Century', *History* 45, no. 150 (February 1959), pp. 16-23.

3 Aveling, *Handle*.

4 C.Z. Wiener, 'The Beleaguered Isle: A Study of Elizabethan and Early Jacobean Anti-Catholicism', *Past and Present* 51 (1971), pp. 27-62.

5 William R. Trimble, 'The Embassy Chapel Question 1625-1660', *Journal of Modern History* 18 (1946), pp. 97-107; W. McGreal, 'The Embassy Chapels', *Aylesford Review* (1965), pp. 66-74.

6 J.S. Hansom, 'Proceedings Against Catholics for Attending Mass at the Spanish Embassy on Palm Sunday 1613-1614' (C.R.S. 9, 1911), pp. 122-6.

7 A.J. Loomie, 'London's Spanish Chapel before and after the Civil War', *Recusant History* 18, no. 4 (October 1987), pp. 402-17; A. Van Der Essen, 'Les Catholiques Londiniens et l'Ambassade d'Espagne, 1633-1637' in Etienne Van Cauwenbergh ed., *Scrinium Lovaniense: Mélanges Historiques* (1961).

8 H.B. Wheatley ed., *The Diary of Samuel Pepys* (1896), vol. 7, p. 247.

9 L. Scouloudi, *Returns of Strangers in the Metropolis 1593, 1627, 1635, 1639* (Huguenot Society Quarto Series 57, 1985); R.E.G. Kirk, *Returns of Aliens: Part 1 1525-1571* (Huguenot Society Quarto Series 10 part 1, 1900); *ibid. Part 2 1571-1597* (Huguenot Society Quarto Series 10 part 2, 1902); *ibid. Part 3 1598-1625* (Huguenot Society Quarto Series 10 part 3, 1907); *Index* (1908). This return is almost wholly concerned with London.

10 Cecil Roth, *A History of the Jews in England* (1941), pp. 159-60, 166.

11 Lady Georgiana Fullerton, *The Life of Luisa de Carvajal* (1873).

12 W.G. Bell, *The Great Fire of London in 1666* (1920).

13 R.M. Fisher, 'Privy Council Coercion and Religious Conformity at the Inns of Court', *Recusant History*15, no. 5 (May 1981), pp. 305-24; W. Prest, *The Inns of Court under Elizabeth I and the Early Stuarts 1590-1640* (1972).

14 F.F. Foster, *The Politics of Stability: A Portrait of the Rulers in Elizabethan London* (1977); I.W. Archer, *The Pursuit of Stability: Social Relations in Elizabethan London* (1991).

15 Many prison lists have been published by the C.R.S. and detailed accounts of life in prison will be found in Gillow and throughout the classic biographies of priests: Anstruther, Birt, Challoner, Foley, Gumbley, Thaddeus, Zimmerman and in the more modern biographies. See also: P. McGrath & J. Rowe, 'The Imprisonment of Catholics under Elizabeth I', *Recusant History* 20, no. 4 (October 1991), pp. 415-35; P. McGrath & J. Rowe, 'The Elizabethan Priests: their Harbourers and Helpers', *Recusant History* 19, no. 3 (May 1989), pp. 209-33. Although these relate to an earlier period, their spirit informed the thinking of the next generation. [See also pp. 46-48 above.]

16 E. Hutton, *Catholicism and English Literature* (1942); M. Eccles, 'Elizabethan Actors: A-D', *Notes and Queries* (1991), pp. 38-49 (includes records of recusant actors and recusant wives); H. Mutschmann & K. Wentersdorf, *Shakespeare and Catholicism* (1952); E.A.G. Honigman & S. Brock, *Playhouse Wills* (1993); J.D. Hahlan, 'Richard Dering, Catholic Musician of Stuart England', *Catholic Historical Review* 46 (1960), pp. 428-52.

17 P.R. Newman, 'Roman Catholics in Pre-Civil War England: the Problem of Definition', *Recusant History* 15, no. 2 (October 1979), pp. 148-52; J.A. Williams, 'English Catholicism under Charles II: the Legal Poisition', *Recusant History* 7, no. 3 (October 1963), pp. 123-37.

18 W.G. Bell, *The Great Fire of London in 1666* (1920).

19 Anthony Kenny ed., *The Responsa Scholarum of the English College, Rome, 1598-1685* (C.R.S. 54 & 55, 1962-1963).

20 R.J. Stonor, *Stonor: a Catholic Sanctuary in the Chilterns from the Fifth Century till To-day* (1951); M. Blundell, *Cavalier: Letters of William Blundell to his Friends* (1933); E.A.B. Barnard, *A Seventeenth-Century Country Gentleman: Sir Francis Throckmorton 1640-1680* (1944); Sir G.H. Ryan & L.J. Redstone, *Timperley of Hintlesham* (1931).

21 B. Zimmerman, *Carmel in England* (1899).

22 Magee, p. 30; J.H. Pollen, 'The Notebook of John Southcote D.D. 1628-36', *Miscellanea* (C.R.S. 1, 1904), p. 114.

BIBLIA SACRA
VETERIS ET NOVI
TESTAMENTI IVXTA
VVLGATAM ÆDI-
TIONEM.

Cum quibusdam Anotationibus Ioannis
Benedicti Parisiensis Theologi.

PARISIIS,
Apud Iacobum Keruer, sub Vnicorne,
in via Iacobea.
1560.

1 The Word: Vulgate Bible with signatures of George Goodwin and Andrew Bromwich

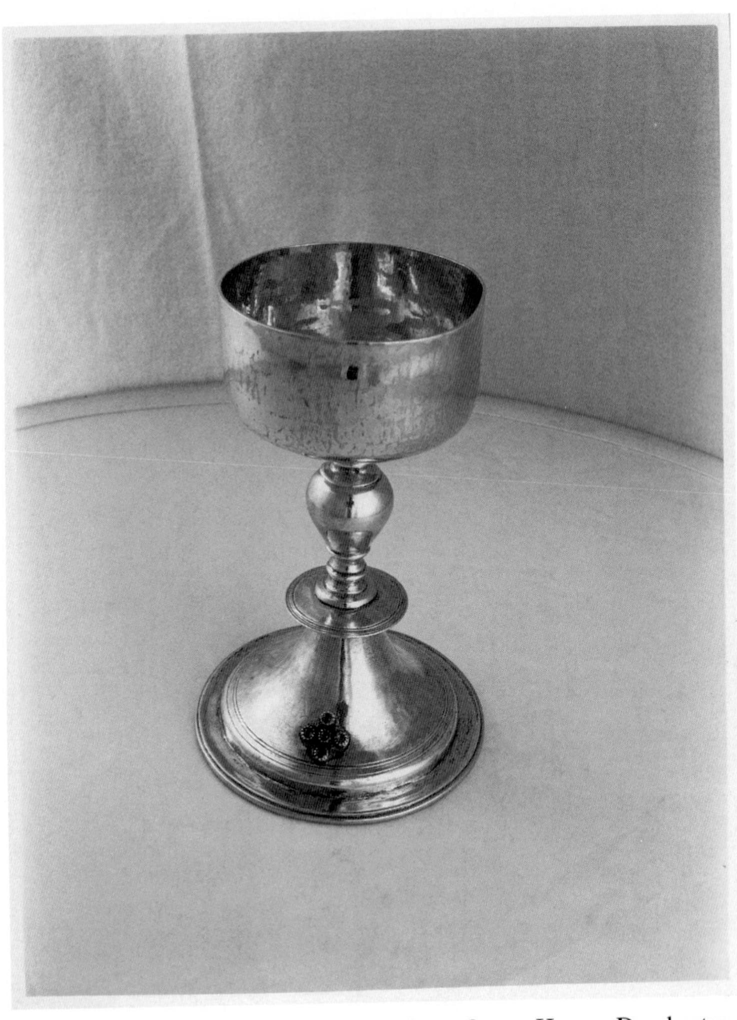

2 The Sacrament: recusant chalice from Overy House, Dorchester-on-Thames

OLD HOUSES in the BUTCHER ROW.
The right hand corner house in this view (which stood on the east side of St Clements lane, near Clements Inn, and
was taken down 30 March 1798) has been suggested to have been the House in which the horrid conspiracy to destroy the
King, and his Children and Parliament, by Gun powder, was determined upon and sworn; and that a book entituled
"The Gun powder Treason," prefaced by Bishop of Lincoln (reprinted 1679) identified it as such; but in respect to this suggestion, it appears, on referring to the book, that the conspirator Thomas Winter, confessed that Catesby, Percy, Wright, Guy Vaux and
himself met merely "behind Saint Clements" (without any further description of the place) where they administered to each other the
oath of secrecy, and after, received the sacrament "in the next room". On this ground, therefore, the identity of the House is still uncertain, and the above houses are inserted only as curious specimens of ancient modes of building in the metropolis.
Pub. Aug. 10. 1798, by N. Smith, Rembrandts Head, Gt Mays Buildings, St Martins Lane, & I. T. Smith, 40, Frith Street, Soho.

3 John Gerard's house (1602–5) in St Clement's Lane, London

4 Boscobel House, Shropshire: attic chapel and priest-hole used by Charles II (1651)

5 Franciscan Masshouse (*c.* 1690), Edgbaston, Birmingham

6 West Grinstead, Sussex: attic chapel (1753).

A note of what is left in the house att
Harvington october the 20th 1696 belonging
to the Chapell, and for the vse of the Clergy
that shall assist the poore of the Parish and
Neighbourhood of Chadsly Corbit, upon a found
setled by Dame Mary Yate late Lady of the
above said Mannor
Church stuffe
Imprimis
one vestment and antipendium of silver stuffe
with gold flowers a whit satine imbrodered vaile
one white taby vestment and antipendium with
a gold stuffe Cross
one white Damaske vestment and plaine satine vaile
one Crimson plushe vestmend and Antipendium
with silver lace
one carnation Indian satine Vestment and An
tipendium laced with silke lace
one purple taby vestment and Antipendium
laced 4 large and 4 lesser peeces of purple sasenet
one purple tafety vestment and Antipendium with
silke and silver lace
one Green taby vestment with a damaske Antipendium
one greene sasenet Vestmen with a green and white
Antipendium
one blake velvet vestment and Antipendium with
a white satine Cross with silver and blake lace
[illegible] vestment with blake and

7 Harvington Hall, Worcestershire: chapel inventory (1696)

Eccleshall, July 17, 1767.

Sir,

IN Pursuance of the above Directions, which I have lately received from his Grace the Lord Archbishop of *Canterbury*; this is to require you, in his Majesty's Name, to make out as correct and complete Lists as possible, of the Papists, or reputed Papists, within your Peculiar Jurisdiction, situated in my Diocese, distinguishing their Sexes, Ages, and Occupations, and how long they have been there resident; which Lists you are desired forthwith to transmit, or certify the Result of your Enquiry into this Point, to me at *Eccleshall.*

I am Sir,

Your obedient humble Servant,

Fred. Lich. *and* Cov.

My Lord

in the Parish of Tipton

Upon strict Enquiry I can find but one Person, who may be liable to a Suspicion of being a Papist. Whether he can be reputed to be such, I leave to your Lordship's better Judgment. His Name is John Pidgeon, of the Age of fifty Years or upwards by Occupation a Victualler. He has resided during his whole Life in or near the Parish: in the former Part of which, being born I believe, of Popish Parents, he was looked upon as a Papist, but for the last twenty Years has not joined in that Communion, nor at all associated with the Papists Men of that Persuasion. Your Lordship's Opinion may be determined by these Circumstances, the Trouble of which, I hope, will be excused in Me, Your faithful humble Servant.

Inquiry 1767

[23] J.C.M. Weale ed., *Registers of the Catholic Chapels Royal and of the Portuguese Embassy Chapel, 1662-1829: Vol. 1 Marriages* (C.R.S. 38, 1941).
[24] *Catholic Ancestor* 5, no. 5 (June 1995), pp. 199-200.
[25] B. Zimmerman, *Carmel in England* (1899); McGreal, 'The Embassy Chapels'.
[26] P.R.O. SP 16/495; referred to in Magee, p. 92.
[27] T.J. McCann ed., *Recusants in the Exchequer Pipe Rolls, 1581-1592* (C.R.S. 71, 1986).
[28] N.M.C. Calthrop ed., *Recusant Roll No. 1 (1592-2)* (C.R.S. 18, 1916); Hugh Bowler ed., *Recusant Roll No. 2 (1593-4)* (C.R.S. 57, 1965); Hugh Bowler ed., *Recusant Rolls No. 3 (1594-5) and No. 4 (1595-6)* (C.R.S. 61, 1970).
[29] J.J. LaRocca, *Jacobean Recusant Rolls for Middlesex 1603-1625: An Abstract in English* (C.R.S. 76, 1997).
[30] J.C. Jeaffreson ed., *Middlesex County Records, 1549-1689,* 4 volumes (1886-1892).
[31] Hugh Bowler, *London Sessions Records 1605-85* (C.R.S. 34, 1934).
[32] Jeaffreson, *Middlesex County Records 3*, pp. 128-59.
[33] J.S. Hansom ed., 'A List of Convicted Recusants in the Reign of King Charles II', *Miscellanea* (C.R.S. 6, 1909), pp. 75-326.
[34] J. Gibson ed., *Oxfordshire and North Berkshire Protestation Returns and Tax Assessments 1641-2* (1994).
[35] A.J.C. Guimraens ed., 'Protestation Returns for the Ossulstone Hundred', *Supplements to the British Archivist* 1 (1913-1920); republished *North Middlesex Family History Society* (1987).
[36] P.R.O. E179/251/1-13. Transcript of 1-3, 5, 8-13 at the Society of Genealogists Library.
[37] P.R.O. SP 16/495.
[38] P.R.O. E179/251/22.
[39] 'A Catalogue of Popish Physicians', *C.A.* 4, no. 3 (November 1992), pp. 111-2, reprinted from John Gee ed., *The Foot out of the Snare* (1624).
[40] P.R.O. E179/143/314, 316.
[41] P.R.O. E179/143/323.
[42] *Committee for Compounding with Delinquents 1643-1660* (H.M.S.O.) 5 volumes: Catholics noted; see also *Committee for the Advance of Money, 1642-1656,* 3 volumes (H.M.S.O., 1888; Kraus reprint, 1967); P.R.O. SP19: Catholics noted in index; J. Lappin, 'Parliament's Government during the English Civil War 1642-1649: Surviving Records in the Public Record Office', *C.A.* 6, no. 4 (February 1997).
[43] A great many of the surviving seventeenth-century City parish registers have been published by the Harleian Society.
[44] M. Gandy, "The Fatal Vespers" or "The Doleful Evensong", 1623', *Catholic Ancestor* 6, no. 2 (June 1996), pp. 65-9; A. Walsham, ' "The Fatall Vesper": Providentialism and Anti-Popery in Late Jacobean London', *Past and Present* 144 (August 1994), pp. 36-87; Foley 1, pp. 85-6.
[45] Guildhall Library, Visitation 1664.
[46] British Library Harleian 280, pp. 157-72 - quoted in Magee.
[47] Guildhall Library, Visitation 1630s (undated),
[48] Guildhall Library, Visitation 1664.
[49] Guildhall Library, Visitation 1679.
[50] See A.C.F. Beales, *Education under Penalty: English Catholic Education from the Reformation to the Fall of James II* (1963), for what little there is to be said about Catholic educational provision in London before the reign of James II; also Michael J. Powers, 'Sir Balthazar Gerbier's Academy of Bethnal Green', *East London Papers* 10 (1967), pp. 19-34: Gerbier's house was attacked by the mob in 1641 as a supposed asylum for Catholics.
[51] *C.A.* 3, no. 5 (June 1991), pp. 207-9.
[52] M. Questier, 'Sources for Conformity in Elizabethan and Jacobean England', *C.A.* 5, no. 5 (June 1995), pp. 187-90.

[53] M. Questier, 'Conformity in the South 1590-1625', *C.A.* 6, no. 3 (November 1996), pp. 95-100: includes London and Middlesex entries.
[54] Magee, pp. 83, 114, 118.
[55] J. Boulton, *Neighbourhood and Society: a London Suburb in the Seventeenth Century* (1987), pp. 7-15.

9

CATHOLICS OF THE SEVENTEENTH CENTURY IN THE BARONY OF KENDAL

A local historian of the Lake District has asserted that

> The Elizabethan middle way in religion was widely, if at first imperfectly, accepted in the north and the people did not long remain attached to the Roman faith,[1]

while another historian has suggested that

> it was in the manor houses of the disgruntled country gentry that the missionary priests of the 1580's and 1590's found their converts and their secret refuges.[2]

The generally accepted view appears to be that of Bossy:

> By the Civil War, except for one or two isolated households of the Howards and a couple of more firmly seated gentry families like the Curwens of Workington and the Stricklands of Sizergh, it [society] had lost all connection with Catholicism.[3]

Solutions have been sought for the mystery of the vanishing Cumbrian Catholics, which include the failure of the clergy to sustain an effective mission to the region:

> Indeed, the organisation of the mission had nourished Lancashire and the North-east at the expense of Cumbria, though this was merely a question of reinforcing success or the survival of the fittest. The Cumbrian mountains had not defended but defeated Catholicism.[4]

This negative view, in so far as it relates to seventeenth-century Catholicism in the Barony of Kendal, is not supported by the available contemporary evidence, nor is the belief that only the Stricklands and their servants were Catholics. Evidence from the constablewick of Skelsmergh and the town of Kendal shows more Catholics in the Barony than was previously thought. The Barony embraced the southern half of the old county of Westmorland, which in 1974 was amalgamated with Cumberland and some small areas of Lancashire and Yorkshire to form the new county of Cumbria. It comprised 400 square miles, half of which was wild and uninhabited moorland called 'Fells'. On three sides these mountainous fells bounded a countryside of many small hills and dales. The area was divided into the civil wards of Lonsdale and Kendal, which were subdivided into constablewicks under the ecclesiastical jurisdiction of the Bishop of Chester as part of the Archdeaconry of Richmond.

Figure 5: The Townships and Parishes of the Barony of Kendal

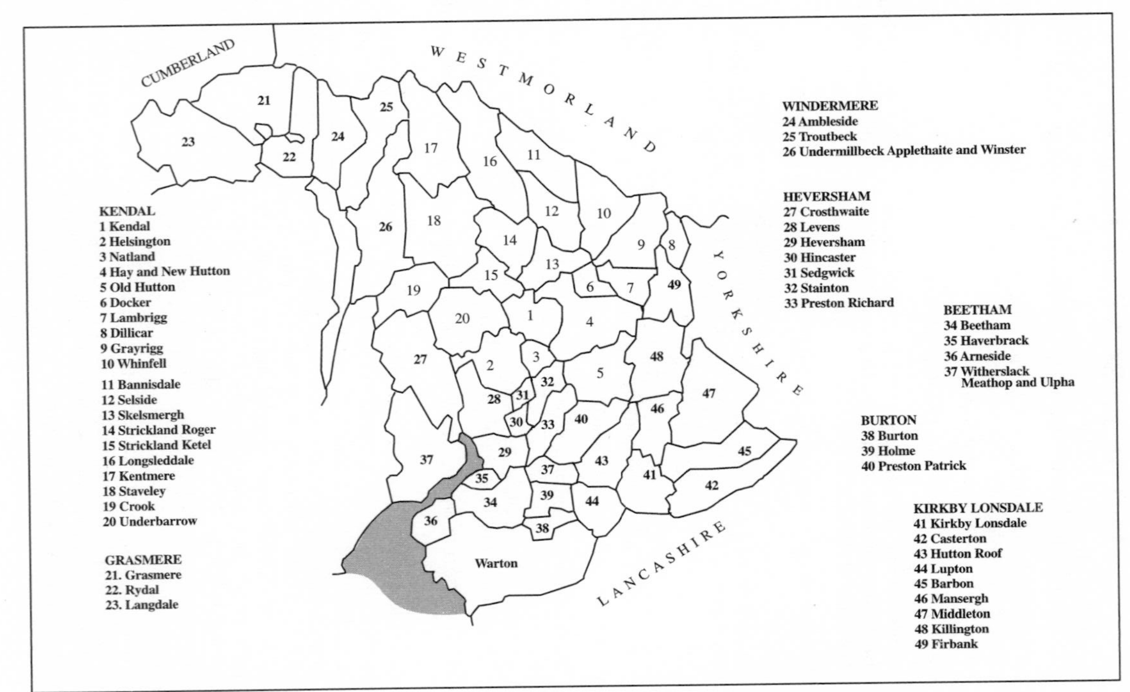
CUMBERLAND
WESTMORLAND
YORKSHIRE
LANCASHIRE
Warton
KENDAL
1 Kendal
2 Helsington
3 Natland
4 Hay and New Hutton
5 Old Hutton
6 Docker
7 Lambrigg
8 Dillicar
9 Grayrigg
10 Whinfell
11 Bannisdale
12 Selside
13 Skelsmergh
14 Strickland Roger
15 Strickland Ketel
16 Longsleddale
17 Kentmere
18 Staveley
19 Crook
20 Underbarrow
GRASMERE
21. Grasmere
22. Rydal
23. Langdale
WINDERMERE
24 Ambleside
25 Troutbeck
26 Undermillbeck Applethaite and Winster
HEVERSHAM
27 Crosthwaite
28 Levens
29 Heversham
30 Hincaster
31 Sedgwick
32 Stainton
33 Preston Richard
BEETHAM
34 Beetham
35 Haverbrack
36 Arneside
37 Witherslack
Meathop and Ulpha
BURTON
38 Burton
39 Holme
40 Preston Patrick
KIRKBY LONSDALE
41 Kirkby Lonsdale
42 Casterton
43 Hutton Roof
44 Lupton
45 Barbon
46 Mansergh
47 Middleton
48 Killington
49 Firbank

The seven Anglican parishes with their 49 townships more or less corresponded to the constablewicks. The county was almost entirely agricultural and pastoral; Kendal was the only manufacturing town, producing coarse cloth, knitted worsted stockings, sailors' hosiery and leather. The majority of the population lived in small hamlets or on scattered farmsteads and their produce of spinning and knitting was sold in Kendal town. The Barony had a port at Milnthorpe and in 1593 it was reported that Richard Taylor of Lyndall in Cartmel often conveyed by boat 'priests and bad persons' to the Isle of Man and Scotland when any search was being made for recusants.[5]

Catholics and Taxation, 1625-1640

Among the 'Town End' manuscripts in Kendal Record Office is a document headed 'This Indenture of Extract', which was the 'Rateing Taxeing and Assessing of the third Subsidies'. Tobias Knipe, gent., was appointed 'High Collector' and the document was dated 1628. The constablewicks were set out as sub-headings and under some appeared the additional words 'Convicted Recusants there', followed by names showing a tax of 8d.[6] 'Statutes at Large' omit the appropriate legislation, but the text is found in 'Statutes of the Realm'. On the accession of Charles I in 1625, 'The First Fruits of most dutiful affection of your loyal and loving Subjects' was a grant by Parliament of two entire Lay Subsidies, which was repeated in 1627 with a grant of five entire subsidies and in 1640 by a further four subsidies.[7]

The Acts provided for an assessment of all persons born 'within the Realm or the King's Dominions in the township or constablewick where they had resided for the most part of the preceding year', but in practice each township by custom nominated two or three men to pay the subsidy on personalty. In a few places it was customary for a landowner to be assessed on the income of 20/- or more from realty '*in terris*' with others on personalty '*in bonis*' worth £3 or more. Both assessments were after payment of debts. Following an examination of the local constables and leading inhabitants from each township, a schedule or roll of assessments was prepared in duplicate by the Commissioners. One copy of the roll was given to the High Collector while the other was returned to the Exchequer.[8]

Aliens and convicted popish recusants aged 17 or above and others aged 21 who had not received Holy Communion within one year were assessed at double the rate of tax being 2s. 8d in the pound on personalty and 4s. in the pound on income from realty; those convicted popish recusants not contributing were rated for a Poll Tax of 8d. The Exchequer, Clerks to the Courts and churchwardens were required to provide lists of convicted recusants for the Commissioners and in theory these rolls of assessments should include all convicted popish recusants capable of paying Poll Tax, with their places of residence for the years 1626, 1628 and 1641. However, 'the disordered passion' of certain members of Parliament over the King's intentions caused Charles to dissolve his 1625 Parliament and letters were written to the Justices of the Peace to exhort people to make the grant.[9] The Exchequer Pells Books record the receipt of tax, thereby verifying its collection,[10] even though not all of the seven or eight rolls of assessments and duplicates have survived. The King's dispute with Parliament may account for the absence of any roll for the first Subsidy.

In the Barony of Kendal two rolls returned into the Exchequer are in the Public Record Office[11] while a further three rolls used by the High Collectors are in Kendal Record Office[12] and include a roll for each of the years previously mentioned. (The names of convicted popish recusants are given in Appendix 1.)

Convicted Popish Recusants in the Rolls

In these five rolls the number of convicted popish recusants is 627, but as some paid Poll Tax on more than one occasion this figure must be reduced to 314 individuals. These were concentrated in certain constablewicks. In the year 1641, as is shown in the table below, 75% were listed in nine of the 48 constablewicks: 50% in six constablewicks to the north of Kendal and 25% in three constablewicks to the south.

Of the convicted popish recusants 90% were beneath the rank of gentry, identified by their descriptions in the list of recusants presented in 1640 for being absent from Church and Communion for six months.

The Gentry

The gentry included Robert Middleton of Burton; Anthony Duckett, William and Hillary Bradley, Ralph Bouskell, Thomas Leyburn and William Thornburgh, all of Beetham; Charles Saule of Stainton, Walter Strickland of Sizergh, John Fleming of Rydal, and John Leyburn of Witherslack. In the northern half of the county the recusant gentry included Cyprian Hilton of Ormside; William Wormley of Shap; John Lawson of Brougham; Thomas Blenkinsop of Brough, and Lancelot Lancaster of Barton.[13] The suggestion that by the Civil War Cumbrian society in Westmorland had lost all connection with Catholicism, except for the Stricklands of Sizergh, is not accurate and the solutions suggested for the alleged mystery of the vanishing Cumbrian Catholics are not really necessary.

Table 18: Convicted Recusants in the Barony of Kendal

Northern Constablewicks	**1626**	**1628**	**1628**	**1641**	**1641**
Docker	0	4	5	6	10
Grayrigg	14	11	27	14	25
Scalthwaite	17	?	12	12	12
Skelsmergh & Patton	6	?	26	19	30
Whinfell	14	12	17	17	22
Whitwell & Selside	10	7	4	4	6
Totals	61	34	91	72	105
Southern Constablewicks					
Beetham	10	10	9	18	28
Helsington	6	2	4	2	3
Witherslack	5	3	4	10	10
Totals	21	15	17	30	41
Kendal	3	12	10	8	11
Combined Totals	85	61	118	110	157
Whole Barony (48 constablewicks)	105	65	126	136	195

Source: K.R.O. WD/TE/110 and WD/RY/Box 102

The constablewicks in the Barony of Kendal might be cited as typical examples for the argument that Catholics 'coagulated' in local groups, at the centre of which a gentleman's house will usually be found.[14] The Ducketts were at Grayrigg Hall, the Thornburghs at Selside Hall, the Leyburns at Skelsmergh, Witherslack and, in the constablewick of Underbarrow, at Cunswick, the Braithwaites at Burneside in Strickland Roger and the Stricklands at Sizergh in the constablewick of Helsington.

The usual explanation for the concentration of Catholics in certain areas is the protection afforded by the local gentry, but it seems more likely it was the priests, themselves members of the gentry families, who gave them the necessary encouragement to remain Catholic. In the constablewick of Skelsmergh and Patton, the manorial hall had been owned by the Leyburn family for generations and in 1629 it was enlarged by John Leyburn while the Anglican chapel was allowed to fall into disrepair, leaving only its walls standing by the end of the 1640s. The representative of the gentry in the constablewick was John Leyburn esquire, one of only three recusants in the Barony who paid at the double rate on realty in 1641, and the importance of the family to the survival of Catholicism in the locality cannot be over-emphasised. They had chapels at Skelsmergh, Cunswick and Witherslack, with a number of the family being ordained priests at Douai. Four of the priests were sons of John Leyburn and two were grandsons. In addition, the education at Douai of James Gandy, alias Leyburn, was paid for by the Leyburn family, and this James Gandy became the first resident priest in Kendal. The failure to repair the Anglican chapel and the fact that the Leyburn family were recusants must have been more than a coincidence and it is probable that the Leyburn family were responsible in part for the high concentration of papists in this constablewick.[15]

In the 1640s one third of those listed as freeholders were convicted popish recusants: John Leyburn esquire, Thomas Gilpin, Nicholas Mawson, James Pickering, Thomas Sledall and Anthony Stevenson.[16] The properties they owned and/or occupied were Skelsmergh Hall, Garthrow, Pond Side, Bowbank, Garnet Folds, Summerhow, and the Mill at Gilthwaiterigg.

Catholic Yeoman Families

A study of three families residing in Skelsmergh reveals an unwavering attachment to Catholicism throughout the seventeenth century.

The **Gilpins**, many of whom were farmers, were the largest recusant family in the constablewick with 13 of its members paying Poll Tax. In 1629 Edward Gilpin compounded for his goods at a yearly rental of £1, Jason Gilpin at £1.10.0., and Christopher Gilpin at £2, which suggests they were customary tenants and not freeholders.[17] Previously, in 1623, Christopher had been presented for marrying his wife Anne without licence or banns and he died at the age of 95.[18] Thomas Gilpin of Skelsmergh Hall, Christopher's son, was a farmer and his name appears on the Recusant Roll of 1650.[19] He was aged 70 in 1692 and neglected to answer the summons for suspected papists to take the Declaration and Oaths in 1696.[20] He probably moved with the Leyburns to Nateby, as a Thomas Gilpin died there in 1708/9.[21] At the turn of the century the Gilpins remaining papists in Skelsmergh were Elizabeth, Ursula and Agnes who married Robert Benson on 7 January 1717/18.[22]

The **Mawsons** were another local recusant family connected with the Leyburns but not dependant on them as tenants. Nicholas Mawson was aged 24 when he inherited one messuage and tenement with 14 acres on the death of his father in 1620.[23] John Mawson, Nicholas' son, was a liveryman and warden of the Goldsmiths' Company and an early banker in London. He was used secretly by the monarch to pay Bishop Leyburn's salary.[24]

John was also one of the co-executors of Bishop Leyburn's will. Nicholas' other son Peter was described as a yeoman in 1657 and was named as a recusant with his wife in 1678.[25] These Mawsons were related to the Pickerings, whose adherence to the faith extended over two hundred years.

The **Pickering** family had many and various links with other local Catholics. John Pickering of Bowbank, yeoman, had his will witnessed in 1572 by Sir James Dugdale, of Strickland Fields, who with Richard Call was reported as using 'them selves as Clarcks att sainge of Masses &c'.[26] Another priest, Robert Middleton, was harboured by Agnes Hodgson in the adjoining constablewick of Selside.[27]

James Pickering, John's son, was presented at the Quarter Sessions in 1606 and at the Archeaconry Court of Richmond for not having his children baptised at his parish church in 1623.[28] His name also appears in the Recusant Rolls of 1624, 1625, 1626 and 1631.[29] In the next generation John Pickering, James's son, and John's wife were presented at the Quarter Sessions in 1657 and were named as recusants in 1678. In the same year, following a search of John's property, the constables scheduled a large gun as having been seized,[30] and in his will of 1680 he bequeathed his residuary estate to his cousin the recusant Peter Mawson, yeoman, and Miles Beck in a form which suggests a bequest for pious uses. (Appendix 2). At his burial the churchwardens were paid 1s. for the cloth which covered his coffin overnight and 1s. 6d. for his coffin. There was evidently no need for secrecy.[31] Another recusant, Thomas Pickering, who had moved to Fawcett Forest, died in 1709. He had petitioned for charity; he had 'lived without being chargeable to the hamlett, but by reason of his old age and infirmity is no longer able to relieve himself without the charity of his neighbours' and it was ordered that 'the sum of ten pence per week be paid aforesaid to the said Thomas Pickering till further order'.[32]

Although it is not possible to produce evidence that John's son and grandson were recusants, his granddaughter Margaret was married by a priest to John Thornburgh and their first child was baptised at Bowbank on the 13th March 1703/4.[33] John's other granddaughter Barbara was married by the same priest to Nicholas Thornburgh, a Catholic, and their first child was baptised at Garnet Folds in Skelsmergh.[34] They later moved to Kendal where Nicholas was an innkeeper.[35] Ultimately Bowbank was sold by John Pickering, junior, and his son, Lancelot, to the diocese of Chester in 1723/4.[36] The administration of the goods of John Pickering of Forest Hall was granted to his principal creditor.[37]

Social Organisation in the Barony of Kendal, 1695

Some idea of the social divisions within the community can be discovered from the census taken in other parts of the Barony in August 1695 under the Acts imposing taxation on marriages, births, deaths, bachelors over 25 years and widowers without children. The relative proportion of each group is as follows:

Status	%
Gentry	1.14
Yeomen	13.05
Husbandmen	13.46
Tradesmen	31.55
Labourers & Servants	20.65
Pensioners & Poor	20.15

Source: K.R.O. WQ/1 - Indictment Book p. 32

The inclusion of Kendal has distorted the percentage for tradesmen but the overall picture for the countryside is an equal split between those with some financial standing and those who were labourers or poor. The few gentry were the lords of the manors, the yeomen were farmers and free tenants required in principle to attend the manorial courts, and the husbandmen were the customary tenant farmers, whose land could be inherited or sold.

The tradesmen formed part of those with financial standing within the community and the 1657 Presentments assist in identifying the trade of a few recusants.[38] Elizabeth Atkinson's husband and Arthur Gilpin were described as wallers. Richard Ayray was a watchmaker, John Harrison a tailor and Robert Nicholson a butcher. Agnes Harrison and Isabel Nicholson, the widows of the tailor and butcher, were described as beggars in 1678, as were the spinsters Elizabeth Elleray and Margaret Warriner.[39] The recusant Thomas Thwaites, carpenter, bought an estate in 1616 from Martin Beck in the adjoining constablewick of Whitwell and Selside for £95[40] and his son John later petitioned to contract for his estate, which had been sequestered prior to his father's death in 1650.[41] Although it is not possible to give the social status of the remaining Poll Tax payers, the names Holme, Jackson, Machell, Summer, Tunstall and Wharton suggest they may have been customary tenants or tradesmen rather than the poor or labourers.

As a social class, the labourers, servants, pensioners and poor, comprising between 40% to 50% of the population, appear rarely to have been convicted of recusancy: it may be that Catholicism had no appeal for this section of the community, or it is more likely that they were ignored by those in authority. In all, a total of 21 convicted popish recusants resident in Kendal were assessed for Poll Tax between 1626 and 1640 and 30 adult recusants paying Poll Tax in 1641. In any event these must have accounted for a significant proportion of the population in Skelsmergh, which was unlikely to have exceeded the 1801 figure of 247. This figure does not include children and persons exempt from payment of the tax.

Kendal is a example of a town in which the number of Catholics increased while those in the countryside decreased. This phenomenon was probably due to the recusancy legislation, which resulted in the minor gentry and the non-gentry landowners being unable to retain ownership of their properties and being forced to move into the town.

The Platt Family

One of the most persistent or obstinate recusants was Oliver Platt who died in 1685/6 at the age of 96. He was probably the son of Peter Platt, a chandler in Kendal. It seems unlikely that Oliver and his wife Ellin were recusants before 1623, as the baptisms of their son, Peter and their daughter, Ann, are recorded in the Kendal parish register. However, in that year Oliver Platt was presented at the Archdeaconry Court for failing to have his children baptised at his parish church.[42]

During the rebuilding of the Black Horse and Rainbow Inn on Highgate, Kendal, in 1836, an oak table and oak panel were found inscribed 'O.P. E.P. 1638', which could indicate that the Platts lived at this property. Certainly it was owned by Robert Stephenson of Dodding Green in 1716, as he charged it with a payment of £6 to the Catholic priest of Kendal for the poor to be distributed on St Thomas's Day.[43] Oliver Platt was in business in Kendal, probably a chandler like his father, and his tokens were dated 1659.[44] Oliver Platt's family were papists for at least five generations and in his 1685/86 will he appointed his widowed daughter-in-law Elizabeth as the sole executrix and residuary beneficiary.[45] Mr Peter Mawson and James Dixon were supervisors and they were probably the recusants Peter Mawson, yeoman, of Skelsmergh and James Dixon, stockinger, who was living on Highgate in 1695. Oliver Platt charged his estate at Garthrow in Skelsmergh with payment of his legacies and his beneficiaries included a nephew who was apprenticed to a pewterer and his grandson Oliver Platt. A later Oliver Platt had a son Peter baptised by the priest, Thomas Roydon, at Summerhow on the 14th January 1717/18. Summerhow was registered by an

Oliver Platt as a papist's estate in 1722[46] and he was listed with 10 others as a papist Freeholder for the 1723 Election.[47]

The Dixon Family

James Dixon, a supervisor of the Platts' 1685/6 will, was a 'stockiner', and he lived amongst the more prosperous tradesmen on Highgate, where he and his wife, Dorothy, were named as recusants.[48] This James Dixon was summoned to appear at the Moot Hall, Kendal, on Saturday 5 June 1680 for the tendering of the Oaths of Supremacy and Allegiance. It seems unlikely that he appeared, as very few did so at this time.[49]

Bishop Leyburn's 1687 list of confirmations at Witherslack (see Appendix 4) includes the names of Nathaniel Dixon, James Dixon and Mary Dixon, of whom Nathaniel can be identified as James Dixon's son and living on Stramongate with his wife, Agnes, and servant Nicholas Dixon in 1695. The baptisms of their children are recorded in Thomas Roydon's registers.[50]

In 1701 there was considerable dissatisfaction with the conduct of the meat trade in Kendal and formal steps were taken to recognise a fraternity of butchers. A constitution was approved with by-laws requiring apprenticeships, wardens and a beadle. Nathaniel Dixon was appointed one of the first wardens and again as warden from 1710 to 1718.[51]

The godparents of Nathaniel's children were his brother Nicholas Dixon, John Leyburn, Elizabeth Nuby, Margaret Atkinson, John Pickering senior, Mary [Pickering], and Margaret Wilkinson. These baptisms are not recorded in the Anglican parish registers except for a 'Margaret' on the date Mary was baptised. Nathaniel Dixon also stood as godfather to James, son of Peter and Ann Borwick, in 1716 and to Rowland, son of Nicholas and Barbara Thornburgh, in 1717, whose marriages the priest Roydon also records. In the 1767 Return of Papists, Peter Borwick is described as a cordwainer, aged 80, as also are members of the Thornborough family.[52]

Nathaniel Dixon, the butcher, owned a dwelling-house, paddock or close in or near Rotten Row Lane, Kendal, at a yearly rent of 1s. and a burgage or dwelling house in Old Hallow Lane, Kendal, 'wherein I do dwell' at 2s. annual rent due to Thomas Fletcher Esq. These properties were registered as a papist's estate and valued at £8 per annum in 1723.[53] Nathaniel Dixon's property, the house on the north side of All Hallows' Lane was purchased by the recusant Peter Borwick, cordwainer, who bequeathed it to his daughter Catherine Borwick in 1764 for life and then to his son James, a currier, who was living in Cockermouth when these children sold it in 1786.[54]

Nathaniel Dixon died in 1728 and his widow Agnes with Roland Atkinson of Firbank, yeoman, entered into the usual bond for the administration of his goods.[55] In 1695 when Nathaniel Dixon was living in Stramongate his neighbours included the Catholic Brian Gant, barber, and his wife Jane and their four children.[56] The Gants' only son John died in 1702, to be followed by Brian in 1705. Jane their daughter was godmother at the baptisms of James Benson, Elizabeth Fox and Margaret Kirby.[57] Nicholas Dixon, Nathaniel's brother, was also a butcher and served as warden between 1702 and 1710 for the Kendal fraternity of butchers. He and his wife Mary, who had been the wife of Thomas Brabin, registered her charge on Beetham Hall as a papist's estate in 1723.[58] This Nicholas stood as godfather at the baptisms of Ellen Benson, his nephew James Dixon, Elizabeth Fox, Ralph Kendal, Margaret Kirby and William Strickland between 1702 and 1711.[59] Another of the Dixon family, Arthur, was probably the butcher and beneficiary mentioned in Robert Stepthenson's will of 1718/19 and who stood as godfather to Catherine Borwick in 1714, Hester Redhead in 1720 and Edward Russell in 1721.[60] It is possible that the Arthur Dixon, who appeared as a butcher in the 1767 Return of Papists as living in Highgate, may have been a son of the earlier Arthur Dixon who was also a tenant of Robert Stephenson. The earliest register of the Kendal Catholic Church records the baptisms of the children of an Arthur and Elizabeth Dixon in 1763 and 1766,[61] and the Platts and Dixons were not the only families which remained loyal to the faith in a town not renowned for its Papist sympathies.

The Borwick Family

The Borwicks were another Catholic family in Kendal and it is probable that Anthony Borwick, the only innholder in Stramongate in 1695, was the father of the recusants Peter Borwick and John Borwick, whose marriage to Isabel Richard was witnessed by Peter Platt, Oliver Platt and Agnes Holmes. The godfather of John Borwick's son, Anthony, was the same Oliver Platt who also stood as a witness to the marriages of Peter Borwick and Ann Pennington in 1714 and Anne Borwick and John Walker in 1715.[62]

The names of the godparents to the children of these marriages, Robert Benson, Ann Holmes, Arthur Dixon, Ann Borwick, Nathaniel Dixon, Sarah Redhead, Nicholas Dixon, Margaret Barrow, Thomas Barrow, and Mary Benson, show that there was a network of families of the common sort, small in number but religiously active.

It is possible to identify the occupations of some of the convicted popish recusants or papists who lived in the other constablewicks and it is known that, in addition to farmers, John Becke was a tanner, James Dennison a tailor, Roger Harrison a miller and John Lumley a saddler.[63]

Priests in Kendal and District

Three Tyburn martyrs, Thomas Sprott alias Parker, Thomas Somers alias Wilson and the bookseller John Duckett were all born in Skelsmergh. Thomas Somers at one time ran a school in Grayrigg.[64] In the 1880's a discovery was made of a secret chamber or hiding-place at Selside Hall:

> In a closet on the first floor of the central block, the farmer showed us that the plank flooring had an aperture cut in it, 2½ feet by 1½ feet, which led underneath by a passage 3 feet long into a vacant space in the partition wall. The hole did not allow the passage of a man's body, but on exploring under the roof we found an aperture through which a man might be let down into a secret cavity contrived in the thickness of the cross hall. The hole in the floor below seemed to be intended for passing in provisions and affording ventilation.[65]

Selside Hall was owned by the Thornburgh family, who were recusants for several generations, and it is probable that Mass was said there.

The identification of priests becomes easier at the turn of the century. The registers of Thomas Roydon record details of 149 baptisms, 41 reconciliations, 38 marriages and 118 deaths, naming some 500 persons over a period commencing in October 1699 and ending in February 1721/22.[66]

The area covered by Roydon's 'Westmorland Circuit' was from Yealand in Lancashire to Penrith in Cumberland and his registers were not the only registers kept by priests serving this community, as it is known that George Leyburn had his own register.[67] Other priests officated at baptisms and marriages within the Barony: they included Nicholas Leyburn, George's brother; a 'Mr Taylor' (probably William Taylor S.J. who was at the adjoining mission known as 'The Manor' of Low Furness); and a 'Mr B'.[68] 'Mr B.' baptised a Strickland, Agnes the daughter of John and Mary Strickland, on 23 Ocotober 1714; Roydon also records the death of a priest, Thomas Weedon of Thurnham, whose name appears in the Kendal parish burial register as 'Mr Thomas Weedon of Syzergh', which suggests that the Strickland family had their own or visiting chaplains.[69] In the 1730s priests known to have been in Kendal include Dom James (Wilfrid) Witham O.S.B. and Dom William Bede Hutton O.S.B.; and the fact that the martyr Thomas Pickering was a laybrother of the same order suggests that the Benedictines may have been active in this area at an earlier date. The Kendal parish register records that a papist priest married John Borwick and Dorothy Jackson, both of Kendal, on 31 May 1739, and that the 'Papist Priest Mr Barnes' married Thomas Coupland and Eliza Holme on 23 April 1745. Robert Stephenson of Skelsmergh gave his house at Dodding Green to the Church as a residence for the priest on the 'Westmorland Circuit' and his charities supported James Gandy, the first resident priest in Kendal.[70] According to tradition Mass was said at the tavern 'Hie Coomber', Horncup Hall and other houses in Kendal, with its first chapel in the down yard of 27 Stramongate in what may have been a disused warehouse.[71]

The tenacity of Catholics in Kendal which has been explored presents a very different picture from that of Bossy quoted above. An effective mission was sustained in this town, even though the number of Catholics was small. At the beginning of this article I took four quotations which I considered to be misleading and in which historians have treated absence of evidence to be evidence of absence, relying on a selection of government or local government returns to under-estimate the strength of Catholicism and to assume that all Catholics were connected with the gentry.

The Poll Tax returns, Subsidy Rolls, Quarter Sessions proceedings, probate records and registers of papists estates can be combined with Bishop Leyburn's lists of Confirmations and Catholic registers to provide evidence to disprove previous estimates of the strength of Catholicism and unproven assumptions relating to their social status. This article has shown that through the correlation of these and other records it is possible to reconstruct the histories of the Catholic families of Kendal, the majority of whom were beneath the rank of gentry.

NOTES

1 C.M.L. Bouch & G.P. Jones, *The Lake Counties, 1500-1830* (1961), p. 174.
2 H.R. Trevor-Roper, *The Gentry, 1540-1640* (1975), p. 31.
3 Bossy, *Catholics*, p. 96.
4 John A. Hilton, 'The Cumbrian Catholics', *Northern History* 16 (1980), pp. 41, 58.
5 C.R.S. 5 (1908), p. 221.
6 K.R.O.WD/TE/110, Town End MSS.
7 Statutes of the Realm 1 Car. I. c.6, 3 Car. I. c.8, 16 Car. I.c.4.
8 Stephen Dowell, *History of Taxation and Taxes in England,* vol. 1, p. 151.
9 P.R.O., SP 16/31/30.
10 P.R.O. E401/1912, 1913 & 1915.
11 P.R.O. E179/195/66 & 71.
12 K.R.O. WD/TE/110 & WD/RY/Box 102. I should like to thank Richard Hall, the archivist, for directing my attention to the Rolls in the Fleming Papers.
13 K.R.O. WD/RY/HMC/173.

14 Bossy, *Catholics*, p. 175.
15 Car. R.O. Machell MSS. 2, p. 117.
16 K.R.O. WD/RY/Box 102 Sir Daniel Fleming's Notebook, pp. 196, 201.
17 C. Talbot ed., *Miscellaneous Catholic Records* (C.R.S. 53, 1960), p. 341.
18 Ches.R.O. EDV/1/25 Correction Book 1623.
19 K.R.O. Levens Hall MSS. Court Rolls; P.R.O. E377/55.
20 Car.R.O. Machell MSS. vol. 2, p. 119; K.R.O. WQ/1/4 Easter 1696.
21 Pres.R.O. WDFC/RC/2 Thomas Roydon, Composite Register, D58.
22 Pres.R.O. WDFC/RC/2 Thomas Roydon, Composite Register, M.
23 J.F. Curwen ed., William Farrar, *Records of the Barony of Kendal*, vol. 1 (1923), p. 263.
24 I am grateful to Mrs Alison Wright, who obtained this information from the Goldsmiths' Company for her research on Bishop Leyburn.
25 K.R.O. WD/RY/HMC/2105.
26 J.H. Pollen ed., *Unpublished Documents relating to the English Martyrs Vol. 1, 1584-1603* (C.R.S. 5, 1908), p. 181.
27 Cornelius Nicolson, *Annals of Kendal* (1861), p. 162.
28 Although the Quarter Session books for this period have not survived, at Carlisle Record Office there are the Hill MSS. and the names of recusants are given in vol. 1, p. 397, vol. 3, pp. 397 & 465; Ches.R.O. EDV/1/25 Correction Book 1623.
29 Hugh Bowler, 'Blessed Thomas Pickering: Some New Facts', *Downside Review* (1940), p. 58.
30 John Curwen, *Records of Kendal* vol. 3 (1926), p. 44.
31 K.R.O. WPP/38, Churchwardens' Accounts.
32 K.R.O. WQ/0/2, p. 217 Christmas 1707.
33 Pres.R.O. WDFC/RC/Thomas Roydon, Composite Register, B37.
34 Pres.R.O. WDFC/RC/Thomas Roydon, Composite Register, B38.
35 K.R.O. Dr. Fahy's papers.
36 K.R.O. WQ/R/P/Box 2, Indenture 21 February 1723/4.
37 Pres.R.O. WR WK, Administrations.
38 K.R.O. WQ/1, Indictment Book, p. 32.
39 K.R.O. WD/RY/HMC/2105.
40 K.R.O. WDX/25/1, Bargain and Sale, 14 July 1615.
41 *Calendar of Committee for Compounding,* Part 4, 2994-2995.
42 Ches.R.O. EDV/1/25, Correction Book 1623, p. 117b.
43 Nicholson, *Annals of Kendal*, p. 221.
44 Nicholson, *Annals of Kendal*, p. 132.
45 Pres.R.O. WR WK,Wills.
46 Pres.R.O. Thomas Roydon, Composite Register B and Baptismal Register 123; K.R.O. WQ/R/P, Box 1, Papist Estate Register, p. 6.
47 Car.R.O. D/Lons/L, Elections 1723.
48 K.R.O. WD/RY/HMC/2105; J.D. Marshall, 'Kendal in the late seventeenth and eighteenth centuries', *Transactions of the Cumberland & Westmorland Antiquarian & Archaeological Society* (1975), p. 188.
49 K.R.O. WD/RY/Box 31.
50 1695 Return; WD/RY/Box 32; Pres.R.O. Roydon's Baptismal Register 2, 7, 34, 55.
51 K.R.O. , Kendal Borough Orders 1696-1764.
52 Pres.R.O. Roydon's Baptismal Register 118 & 119; Composite Register M25 & M6.
53 K.R.O., WQ/R/P Papists Estate Register, p. 3; Curwen, *Records of Kendal*, vol. 3, p. 50.
54 K.R.O. , WQ/R/P Box 2, Indenture 11 December 1786.
55 Pres.R.O. WR WK Administrations.
56 K.R.O. , 1695 Returns WD/RY/Box 31.
57 Pres.R.O. Roydon's Baptismal Register, pp. 130, 57, 76.

[58] K.R.O. , WQ/R/P Papists Estates Register, p. 27.
[59] Pres.R.O. Roydon's Baptismal Register, pp. 24, 55, 57, 63, 76, 89.
[60] Pres.R.O. Roydon's Baptismal Register, pp. 104, 140, 145.
[61] The original register was lodged at the P.R.O. but there is a microfilm copy at K.R.O.
[62] Pres.R.O. Roydon's Composite Register, M25, M30.
[63] K.R.O. , Browne MSS. vol. 15, p. 2; K.R.O. WQ/1/4 Indictments 1691.
[64] Anstruther 1, p. 329; Anstruther 2, p. 302.
[65] M.W. Taylor, 'The Old Manorial Halls of Westmorland and Cumberland', *Cumberland & Westmorland Antiquarian & Archaeological Society Extra Series* 8 (1892), p. 228.
[66] Pres.R.O. Thomas Roydon's Registers.
[67] Pres. R.O. Composite Register B52, M16, D45.
[68] Pres. R.O. Composite Register, M6, M8, B97.
[69] Pres. R.O. Composite Register D36 & Register of Deaths 37.
[70] Brian C. Foley, *Some People of the Penal Times* (1991), p. 39.
[71] J.F. Curwen, *Kirkbie Kendall* (1900), pp. 190, 361, 395.

APPENDIX 1: LAY SUBSIDIES 1625 - 1641

Convicted Recusants in the Lay Subsidies for the Kendal and Londsdale wards, Westmorland, from 1625 to 1641.

*	Name in brackets given
N	Named in return
D	Name deleted in return
X	No return for township
A	1625 Act 2nd subsidy paid 1626
B	1627 Act 1st and 2nd Subsidy paid 1628
C	1627 Act 3rd Subsidy paid 1628
D	1640 Act 1st and 2nd Subsidy paid 1641
E	1640 Act 3rd and 4th Subsidy paid in 1641

KENDAL WARD	**1626**	**1628**		**1641**	
Beetham and Farleton	**A**	**B**	**C**	**D**	**E**
Alice Borwick	-	-	-	-	N
John Borwick	-	-	-	-	N
and his wife	-	-	-	-	N
Anne Bouskell	-	-	-	N	N
Francis Bradley	-	-	-	N	N
Hillarie Bradley	N	N	N	N	N
and [Eliz:] his wife	N	N	N	N	N*
Thomas Bradley	-	-	-	-	N
William Bradley	N	N	N	N	N
[Elizabeth] his wife	-	N	N	N	N*
John Buskell	-	-	-	-	N
Ralph Buskell	-	-	-	N	N
and his wife	-	-	-	N	N
Richard Croxton	-	-	-	N	N
and his wife	-	-	-	N	N
Francis Dabridgcourt	-	-	-	N	N
Anne Ducket	N	N	N	N	N
Anthony Ducket	N	N	N	N	N
and his wife	-	-	-	N	N
Charles Ducket	-	-	-	N	N
Christopher Helme	N	N	N	-	N
Richard Hutchinson	-	-	-	-	N

	A	B	C	D	E
Dorothie Johnson	-	-	-	N	N
Grace Johnson	-	N	-	-	-
Thomas Laybourne	N	N	N	N	N
and [Marye] his wife	N	N*	N*	N	N*
Francis Middleton	-	-	-	-	N
Ellin Pollen	-	-	-	-	N
Lucie Spence	-	-	-	-	N
Jamie Smith	N	-	D	-	-
and his wife	N	-	-	-	-
Crosthwait and Lyth					
Dothie Wilkinson	-	-	-	N	-
Katherine Wales	-	-	-	-	N
Docker					
Anthone Beethome	-	-	-	-	N
Marie Duckett	-	-	-	N	N
Margarie Gilpin	-	-	N	-	-
Alexander Hewetson	-	N	N	-	-
Myles Hewetson	-	N	N	-	-
Andrew Moser	-	-	-	N	N
Agnes Thompson	-	-	-	-	N
Anthonie Tunstall	-	-	-	-	N
Dorothie Warriner	-	-	-	-	N
John Washinton	-	N	N	N	N
and Jane or Jenet his wife	-	N	N	N	N
Randall Washington	-	-	-	N	N
Marian his wife	-	-	-	N	N
Grayrigge					
Anthonie Duckett Esquire a convicted recusant in lands £6	See below			N	N
Francis Bennett	-	-	-	-	N
Dorothie Bennison	-	-	-	-	N
Roger Borwicke	-	-	-	-	N
Isabell Boulton	-	-	-	-	N
Priscilla Cowpland	-	-	-	-	N

	A	B	C	D	E
Jane Dennison	-	-	N	-	-
Margaret Dennison	N	-	N	-	-
Thomas Denison	-	-	-	N	N
Elinor Dickonson	-	D	N	-	-
Alice Dover	-	-	N	-	-
Alice Dowker	-	-	N	-	-
Anthony Ducket Esq.	N	N	N	See above	
and Elizabeth his wife	N	N	N	N	N
Francis Ducket	N	N	N	-	N
James Duckett	-	-	-	N	N
Marie his wife	-	-	-	N	N
Jane ye Lady Ducket	N	N	N	-	-
Jane Ducket	N	-	-	-	-
Katerine Ducket	N	N	N	N	N
Will[ia]m Ducket	N	N	N	-	-
Sibell Ewan	-	-	N	-	-
Jane the wife of Michaell Fairer	N	-	N	-	N
Marian Gilpin	-	-	N	-	-
Marie Hinde	-	-	-	-	N
Richard Hutchinson	-	-	N	-	-
Issabell Johnson	-	-	N	-	-
James Johnson	-	-	-	N	N
Thomas Johnson	-	-	N	-	N
Francis Kitchin	-	-	N	-	-
Margaret Lupton	-	-	-	N	N
Andrew Moser	-	-	N	-	-
Thomas Punder	-	N	N	-	-
Richard Robson	-	-	N	-	-
Alice Shawe	-	-	N	-	-
Anne the wife of George Sheppard	N	-	-	-	-
Issabell Sleddall	-	-	-	-	N
Agnes Sum[m]ers	-	-	-	-	N
Thomas Tomlinson	-	N	N	-	-

	A	B	C	D	E
Anne Washington	N	N	N	N	N
Francis Washington	-	-	-	N	N
JohnWashington	-	-	-	N	N
James Washington	-	-	N	N	N
Randall Washington	N	-	-	-	-
Richard Washington	N	N	N	N	N
Thomas Washington	N	N	N	N	N
Gressmire					
John Fleeming Esq.	N	-	-	-	-
Helsington					
Thomas Dodgson	-	-	-	N	N
[Agnes] his wife	-	-	-	N	N*
Francis Ducket	N	-	-	-	-
and Mary his wife	N	-	-	-	-
George Maychell	N	-	N	-	-
Margaret his wife	-	-	N	-	-
Margaret Moore	N	-	-	-	-
John Strickland	N	N	N	-	-
and Anne his wife	N	N	N	-	-
Walter Strickland gent.	-	-	-	-	N
Kirkby Kendall					
Katherine Ayrey	-	N	-	-	-
Richard Ayray	-	-	-	N	N
Anthony Bethome	-	N	N	-	-
Margaret Hodgson	-	-	-	N	N
Agnes the wife of Rowland Jeninges	N	N	N	-	-
Isabell wife of Will[iam] Jennings	-	N	N	-	-
Margaret Moore	-	-	-	-	N
Henry Pearson	-	N	N	-	-
Richard Pearson	-	N	N	-	-
and [Agnes] his wife	-	N	N*	-	-
Oliver Platt	N	N	N	N	N
[Ellin] his wife	N	N	N	N*	N*

	A	B	C	D	E
Peter Platt	-	-	-	N	N
Elizabeth his wife	-	-	-	N	N
John Saule	-	-	-	N	N
Dorothie his wife	-	-	-	N	N
Frances Taylor	-	-	-	-	N
Jane Wilkinson	-	-	-	-	N
John Wilkinson	-	N	-	-	-
Will[ia]m Wilkinson	-	N	N	-	-
and his wife	-	N	N	-	-
Lamrigge					
Will[ia]m Warrin[er]	-	-	N	-	-
Anthony Beethome		-	-	N	-
Natland					
James Mackereth	N	-	-	-	-
Tabitha Williamson	N	-	-	-	-
John Strickland	-	-	-	N	N
Watsfeild and Graveshipp					
Anthonie Fletcher	-	-	-	-	N
and his wife	-	-	-	-	N
Thomas Helme	-	-	-	N	N
[Ellin] his wife	-	-	-	N	N*
Agnes Stainbanch	-	-	-	-	N
Ellin Stainbanch widdowe	-	-	-	N	N
Over Staveley					
Jervice Strickland	N	X	-	-	-
George Strickland	-	X	N	-	-
Rydall and Loughrigge					
John Fleming Esq. in landes £6 [a convicted recusant]	N	N	N	N	N
Dorothie Barbon	-	-	-	N	N
Salamon Benson	-	-	-	N	N
Robert Gardiner	-	-	-	N	N
Edward Harrison	-	-	-	N	N
Katerine Harrison	-	-	-	-	N

	A	B	C	D	E
Lancelot Harrison	-	-	-	-	N
Richard Harison	-	-	-	N	N
Richard Willson	-	-	-	-	N
Skatthwaiterigge Hay and Hutton in the Haye					
Agnes, wife of Tho[mas] Atkinson	N	X	N	N	N
Edward Atkinson	N	X	N	-	-
John Atkinson	N	X	N	N	N
Alice his wife	-	X	-	N	-
Thomas Atkinson	N	X	-	N	-
Agnes Becke	-	X	-	-	N
Annas Becke	-	X	-	-	N
Ellin Becke	-	X	-	-	N
John Becke	N	X	N	N	N
Miles Becke	N	X	N	-	-
and Ellinor his wife	N	X	N	N	-
Richard Becke	N	X	D	N	N
Walter Becke	-	X	-	N	N
James Benson	N	X	-	-	-
Anthony Fletcher	N	X	N	-	-
and Ellin or Ellinor his wife	N	X	N	-	-
Anthony Hodgson	N	X	N	-	-
and Cicily his wife	N	X	N	-	N
John Hodgson	N	X	N	-	-
and Alice his wife	N	X	N	-	-
Katherine Hodgson	N	X	-	N	N
Margaret Hodgson	-	X	-	N	N
Anne Kilner	N	X	D	-	-
Jane Nicholson	-	X	-	-	N
James Nicolson	-	X	-	N	-
Eliz: Speight	-	X	-	N	N

	A	B	C	D	E
Skelsmergh & Patton					
John [Leybourne] [in lands] £3	-	X	N		
Esquier a convicted recusant in goods £1		X		N	N
Anthony Atkinson	-	X	D	-	-
and Issabell his wife	-	X	N	-	-
Jenet Atkinson	-	X	N	-	-
Francis Ducket	-	X	N	-	-
and Marie his wife	-	X	N	-	-
Thomas Ducket	-	X	N	-	-
James Edmundson	-	X	N	-	N
John Edmundson	-	X	D	-	N
and Agnes his wife	-	X	D	-	-
Jane wife of John Edmunson	-	X	-	-	N
Agnes Garnett	-	X	-	N	N
Wife of John Garnett	-	X	-	-	N
Thomas Garnet	-	X	-	-	N
Agnes the wife of Will(ia)m Gilpin	-	X	N	-	-
Arthur Gilpin	-	X	N	-	-
Bartho Gilpin	-	X	N	-	-
Christopher Gilpin	N	X	-	-	-
and Anne his wife	N	X	-	-	-
Edward Gilpin	N	X	-	-	-
and Francis his wife	N	X	-	-	-
Jason Gilpin	N	X	-	N	N
and Alice his wife	N	X	-	-	-
John Gilpin	-	X	N	-	-
Elizabeth his wife	-	X	N	-	-
George Gilpin	-	X	N	-	-
Thomas Gilpin	-	X	N	-	-
Richard Harrison th[e] elder	-	X	N	-	-
Richard Harrson	N	X	N	-	N
Anne Helme	-	X	-	-	N
[Anne] the wife of John Jackson	-	X	N*	N	-

	A	B	C	D	E
John Jackson	-	X	-	-	N
Jane Maichell ux[or]	-	X	-	-	N
Margaret Mowson	N	X	N	-	-
Nicholas Mowson	N	X	N	N	N
and Alice or Agnes his wife	N	X	N	N	N
Robert Mowson	N	X	N	N	N
Elizabeth Mowson	N	X	N	-	-
James Nicolson	-	X	D	-	-
Dorothie Patch	-	X	D	-	N
Jenet Patch	-	X	D	-	N
Joseph Patch	-	X	D	-	-
William Patch	-	X	-	-	N
James Pickeringe	N	X	-	N	N
and [Issabell] his wife	N*	X	-	N	N
John Pickeringe	-	X	-	N	N
Anne his wife	-	X	-	N	N
Elizabeth Pickeringe	-	X	-	-	N
Issabell Pickeringe	-	X	-	-	N
Lancelote Pickeringe	-	X	-	N	N
Margaret his wife	-	X	-	N	N
Thomas Sleddall	-	X	-	N	N
Dorothie his wife	-	X	-	N	N
Anthonie Stevenson	-	X	-	N	N
Anne his wife	-	X	-	N	N
Anthony Sum[m]er	-	X	N	-	-
Edward Thwaites	-	X	N	-	-
Margaret Thwaites	-	X	N	-	-
Thomas Tunstall	-	X	D	-	-
Emme his wife	-	X	N	-	-
Katerine Waler	-	X	N	-	-
William Warton	N	X	-	-	-
and Alice his wife	N	X	-	-	-
Anthony Wharton	-	X	-	N	-
and his wife	-	X	-	N	-

	A	B	C	D	E
Stainton					
Charles Saule	-	-	-	N	N
Jane his wife	-	-	-	N	N
Katherine Helme	-	-	-	-	N
Charles Birkenhead	-	-	-	-	N
Thomas Birkenhead	-	-	-	N	N
[Jenet] his wife	-	-	-	N	N*
Strickland Ketle and Strickland Roger					
Roger Walker	N	X	N	N	N
[Agnes] his wife	N	X	N*	-	-
Richard Armstrong	N	X	N	-	-
[Elizabeth] his wife	N	X	N*	-	-
Cicilie Newbie	N	X	D	-	-
Bernard Walker	-	-	N	N	-
Margaret his wife	-	-	-	N	-
Alice Becke	-	-	N	-	-
Frances Chamley	-	-	-	N	N
Margaret [wife of Mr] Hastwhitle	-	-	-	N	N*
Underbarrow and Bradley Feild					
Jane Wilkinson	N	-	-	-	-
Randall Newby	-	N	-	-	-
Dorothie Wilkinson	-	N	-	-	N
Whinfell					
Dorothie Atkinson	-	-	-	N	N
Hugh Ayrey	-	-	N	-	-
Thomas Ayrey	N	N	N	-	-
James Dennison	N	N	N	-	N
and [Margaret] his wife	N	N*	N*	-	N*
John Fawcet	N	N	N	-	-
and [Mabell] his wife	N	N*	N*	-	-
Bartholemew Gillpin	-	-	-	N	N
Margaret his wife	-	-	-	N	N

	A	B	C	D	E
Christopher Gillpin	-	-	-	N	N
[Anne] his wife	-	-	-	N	N*
Thomas Gillpin	-	-	-	N	N
Margaret or Mary his wife	-	-	-	N	N
Agnes Helme	-	-	-	-	N
Isabell the wife of Richard Helme	-	N	N	-	N
Cicilia Lickbarrowe	-	-	-	-	N
Thomas Mathew	N	-	N	-	-
[Issabell] his wife	N	-	N*	-	-
William Newbie	N	N	N	N	N
and [Jennett] his wife	N	N*	N*	N*	N*
Margaret Nicholson	-	-	-	N	N
Richard Nicholson	-	-	-	-	N
James Pearson	-	-	-	N	-
Agnes his wife	-	-	-	N	-
Richard Pearson	N	N	N	N	N
and [Mabell] his wife	N	N*	N*	N*	N*
Agnes Simpson	-	-	-	-	N
Robert Stainbancke	-	-	N	-	-
Dorotha his wife	-	-	N	-	-
Anne the wife of Myles Stevenson	-	N	N	-	-
John Stephenson	-	-	-	N	N
Nicholas Sum[m]er	N	-	-	-	-
and his daughter	N	-	-	-	-
Anthony Wharton	N	N	N	-	-
William Warton	-	-	-	N	N
Anthonie Wilkinson	-	-	-	N	N
Whitwell and Selside					
Issabell the wife of Edward Dodding	-	-	N	-	-
Agnes Gilpin wife of [William]	N*	N*	-	N	N
Arthure Gilpin	N	N	-	N	N

	A	B	C	D	E
Bartholemew Gilpin	N	N	-	-	-
Dorothie Gilpin	-	-	-	N	N
George Gilpin	N	N	-	-	N
Thomas Gilpin	N	-	-	-	-
John Hayton [or Heyton or Leyton]	N	N	N	-	N
Issabell Simme	-	-	N	-	-
Margaret Thomson	N	-	-	-	-
Thomas Thornburgh	-	-	N	-	-
Jane Thornburg	-	-	N	-	
Thomas Thwaites	N	N	-	-	N
Emme Tunstall wife of Tho[mas]	N	N	-	-	-
Thomas Tunstall	-	-	-	N	N
Issabell Ward wife of Edw: Ward	N	D	-	-	-
Witherslacke Methop and Ovey					
William Bethome	N	-	N	-	-
Thomas Bradley	N	N	N	-	-
Ellin Calvert	-	-	-	N	N
Grace Crosfeild	-	-	-	N	N
Rowland Crossfeild	-	-	-	N	N
Guy Cowp(er)thait	-	N	N	-	-
Marye his wife	-	N	-	-	-
Marie Curwen	N	-	N	-	-
Alice Griggson	-	-	-	N	N
Walter Kendal	-	-	-	N	N
Guy Kitchin	N	-	-	-	-
John Labourne Esqr	N	-	-	-	-
Ux[or] John Laybourne Ar[miger]	-	-	-	N	N
Christopher Skirret	-	-	-	N	N
William Thornburgh gent.	-	-	-	N	N
Katherine Ux[or]	-	-	-	N	N
Row[land]Thorneburgh	-	-	-	N	N

	A	B	C	D	E
LONSDALE WARD					
Burton					
Robert Middleton gent.	-	-	-	-	N
and his wife	-	-	-	-	N
Firbancke					
George Atkinson	-	-	-	N	N
[Bridgett] his wife	-	-	-	N	N
Hutton Roofe and Casterton					
Mary the wife of John Wood	-	N	D	-	-
Elizabeth Middleton	-	-	D	-	-
Killington					
Lucie Kitson	-	-	-	N	N
Kirby Lonsdale					
Thomas Banckes	-	-	-	-	N
and his wife	-	-	-	-	N
Middleton					
Joane the wife of Edward Middleton	-	N	-	-	-
Frances [the wife of Tho:], Pickeringe	-	-	-	N	N*
Bridgett Wood	-	-	-	N	N

APPENDIX 2: WILL OF JOHN PICKERING

Abstract of the Will and Inventory of John Pickering elder of Bowbank in Skelsmergh, yeoman, dated 1 March 1679/80.

Legacies charged on Bowbank:

1. Andrew Wharton my nephew (if he will accept) £5
   James Wharton his brother 50/-
   his sister Dorothy Cowper 20/-
2. Richard Pearson my nephew (if he will accept) £3
   Thomas Pearson 20/-
   James Pearson 20/-
3. Elinor Robinson my neece £3
   her daughter 10/-
   Dorothy Robinson my god-daughter 10/-
   John Robinson 20/-
4. Margaret Beck £17 and my featherbed upon condition 'that they and every of the before mentioned do give security of all bonds whatsoever because I believe all are discharged'.
5. Godson John Pickering son of Thomas Pickering £2
6. Godson John Gilpin
   God-daughter Margaret Atkinson 20/-
   John Bowser
   Nicholas Barns
   Alice Brabin 5/-
7. The poor

Supervisors cousin Peter Mowson and Miles Beck 'desiring anythin remanes to bestowe them according to my mind'.
Executors Rowland Atkinson, John Braban.
Witnesses James Ayrey, Nicholson Braban, John Brabin.
Signed and sealed by John Pickeringe.

APPENDIX 3: SOCIAL GROUPING OF KENDAL CATHOLICS

Certificates and Assessments of Inhabitants (A: Wives; B: Widows and Spinsters; C: Children.)

Class	Barbon	Burton	Casterton	Dillicar	Firbank	Killington	Kirby Kendal	Kirby Lonsdale	Lupton	Mansergh	Middleton
Gentry	-	-	-	-	-	2	11	1	-	1	-
A	-	-	-	-	-	-	9	1	-	-	-
B	-	-	-	-	-	-	-	-	-	1	-
C	-	-	-	-	-	2	16	5	-	-	-
Total						**4**	**36**	**7**		**2**	
Yeomen	16	15	14	4	24	16	21	37	3	10	15
A	7	11	11	4	12	12	17	31	1	5	8
B	15	3	3	-	3	1	-	14	-	11	-
C	11	15	16	2	8	13	29	78	-	18	26
Total	**49**	**44**	**44**	**10**	**47**	**42**	**67**	**160**	**4**	**44**	**49**
Husbandmen	20	5	19	1	14	15	-	36	36	13	31
A	12	5	14	-	2	13	-	30	27	10	15
B	-	3	4	-	2	1	-	8	8	11	8
C	32	13	19	-	2	17	-	65	29	17	23
Total	**64**	**26**	**56**	**1**	**20**	**46**		**139**	**100**	**51**	**77**
Tradesmen	-	22	-	1	5	9	366	-	14	-	-
A	-	15	-	-	1	6	244	-	8	-	-
B	-	3	-	-	-	1	141	-	1	-	-
C	-	18	-	-	-	7	491	-	6	-	-
Total		**58**		**1**	**6**	**23**	**1242**		**29**		
Labourers\Servants	24	5	4	7	8	19	214	41	3	22	40
A	12	3	-	2	-	7	28	13	-	6	24
B	12	-	9	5	4	12	189	46	1	-	14
C	9	-	-	2	-	4	42	22	-	11	26
Total	**57**	**8**	**13**	**16**	**12**	**42**	**473**	**122**	**4**	**39**	**104**
Pensioners \ Poor	10	20	19	-	-	18	80	29	-	9	20
A	8	19	12	-	-	13	65	28	-	8	17
B	8	6	7	-	-	12	75	14	-	6	22
C	28	19	9	-	-	34	151	54	-	11	37
Total	**54**	**64**	**47**			**77**	**371**	**125**		**34**	**96**
Grand Total	224	200	160	28	85	236	2189	553	137	170	326

APPENDIX 4: CONFIRMATIONS BY BISHOP LEYBURN ON 25, 28 AND 29 AUGUST 1687

w = Witherslack d = Dodding Green s = Sizergh

..IGHFEILD	w
ADISON	
James	w
Christopher	w
ARTHERWEIGHT	
James	w
ATKINSON	
Agnes	w
Elizabeth	s
Jane	d
Margaret	w
Margaret	d
Margaret	s
Robert	d
BALY	
Catherine	s
BEAMENT	
Elizabeth	s
BIRKETT	
Elizabeth	w
John	w
Marie	w
BORWICK	
Anthony	w
Catherine	w
Martha	w
Mary	w
BOUSKELL	
Agnes	w
Catherine	w
Jasper	w
BOWS	
Ellen	w
Mary	w
BRABANT	
Elizabeth	s
John	s
Michael	s
BRADSHAW	
John	s
BRATHWAIT	
Agnes	d
Phillip	d
Winifred	s
BROWN	
Elizabeth	d
BUSH	
Genet	w
BURTON	
Jane	w
COWPER	
James	w
CRAGGS	
Ann	s
CROFT	
Barbarie	s
DAWSON	
Elizabeth	w
DENISON	
Agnes	d
Andrew	w
Anthony	d
Edward	d
Isabel	w
James	w
James	w
Jane	d
Margaret	d
Marie	w
DICKINSON	
John	w
DIXON	
Ellen	w
Isabel	w
James	w
John	d
Mary	w
Nathaniel	w
Robert	d
DODSWORTH	
Winifred	d
DUCKET	
Dorothy	w
Elizabeth	d
Mary	w
ELERE	
Elizabeth	w
ELLWOOD	
Agnes	w
ESKIN	
David	w
FAWCETT	
Isabel	w
FLEMING	
Catherine	w
FOXCROFT	
George	w
Mary	w
GANT	
Dorothy	d
Jane	d
Mary	d
GARNETT	
Agnes	w
Anthony	w
Dorothy	w
Dorothy	w
James	w
Marie	
Mary	d
Thomas	
GASTELL	
Jane	w
Margaret	w
GILPIN	
Ann	w
Ann	d
Elizabeth	w
Elizabeth	d
Francis	w
John	w
Margaret	w
Robert	w
Thomas	w
Ursuly	w
GOLD	
Elizabeth	d
GORTHSTHROP	
William	w
HALL	
William	w
HARRISON	
Agnes	d
Roger	d
HELM	
Robert	w
HERIMON	
Margaret	w
HEWITSON	
John	w
HICHENON	
Francis	w
HILTON	
George	w
John	w
Marie	s
HOLME	
Agnes	d
Alice	w
Dorothy	w
Dorothy	d
Edward	w
George	w
James	w
Robert	w
HOWARD	
Catherine	w
Lucy	w
JACKSON	
Margaret	d
JOBSON	
Elizabeth	w

KENDALL
John w

KERKHEM
Dorothy w

KILNER
Margaret w

KNIPE
Ann w
Edward w
Marie w
Mary w
Thomas w

LANGTHORNE
Elizabeth w

LAYFIELD
Elizabeth w
Isabel w
John w

LEBRON
Clare w
Teresa w
Winifred w

LEVENS
Marie s

LEWCAS
Dorothy w

LOWTHER
Ann w

MACHELL
Agnes w
Jane w
Lancelot w
Lancelot w
Margaret w

MALIN
Anne w
James w
John w

MALTEN
Monica w

MOUNT
James w

NICKELSON
Dorothy w
Isabel w
Margaret d
Robert w

NOBLET
Margaret w

PARKINSON
Christopher w
Cuthbert w
Ellen w
Jude w
Richard w
William w

PATTIM
Thomas w

PEARSON
Thomas w

PICKERING
Cecily s
James w
John w
Lancelot s
Margaret w
Margaret w
Mary w
Thomas s
Thomas s

PLATT
Ann w
Mary w
Peter w

PRESTON
Mary w

REDER
Ellen w

ROWLANDSON
Ann w
William d

RUMLEY
Henry w
John w
Margaret w

SELBY
Elizabeth w

SHEDALL
Mary w

SCHENTON
John w

SHERSIKALL
Ann w

SHOROCK
John w

SKIRRET
Margaret w

STEPHENSON
Robert w

STRICKLAND
Francis s
John s
Luke s
Thomas s

STURDIE
Gregory s

TARBUCK
Edward w
Margaret w
William w

THORNBURGH
Catherine w
Dorothy d
Frances d
Frances d
George w
Isabel d
James w
John d
Mary w
Nicholas w
Rowland jun w
Thomas w
William w

TOWTELL
Alice w

WARD
Ann w

WILKINSON
Ann w
Bridget s
Dorothy d
Elizabeth s
John s
Margaret d
Mary w
Mary w

WILSON
Elizabeth d
Margaret w
Margaret w

These lists differ from the corresponding ones in *Bishop Leyburn's Confirmation Register of 1687*, ed. J. A. Hilton and others (North-West Catholic History Society, Wigan, 1997), pp. 86-87, 93-95. List 21, p. 86, is there given as [Corby] and List 22, p. 87, as Dodding Green and Sizergh. But in the MS, List 21 is not said to be of candidates from Corby and is in a different hand from List 20, pp. 84-85, which is headed 'Confirmed at Corby August 22th'. List 22 is all in one hand but is endorsed 'Doddin Green and Sizer Westmorland Aug. 25'. It seems likely that List 21 is of names from Dodding Green and List 22 of names from Sizergh, and that the endorsement refers to both. In the lists above, therefore, **d** indicates names from List 21 and **s** names from List 22. There is no question about List 24, all the leaves of which are identified in the MS as containing names from Witherslack (**w**). List 23, pp. 88-92, is of those confirmed at Callaly, Northumberland, on 16 August.

10

CATHOLICS IN THE VILLAGE COMMUNITY: MADELEY, SHROPSHIRE, 1630-1770

The diversity and particularity of Protestant nonconformity has required that it be studied in terms of local congregations and local leaders. The evidence is not only the long and lovingly preserved records of persecution and discrimination on religious grounds, but also those produced by the Church of England hegemony. Recent work shows that Protestant dissenters were not isolated groups in post-Restoration England, but were to a large extent part of the wider economic communities in which they lived. The Corporation Acts were largely disregarded in places where they dominated the urban economy.[1] Recent study of parish registers for demographic purposes has revealed, incidentally, that moderate nonconformists used religious rites of passage offered by the Established Church, such as baptism and burial, if these did not require them to compromise their beliefs. The extensive business archives left by Quakers, the most select

Figure 6: Map of the Parish of Madeley, Shropshire

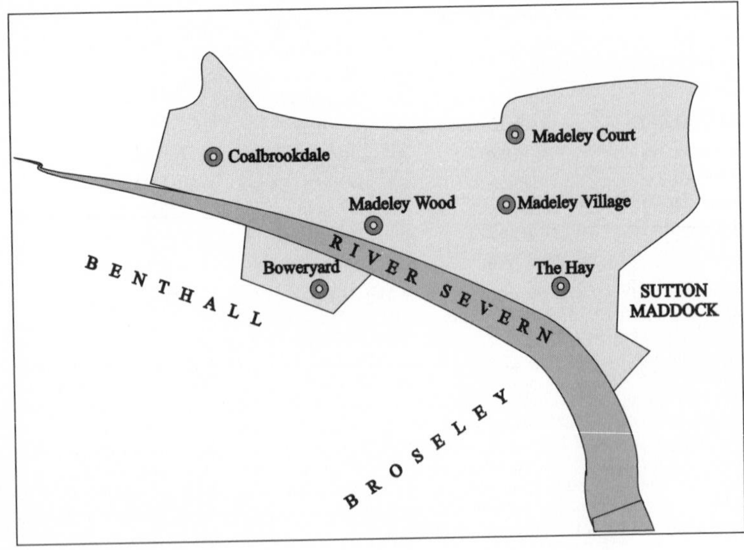

and doctrinally distinctive of the major Protestant nonconformist sects, show that, while they were typically business partners one with another in terms of capital investment, they sold almost all of what they produced in the wider world. The conformist corporation of Bridgnorth, for example, placed orders with the Darbys of Coalbrookdale for parts for their waterworks from 1715 onwards, and later leased the town mills to the Darbys as the site for an iron forge.[2] In order to maintain economic relationships some form of socialising would be necessary. A recent study of the Hearth Tax returns for Bedfordshire, Cambridgeshire and Huntingdonshire argues for the successful integration of Protestant dissenters within their communities, and identifies numerous occasions in which they performed traditional neighbourly functions for parishioners outside their sects.[3]

The involvement of Protestant nonconformists with the rest of society can be seen as a consequence of the rapid, though unsteady, decline in religious tension, and the retreat by the sects themselves from evangelisation into quietism as Republic gave way to restored Monarchy. The composition of the Protestant nonconformist congregations in post-Restoration England is shown to be almost exclusively non-aristocratic. Those in the countryside who were most socially distinguished were merely members of parish élites, some yeomen, others gentlemen.[4]

Traditionally, the study of Catholics focused on the operation of the penal laws and on the record of persecution, and the result has on the whole been an emphasis on separation. If however we make use of the records of the parish, it is possible that the new model of integration and non-aristocratic composition which has been demonstrated for Protestant Dissent could also prove to be applicable to Catholics.

On the other hand, Protestant nonconformists enjoyed a measure of religious toleration after 1689, and were not associated in the popular mind with foreign enemies like France and Spain, or with the repressive measures of the Inquisition. Catholics were identified with the later Stuarts, and experienced a much longer period of persecution, following a steeper and even more rocky path towards toleration.

Yet common sense would suggest that, as most Catholics had to earn their income in the outside world, they must have been integrated to a considerable extent. How could, for example, Alborough Turner, landlady of The Crown on Bridgnorth High Street, and seemingly the only Catholic in the town in the 1630s, have made a living if she had not been integrated into the Protestant economic community? Would Thomas Wigmore and Abraham Ankers, brickmakers, of Newport in Shropshire, only have sold bricks to Catholics? Did Nathaniel Bostocke, physician of Prees in the same county, only minister to Catholics?[5]

The main objective of this paper is to explore the extent to which there was a coming together amongst non-aristocratic groups within Madeley parish. Did Catholics and Protestants work together? Did Catholics play their part in social control of the communities in which they lived through membership of administrative bodies at the parish level? Did Catholics who did not marry Catholics from their own village marry Catholics from other villages, or did they marry Protestants from their own village? Were there friendships between Catholics and Protestants? Did Catholics use the services of the Church of England? Finally, if evidence of such behaviour can be found, is it a characteristic of an open village rather than a closed village where there was a dominant Catholic landlord?

The Parish of Madeley

Madeley in Shropshire offers an interesting opportunity to study these questions, since it contained on the one hand a substantial number of non-aristocratic Catholics and on the other a well stocked 'parish chest'. It has been the subject of a considerable number of studies because of its importance in the history of both iron manufacture and of Methodism

Madeley is situated on the River Severn seven miles upriver from Bridgnorth on the south-western fringes of the east Shropshire coalfield. Like most Shropshire parishes, it contained several settlements by the second quarter of the seventeenth century, but untypically two of the three were already partly industrial in nature. Clustered around the church was a failed medieval town whose inhabitants were primarily involved in a form of sheep-corn husbandry like other communities in the triangle of land between Watling Street, the River Severn and the Staffordshire border. Close by was Madeley Court, the manor house of the Brooke family. A mile to the west, on or close to the banks of the Severn, was Madeley Wood, a settlement of coalminers working in pits owned and operated by the Brooke family, who were lords of the manor.[6] The pits were administered through their estate managers, and supplied fuel to towns and villages as far apart as Shrewsbury and Gloucester. This was a relatively recent development, for there was little mining activity in the parish before the middle of Queen Elizabeth I's reign.[7]

Half a mile to the north of Madeley Wood was Coalbrookdale, the site of a blast furnace, forge and other works, probably constructed by the Brookes in about 1615 in association with a project for making steel by the cementation process. Skilled metal workers lived in this area.[8] At the mouth of the valley, and on the opposite bank of the river in the Boweryard, were small communities of barge owners and barge operators who brought in the raw materials needed by the iron works, and shipped out the coal, steel and other industrial goods produced in Madeley and its adjacent parishes.

During the period covered by this chapter, in response to industrial development the population of Madeley more than doubled. Although all three settlements grew in size, much of the population increase was concentrated in Madeley Wood. Here coal obtained from drift mines bored into the sides of what was later to become known as the Ironbridge Gorge could be easily transported to quays on the banks of the Severn, and miners could build cottages on the common land of the village, some of which was situated on the slopes leading down to the river.[9]

The initial patron of the Catholic community at Madeley was probably Sir Basil Brooke (1576-1646), though he was not formally presented as a Catholic until the Middlesex Quarter Sessions of 1640.[10] There is no clear evidence of the recusancy of Sir Basil's father, although it was claimed by Richard Bub, a deponent in a court case, that in 1603 a priest called Rogers had 'frequented Mr John Brooke, father to Sir Basil'.[11] There is nothing particularly Catholic about John's will or that of his wife Ann, daughter of Francis Shirley of Leicestershire,[12] and Richard Bub did not encounter Rogers till some years after John Brooke's death.[13] There are, however, some pieces of circumstantial evidence in addition to Bub's testimony. The names of two of John Brooke's Madeley tenants, Margaret Charlton and Richard Moore, appear in the Recusant Roll for 1592-93, and Brooke himself was never chosen to serve as a justice of the peace or sheriff for the county. Admittedly he served twice as bailiff of Wenlock, but not after 1580 when sanctions were tightened against those suspected of Catholic sympathies.

Sir Basil had a most distinguished career as a courtier, as a leader of the lay Catholic community, and as an industrialist and innovator. In the late 1630s he was Treasurer of Queen Henrietta Maria's household and helped to co-ordinate the campaign against the imposition of Catholic episcopal discipline on the laity in the person of Richard Smith, Bishop of Chalcedon. Brooke's personal contributions towards the development of steel-making techniques in various places in England and his coalmining ventures at Madeley have been described elsewhere. He also leased the Queen's ironworks in the Forest of Dean for many years, had an interest in copper mining in Ireland, and was involved in a wide range of other projects such as prospecting for alum, developing soap manufacture and encouraging England's North Sea fisheries.[14]

Madeley had all the qualities of a closed parish. The Brookes owned almost the entire area of the manor, had the manor house as their principal residence outside London, and held the great tithes and the advowson. Sir Basil spent most of his time at Court, but the manor was carefully and conscientiously administered. This he achieved using a hierarchy of agents, most of whom were brought in from outside, and subsequently exposed as Catholics.[15]

In contrast, Church of England discipline was lax. A presentment was made in 1618 to the Consistory Court that there had been morris dancing during the time of evening prayer. Two years later it was alleged that the parish clerk was not performing his services satisfactorily, being only fourteen years of age, whereas Richard Phillips, vicar in the late 1630s, was an ex-soldier with no training as a minister, unlearned, immoral and abusive towards his parishioners

Sir Basil had become one of the foremost Catholics in England by the 1630s. It was thanks to his own abilities, rather than to his ancestry or to the size of his landed estates, for both were modest He was able to arrange marriages for his sons and daughters with notable Catholic aristocratic families, and Sir Basil's business partners were in the main members of leading English Catholic families.[16] At the outbreak of the first Bishops' War with Scotland in 1639, he was one of the small committee authorised to draw up a letter in the Queen's name appealing for donations from the Catholic peerage, gentry and priests.[17]

In 1641, after the Irish revolt, Sir Basil was accused of planning a similar Catholic uprising in England and spent most, if not all, of the last five years of his life in prison. Even so, in 1643, though incarcerated in the Tower, he was thought to have been the mastermind behind a plot to betray London to the Royalists.[18]

Despite his overtly Catholic position, Sir Basil was not prosecuted as a Catholic until 1640, and no lists of recusants living at Madeley have been found until after 1660. As a result it is impossible to ascertain the number of Catholics living there in the first half of the seventeenth century. On the face of it, there were none. Nobody living in Madeley was named in the Recusant Rolls for the county in periods of persecution such as the late 1620s and the early 1640s. The Acta books of the Hereford diocese contain the names of Catholics living in the adjacent manor of Benthall, but cases in the Consistory Court relating to Madeley are exclusively concerned with laxity in religious observance or with immorality on the part of individual parishioners.[19]

Catholics in Madeley 1640-1660

Lack of interest in reporting Catholics is apparent even in the 1640s. In 1641 the parishioners petitioned Parliament asking for pressure to be put on Sir Basil Brooke to remove Richard Phillips, the incumbent. One of the many charges against Phillips was that he had leased the lesser tithes to William Webb, one of Brooke's agents. Webb's widow and eldest son were subsequently arraigned as recusants. Given the political atmosphere at Westminster, allegations that Phillips had turned a blind eye to Roman Catholicism in the parish or, even worse, had collaborated with the Brookes or their agents would have been the most convincing evidence in support of the petition. Surprisingly there is no mention of recusancy in the petition itself.[20]

In 1644 or 1645 the parishioners petitioned Sir Basil, who was still in prison, wanting his approval for the appointment of Michael Richards as vicar in succession to Phillips, who had died. Richards, the son of a freeholder or tenant farmer in an adjacent parish, had been performing the duties of vicar unofficially for the past few months, was 'very honest and civil' and 'painful and industrious in his calling'. This petition was signed by all the substantial parishioners, including people who were to be presented in the 1660s as recusants. At the top of the list of signatories were William Webb and Francis Woolf, who managed Sir Basil's ironworks and helped Charles II after the Battle of Worcester.[21] Presumably Catholics felt that Michael Richards was a safe successor to Phillips, which is perhaps hinted at in the phrase 'very honest and civil' and in the emphasis that he was a local man. It is also perhaps of some significance that they had not signed the earlier petition, which might have led to the replacement of Phillips by a vehemently Protestant outsider.

Four years later, in 1648, there was an acrimonious dispute over the Brookes' industrial undertakings. These had been under various short term tenancies from 1645, when the Ironbridge Gorge area had been overrun by Parliament's forces and the property sequestrated. Two groups contended for a lease from the sequestration committee for Shropshire: one comprised a number of Protestant tenants of Sir Basil Brooke led by Michael Richards, the vicar, while the other consisted of four Shropshire Protestant squires probably acting as a front for the Brooke family itself. They were led by Sir Basil's closest Protestant relation, Edward Cludd. The sequestrators took evidence from the Brookes' workmen and agents, including Francis Woolf, but despite bitter recriminations only the landowners (none of whom lived in Madeley) were accused of Catholicism. Recusancy was not used as a charge against anybody living in the parish.[22]

The Protestation oath in 1642 provides evidence almost for the first time of the hidden Catholic presence in the parish. The vicar and churchwardens did not present a list of those who refused to sign, but the names of some of them can be discovered by comparing the signatures to the Protestation with those on a list compiled a month earlier of people who had contributed towards the relief of the Irish Protestants evicted from their lands during the uprising which had begun in October 1641. Those missing from the Protestation list are Francis Woolf, senior and junior, gentlemen, Mr William Webb, Mr Francis Frisby, Joseph Goodman, Roger Rowley, Richard Shentall, John York and Thomas Phillips.[23] All except Frisby, York and Phillips were later presented as recusants, or had wives who were.

Others who were subsequently presented to the Consistory Court at Hereford as recusants can be identified in the short list of those who failed to pay their church lewn in 1641 and/or 1642. Yet others were amongst those parishioners who obtained substitutes for themselves in the 1630s, when it was their farm's turn to provide a churchwarden for the year, a position which required them to swear an oath of allegiance to the Church of England. Of the six who declined the honour between 1630 and 1638, four (Francis Woolf I, Roger Rowley, John Charlton and John Cooper) were presented as recusants at some time in their lives or had female relations who were. Francis Brooke may possibly be in the same category, though, being a trowman, he probably declined because he could expect to be away from home on Sundays.[24] Presumably the other four who refused also made excuses of this nature or else they would have been laying themselves open to accusations of Catholicism, even if they were still attending church from time to time.

The influence of the Brookes probably explained why there was silence concerning recusants in the 1630s, but it does not explain why the same attitude of 'turning a blind eye' persisted throughout the vicissitudes of the 1640s, when one can presume that much, if not all, of the seigneurial power of Catholic landowners at the parish level was cancelled out by the tight control Parliament maintained over sequestrated Catholic estates. It is difficult to imagine that traditional connivance would continue during the Interregnum given the extraordinary nature of the times. What broke the mould can only be a matter of guesswork, but it is possible that defeat in the struggle for the

Brookes' industrial interests turned the vicar and Protestant tenants like Harry Bowdler into determined anti-Catholics for the first time.

Catholics in Madeley after 1660

Recusancy in Madeley was out in the open after the Restoration. Catholics were presented before the Consistory Court of the diocese of Hereford from 1664 onwards for various offences, but how large was the recusant population of Madeley? According to the Compton Census there were 51 Catholics living there in 1676, but they are not identified by name. This figure represents approximately 12% of the adult inhabitants of the parish, and just under 20% of the Catholic population of the county as a whole over the age of twelve. Parish constables' presentments to Wenlock Quarter Sessions in 1682 give only 33 names, but some people suspected of recusancy were almost certainly included among the eight additional people presented for non-attendance at church. Stagles and Lloyd regarded this group as Protestant dissenters, but according to the Compton Census there were no Nonconformists living in Madeley in 1676.[25] Moreover, as Peter Challinor has shown in his study of Cheshire constables' returns, Catholics in considerable numbers were presented before Quarter Sessions in the early 1680s as absentees from church rather than as recusants.[26] This also happened in the case of Madeley in 1682, when members of the Woolf family were presented for not attending the parish church for a space of twelve months rather than, as in 1677, for recusancy. It therefore seems far more likely that the Madeley non-attenders were recusants rather than Protestant dissenters, though some could have been indicating an indifference towards religion in general. Less than thirty years later eight inhabitants of Bridgnorth were required to appear before the town's Quarter Sessions court for refusing to attend any form of religious worship.[27] However some of the Madeley eight were subsequently presented for practising some religion other than that of the Church of England, and in their case indifference is almost certainly not the answer. Two other contingencies further erode the difference between the figure given in the Compton Census and that in the constables' presentments: the latter did not include children between the ages of twelve and fifteen, and the Brooke family were in residence at Madeley Court in 1676 but not in the early 1680s.[28] If all these factors are taken into account, the figures for 1676 and 1682 are not irreconcilable.

The names presented to the Wenlock justices in 1682 can be supplemented by a plethora of others to be found in the

Consistory Court records for the period 1664 to 1686. The number presented at any one time varied markedly over time, reaching a peak of 54 in 1684. The fact that it did vary even during the peak of anti-Catholic frenzy of the Popish Plot and the Exclusion Crisis suggests a measure of occasional conformity to be expected in times of peril, though such an upsurge is not apparent in an increase in baptisms recorded in the Madeley parish register for 1678 or 1684. Unfortunately the years in between are missing.

If the names from all sources are collated, a list of 135 adults who refused either to attend church, or to take communion at Easter, or both, can be compiled for the period 1664 to 1686. This may represent an upper limit to the number of Madeley Catholics, though it is possible that the number of non-Catholic non-attenders included in the 135 was exceeded by the number of Catholics who attended the parish church sufficiently to avoid all charges of recusancy or non-attendance. The only person summoned before the Consistory Court for whom there is any evidence that he may have been a Protestant dissenter is John Betton of Madeley Wood. However, the fact that the only occasion on which he was presented was the year after the Compton Census had been taken makes this improbable. Betton, though only the son of a coalminer, was in some form of holy orders, and also intermittently at odds with the vicar. At various times between 1664 and 1695 he was accused of keeping a school without licence, performing clandestine marriages, and refusing to take communion. In the secular courts he was charged with assaulting his mother. Betton's married status precludes him from being the Catholic priest, but it is possible that he was a Church of England minister who had converted to Catholicism.[29]

The occupations of the male recusants living in Madeley can very largely be ascertained from the poll tax schedule of 1660, the royal aid of 1661, and entries in the parish register.[30] These show that socially recusants were a very variegated group - not simply the aristocratic household at Madeley Court and its servants. Indeed they may have comprised the most diverse collection of Catholics living in a Midland village at that time. At the top were the Brooke family. Below them were members of three very minor gentry families (the Purcells, the Webbs and the Woolfs) who were the Brookes' tenants. Below them, but still part of the 'middling sort' were yeomen farmers, some of whom, like the Goodmans, were newcomers, others, like the Rowleys, resident in the parish by the latter part of Queen Elizabeth's reign. Thirdly there were people whose livelihood derived partly or wholly from non-agricultural activities, both skilled workers and labourers.

The final category were people described as servants who were attached to the aristocratic and gentry households, though in the case of those employed by the gentry they would very largely have been servants in husbandry rather than household servants, as all three families were actively involved in farming.[31] The only category under-represented is retailers. None of the Madeley mercers appears to have been a Catholic, though one of the butchers was.

The Distribution of Catholics in Madeley

As a group, Catholics do represent a reasonable cross-section of the Madeley society, but they were not a representative cross-section in a topographical or occupational sense. Considerable numbers lived in Madeley Town and in Coalbrookdale, very few in Madeley Wood: only three of the coalminers living in the parish between 1660 and 1700 appear to have been Catholics. Catholics formed 100% of the aristocrats living in the parish, not simply the Brooke family and their relatives like the Guildfords and Mrs Dorothy Starkey, but also unrelated Catholics like John and Richard Giffard who were temporary lodgers at Madeley Court between 1679 and 1682. Among the rich farmers Catholics were less numerous, but nevertheless a significant minority which included not only the Webbs, the Woolfs and the Purcells, who claimed gentility, but also the Stanleys and the Twyfords, who had acquired that status by 1700, and the Rowleys and Goodmans, who were invariably described as yeomen or husbandmen. Of these, only the Stanleys were freeholders. The parallel hierarchy of Protestant tenant farmers was headed by the Ashwoods and the Bowdlers, who not long after the Restoration were described in some documents as gentlemen.

Another concentration of Catholics was to be found among the skilled workers in the iron and steel undertakings in Coalbrookdale: Thomas Glasbrook senior and junior, William Glasbrook, William Maybury, William Hallam, and probably Richard Rubery alias Mihill, whose daughters found places as servants with Catholic families. One was taken in as a child in 1651 by the Rowleys when her father apparently deserted her. Another suffered some kind of debilitating illness whilst away from the parish. She was brought back to Madeley, still presumably her place of settlement, and lodged with William Morris alias Davies, a recusant, who was paid regular sums for her upkeep by the overseers of the poor.[32] Francis Woolf, the manager of all the Brookes' industrial undertakings in the parish, has already been mentioned. His successor Lawrence Wellington was accused of refusing to attend church on a single occasion, but seems to have conformed by the mid 1680s.[33]

The Madeley parish registers are available from 1645 onwards. Although incomplete, particularly between 1676 and 1695, gaps can largely be plugged using Bishops' Transcripts. There is also what appears to be a duplicate of the register for the period 1696 to 1706, but it is in fact a data book which the parish constables used in calculating payments towards the birth, marriage and death tax. This includes births of Catholic children who had not been baptised in the parish church. Another important source is Easter Books which survive intermittently between 1649 and 1720, in which the vicar kept a record of his income from tithes and other sources, and also the accounts of the churchwardens and the overseers of the poor including some parish rate schedules for the same period.[34]

Estate material is extremely disappointing, comprising only a very full, but damaged, manorial court roll for 1677 and a number of less informative ones for the second decade of the eighteenth century, and some papers relating to the sale of land at the very beginning of the eighteenth century.[35] Wills, executors' accounts and probate inventories in the archives of the diocese and of the Prerogative Court of Canterbury are much more common after 1660 than before, whereas the Acta books at Hereford provide some detail concerning not only family relationships but also offences against ecclesiastical law other than those relating to recusancy discussed above. The records of lay courts of law are much less informative. Shropshire Quarter Sessions papers are severely limited in content before the middle of the eighteenth century, whereas Wenlock Quarter Sessions rarely met. Wenlock bailiff court papers are of some value from 1610 onwards, but their jurisdiction was confined almost exclusively to disputes over debts and the misappropriation of goods. Moreover, the detail in the paperwork accompanying bailiffs' court cases becomes less full over time.[36] Family reconstitution by collating all the sources shows that Catholic parish gentry families, although in other respects much closer to the yeomanry than to the aristocracy, tended to follow the examples of their superiors when it came to marriage, choosing Catholics of their own socio-economic group living in other parishes. This is fully apparent from the family trees of the Woolf, Heatherley and Purcell families. What has been less well known until these sources were examined is that lesser families frequently married Protestants, their marriages being recorded in the Church of England parish register. The records of baptism among Catholics below the rank of gentry show that practice varied. Some families like the Duddalls and the Goodmans had none of their children baptised in accordance with Church of England rites, others like the Morris alias Davies family and the Glasbrookes had some baptised, some not. In the late 1640s and early 1650s, such baptism was more common than in the last quarter of the century, with families like the Stanleys and the Goodmans having all their children baptised by Michael Richards, the Church of England minister, but this may have been because they had yet to be converted. Burial posed less of a problem provided that the deceased had received the last rites from the Catholic priest. Most Catholics living in Madeley were buried in the church or churchyard, including even the priests John Woolf and Henry Harnage, but some like Mary Farmer were buried in Catholic holy ground at White Ladies, a former nunnery on the Staffordshire border ten miles away.

Registers of baptisms, marriages and burials, supplemented by other sources such as wills and Easter books enable something to be said about how the faith was (or was not) carried down the generations, and also when and why conversion took place.

The Cawcock and York Families

In 1767 ten of the Catholic inhabitants of Madeley were members of the York family. Many, possibly all, were descendants of Mary Cawcock, who had married the blacksmith John York in 1680.[37] Mary was the daughter of Eleanor Cawcock, wife of Robert, a labourer. She herself was probably the daughter of John Ames, labourer, who as an elderly widower was living with her and her husband in 1660. (In the early 1650s when John's wife had been alive the two households had been separate.) Neither John York or Robert Cawcock was accused of recusancy, but John Ames, Eleanor Cawcock and Mary York née Cawcock were. Only three of Mary and John York's six or more children were baptised by the Protestant minister, though two of the three were Catholics by the end of their lives. Two others were buried unbaptised during the period when the Act authorising the birth, marriage and death tax was in force.

The Blest Family

A similar process can be seen at work in the Blest family. Richard Blest was not at any time accused of recusancy in the Consistory Court; his wife Sarah, however, was the daughter of Jane Cooper who, as the wife of John Cooper, weaver, was named in the first list of recusants presented to the Court in 1664. She appears in every list thereafter, and was joined by Sarah in

1680, when she came of age to be presented before the court. Richard and Sarah married in 1683. Only one of their children was baptised by the Protestant minister, a son who died soon after birth, but this did not prevent Richard serving as one of the churchwardens in 1706. Soon afterwards, however, he must have revealed his true religious beliefs as his freehold farm of 31 acres, acquired from the Brooke family in about 1705, was registered as property owned by a recusant in 1716.[38]

The Stanley Family

A more complex story emerges from records relating to the Stanley family who were substantial freehold farmers in Coalbrookdale. Captain Thomas Stanley, probably an officer for Parliament during the Civil War, and his wife Catherine had their children baptised by Michael Richards, the Church of England minister, in the late 1640s and early 1650s, but following her husband's death in 1670 Catherine Stanley and her son Thomas were consistently presented as recusants. This Thomas Stanley's first two wives were apparently either Catholics or willing for their children to be brought up as Catholics: there are several burials of young Stanleys (but no baptisms) recorded in the parish register, and two births in the birth, marriage and death register of 1696-1706. In 1710 Thomas married for the third time, presumably to a convinced Protestant, as the children of that marriage were baptised in the parish church from 1712 onwards. The date of Thomas Stanley(II)'s conversion is not known, but unlike Richard Blest, his lands were not registered as belonging to a papist in 1716. As he did not serve as churchwarden for the first time until two years later, when he was over sixty years of age, conversion to Protestantism had probably taken place only recently. What may be of significance in the case of Thomas Stanley's third marriage is that as a result he acquired a male heir who survived infancy. This was possibly taken as confirmation that he had taken the correct decision by changing his religion. There is no evidence of backsliding thereafter.[39]

Changing Allegiance

In other cases the non-transference rather than the transference of the faith can sometimes be imputed. The daughter of Joan Bowen, widow, for example, did not carry Catholicism into the Vaughan family. Usually, however, the evidence is too slight for the whole process to be discerned. The Twyfords were one of the most committed Catholic families amongst the yeomen farmer group. Richard Twyford and his wife Jane, who died in 1682 and

1700 respectively, were presented as recusants from 1672, but there is no clear evidence that Luke their son was ever a recusant. He did not marry, and so had no children to be baptised. He was never presented before Wenlock Quarter Sessions or the Consistory Court and there is nothing Catholic about his will other than that he named John Heatherley as his friend. His sister Mary, however, who married the Protestant yeoman farmer Roger Roe in 1684, was presented in 1685 and none of their children was baptised by the Protestant minister, though several were buried in Madeley church. There is no evidence that Roger, who was churchwarden between 1716 and 1718, was a convert, and nothing is known about their only surviving child Mary, who married Richard Jones, a blacksmith from Burrington in Herefordshire.

Roger's brother William had also apparently married a Catholic, or somebody he suspected of Catholicism, as his will includes a clause ordering his executors (which did not include his wife Lucy) to ensure that his only daughter Elizabeth was brought up in the Church of England. William's wife was almost certainly Lucy Griffiths, as members of the Griffiths family were part of his household in the years immediately before his death. If so, he had probably met Lucy whilst living in the Catholic household of John Heatherley where they had both been servants in 1706. A pointer to Lucy's religious affiliations is that within two years of her husband's death she had moved in with the Goodmans, one of the most consistently Catholic families in the parish. What subsequently happened to the daughter is not known. The Easter Books come to an end within two years of William's death, and neither her marriage nor her burial is to be found in the Madeley parish register.[40]

Catholic Servants in Madeley

Stronger, though still largely circumstantial, evidence of the perils Protestants faced in taking up service in Catholic households is to be found elsewhere in the Madeley evidence, but first it is necessary to examine the composition of the servant class in the parish. If the Madeley Easter Books are compared with the Consistory Court papers, it is apparent that some servants living with aristocratic and prosperous farming families in the late seventeenth century were Catholics and others not. Some of the Catholic servants, like Sarah Duddall and Abigail and Ann Strutton, can be identified as the children of Catholic families living in the parish, but most cannot. The Consistory Court papers for Hereford diocese suggest that they did not come from Catholic families living to the west and south of Madeley, and there is no clear correlation with data concerning recusants presented in Coventry and Lichfield diocese, which lay to the east and north. But if the servants were not Catholics when first employed, there were pressures to convert whilst living in a Catholic household. The most clear-cut example is provided by Joseph Littlemore of Dawley who, in the Coventry and Lichfield returns of 1706, is alleged to have been 'a servant sometimes at Madeley Court and there seduced'. The first part of the statement is confirmed by an entry in the Madeley Easter Book, which shows he had been living in the Purcell household at Madeley Court in the mid-1680s, the Brookes having chosen to live elsewhere *c.*1680.[41]

The case of John Farmer provides fuller, if less direct, evidence of somebody who may have been won over to the faith as a result of residence at Madeley Court. He was a servant there in the 1670s, but he was never presented as a recusant. In 1684 he married Mary Worcellor, a fellow-servant who was a Catholic, and in the following year he was presented as a recusant for the first time (together with his wife). By the early 1690s John Farmer was tenant of a substantial farm belonging to the estate, on which he grazed a herd of nearly twenty cows. In 1695 his wife was buried in the Catholic graveyard at White Ladies. When he himself died in 1707 without male heirs, the executor was his brother Thomas Farmer of Diddlebury, who was apparently not a Catholic.[42]

Another example of a man who may have acquired a tenancy as a result of becoming a Catholic is Richard Blest discussed above, who seems to have begun life as a shoemaker, but there is no evidence that he had ever been in service in a Catholic household. Shropshire certainly provides evidence that Protestant clergy saw the Catholic gentry as winning converts using the bait of tenancies. The vicar of Lydbury North wrote as follows in 1767 of Edmund Plowden of Plowden:

> If he gets a Protestant servant into his family, he seldom fails of recusing him, partly by meat and drink, partly by indulgence and diversion, and very often by marriage. Then he settles them in some of his farms or cottages and for the most part maintains them afterwards.[43]

If the Brookes were trying to surround themselves with Catholic tenants in the post-Restoration period, some success had been achieved by the end of the century. Whereas in 1673 only three of the principal tenants were Catholics, by 1702 almost 50% of the Madeley estate belonging to the Brooke family was in the hands of ten tenants who were either Catholics or who had close relations who were.[44] The obverse of this should not, however, be forgotten. Over 50% of the Brookes' land was farmed by Protestants, some of whom had been their tenants for generations.

Madeley Catholics and their Neighbours

Turning to matters external to the household and the farm, Catholics in Madeley contributed towards the re-edification of the church in which the Protestants worshipped. In 1711, for example, the Purcells and the Heatherleys headed the list of those paying for the construction of an extension to accommodate the growing population of coalminers and metal workers.[45] They presumably assumed that the church would revert to Rome in the fullness of time, though they may have been influenced by the more short-term consideration of 'purchasing the sympathy of the Anglicans', like their Wolverhampton co-religionists who, later in the century, made donations towards the building of the new church of St John. Catholics were less keen to pay tithes, but this was equally true of some of their conformist neighbours. However, they paid up when sufficient pressure was applied as they did not disapprove of tithes as a matter of principle. Here a clear contrast can be drawn with the Quakers living in the adjacent parish of Broseley, who refused outright and suffered grievously for their offence. What is surprising, however, is the Madeley Catholics' behaviour with regard to 'churching'. Unfortunately it was only between 1672 to 1686 that the incumbent kept a complete record of his receipts from the parish, but during this period even those families which were most consistently Catholic like the Goodmans, the Duddalls and the Struttons, had their wives churched.[46] Moreover, the minister was willing to perform the ceremony even though he had not baptised the child. Catholic women were evidently not excluded from this social occasion.

The integration of the Catholics into the village community in a non-religious sense is apparent when other classes of documents are examined. Mrs Dorothy Starkey, Sir Basil Brooke's daughter and widow of Hugh Starkey of Darley, Cheshire, leased a house from Michael Richards, the vicar. Giles Goodman obtained schooling for his son from Richards' successor. Catholics frequently served as overseers of the poor, even at the height of the Exclusion Crisis, and out of the sixteen parishioners named as trustees to administer the stock of the poor in 1695, six were Catholics. Catholics served occasionally as churchwardens Francis Rowley in 1672 and Giles Webb in 1674, for example though the normal practice was to hire a substitute.[47] Catholics appraised the goods of their neighbours for purposes of probate, and collected the land tax and the birth, marriage and death tax.

They also served as constables of the parish and jurors in the manorial court, but the poverty of source material relating to manorial administration makes it impossible to ascertain how often this occurred.[48]

Madeley Catholics and their Priests

In Madeley as elsewhere it is difficult to establish what pastoral care was available to the Catholics. Two priests, William Pegg alias Hastings and Henry Harnage, one serving the great house and the other lesser folk, are known to have been living at Madeley in 1693, but nothing is presently known about the earlier part of the century.[49] There must have been a priest in the parish or close by in the reigns of Charles II and James II, but none of the servants recorded in the Easter Books, the presentments to the Consistory Court, or the 1660 Poll Tax as living at Madeley Court or in the houses of John Purcell, Francis Woolf or Giles Webb have surnames which are known aliases of priests. Most stayed for only a year or so, and were therefore almost certainly servants in husbandry, but there were a few who remained much longer in the parish. John Adderley, who was in Francis Woolf's household between 1678 and 1685, looks initially to be the most likely candidate, but he was in fact John Heatherley, who married Francis Woolf II's daughter and eventual heiress. Other male servants who could have been priests are Nicholas Clarke (1649-1660), Richard Giffard (1679-1685), Henry Poole (1670-1684), Richard Poole (1670-1677) and Edward Williams (1649-1662). The Woolf family produced two priests during the course of the seventeenth century, but there is no evidence that they worked in Madeley before Harnage and Pegg. Lawrence Woolf O.S.B. (who died in 1697) was described as overseas in the will of his father Francis Woolf I proved in 1667, and John Woolf S.J., Francis II's son, who was buried in Madeley church or churchyard in 1735, seems only to have spent his declining years in Madeley.[50]

The most significant event for Madeley Catholics in the first half of the eighteenth century must have been the departure of the Brookes. The last of the senior line of the family died in 1699. In 1705 his cousin Comberford Brooke sold almost the whole of the Madeley estate, including Madeley Court itself, mainly to Protestants, but not the manorial rights which were divided between his two daughters and co-heiresses, one of whom married a Protestant. The other married a son of John Giffard of London, merchant, a younger son of the Giffards of Chillington. By the mid-1760s her portion of the manor was divided between their four daughters, each of whom owned an eighth. The sale of the estate was occasioned, not by the cumulative burden of recusancy fines, but by the vast debts incurred by Sir Basil's great-grandson, Basil Brooke, D.C.L., during the 1690s in searching for new deposits of coal and iron-ore.[51] Thus landownership fragmented in the manor and seignorial control declined.

As in other areas where there had been an aristocratic Catholic landowner, recusancy lingered on, but at Madeley it seems to have retained its strength, not gradually withered away. A priest lived firstly at The Hay, the Purcells' residence, and later at Madeley Wood, where most of the Catholics were living in the second half of the eighteenth century. Pegg left Madeley for Shrewsbury in about 1700, but Harnage remained there until his death in 1737. Towards the end of his life he was probably assisted by John Woolf, the last of his line, an elderly man who had returned to his home parish in or before 1731, when he witnessed the will of his niece Mary Heatherley. Between 1738 and 1755 Joseph Valentine was resident at The Hay. He had been brought up in Italy and in his first year at Madeley his command of English was so poor that he could not preach. Instead Mr Purcell 'read some pious book to the congregation to supply his deficiency in that point'. He overlapped with Edward Matthews, who served the villagers from 1750 to 1769 or later. Possibly what can be discerned is the practice of the 1690s, one priest for the gentry and one for the people, persisting until the Purcells left The Hay in the mid-1750s.[52]

Madeley Catholics in the Middle of the Eighteenth Century

The succession of priests in the middle years of the eighteenth century is much easier to trace than the composition of the lay Catholic community in Madeley and its relations with the Protestants, as few of the parish administrative documents survive. Those Catholics who had freehold land or annuities deriving from it can be identified using materials compiled after the Jacobite uprising of 1715, and these can be updated from documents relating to land sales retained by the Shropshire Quarter Sessions court, but most ordinary Catholics were tenants and therefore cannot be traced by this method. In 1767, however, a new diocesan listing gives sufficiently detailed information, not only to reconstruct the recusant community as it was then, but also to project it back in time to a limited extent using such records as do exist for the fallow period — wills, the parish registers, and the papers of Catholic clergy and administrators who staffed and financed the hidden church.[53]

In 1716 the vicar had reported to his bishop that there were sixteen Catholic families resident in the parish. This probably meant that the congregation was a similar size to that of the 1680s but, as with the Compton Census, the families concerned are not named. In 1767, however, there were 41 Catholic men and women over the age of twelve and 31 children living in the parish. The majority of the adult males were manual workers: three blacksmiths, two coal-miners, an engineer, a butcher, a carpenter, and a weaver. Though there are no boatmen, the profile is not markedly dissimilar to that of the Madeley manual workers who fell foul of the Consistory Court in the 1670s and 1680s. However, the seventeenth-century manual workers were one of four non-aristocratic social groups living in the parish. The skilled iron-workers and servants had very largely disappeared. As for the farmers, they had either died out like the Twyfords, or had conformed like the Stanleys and possibly the Blests, though the complete absence of documents on most of the minor estates into which Madeley was divided after 1705 makes it impossible to be more precise. The sole survivor was John Hill, husbandman, but he was almost certainly one of a family of coal-miners who also had a smallholding, not one of the parish élite.

The sole lay recusant of substance living in Madeley in 1767 was the steward, Thomas Slaughter, whose son had married Barbara, one of the four daughters of John and Rose Giffard. Thomas Slaughter senior presumably enjoyed the title steward because he managed Barbara's lands in the manor, and possibly those of her three sisters, but he himself had no landed estate in Madeley other than an interest in a row of cottages which had been built on the common. It also seems unlikely that the combined estate of the four sisters amounted to much more than two hundred out of the five thousand acres owned by the Brookes in the 1690s.[54] The other Catholic gentry families had died out or had left the parish, and it is this, together with the sale of Madeley Court to the Protestant Astley family, which explains why there are no servants in the 1767 list. Barbara, the last member of the Webb family, had died in 1707. The Heatherleys had sold up in 1765, the Purcells ten years earlier, though one of the younger sons of the Purcell family had married a Broseley heiress and is recorded in the 1767 list under that parish.[55] The minor gentry had, however, made some provision for the Catholics who lived after them. Barbara Webb left £3 to the priest Henry Harnage, Mary Heatherley £10. The purpose is not stated, and the assumption must be that it was to pay for Masses to be offered up for the repose of their souls, but possibly it was to put into the common purse for the benefit of the ministry. Mrs. Webb also left £20 in John Heatherley's hands, presumably for Catholic uses, and £3 a year to apprentice young

Catholic boys. John Heatherley himself left £100 to be invested to offer Masses for the souls of his wife and himself; his son, another John, £200 for the use of the priest. Sarah Brayne, Mary's niece and the main beneficiary of her will, also appears to have left money to the Church, but it was subject to litigation and may not have reached its intended beneficiaries.[56]

The ages of the Catholic population in 1767 ranged from over eighty to less than one year. Women above the age of sixteen outnumbered men by 17 to 16. Apart from three girls in their teens who were living with one or both of their parents, all the unmarried women and widows were in gainful employment. Two kept inns, one was a nurse, one a mantua-maker, one a shopkeeper and one a spinner. Eight of the seventeen were married women. Only four had Catholic husbands, but three of the remainder had brought their children up in the faith. The same pattern applies to males. Five of the nine married men did not have Catholic wives, but all had Catholic children.

With the single exception of Thomas and Mary Moseley, who had settled in Madeley in 1761, all the Catholic families had one parent who had been resident in the parish since birth. In fact 65 of the 72 persons named had been born in the parish. This is a completely different pattern from that which emerges from analysis of the much smaller Catholic community living in the neighbouring coalmining parish of Broseley. Only one of the seven Broseley Catholics had been born in the parish. Five were wives or widows of industrial workers or boatmen, but none had apparently brought up their children as Catholics. The two males were Edward Purcell, gent., mentioned above, and John Weaver, a collier, whose family, resident in adjacent chapelry of Benthall since the mid-seventeenth century, had had a longstanding commitment to Catholicism.[57]

The Goodman and Strutton Families

Only two of the surnames in the 1767 list are familiar from the seventeenth-century lists of recusants, Goodman and Strutton, but there is considerable evidence that two of the other families mentioned the Yorks and the Hills had converted by 1700. Also, a few connections can be made with recusant families represented in earlier lists using wills, Church of England marriage registers and early eighteenth-century Easter Books. Ann, the wife of Francis Astbury, collier, for example, was a Goodman. Given her place in the 1767 list, which appears to group families together, she was the daughter of Giles Goodman(II), an engineer, the grandson of Giles Goodman, yeoman, who was presented for recusancy before the Consistory Court in 1685. The Goodmans appear to have declined in status during the course of the eighteenth century. In the 1720s Giles Goodman(II)'s uncles were members of the parish elite. At his death in 1733 John Goodman had a very substantial farm, whereas Basil Goodman managed coalworks belonging to the Purcells drained by one of the earliest steam engines to be constructed in the east Shropshire coalfield. John died without male heirs whilst Basil appears to have conformed. Nevertheless seven Goodmans are named as Catholics in 1767.

There are, however, only three Struttons, even though the parish registers show that there was no shortage of heirs. Eleanor Strutton, described as innkeeper, was the widow of Richard Strutton, butcher (who had died in 1739 and who was almost certainly the son of Sampson Strutton who owned a cottage in 1716). Richard left all his goods to his widow but only a shilling each to his children, who are not even mentioned by name. None of the children are named in the 1767 list. The other Struttons, Thomas and his young daughter Mary, were probably not the descendants of Eleanor and Richard as their names are not adjacent to hers in the list.[58] The connections between the Hills, and all but the most elderly of the Yorks, and their seventeenth-century ancestors cannot, however, be determined because of the large numbers of Protestants with the same surnames living in Madeley parish in the early and mid eighteenth century.

Madeley Catholics and the Parish Church

As in the Restoration period, Catholic families appear to have made intermittent use of Protestant rites, though in the absence of Easter Books, only a limited number of rites can be monitored. Marriages are not surprisingly the commonest rites, given that so many Madeley Catholics married Protestants. Nevertheless, some marriages are not recorded, even though, as in the case of the Green and Stockings families, both partners and all their children were born in Madeley. Registers of adjacent parishes have also been searched without success, but as all the partners were Catholics, and as both marriages took place before Hardwicke's Marriage Act, the ceremonies need not have taken place within a parish church.

Throughout the period 1720-1767, the burials of Catholics of all classes and statuses were recorded in the parish register. These included members of the Woolf and Heatherley families in 1720, 1724, 1732, 1735, and 1761, the wife of Sampson Strutton the butcher in 1709, the daughter of Giles Goodman, engineer, in 1746, and the son of Thomas Hill collier in 1727 — but only in a single case does the parish clerk record that the burial service was 'without the Office'.

The two aged coalminers in the 1767 list, John and Robert York, were baptised by the vicar in 1687 and 1691, as were some York children of the next generation, but none of the children of William Goodman shoemaker (buried 1763), of John Heatherley gent. (buried 1720) or of the Hill family. The number of such baptisms becomes fewer in the middle of the eighteenth century, possibly reflecting a stronger and more confident Catholic priestly presence in the parish, but correlation between the Madeley 1767 return and the registers of the Church of England parish reveals that some Catholic children had been baptised in the parish church in the past ten or so years.[59] Possibly their parents had converted or been reconciled to Catholicism since the first baptisms had taken place. This may have the case with the family of Thomas and Mary Hodgkiss. Only their eldest child, Sarah, is not included in the 1767 list of Catholics, and she was the only one to have been baptised in the parish church. However, the baptismal record of the children of John York, collier, raises questions to which as yet there are no answers. Winifred, the only child of his first marriage, is named in the list of papists, but none of the children of his second and third marriages other than Elizabeth, aged 4 in 1767. This is not the case of a recent conversion. Her brother John, baptised on 9 April 1765, was not included in the list of recusants.

John Fletcher, Vicar of Madeley, and the Catholics

The baptism of Catholic children in the parish church of Madeley at this time is particularly interesting, since the vicar from 1760 until his death in 1785 was John Fletcher, famous by the end of his life as a Methodist zealot of national importance. His attempts to evangelise his parish involved him in disputes with local Catholics. In 1762 Fletcher was disturbed in his devotions by a mob. They were not apparently Catholics, but their leader, Mr Thomas Haughton junior, was. Entering the house of a Mrs Matthews, where Fletcher and his supporters were holding a prayer meeting, Haughton and his companions tried to disrupt the proceedings, but were apparently persuaded to withdraw before violence could break out. Fletcher then attempted to present Haughton before the Consistory Court to answer charges of blasphemy, drunkenness and disrespect towards the royal family, but his efforts were obstructed by the churchwardens. When, in his own words, 'I went to Ludlow to the Bishop's visitation, and thought the occasion favourable for my purpose, the churchwardens, when we were on the spot, refused to support me, and the court paid no regards to my presentation'. Unfortunately the churchwardens' names are not known, but as it was customary in Madeley for the office to circulate amongst the minor landowners and principal tenants, who presumably formed the parish vestry, opposition is not altogether surprising. He disparaged them as the 'half-gentlemen of the parish'. By implication he associated them with support for swearing, drunkenness and other sins and later stated that he counted none of the farmers of the village as God-fearing.[60]

Seven years later Mr Matthews, the Catholic priest, succeeded in converting two families who had been John Fletcher's parishioners. This caused Fletcher to oppose the construction of a new Catholic place of worship which was to be erected behind the priest's house in High Street, Madeley Wood, on land belonging to the descendants of the Brookes. In this he failed, but what materialised must have been a powerful affront to evangelical Protestantism, a large building costing almost £500 and capable of holding a congregation of 200. Much of the money was provided by aristocrats, many of whom lived at a distance: the Duke and Duchess of Norfolk, for example, contributed £35 and Lady Stourton £40, whereas the Shropshire gentry as a whole only gave at the most £66.[61]

Fletcher then took the spiritual initiative, determined to 'strip the whore of Babylon and expose her nakedness'. In a letter which was published he attacked the Catholic Church in general for its dangerous principles, for encouraging profanity and, somewhat bizarrely, for interfering with the freedom of others to practise their faith. The Catholics held meetings to discuss how to best counter the attack, and Fletcher claims that he was threatened with violence by 'one of their bloody bullies'. He replied with a sermon denouncing the Church and all its works, which provoked a counter-blast from Thomas Slaughter, the steward, who stood in the churchyard after the sermon and called out several times that 'There was not one word of truth in the whole of my discourse, and that he would prove it'.[62] Additionally he promised to produce a Catholic priest who would answer both the sermon and the letter, presumably his brother James who was chaplain to the Earl of Shrewsbury at Longford Hall. Thomas Slaughter, as we have seen, was the most notable Catholic in Madeley, but his Catholicism did not prevent him from playing an important part in the running of the parish. He was a member of the vestry from 1768 to 1773, a period before and after the demonstration in the churchyard. He also served as overseer of the poor in 1773-74 with Abraham Darby III, the Quaker ironmaster.[63]

There is no evidence that the confrontation between priest and minister took place, but Fletcher seems to have been so discomfited by the encounter with Slaughter that he left the parish for some months. He travelled first to Wales, and then to France and Italy where he conducted research into 'the gross and absurd practices of the priests and other clergy', even attending the Pope's private chapel in Rome. Behind the confrontations of 1762 and 1769 we may see an open village taking action in defence of its freedom from seignorial or, in this case, clerical, control. Fletcher's attack on irreligion in Madeley had concentrated on popular culture drinking and impolite language in the case of the Haughton incident, but also Sunday as a day of leisure, popular sports such as bull-baiting, and even children's games. His initiative appears, from Fletcher's correspondence, to have produced considerable resistance from both Protestants and Catholics, which was probably intensified by the fact that some of his early supporters appear, like him, to have been newcomers to the village.[64] Moreover, the village élite, having experienced a serious uprising of coalminers in 1756, would probably have been wary of antagonising the poor by attacking their popular culture. But why should Catholics have taken the lead in what seems to have been the chief confrontation between the incumbent and the inhabitants of the parish? Perhaps Haughton and Slaughter were being used as surrogates by the Protestant leaders of the village community. Possibly the *quid pro quo* was that the Protestants would not object to the opening of the new Catholic chapel in Madeley Wood on land given to the Catholic church by the mother-in-law of Slaughter's son. Seignorial influence, however, was almost certainly not a factor. In 1769 the owner of Madeley Court was a Protestant as were all the substantial landholders. Slaughter's standing derived not from his own resources but presumably from the backing of the parish élite.

The parish records have made it possible to analyse the complex web of relationships which linked Catholics below the rank of gentry to their neighbours. Many more linkages could be established, but it is already evident that, if separation was the characteristic of some of the gentry, integration was the model at parish level, in secular and community affairs at least, in a village that was first closed and then open. In this they were more similar to the Protestant dissenters than might be thought, and their Catholicism did not exist in isolation, but was part of the culture of their time and location.

ABBREVIATIONS

Mutton Norman Mutton ed., 'Shropshire recusants in 1706, 1767 and 1780', *Worcs. Rec.* 24, 25, 26 (1974-75).

Tyerman L. Tyerman, *Wesley's Designated Successor* (1882)

NOTES

1 J. Hurwich, 'Coventry Dissenters and Politics 1660-1720', *Midland History* 4, no. 1 (1977), pp. 30-1.
2 Sh.R.O. 4001.
3 Spufford.
4 The term 'non-aristocratic' is used deliberately in preference to 'sub-gentry' because of the similarity in lifestyle between the 'parish gentry' and the richer yeomen.
5 M.D.G. Wanklyn ed., 'Shropshire Recusants in 1635', *Midland Catholic History* 3 (1993), pp. 8-14.
6 V.C.H. Shropshire 11, pp. 21-56.
7 Wanklyn, *Darby*.
8 *Shropshire Natural History and Archaeological Society Newsletter* 44 (1973).
9 S. Sogner, 'Aspects of the Demographic Situation in Seventeen Shropshire Parishes', *Population Studies* (1964); V.C.H. Shropshire 2, p. 225.
10 P.R.O. SP 23/64, f. 825; J. Randall, *History of Madeley* (1880), pp. 24-5; Dictionary of National Biography.
11 M.M.C. Calthrop, *Recusant Roll No. 1* (C.R.S. 18, 1916); Hugh Bowler, *Recusant Roll No. 2*(C.R.S. 57, 1965); *ibid., Recusant Rolls Nos. 3 & 4* (C.R.S. 61, 1970); P.R.O. SP 14/28/112/I.
12 P.R.O. PROB 11, 1599 (13 Kidd) and 1610 (14 Wingfield).
13 P. Caraman, *Henry Garnet* (1964), p. 320.
14 H.R. Schubert, *The History of the British Iron and Steel Industry* (1957), pp. 324-5; Wanklyn, *Darby*, pp. 3-6. There are also many references to Sir Basil's commercial and industrial undertakings in the Calendars of State Papers, in particular the C.S.P.D. for 1635, 1636, and 1625-49 Addenda, and the Calendar of State Papers Ireland 1615-25. There is an adequate account of his political and religious activities in the *Dictionary of National Biography.*
15 P.R.O. SP 23/165, ff. 177-230; SP 23/237, ff. 69-70.
16 Sh.R.O. Hardwicke's pedigrees.
17 M.J. Havran, *The Catholics and Caroline England* (1962), p. 153. Brooke and Sir Kenelm Digby signed a receipt for £312 9s. 2d. donated by Charles Townley (J.R.L. MSS 737).
18 *Dictionary of National Biography*; C.V. Wedgwood, *The King's War* (1958), pp. 284-6.
19 P.R.O. 337/35, 49; H.W.R.O. Hereford Diocese Records, Acta Books, box 1.
20 Sh.R.O. 4925.
21 Sh.R.O. 2280/1/1.
22 V.C.H. *Shropshire* 11, p. 46; P.R.O. SP 23/165, ff. 177-238.
23 Lords R.O. Protestation Returns for Oxford and Shropshire, ff. 194-5.
24 Sh. R.O. 2280/2/42.
25 L.C. Lloyd ed., *The Borough of Much Wenlock 1468-1968* (1968), pp. 32-4; *Transactions of the Shropshire Natural History and Archaeological Society* 2nd Series 1 (1889).

[26] P. Challinor, *The Structure of Politics in Cheshire 1660-1714* (Ph.D. Wolverhampton Polytechnic, 1983), pp. 93-5.
[27] Sh.R.O. 4001/J (Quarter Sessions files, Box 3, 1709).
[28] Sh.R.O. 2280/2/3,4; Much Wenlock Corn Exchange, Wenlock Borough Archives, Quarter Sessions papers, 1682, unfoliated.
[29] *Ibid.*, 1681/82, unfoliated; H.W.R.O. Hereford Diocese Records, Acta Books, boxes 3-6.
[30] P.R.O. E179/168/214, 219.
[31] Their heavy involvement in farming is apparent from the surviving seventeenth century Easter books: Sh.R.O. 2280/2/1-4.
[32] Sh.R.O. 2280/2/42 unfoliated, 1685 and after.
[33] *Ibid.*; *Worcs. Rec.* 53 (1989), pp. 33; *Worcs. Rec.* 54 (1989), pp. 31-3.
[34] H.W.R.O. Foley MSS.; H.W.R.O. Hereford Diocese Records, Bishops' Transcripts, 1638, 1678, 1684-95; Sh.R.O. 2280/2/2-9; Sh. R.O. transcripts of Madeley parish registers.
[35] Sh.R.O. 210/1; 2280/14/2; 516/11, 749, 1987/19/3.
[36] Much Wenlock Corn Exchange, Bailiffs' Court Papers, 1611-1734.
[37] In the reconstitutions which follow the listings of papists used unless otherwise referenced are those of 1706, 1767 and 1780 in the House of Lords. The 1767 returns are the originals located in L.J.R.O., which give names (transcription: Mutton); Mutton 25, pp. 36-9.
[38] The Shropshire section is printed in *Transactions of the Shropshire Archaeological Society* 2nd Series 1 (1889) as footnotes to the Compton Census.
[39] A Thomas Stanley was captain of a company of Shropshire infantry in 1645 and 1646, and fought at the siege of Chester : P.R.O. SP 28/224, f. 48; R. Morris, *The Siege of Chester* (1924), p. 164; *Worcs. Rec.* 54 (1989), pp. 26, 28, 30, 32-3; Sh.R.O. transcripts of Madeley parish registers.
[40] H.W.R.O. Hereford Diocese Probate Records, will of William Roe 1718; Sh.R.O. 2280/2/9.
[41] Mutton 24, p. 22; Sh.R.O. 2280/2/5 1685-6.
[42] H.W.R.O. Hereford Diocese Records, marriage licences 1684; letters of administration of John Farmer 1707; Sh.R.O. transcript of Madeley parish registers 24 September 1695.
[43] William Price, 'Three Jesuits at Plowden Hall', *Recusant History* 10 (1969-70), p. 169.
[44] Sh.R.O. 210/1.
[45] Sh.R.O. 2280/2/42.
[46] Sh.R.O. 2280/2/3.
[47] Sh.R.O. 2280/8/10; 2280/2/42.
[48] Sh.R.O. 2280/14/2; 210/1; transcripts of parish registers.
[49] Bossy, *Catholics*, p. 260.
[50] Sh.R.O. 2280/2/2,3; P.R.O. PROB 11 1667; Bellenger, *Priests*, p. 124; H.W.R.O. Probate Records, will of Mary Heatherley née Woolf, proved 1733.
[51] Wanklyn, *Darby*, p. 4; P.R.O. C5/180/133 (I am grateful to Mr. G. Baugh, editor of the V.C.H. *Shropshire* for the Court of Chancery reference).
[52] Anstruther 3, p. 92; Anstruther 4, p. 265.
[53] H.W.R.O. Diocese of Hereford Records, papist returns for 1767 (printed Mutton 25, pp. 28-42, pp. 21-4; *Transactions of the Shropshire Archaeological Society* 2nd Series 1 (1889), p. 90; Sh.R.O. Quarter Sessions files parcel 282, register of papist deeds.
[54] V.C.H. *Shropshire* 11, p. 36; Sh.R.O. 1681/135/4. A fine levied in the 1770s (Sh.R.O. 1681/135/1) suggests that the manorial lords combined had the freehold of as many as 50 cottages.
[55] H.W.R.O. Hereford Diocese Probate Records, 14 September 1708; B.A.A. A.268; V.C.H. *Shropshire* 11, p. 67; Mutton 25, p. 30.
[56] H.W.R.O. Hereford Diocese Probate Records 1707, 1733; B.A.A. A.188-94, 254, 268, 288.

[57] Mutton 25, pp. 30, 36-9.
[58] H.W.R.O. will of Richard Strutton, butcher, proved 3 June 1740.
[59] Sh.R.O. Madeley parish register 1749, burial of Christina Price, a papist; Mutton 25, pp. 31-2, 36, 40-1.
[60] Mutton 25, p. 62; Fletcher's letters describing this and other conflicts within the parish are printed in Tyerman; His disparaging comments concerning the parish élite are printed on pages 76 and 79. See also R.F.Skinner, *Nonconformity in Shropshire 1662-1816* (1964); J. Benson, *The Life of Mr John William de Fléchère.*
[61] *Ibid.*, pp. 156-9; B.A.A. A.449, 459-63.
[62] Tyerman, pp. 156, 158-60; V.C.H. *Shropshire* 11, pp. 61, 69.
[63] Sh.R.O. 2280/6/95, ff. 1-5; B.S. Trinder, *The Industrial Revolution in Shropshire* (2nd edition, Chichester, 1981), pp. 227-8.
[64] Tyerman, pp. 65, 70-1, 83. Attempts were made to expel one of his supporters from the parish, seemingly because he did not have a settlement there (*ibid.*, p. 76).

11

'CHIEFLY OF LOW RANK': THE CATHOLICS OF NORTH-EAST ENGLAND, 1705-1814

In his sermon 'The Second Spring', given at the first Synod of Westminster in 1852, Newman reduced the Fathers to tears with a description of what he supposed Catholic life had been like in 1800. The English Catholic community, he said, had dwindled to 'a few adherents of the Old Religion' who, 'though noble of bearing and said to be of good family', went 'silently and sorrowfully about'. They lived in old-fashioned mansions of gloomy appearance behind high walls, iron gates and yew hedges. Others

> were ... found in corners, and alleys, and cellars, and the housetops, or in the recesses of the country; cut off from the populous world around them, and dimly seen, as if through a mist or in twilight, as ghosts flitting to and fro.[1]

Newman's hyperbole was perhaps excusable, given that the occasion on which he spoke marked the culmination of the progress of English Catholicism from the darkest days of persecution to those of a newly-restored hierarchy. His portrayal has, however, proved difficult to modify, despite evidence that has since become available.

Some of that evidence will be presented here and it comes from north-east England. The term 'north-east' is used to distinguish the region from the Anglican diocese of Durham, the counties of Northumberland and Durham, and the Catholic Northern Vicariate, none of which would be appropriate. The diocese included Alston in Cumberland and Craike in Yorkshire, but excluded Hexham and its shire which was in the diocese of York. Berwick and its shire lay outside Northumberland. Hexham and Berwick, however, figure in the Catholic life of the region and cannot sensibly be left out. The region formed only the eastern part of the Catholic Vicariate of the Northern District, which comprised all England between the Humber and the Tweed. Hence the area covered here is that lying east of the Pennines between the Rivers Tweed and Tees, including Berwick. This is generally agreed to be a cohesive region, encompassed as it is on three sides by substantial physical and psychological boundaries. Only in the south is the border less palpable, though no doubt a Yorkshireman would have little hesitation in pointing to the Tees as the northern frontier of civilised life.

There were around a dozen head-counts of the Roman Catholics in north-east England between the Revolution of 1688

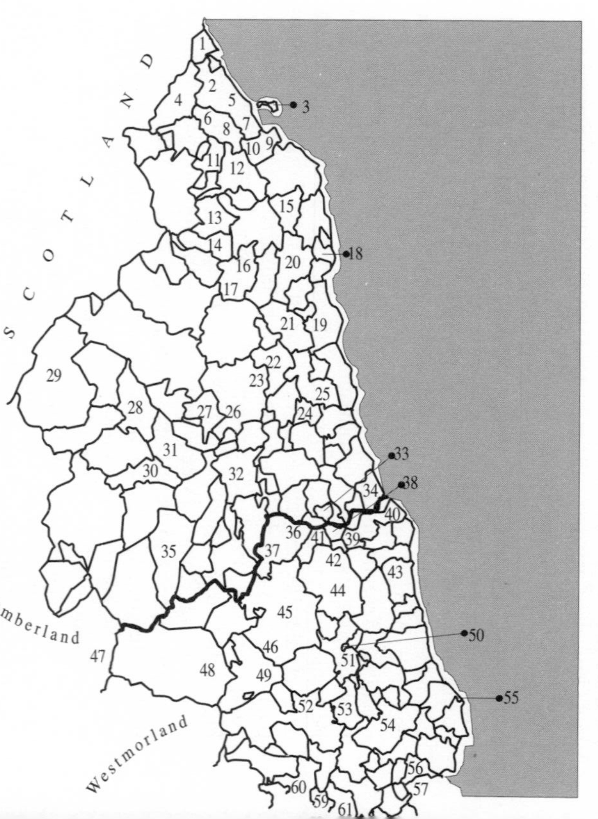

Figure 7: Catholics of the North-East

and the end of the Napoleonic Wars the 'long eighteenth century'. Since no other minority religious group was enumerated as often, the English Catholic body is the one in the period about which we can know most. Much of the data, admittedly, was collected using different criteria and was not gathered by the same authority. Some surveys were made by Anglican officials and others by Catholics; some counted all papists, others communicants only, and yet others heads of households.[2] Eight surveys, however, were conducted by Anglican parochial officials using the same criteria, and hence form a coherent series which can be used to define the social character of the northern Catholics of the period. These were: the Parliamentary Returns of Papists made in 1705, 1767 and 1780;[3] and the Episcopal Visitation Returns of Durham made in 173[2],[4] 1774, 1792, 1810 and 1814.[5]

It was a duty of Anglican clergymen and churchwardens to identify Dissenters and Catholics, and they would be no less efficient in counting them when asked to do so than they would when collecting church revenues. Almost half the parishes of the diocese contained around one hundred families; with such small populations to monitor the authorities would indeed have had to be careless not to have known who was who. In 1705 the vicar of Horton reported there were no papists in his parish to his 'great comfort and satisfaction'; the vicar of Ingram clearly had little difficulty in coping, for he wished 'the Dissenters were as soon numbered'.[6] In 1814, the rector of Falstone (with 147 families) observed 'The Idea or Meaning of Popery is, I believe, not in the least comprehended in this Chapelry'. The rector of Kirkhaugh could not recall one Catholic inhabitant in thirty years. The vicar of Ilderton knew there had been no Catholic residents in his parish between 1764 and 1810. If anyone had any doubts about the matter, he could have followed the example of a vicar of Ryton who wrote to the Catholic priest at Stella asking for the information, 'tonight if possible'. A vicar of Lanchester was the only clergyman who declined to count the papists at his bishop's behest but that was because, as he bravely declared, 'to number them would be thought invidious'. A vicar of Ryton gave an imprecise number because the number was so large: 'I do not know the number of papists but it is considerable, not less, as I suppose, than 400'. Similarly, the vicar of Whittingham reported simply that 'most' of the inhabitants of Callaly were papists. The majority of parishes missing from the returns had no history of Roman Catholicism, as was confirmed by a diocesan official in 1767 when he endorsed the bundle of returns sent up to London: 'There are no papists or reputed Papists in such of the parishes within the Diocese of Durham as are not mentioned herein'. Finally, while a number of returns made in 1705 omitted children, women and servants, the overwhelming majority of returns made thereafter included all Catholics whatever age or social standing.

In short, there is no reason to doubt the reliability of this material, nor except on rare occasions, is there any justification for amending the stated figures. Yet the 1767 figures have been 'corrected' to take account of the poor 'conditions of eighteenth century statistical enquiry', and to add as much as 15% to the stated population.[7] In the case of the north-east this is wholly unjustified. Taken as a whole, the returns provide the information necessary for a methodical and detailed reconstruction of the demographic, economic and social character of the Roman Catholics of north-east England in the last years of the recusant era, when, it should be noted, there was a negligible Irish presence in the region.

Synopsis of the Returns

In March 1705 the House of Lords, alarmed at the apparent growth and strength of Popery, ordered the diocesan clergy to conduct a census of the English Catholics.[8] Most of the returns from the parishes of County Durham have survived, but only half from the Northumbrian parishes in which Catholics groups are known to have lived are extant, and the returns from Hexhamshire went to York. These deficiencies do not, however, render the returns entirely useless, as will be seen. Evidently, the power and influence of the Catholics was of greater interest than mere numbers or religious practice, for the census was concerned entirely with their 'qualities, estates and abodes' and there is no reference to priests or chapels. In that respect the census showed that the northern Catholics could not be counted among the wealthiest in the population nor were they a threat to civil order. The vicar of Chatton reported the few papists in his parish as behaving 'themselves very civilly, with a mighty reservedness'. But the census did confirm what members of the House of Lords suspected, that the small Catholic population was well-established, confident and possessed of a capacity for growth.

Although they fall outside the scope of this study, the registers compiled under the Registration of Papists' Estates Act, 1716 (1 Geo. I c.55), passed in the wake of the Jacobite Rising of 1715, must be noticed because they facilitate the identification of those with and those without capital resources.[9]

The number and whereabouts of the north-eastern Catholics were next investigated by Edward Chandler, Bishop of Durham, in 173[2]. Out of the one hundred and fifty Anglican parishes in the diocese, twenty-one are missing from the extant record but half of those are from parishes having no history of Catholicism; the resultant shortfall in the total is estimated at about 675 Catholics. At any rate, it is quite clear from this survey and that of 1767 that the Catholic community survived the Jacobite Risings almost unscathed although they were meant to have been subjected to severe penalties for their loyalty to the Stuarts. It is also clear that the Catholics of the region were served by an extensively distributed mission; there were some thirty-four mission-stations and their disposition would remain essentially unchanged for a century; fifteen dame-schools would be functioning before the first Relief Act.[10]

By far the most important, and virtually comprehensive, censuses of the Catholic population in the north-east during the period were those of 1767, taken in response to press criticism that the bishops had failed to contain the spread of Popery;[11] a similar enquiry made in 1780 in an attempt to prove the Protestant fears about the growth of Catholicism after the Catholic Relief Act of 1778 were unfounded; and four routine Episcopal Visitations made between 1774 and 1814. Between them, these provide extensive sociological data on the Catholics at the time of the Relief Acts. Although strictly speaking they fall outside the overall period of this book, the visitation returns of 1810 and 1814 were the last to be taken before the Catholic Emancipation Act, and cannot therefore be excluded. Since, however, they are almost identical they are treated as one in the analysis.[12]

Population Trends

The series of returns shows that the Catholic population of the north-east rose significantly in the first half of the eighteenth century, but then fell back so that at the end of the war in 1814/5 it numbered about the same as it had over a century before. The Catholic population of 1705 has been calculated by comparison with later years. That is, the number of Catholics in parishes for which there is a complete series of returns from 1705 to 1814 represents about half the total on each occasion. The figure from those parishes in 1705 was 1,279, which, if it conforms to the pattern, would give a total of around 2,588 Catholics, or 1.2% of the population. While tenable, this figure may be a little low, given that Bishop John Leyburn had confirmed 2,727 people in the region in 1687. Celia Fiennes, on a visit to Durham city in 1697, noted that there were 'many Papists in the town, popishly affected and daily increase'. At any rate, the census of 1705 showed that the Catholic population was widespread and vigorous. In 1724 Daniel Defoe reported Durham city to be full of Catholics

> who live peaceably and disturb no body, and no body them. For, we being there on a holiday, saw them going as publicly to Mass as the Dissenters did on other ways to their meeting-house.[13]

The population of the region in 1767 was about 235,000 of which the Catholics represented 2%. That was the largest proportion achieved in the period; in 1810 the Catholics represented only 1% of the population of 350,000.

The rise and fall of the Catholic population over the period is not easy to explain, indeed it is contradictory. The rise occurred in the period of the two Jacobite Risings when Catholic numbers

Table 19: Catholic Population of North-East England, 1705-1814

	1705	1732	1767	1774	1780	1792	1810/4
County Totals							
County Durham	958	1658	2723	2700	2426	1998	1678
Northumberland	446	1324	2165	2331	2241	1895	1861
Hexhamshire	172	105	318	*N*	200	*N*	233
Recorded totals	1576	3087	5206	5031	4867	3893	3772
Estimated totals	2558	3858	5206	5281	4867	4108	3772
Totals from parishes for which a complete set exists	1279	1887	2597	2534	2459	1990	1498
Totals from selected urban parishes							
Alnwick	[9]	(8)	70	(17)	93	60	40
Berwick	0	(2)	12	(1)	13	35	60
Durham City	64	314	420	(87)	336	198	150
Morpeth	13		86	few	77	60	50
Sunderland	14	(2)	113	(10)	174	180	68
Totals from selected rural parishes							
Felton	28	(10)	76	(15)	75	76	111
Kirkwhelpington	4	(14)	89	(12)	106	(10)	some
Lanchester	35	135	284	(71)	276	313	320
Ryton	183		447	(100)	334	359	400
Whittingham	56	(42)	199	(39)	257	194	136

Key: (families), [no women listed], N: missing returns.

Sources: Parliamentary and Episcopal Visitation Returns for the Dioceses of Durham. For Hexamshire see C.R.S. 32 (1706); *Yorkshire Archaeological Society* 75 (1835); *The Rosary* 14, No 6 (1811); D Milburn, *A History of Ushaw College* (1964), p.90 n4 (1781); Parliamentary Returns of Papists, 1767, Diocese of York.

might have been expected to fall as a reflection of their unpopularity and consequent self-effacement. It seems, however, that the relatively newly-established mission, under the enthusiastic patronage of the gentry, imbued the Catholic body with a self-confidence which encouraged cohesion and growth against the odds. The fall in Catholic numbers later in the century took place contrary to their potential for natural growth and when the social characteristics of the northern Catholics were similar to those of the population in general.

The decline undoubtedly took place and it was widely remarked upon. The visitation returns from Lamesley, Whickham, Newcastle St Andrew, Newcastle St Ann, Darlington, Stamfordham and Sunderland all noted the fall. In 1810 the curate of Belford observed that the children of the half-dozen Catholics were beginning to attend the established church, and in 1814 the vicar of Chollerton noticed the same development. One of the two Catholic inhabitants of Warkworth often attended the parish church. The vicar of Sockburn rejoiced that he had only one Catholic woman, aged eighty, in his parish, while 'at the last visitation holden by Bishop Thurlow there were two Popish families'. In 1792 the curate of Carham said it was 'a rarity' to see a Catholic in the parish; there had been five in 1780.

Disruptions to the Catholic mission were partly responsible for the decline. The chapel at Hesleyside was closed for financial reasons and in 1774 the vicar of Simonburn reported that there was 'no Mass-house, thank God, in the parish'. In 1810 he expressed his delight at having 'no Popish school or Seminary in my parish', and went on,

> I hope the number of Papists does not increase with us: and I am happy that I have converted one large family to the Communion of our Church.

In 1814 there were no more than twenty Catholics in the parish; there had been around eighty in 1780. In 1810 the curate of Kyloe and Lowick anticipated gains:

> Mr Clavering of Berrington having sold his Estate lately, they will soon disappear in that quarter, and as the Haggerstone family do not scruple to take a good Tenant from among the Protestants, they are, I think, upon the decrease in both parishes.

Similarly, the curate of Netherwitton remarked in 1774 that

> a Protestant Gentleman having about 2 years ago married one of the coheiresses of the Principal Roman Catholic family [Thornton], the P[opish] Priest had been sent out of the Chapelry and that Interest is now on the decline and some converts have been made.

The Catholic community of one hundred in 1767 declined to seventy in 1792; a report of 1827 said 'few Catholics are now remaining here'. In Kirkwhelpington it was noted in 1792 that Catholic numbers had fallen each year since the apostasy of Sir John Swinburne to the Church of England, and the Catholic community of Felling was decimated following the secession of Charles Brandling, the Catholic squire.

These examples show that contributory factors to the decline of the Catholic population included isolation, a lack of pastoral care and the apostasy or temporary insolvency of a Catholic landowner bringing about the closure of a chapel and the dismissal of the chaplain. Areas which maintained their Catholic populations were those sizeable rural enclaves with a relatively settled community. In Ryton and Lanchester, where the Church was visible and strong, and where the Catholic population was long-established, numbers held up. In those, usually urban, areas where the Catholic population was less settled, or where there was a small Catholic presence in a rural parish, or where the church was inconspicuous, numbers fell. In Darlington there was a small and apparently well-established Catholic community, but it was only served by a monthly supply mission until 1824; the Catholic population fell by 70%, yet over half the Catholics were aged under thirty in 1767 and could have been expected to reproduce themselves. Similarly, a large rural Catholic community could fall markedly if the Catholic landowner, and hence principal employer, left the Church. There were exceptions to the general pattern; a small urban group of Catholics could flourish, given an active missioner, which was the case at Berwick towards the end of the century and at North Shields some years later.

To some extent, war and the demographic change associated with industrial development also served to hinder the growth of the small Catholic body. Moreover, though there were only 1,873 Methodists in County Durham in 1767 (concentrated on Tyneside and in the western dales), the rapid proliferation of Methodism later in the century suggests that the legal disabilities and political uncertainties associated with Catholicism were also important influences.[14] It was certainly not a time for zealous evangelism, living as Catholics did in a state of informal toleration. Such a policy would have been seen by many Protestants as provocative, just as many Catholic lay gentlemen would have considered it inexpedient for their chaplains to be seen casting about for converts in their localities. It is clear, at any rate, that there were few conversions except through marriage. The vicar of Esh remarked in 1792 that Catholic 'numbers have not increased except by the ordinary methods of population rise'.

The few and ageing priests had to be content to minister to existing Catholics but, despite their best efforts, they were fighting a losing battle in the towns and remoter areas. They were unable to visit regularly those Catholics living in the widely scattered farmsteads and hamlets of the region. Yet the maintenance of the faith depended on such support because religious practice is very difficult to sustain in isolation. A solitary, remotely-located family would almost inevitably leave the Church in one or two generations without regular encouragement to persevere. In Bothal in 1792 the Catholics were 'an old man and his wife and their son and his wife but the children of the latter have been baptised in the Church [of England]'. Missionary discretion had to be kept up even after the first stage of Relief had been achieved; the Gordon Riots reminded Catholics not to over-reach themselves, and the ill-tempered debate on the Catholic Question would continue for a further fifty years. Protestant England would prove extremely reluctant to grant formal and civil political liberty to Papists in 1829 despite having welcomed numbers of exiled French priests and accepted the repatriation of the English colleges and convents from the Continent after the French Revolution.

Distribution and Density

In general, the small Catholic population was widely dispersed throughout the region. Almost 90% of Anglican parishes reported Catholic inhabitancy at one time or another. There were, however, some populous parishes, mostly in the remote western uplands, which had no Catholic residents at all, and the best example is Stanhope in Weardale (population 5,000), which was, in any case, assiduously evangelised by John Wesley.

The principal, and unsurprising, feature of the distribution of the Catholics in the north-east was that the largest groups were to be found in the vicinity of the Catholic missions. A mission-station was generally established by a country gentleman on his estate and the nucleus of the congregation was formed from the members of the household and estate workers. The geographical range of the mission quickly expanded so that some were attended from considerable distances by people unconnected with the patron. Before a resident missioner was appointed at Berwick, for example, the Catholics travelled to Haggerston Castle for Sunday Mass, a tiring round trip of over twelve miles. Alternatively, of course, the missioner could do the travelling; in 1805 the Berwick missioner said he had 'walked no less than 1,000 miles' on missionary duty in the previous year.[15] That was exceptional, for most Catholics lived within range of a chapel.

Nonetheless, the widespread distribution of the Catholic population necessarily involved substantial amounts of walking or riding if those in the remoter areas were to practise their faith regularly.

Table 20: Residential Density of Catholic Families in North-East England (Selected Parishes)

	Total No. of families	No. of RC families	% of RC families
County Durham Parishes:			
Croxdale	100	50	50
Merrington	53	11	20
Ryton	600	100	16
Lanchester	593	77	13
Durham City (6 parishes)	1,000	100	10
Northumberland Parishes:			
Netherwitton	110	24	22
Ancroft-cum-Kyloe	274	42	15
Whittingham	242	39	16
Lowick	297	10	3.3
Newcastle-upon-Tyne (4 parishes)	5,285	84	1.6
Totals:			
County Durham	25,000	600	2.4
Northumberland	27,131	518	1.9

Source: 1774 Durham Episcopal Visitation Return.

Normally, the Episcopal Visitation questionnaire enquired about the number of individual Catholics in the parishes, but in 1774 it asked for the number of families, thus revealing the average size of a family to be four persons. Since it also asked for the total number of families in the parish, a direct measurement of residential density can be calculated for the Catholic population. The average size of the Anglican parish in the North at this time, however, was over ten thousand acres, and so the parish is not always the most useful geographical unit by which to illustrate the residential density of the population, although that is how the information was collected.[16] In 1750 the Catholic chaplains at Haggerston Castle and Berrington Hall reported that a total of some 230 people of all ages attended one or other of the two chapels. That figure was corroborated in 1767, allowing for growth, when the four parishes of Ancroft, Belford, Holy Island and Lowick returned 256 Catholics (56 families in 1774).

The two principal returns came from Lowick and the chapelry of Kyloe in Ancroft. The villages of Kyloe and nearby Fenwick (where there was a Catholic school) belonged to the Haggerstons, as did Lowick, two and a half miles to the west. Haggerston and Berrington (which belonged to the Claverings) lay about three miles to the north. Virtually all the Catholics of the area lived in those five villages, and so the geographical spread and residential density of the Catholic population is distorted when taking the parish as the base unit of measurement. Six per cent of the families of Hartburn parish were Catholic, but if the village and chapelry of Netherwitton is taken separately (as it usually was) then the distribution of Catholic families is seen to be concentrated, for it amounts to 22% of the chapelry's population. In the same way, most of the Catholic families in the parish of Whittingham lived in settlements close to Callaly Castle. Such concentrations are to be attributed to the presence of Catholic gentry houses and chapels: the Thorntons at Netherwitton, Salvins at Croxdale, Smythes in Esh (Lanchester), Silvertops in Stella (Ryton), and so on. Although in no parish did the Catholics form a majority of inhabitants, a few villages associated with Catholic gentry estates did have relatively large Catholic communities; apart from those enclaves, the remainder of the Catholic population was distributed thinly. None of the towns of the region, except Durham, had a large Catholic community. The Catholic body, then, was not a conspicuous component of the region's population.

Geographical Mobility

In 1767 parish officials were asked to state how long the Catholics had been resident in their present domiciles. Clearly, the overwhelming majority of children under fifteen years of age were living where they had been born, or had moved with their parents, and that group, which is about a third of the whole, can be excluded from any analysis of free geographical mobility.

This shows that just under half the Catholic adults in each county were living in their native parishes, and about a third had moved into their present localities within the previous ten years. Although the rural Catholics were considerably more settled than those in the urban areas, that was not invariably the case; the Catholics of Ellingham and Lanchester were as likely to be newcomers as long-term residents. A close analysis indicates that the geographical mobility of the northern Catholics was governed largely by economic circumstances rather than by religious considerations. Agriculture had long been, and would remain for some time, the staple industry in such places as Croxdale, Kyloe and Whittingham, just as coal-mining had a long history in Ryton. The populations of those parishes were therefore unlikely to change markedly. The towns, on the other hand, were fast-growing industrial and commercial centres which had a relatively mobile and young population (half the Catholics of Newcastle and two thirds of those in Alnwick were under thirty years of age).

Table 21: Geographical Mobility of Adult Catholics of North-East England, 1767

	Percentage of adults resident in their present parishes	
	Under 10 years %	**Since birth or over 20 years %**
County Durham (10% unknown)	33	44
Northumberland (17% unknown)	28	47
Selected parishes:		
Alnwick	65	19
Croxdale	22	68
Durham City (6 parishes)	42	43
Ellingham	43	39
Kyloe & Lowick	14	78
Lanchester	35	45
Newcastle-upon-Tyne (4 parishes)	60	21
Ryton	14	69
Sunderland (3 parishes)	50	17
Whittingham	26	63

Source: Returns of Papists, 1767, diocese of Durham.

Table 22 shows, not surprisingly, that the young were the most mobile and the old were the most settled groups in society. On reaching working (or marriageable) age, individuals moved away from their native parishes if suitable opportunities did not occur locally. A readiness to move about was maintained throughout a working life, but as people got older, they became less likely to move. Commonplace as this conclusion is, it does at least indicate that the pattern of geographical mobility exhibited by the Catholics of the north-east was similar to that which might be expected of any economically-active population. There is nothing to indicate that there was any large scale movement into the Catholic strongholds, nor were the Catholics constrained or inhibited from moving into new localities to seek work or a spouse.

Table 22: Geographical Mobility of Northumbrian Catholic Adults, 1767

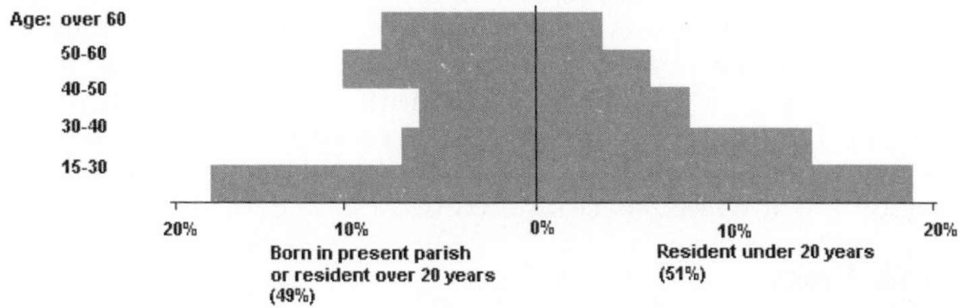

However, religious practice is at greater risk when a population is mobile or when social change is taking place.[17] A family moving from a rural area into an urban centre has to be able to reconnect with the Church after moving. If the Church's organisation is weak or inconspicuous, or if regular religious services are not maintained, the chances are that the family will be lost. Obviously a number of migrant did reconnect, but there was no overall increase in the urban Catholic population until the 1820s at the earliest, yet it was into the towns that the population had been moving since late in the previous century. Hence, leakage as the result of migration was another factor contributing to the decline in overall Catholic numbers.[18]

Age and Gender Profile

Table 23: Age and Gender Profile of North-Eastern Catholics, 1767

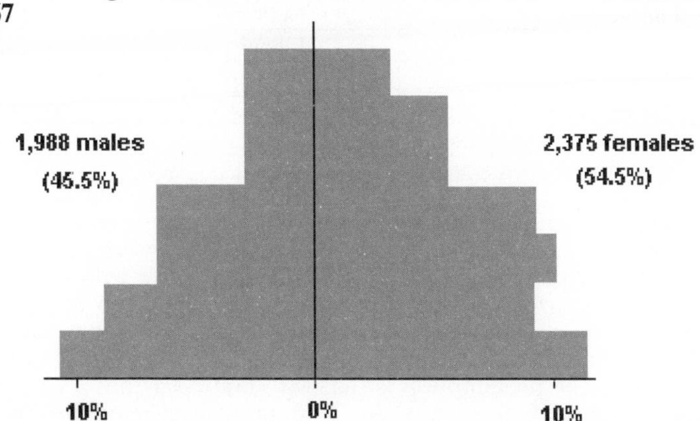

The age and sex of 90% of the north-eastern Catholics in 1767 is known. Table 23 shows that the age pattern was pyramidal and that the sexes were in rough balance. About 40% were aged between twenty and forty, and it is from this group that natural increase was to be expected. Since the composition of the Catholic population was clearly suited to growth, the decline in numbers over the next half-century cannot be attributed in the same to a lack of fecundity or a shortage of suitable Catholic mates in the same age group. The structure of the Catholic population of the north-east was remarkably similar to that of the nation as a whole, as computed in 1750 and 1815.[19]

Marital Patterns

The 1767 returns give the marital status of 94% of the Catholics of the region. Children up to the age of fifteen years (the age at which the majority seem to have become economically active) represent a third of the whole. 30% were single men and women; 5% were widows or widowers; and 30% were married. The large numbers of single people indicates that Catholics followed the national practice for a first marriage to take place in the middle to late twenties. Of major significance for present purposes, however, is the extent to which Catholics married within their own church, or sought a spouse without regard to ecclesiastical affiliation.

Table 24: Marriages in which only one partner was R.C.: North-East England, 1767

County Durham	44%	Northumberland	45%
Lanchester	26%	Netherwitton	17%
Croxdale	28%	Ellingham	42%
Ryton	44%	Newcastle (4 parishes)	42%
Durham City (6 parishes)	50%	Alnwick	65%
Sunderland (3 parishes)	57%	Longhorsley	84%

Sample: 916 married couples, i.e., all those listed as being married.

Table 24 shows that just over half of all marriages were between Catholics and hence the remainder were apparently 'mixed'. Mixed marriages are difficult to identify with certainty, since the returning officer may not have intended to imply one, whereas one may be inferred from the way the entry is written. In Durham there was 'the wife and daughter of a Mr Hanby, a Plumber'. The presumption is that Mr Hanby was not a Catholic. Also in Durham there was 'Mr Walton, a teacher of the French language, and his infant son'. Is it justified to assume this to be a mixed marriage because the wife is not mentioned? Mr Walton may have been a widower, or perhaps the vicar did not think to mention the wife, assuming it to be obvious. There are some difficulties, then, but these are mostly to do with a minority of cases in which the husband is Catholic but the wife is (apparently) not.

In the north-east, mixed marriages were almost as common as those between two Roman Catholics. As perhaps was to be expected, the highest incidence of mixed marriages occurred in the towns, but no other correlation can be established. The number of mixed marriages was relatively high in such Catholic strongholds as Croxdale and Ellingham. In the parish of Netherwitton where the large Catholic population was well established, only 17% of marriages were mixed, but in Longhorsley which also had a relatively large settled Catholic community, only 16% of marriages were between two Catholics. In the small and less settled Catholic population of Newcastle, over half the marriages were between two Catholics. This pattern was not uncommon. The Revd. Joseph Berington noted that mixed marriages were 'now very usual' in the south, and in 1803 the Vicar Apostolic of the Western District reported an increase in mixed marriages as well as a decline in attendance at the sacraments and a general relaxation of the barriers between Catholics and Protestants.[20]

The implications of a generally high incidence of mixed marriages are twofold. Firstly, it suggests that since the choice of marriage partner was not restricted to their co-religionists, the Catholics were securely based in society, and were neither insular or ostracised. Secondly the growth in the Catholic population would be affected, and the outcome of a mixed marriage was various. In 1792 the vicar of Lanchester said:

> During a residence of 13 years in the parish there have been four instances of Protestants marrying Papists and turning to their Communion, whilst I have only got one from them in a similar instance.

In Norton that year one wife was 'perverted to Popery on her marriage. The two sisters of the husband came over to the Communion of our Church on their marriages'. In 1801 there was a large family in Wolsingham in which the father and sons were Catholic while the wife and daughters were Anglican; in Longhoughton the opposite was the case. In Ellingham in 1810 it was reported that

> The wives and daughters of two other farmers are Papists: but the fathers and sons of the established church. Several instances of the same kind occur among the Cottagers and married servants of Mr Haggerston, and one or two where the husband is a Roman Catholic and the wife of the established church. I am not aware of any persons

having lately been perverted to Popery in this parish. Where however the parents of any new born child, dependent on the Haggerston family are of different persuasions as above mentioned, the children are mostly baptized by the Roman Catholic priest.

In Warkworth in 1792 a farmer called Thomas Wilson, 'being the son of Protestant parents' married a Catholic and since then he appeared 'to be a Papist, as he had had his son baptized by a popish priest'. This was a constant theme in the reports about the northern Catholics. In 1732 the vicar of Gainford expressed great irritation with the Catholics in his parish who, among other things, were 'wont to be marryed by a Popish Priest without Banns or License'. He sought his bishop's advice on another matter:

When a Papist [of Piercebridge] chances to marry a Protestant, the Papist for the most part causes the children to be baptized by a Popish Priest and to be brought up in his own religion. The vicar of Gainford, to prevent the mischief last mentioned, has several times required the parties to observe this Rule, viz: That the boys should follow the Religion of the father and the girls that of the mother. But the Papists will not keep to the Rule.

He went on to complain about another stratagem:

Francis Jakes, a poor man of the said town, was lately seduced to the Roman Catholic Religion, probably by some of the family at Cliff, the seat of a Roman Catholic gentleman near Piercebridge in Yorkshire. That the said Jakes sends two of his children to be brought up Papists on consideration (as the report is) of their being taught to read and write gratis.[21]

He concluded with a plea for advice on how to 'restrain the aforesaid practices tending to increase the Popish party' in his parish. It is not known whether the bishop came to the vicar's assistance; probably not, because Mr Witham and his chaplain at Cliffe Hall continued as before. These examples show that a mixed marriage could result in apostasy, recruitment, or have no effect on religious affiliations. Since Catholic numbers fell in the period, however, it seems as if losses through mixed marriage outnumbered gains.

Socio-Economic Status

The English social pyramid, though steep in terms of income, was almost flat above the base and the number of individuals holding a social rank was very small. The 1705 returns taken in conjunction with the returns made in accordance with the Registration of Papists' Estates Act (1716) show that there were three, more or less distinct, groupings. There was a tiny group

(3%) of wealthy landowners and annuitants (mostly widows), with incomes of between £100 and £4,000 a year. Then there was a small group (7%) of tradesmen, lesser gentry and farmers, in possession of property such as house, shops and smallholdings which yielded incomes of under £100 a year. The professions were represented by one or two attorneys, physicians and a handful of stewards, agents or factors of gentry estates.

The majority (90%) were ordinary folk without any capital resources to speak of, and most of them earned a living on the land in one way or another. Large numbers of yeomen, husbandmen and herdsmen are listed in 1705; millers, cottagers and agricultural day-labourers were also to be found in most rural parishes. The urban parishes listed wrights of various kinds in addition to numbers of butchers, shoemakers, carpenters and innkeepers. Master mariners worked out of the ports and pitmen, sinkers and staithemen worked in the coalmines. There was a goldsmith, a tobacconist, a schoolmaster, a music teacher and the wife of a Yorkshire rector. Finally, servants and labourers appear in all parish returns; one or two individuals received parish alms and there was one Catholic prisoner in Newcastle gaol. At the beginning of the eighteenth century, then, the socio-economic structure of the northern Catholic community was similar to that of the population as a whole: Catholics were to be found at all social levels and in all situations. Anti-Catholicism was expressed from time to time but on only one occasion did this have a significant economic effect. Ambrose Crowley was compelled to move his ironworks from Sunderland to Ryton in 1690 because 'many of his workmen were foreigners and Catholics, and they did not altogether meet with a friendly reception', but that was in the unsettled period after the Revolution.[22]

The socio-economic structure of the north-eastern Catholics was unaltered at the time of the Relief Acts. In 1767 there were farmers and merchants, doctors and teachers, labourers, publicans and shopkeepers. Industry was represented by managers, wheelwrights, enginewrights, millwrights, and so on. Unskilled, semi-skilled and skilled jobs were listed together with gardeners, seafarers, miners and servants. The breeches-maker, mantua-maker, cheese-seller, petticoat-quilter, lint-heckler, tallow-chandler and flax-dresser appeared with the goldsmith, milliner, clockmaker, clerk, midwife, apothecary, nurse, barber, fiddler and fortune-teller. Catholics were therefore to be found in most, if not all, occupations available in the region. But whether they were under-or over-represented in any particular occupation can be ascertained in a general way only because of the absence of directly comparable material.

Table 25: Occupations of North-Eastern Catholics in 1767 compared with National Distribution in 1801

	Percentage of population engaged	
	Britain %	R.C.s in the North-East %
Agriculture, fishing & forestry	36	16
Manufacturing, mining, building	30	47
Trade & transport	11	6
Domestic & personal	11	24
Professional, public service & gentry	12	7

Sources: 1767 Returns of Papists, Diocese of Durham; 1810 National Census.

It can be seen from Table 25 that the Catholics were not languishing in the gaols or the workhouse but were gainfully employed. But they were under-represented in agriculture, public service and in the professional and commercial classes. Since the professions were closed to them under the penal laws, it is perhaps more surprising that any Catholics at all managed to follow a professional career. Durham city was notorious for the high number of Catholic doctors in practice there at this time.[23] The reduced number in agriculture and trade was doubtless because those were capital-intensive occupations. For the most part, the region's Catholics were predominantly of what has come to be known as the working class and hence were over-represented in the manufacturing and service sectors. It is striking how often the Anglican clergy referred to the Catholics as 'chiefly of low rank', 'mostly servants, mechanics and labourers', 'none of them of any Note', 'not persons of much condition in life', 'plebeians' or 'common people'. The Catholic priest Joseph Berington, who gave an account of the English Catholics in 1780, held a similar view:

> The inferior orders are little distinguishable from the corresponding classes of their Protestant neighbours. Here the broad features of distinction almost disappear industry, association, necessity, obliterate the characteristic traits. Generally speaking, they are farmers [i.e., farm-workers], shop-keepers, artisans and labourers.[24]

Conclusions

Several inter-related conclusions can be drawn from this analysis. In every respect the Catholics of north-eastern England in the eighteenth century showed social characteristics virtually indistinguishable from those of their neighbours. They were represented at every social level and in almost all localities; their ages and gender were typical; their employment, residential and marital problems indicate they were securely integrated into local society. The Catholics lived openly and they had achieved a large degree of economic autonomy and social acceptance long before their political emancipation in 1829. Total exclusion was maintained only in the professions and political life but otherwise Catholics were free to engage in productive employment appropriate to their social and financial condition. This was by no means peculiar to the north-east, for a similar situation obtained in North Yorkshire, York, Birmingham, Lancashire and Staffordshire. Although it has been observed that the Catholics of this time 'were well-assimilated into local life, but beyond that they did not venture', there is no evidence of a Catholic ghetto in the north-east, nor was there a Catholic sub-culture, except perhaps among the lay gentry, who for the most part married within their own small circle and took their leisure in the same kind of company.[25]

Catholics were not particularly conspicuous in their religious practice, the one thing that set them apart from their contemporaries. To a large extent that was their surety; they found it possible to live in peace because they practised their religion discreetly while at the same time managing to avoid any tendency to insularity. In 1777 Pope Pius VI agreed to reduce the number of holydays in England because they could not be observed by Catholics working in a predominantly Protestant world, and in 1814 a group of laymen appealed for a relaxation of the abstinence laws for the various vigils and ember and rogation days for similar reasons:

> Living as we daily do in intercourse with our Protestant citizens, employed as the great bulk of the Catholic Manufacturers are by Protestant Capitalists, engaged as many Catholics are in the pursuits of Agriculture, mining and Commerce, where they are daily and hourly intermixed with their Protestant neighbours and from which their presence cannot without the greatest difficulties to their families and their masters be dispensed with, difficulties so great and so multiplying from the high price of labour, the increased application of machinery and the constant and daily intercourse between persons of different religions, as to render some of these regulations. ......so difficult of observance particularly the Saturdays and Wednesdays, arising from the circumstances of their being the general market days thro'out Great Britain....[26]

The appeal was successful and, in the subsequent political campaigns for their relief and emancipation, Catholic leaders could justifiably emphasise their social congruity with their fellow-citizens.

The notion that by the eighteenth century the English Catholic body was reduced to an insignificant and segregated group of decaying gentry is therefore wide of the mark. As has been shown, the recusants of the north-east were sturdy and self-assured; their discretion should not be understood as submission. Only eleven years after the Gordon Riots, which followed the first Catholic Relief Act, a second and more extensive Relief Bill was enacted, and that would lead to a post-war increase in the Catholic population; the Status Animarum of the Vicariate for 1830 estimated the number of Catholics in the region to be 20,000 (even before the Irish influx).[27] Thus the foundations of the Catholic Revival of the nineteenth century were laid in the eighteenth; the 'Second Spring' could not possibly have taken place without the steady, if unobtrusive, consolidation of the mission by the last of the English Catholic recusants, who were, overwhelmingly, below the rank of gentry.

NOTES

1 Denis Gwynn, *The Second Spring 1818-1852* (1942), pp. 11-3. Newman also spoke of the 'resurrection' of the English Catholic Church brought about in his view by the Oxford Movement and the Irish influx.

2 Catholic surveys not examined here, because of their deficiencies include: Bishop D. Williams' Visitation and Confirmation, 1728 (C.R.S. 25, 100); List of Non-Jurors of County Durham, 1744 (Ushaw, W.V. Smith Papers); Jubilee Returns by Jesuit Missioners, 1750 (Foley 5, Series 12, 666-7); Bishop F. Petre's Estimate, 1773 (J.H. Whyte, 'The Vicars Apostolics' Returns of 1773', *Recusant History* 9, no. 4 (1968), pp. 205-14); Bishop M. Gibson's *Relatio* of 1787 (abbreviated in Leo Gooch, 'The Last Recusants of the North East: the Reports of 1780 and 1787', *N.C.H.* 27 (1988), pp. 7-11). It is clear from the surveys made by the Vicars Apostolic, that they knew less about their own people than did the Anglican clergy.

3 Lords R.O. Main Papers, Returns of Papists 1705/6 Dioceses of Durham and York; E.S. Worrall ed., *Returns of Papists, 1767, Vol. 2, Dioceses of England and Wales except Chester* (C.R.S. Occasional Publications 2, 1989); Lords R.O. Main Papers, Returns of Papists, 1780.

4 Durham University Library, Archives and Special Collections, Bishop Edward Chandler's Parochial Returns & Remarks on his Visitation 173[2]. From internal evidence this can be dated at approximately 1732 and hence would have been his primary Visitation.

5 Durham University Library, Archives and Special Collections, Auckland Castle Episcopal Records: Clergy Visitation Returns, 1774 (to Bishop Egerton); 1792, 1810, 1814 (to Bishop Barrington.

6 Hence extracts from the returns are identified in the text by parish and year without further footnotes.

7 E.g. Bossy, *Catholics*, p. 184.

8 *Journals of the House of Lords* 17, 685/6, 720/1.

9 The registers compiled under this Act have been published: *Northumberland* (Surtees Society, 131, 1918), *Co. Durham* (Surtees Society 173 & 175, 1962 & 1965). For the general political and social background see, Colin Haydon, *Anti-Catholicism in Eighteenth Century England c. 1714-1780* (1993).

10 Leo Gooch, *From Jacobite to Radical: the Catholics of North East England 1688-1850* (Ph.D. University of Durham, 1989), part 2, chapter 1.

11 For critical press comment see, *inter alia*, *The Monthly Review* 32 (1765), pp. 370, 472, 479-80; 35 (1766), pp. 246-7, 487; 37 (1767), pp. 317-8. Thomas Hollis, a

zealous Low-Church Whig, published a 'Plan for Preventing the Growth of Popery in England' in *The London Chronicle* on 22-24 September 1768, in which he advocated the introduction of new penal laws.

12 The question asked at the Visitation of 1792, and with minor variations in other years, was:

Are there any reputed papists in your parish or chapelry? How many, and of what rank? Have any persons lately perverted to popery; by whom; and by what means? Is there any place in your parish or chapelry in which they assemble for divine worship, and where is it? Doth any popish priest reside in your parish, or resort to it? And by what name doth he go? Is there any popish school in your parish to which the children of Protestant parents are admitted? Hath any Visitation or confirmation been holden in your parish lately by any popish bishop?

13 F.J. Vaughan, 'Bishop Leyburn and his Confirmation Register of 1687', *N.C.H.* 12 (1980), pp. 14-8; Celia Fiennes, *Through England on a Side-saddle in the Time of William and Mary* (1888 ed.), p. 180; Daniel Defoe, *A Tour thro' the Whole Island of Great Britain* (1724), p. 9.

14 S. Ayling, *John Wesley* (1979), pp. 242, 310.

15 Ushaw, Eyre MSS. No. 88, Philip Besnier to Thomas Eyre.

16 A.D. Gilbert, *Religion and Society in Industrial England* (1976), p. 101.

17 R. Currie et al, *Churches and Churchgoers: Patterns of Church Growth in the British Isles since 1700* (1977), pp. 7, 103. (This work is unreliable on Catholic numbers, e.g. p. 21, Table 2.3.)

18 See Bossy, *Catholics*, pp. 300-1 for comparable mobility patterns in Staffordshire.

19 Michael Rose, *The Economic History of Britain since 1700, Volume 1, 1700-1860*, pp. 22-3.

20 Joseph Berington, *The State and Behaviour of English Catholics from the Reformation to the Year 1780* (1780), p. 118; J.P. Chinnici, *The English Catholic Enlightenment 1780-1850* (1980), p. 70.

21 W.R. Ward, *Religion and Society in England 1790-1850* (1972), p. 25.

22 Michael W. Flinn, *Men of Iron* (1962), pp. 40-1; W. Mitchell, *History of Sunderland* (1919), p. 68.

23 William V. Smith, 'Recusant Doctors in Northumberland and Durham, 1650-1790', *N.C.H.* 23 (1986), pp. 15-26.

24 Berington, *State and Behaviour of English Catholics*. Berington also noted the fall in the overall number of Catholics: ibid., pp. 111-24.

25 Aveling, *York*, chapters 4 & 5; Aveling, *North*, pp. 400-3; J. Hugh Aveling, 'Some Aspects of Yorkshire Catholic Recusant History', *Studies in Church History* 4 (1967), pp. 118-21; Bossy, *Catholics*, chapter 13; Judith F. Champ, 'St. Martin's Parish, Birmingham, in 1767: A Study of Urban Catholicism', *Recusant History* 15, no. 5 (1981); George Connolly, 'The Transubstantiation of Myth: Towards a New Popular History of Nineteenth Century Catholicism in England', *Journal of Ecclesiastical History* 35, no. 1 (1984); D. Holmes, *More Roman than Rome* (1978), pp. 21-3.

26 Ushaw DIO 11; J. P. Chinnici, *The English Catholic Enlightenment* (Shepherdstown, U.S.A., 1980), pp. 68-9.

27 J. Lenders, 'Statistics of the Diocese of Hexham and Newcastle 1830-1930', (n.d.), in Northumberland Record Office RCD 2/1.

Part Three: Catholics on the Eve of the Relief Acts

12

1767—THE SOURCES

By the end of the eighteenth century there is much more evidence from the Catholic community itself and this evidence can be placed in the context of the Returns of Papists made by the Anglican Bishops to the House of Lords in 1767.[1] The Returns were analysed in depth by the late J. A. Lesourd in 1978 but regrettably his work has never been translated or published in England.[2] Lesourd was mainly concerned to provide a statistical analysis and, while making use of his work, this study will use the returns rather to reconstruct individual Catholic congregations and with the help of other evidence to penetrate the experience of Catholics on the eve of the Relief Acts of 1778 and 1791.

The returns, as printed by the Catholic Record Society from the summary in the House of Lords, list 66,690 papists, men, women and children, excluding those in the Welsh dioceses. They come from 2,537 places (parishes, chapelries and townships) in 22 dioceses, that is, less than half of the parishes of England. The question arises whether the returns we do not have were nil returns or missing returns. Original returns to this enquiry have survived in some dioceses. Those from Worcester Diocese show that nil returns were made by 152 parishes and these are with a very few exceptions the 'missing' parishes in the House of Lords summary. Again, 420 parishes of Lichfield diocese declared 'there are no papists or reputed papists' while 209 parishes reported 4,949 papists or reputed papists. Despite omissions, we probably have information from most parishes where Catholics lived, at least in the provinces. All dioceses included details of age and residence, while all but Chichester included occupations. However, this information was not given systematically.[3]

Lesourd looked at the figures by county instead of by diocese, and found nine which reported less than a hundred papists: Cambridge, Cornwall, Cumberland, Hertford, Huntingdon, Kent, Northamptonshire, Rutland and Westmorland, all, be it noted, areas which were predominantly rural and becoming more so. There had been little change in distribution in these areas since 1600. In contrast, some returns from Durham, Lancashire, the dioceses of Lichfield and Worcester and Yorkshire were of large numbers and revealed new centres.[4]

Table 26: Information provided by Dioceses to the House of Lords, 1767

Diocese	**Papists**	**Returns**
Bath & Wells	383	42
Bristol	1,018	46
Canterbury	271	36
Carlisle (initials)	173	23
Chester (names)	25,139	497
Chichester	548	63
Durham (names)	4,916	132
Ely	7	2
Exeter (names)	291	50
Gloucester	316	49
Hereford (names)	565	114
Lichfield	4,949	209
Lincoln	1,642	206
London*	12,320	98
Norwich	1,279	168
Oxford	803	85
Peterborough	125	46
Rochester	212	21
Salisbury	1,197	85
Winchester	1,760	127
Worcester	2,187	110
York (initials)	6,589	356
Totals	66,690	2,537

Source: Worrall, *The Returns of Papists 1767,* volumes 1 and 2. Chichester: Bishop's figure 846. York: Archbishop's figure 6545.

Mapping the returns to the 1767 enquiry shows how greatly the concentration of Catholics varied within short distances. In south-west Warwickshire there were a number of Catholic missions but in north-east Warwickshire virtually none. In Hampshire, Catholics were found along the coastal strip from Portsmouth to Chichester and around Winchester but few in the rest of the county. The Essex missions were grouped in the south-west of the county. In the north-west of England the missions were concentrated around the Barony of Kendal and in Cheshire in the Wirral peninsula. In Lancashire the great majority of the missions were in the west of the county.

The Reliability of the 1767 Returns

The lists include men, women and children, even infants, making this a real attempt at a census. Previous listings were made for legal or pastoral reasons and identified particular groups of Catholics, usually adults only. For this reason there can be no numerical comparison between the Compton census of 1676 and the returns of 1767, or indeed any other return made in the intermediate period unless care is taken to compare only like with like by, for example, leaving the children out of account, comparing parish only with parish, township only with township, and by recognising omissions. While the returns offer only very insecure statistics, they can nevertheless yield a rich return of information and understanding of the generality of Catholics.

Letters were sent out to bishops on 4 July and the returns were to be made by Michaelmas. The necessary administrative structure to carry out the survey was already in place, since the Church of England bishops were accustomed to collecting such information from incumbents of the parishes and chapels in the dioceses. In the London parishes of St James and St Giles, the incumbents said, understandably, that the numbers were too large to give details of name, occupation and length of residence, but they did claim to have at least made a count of the Catholics in all the streets, alleys and courts. In general, the information provided for London is much less satisfactory than elsewhere and the ignorance of the incumbents contrasts with the detailed knowledge in many rural parishes. In many cases two or three families were given together, perhaps indicating multi-occupancy; information concerning length of residence is especially defective, and almost nothing is said about children other than their numbers. Collective entries are made for poorer people, for example labourers, dockers and oyster-women. Nevertheless, the references to persons who refused to give account of themselves suggest that some house-to-house visiting was attempted.[5] Elsewhere considerable efforts were made to make a careful return even where the numbers were large. Liverpool had an organised team of local officers for the administration of what was already a town of some 30,000 inhabitants, and was able to carry through the operation quickly and efficiently. A team of seventeen men was appointed and each man was responsible for collecting the information from a group of streets and yards. The collectors of information were generally middle-class men who were regularly involved in local government. Two were serving churchwardens, two were sidesmen, five were overseers of the poor, and one was a tax collector. The team was organised by Mr Tillinghast, the chief rate collector. The work was carried out between 16th September and 19th October 1767 and produced a list of over 1,500 men, women and children with only one error of double counting. This was one of many similar tasks which Mr Tillinghast and his colleagues were constantly required to perform.[6]

Individual incumbents were anxious to demonstrate their diligence to the Bishops. The minister at Chipping, Lancashire, remarked:

> It was not difficult for me to comply with your lordship's request as I have more than once taken the number of Protestants and Papists. As to the exact age of everyone, it would be impossible to know it except by their own account which is not to be relied upon. They are few, if any, but I personally know them as they are all natives of this parish or neighbourhood.

He listed 186 papists but excluded the priest 'lately a month or more absent, at London as is commonly reported'.[7] At Bolam, Northumberland, the minister went to see the persons concerned to get full details.[8] At Fowey, Cornwall, the incumbent reported

> John Couch, formerly a brewer in London but has for forty years lived in Fowey on the income of his estates with Anne his wife and his son. The eldest brother is a Jesuit in Hungary, and the youngest is still abroad at school at some popish seminary and is designed for a surgeon.

He adds that John Couch's predecessors had been papists for many generations. In this fishing town of 127 families in 1745 such matters were evidently commonly known. The great majority of the incumbents had only a few Catholics to report. One thousand individual returns listed less than five papists and a further 600 between five and nine, or in other words one or two families.[9]

Sometimes the lists of Easter communicants at a Catholic mission can be correlated with the return of 1767 to test its reliability . This is possible in the case of a cluster of three Mass centres associated with Chillington Hall which lay in the parish of Brewood, Staffordshire. The annual lists of communicants from 1758-1848 have survived. If we compare the numbers of communicants in 1767 with the numbers of persons over fourteen reported to the House of Lords the two were much the same, 243 persons over the age 14 on the return, and 233 on the communion list. As so often, comparison of numbers by itself is deceptive, for a name-by-name comparison of the two lists shows that only 146 persons are actually common to both lists. Among those who appear in the return but did not make their Easter communion in 1767 were some Catholic families who appeared frequently in the Catholic registers, for example the families of Howell, Read, Styche and Yates. There may be many possible reasons to account for their absence from Communion. The return shows that some of the Catholics concerned were elderly. Some may have gone to communion elsewhere, for there were many alternative Mass centres in the area, and the Howells and the Cauzers, for example, had Catholic relatives in Wolverhampton. Having allowed for all these, is it going too far to suggest that we have identified some of the less committed Catholics? These may comprise a group of Catholics whose neighbours thought of them as Catholics, who perhaps thought of themselves as Catholics but who did not fulfill their Easter duties. Were all the Catholics listed in 1767 what we should call today 'practising Catholics'?

The reverse comparison shows that there were 86 communicants who do not appear in the 1767 return for Brewood. Of these, 16 can be found in the returns of surrounding parishes of Penkridge, Codsall, Stretton and Blymhill, revealing Catholic families who can be shown to have travelled in from elsewhere to make their communion. Most of these are from parishes north of Brewood, hardly surprisingly, as there were three more Mass centres south of Brewood and another three to the west, but none to the north. We are left with 70 persons who communicated but whose residence is unknown.[10]

The numbers of Catholics need to be placed in the context of parish population, but such figures for this period are hard to come by, even in the crudest form, especially for rural parishes. By 1767, contemporary estimates of the size of towns were becoming more reliable and the Church of England *Comperta* give some information about the total number of families or inhabitants in individual parishes, as well as of papists and Dissenters. Although coverage and chronology are not regular, these have been used in what follows as a rough guide in default of better.[11] It was, after all, to the Church of England incumbents and the parishes that the government turned when systematic decennial censuses began in 1801.

Records created by the Catholics themselves, and in particular the administrative records of the clergy, are particularly useful in building mission histories. The bishops' authority over priests was well established, even though England was a missionary country and there were no formal Catholic parishes, and the bishops were in practice usually responsible for the appointment of priests as well as the grant of their faculties. After 1753 this applied to regular as well as secular clergy. The correspondence of the bishops and that of the superiors of the religious orders, together with the accounts of the funds held for both the secular clergy and the regular priests provide details of pastoral care of the laity.[12]

About 40 Catholic registers have survived from before 1770. While a few were little more than the personal notebooks of the priest, most were systematically kept and increasingly required by the Vicars Apostolic. Registers have the advantage of being 'mission based', provide information about the vital events in the lives of Catholic families, and, in combination with other material, reveal the differences between congregations.[13]

NOTES

1 Worrall, p. 33.
2 Lesourd: all references are to the first volume.
3 Worrall, p. 101. Original returns include: L.J.R.O. K56 & B/A/12; H.W.R.O. 2877 ii; those for Staffordshire are published in Michael Greenslade ed., 'The 1767 Return of Staffordshire Papists', *Staffs. C.H.* 17 (1977), pp. 1-57. The original returns for Norwich Diocese are transcribed and published in Joy Rowe, *Religious Dissent in East Anglia 3* (Centre for East Anglia Studies, 1996), pp. 202-34; the returns for Lincoln Diocese are in L.R.O. but are, like the House of Lords version, in summary form (ex. inf. archivist); the original returns for Northumberland are in Northumberland Record Office (ex. inf. Robin Gard); the original returns for London Diocese are in Lambeth Palace Library and have been transcribed by Julia Bellord (transcript and index in W.A.A. and Guildhall Library).
4 Lesourd, pp. 131-2; Worall 2, pp. vii-ix.
5 Worrall 2, pp. 140-4.
6 Worrall 1, pp. 9-22; *Liverpool Registers*, pp. 178-253 (analysis by C. Bennett).
7 Worrall 1, p. 104.
8 Worrall 2, p. 7.
9 Worrall 2, p. 178.
10 B.A.A. Easter Communion List 1767, Brewood, not yet listed; Worrall 2, pp. 84-6; Rowlands. Analysis by C. Coleman.
11 Printed Visitations are too numerous to list, but those which have been used in this work include: Thomas Trappes-Lomax, 'Archbishop Blackburne's Visitation Return of the Diocese of York', *Miscellanea* (C.R.S. 32, 1932), p. 380; F.R. Raines, *Notitia Cestriensis: historical notes of the Rt. Rev. Francis Gastrel* (Chetham Society Old Series, 4 volumes, 1845-1850); *The Archdeanery of Richmond in the Eighteenth Century, Bishop Gastrel's Notitia: The Yorkshire Parishes* (Yorkshire Record Society 146, 1990); E. Lloyd Jukes ed., *Visitation Returns 1738 and 1761* (Oxfordshire Record Society, 1957); W. Ward ed., *Parson and Parish in Eighteenth Century Hampshire: Replies to Bishops' Visitations* (Hampshire Record Series 13, 1995); Leo Gooch, 'Bishop Edward Chandler's Parochial Returns and Remarks on his Visitation (1732)', *Recusant History* 15 (1979-80), pp. 29-81.
12 W.A.A. Vol. 40, 59; Bellenger, *Scrolls*, p. 96. For the location and listings of the records of the Vicars Apostolic, the religious orders and related collections see the *Directory of Catholic Archives in the U.K.* (3rd edition, 1994).
13 See Michael Gandy, *Catholic Missions and Registers 1700-1880,* 6 volumes (privately printed, 1993); also Steel & Samuels, pp. 799-956.

13

1767—RELIGIOUS LIFE

The 1767 Returns recorded 249 secular and regular priests in the provinces and 25 in London. This enquiry was taking place against the background of the prosecution of fifteen priests and nine Catholic teachers, the temporary closure of at least four Masshouses in London and the expulsion of the Jesuits from France and Spain.[1] Incumbents were aware that to name a man as a priest was in effect to lay a legal charge against him. Many covered themselves by using adjectives such as 'reputed', 'supposed' and 'alleged', but this need not be taken to express any doubt about the fact. The returns from the diocese of Worcester omit all priests, perhaps for this reason.

Priests were in most cases well known to the Anglican incumbents, at least in the provinces. Some refer to them (correctly) as 'secular', 'Jesuit', 'monk' or 'friar'. Edward Dicconson of Winwick gave the parson a list of his household omitting the priest, but the parson remedied the omission from his own knowledge.[2] At Hathersage, Derbyshire, in 1751 the incumbent reported 'A person who calls himself Wilson is said to officiate as priest'. The Catholic records show that this refers to Thomas Wilson who had lived in Hathersage since 1743, was imprisoned after the '45 and then returned to Hathersage, where at the age of 50 he was listed on the 1767 return and where he died after forty years' service.[3] Six years after the 1767 return, in 1773, the Vicars Apostolic reported to Rome a total of 386 active missionaries including secular, Jesuit and other regular priests. According to this list they were responsible for about 59,000 Catholics, but it should not be taken as incontrovertible.[4]

Many priests had a regular circuit or riding, visiting small groups and saying Mass in a cottage or farmhouse. At Gooseford in Kidlington parish, Oxfordshire, a priest came once a month and 'officiates in a little room in an alehouse', visiting other places on other Sundays. In 1729 the priest who helped Bishop Stonor at Old Heythrop, Oxfordshire, had to ride four score miles every week 'twenty-two of which he was obliged to ride Gratis.'[5] The important word here is 'obliged': these were places where the District was committed to provide Mass whether it was endowed or not. The riding mission at Bacton, Suffolk, replaced an older gentry centre at Coulsey Wood. Mass was said at Thelveton, Stoke Ash, Cotton, Bacton and Haughley. Catholics from Thelnetham, Thornham Magna, Walsham and Thwaite came to Bacton to make their Easter Communion.[6] Occasionally it was difficult to find suitable priests for riding missions. A Jesuit wrote:

> J. Gage [S.J] goes once a year on a weekday but I was told [by the patron] that I must go on Sundays or not at all. Mr Reethley said I could not supply Sunbury too. Billing [another Jesuit priest] is unwilling to go to either place, as he would have to stay overnight. Mr Gage can go in the morning and do both.[7]

Bishop Witham in a pastoral letter in 1704 urged his priests not 'to take on too large a circuit when others near at hand might supply, and so expose the flock to want of hearing'.[8]

The records of the Jesuit Residence of St George at Worcester show that the salaries and board of the four priests were met from Jesuit funds, not from the contributions of the generality of the faithful, even the gentry. Jesuits were not permitted by the rules of the order to receive Mass stipends or offerings. Mass centres were moved from house to house, and when one place became inconvenient another was found for what was essentially a mission rather than a chaplaincy.

The accounts show payments for wine, candles, bread, books and writing accounts for the whole Residence. Altar breads, a thousand at a time, were sent from London regularly, also 'directories' (Persons' *Christian Directory*?) and catechisms.[9] The secular clergy did receive offerings and endowments from people of modest status but it has been insufficiently emphasised that much of the financing of missions came not from lay people but from the clergy themselves, both from individuals leaving bequests to endow missions and from accumulated funds and investments in public funds managed by the clergy as a body. The common people were the recipients of a service rather than its providers.

The Sacramental Life of Catholics in the Eighteenth Century

Some Catholics could hear Mass weekly. At Godington, Oxfordshire, the Catholics, 'all common people, assemble for worship at Mr Davis' most Sabbath days and the priest resides there'.[10] Others were visited more or less frequently. The priest Mr Hulme came once a month from Manchester to Macclesfield where there were 37 Catholics.[11] The replies of the Anglican incumbents in Oxfordshire to Bishop Secker in 1738 reveal a priest visiting Cassington 'occasionally', Heath once per month, 'sometimes' Hardwick and Somerton, where there was Mass in the chapel of the ruined house of the Fermors. There were also resident priests at Watlington and Kiddington. In contrast at Mapledurham there were no less than three resident chaplains attendant upon three Catholic gentlewomen. The parish had 70 houses and 23 cottages in all, and a total population of 430 of whom 47 were Catholics. By 1767 there was one priest and 29 adults.[12]

There are references to small groups praying together without a priest. At Bath, in 1667 'a dozen simple women' and three or four men had been found 'at their beads'; and at Somersley, Lincolnshire, the papists sometimes met in the open air at the ancient cross in the churchyard.[13]

The inventories of vestments and missions such as Oscott, Staffordshire, and Bryn, Lancashire, show that the missions possessed all that was needed for the full liturgical cycle, including the services of Holy Week. There were tabernacles, ciboria, thuribles, monstrances, incense-boats, silver candlesticks, flower vases, and devotional paintings of the stations of the cross and of the saints; and small paper 'holy pictures' were distributed to children and servants. The full celebration of the liturgy of the Church was as much a feature of the independent Mass centres as of those of the gentry.[14]

It is not clear how frequently lay Catholics received holy communion at Mass, nor how far communion was received on separate occasions. Crichton argues that for most people communion was often received outside the Mass itself in a separate ceremony before or after Mass, as was usual in Continental churches at this time. Some rather obscure remarks by William Statham of Sheffield about the separate provision of communion for the sick at Hathersage suggest that for him at least this was not a familiar practice. Crichton also suggests that most Catholics received communion only a few times a year, at Christmas, Easter and Whitsuntide. On the other hand the Bona Mors society and other confraternities committed their members to monthly confession and communion. Henry Houghton at West Grinstead enrolled his people in the Bona Mors Society at the time of their first communion. Confession was regarded as an essential preliminary before communion, preferably on the evening before receiving, and communion under both kinds was forbidden to the laity. Communicants were required to fast from midnight, wash their hands, receive on the tongue, swallow, not chew, the Species, and remain in private prayer for at least one quarter of an hour.[15]

Catholics and their Prayer-Books

From the beginning of the eighteenth century, under the influence of Gother and Challoner, many prayer-books had been published for the use of the generality of the congregation. In

1718 Gother published a complete missal in Latin and English, the first complete translation of the Mass in England. Short Latin phrases which occurred frequently in the Mass were listed and translated to mark the stages of the Mass and prayers in English were said before and after Communion, but it remained the case that the laypeople were 'at Mass' rather than participating in the action. The *Manual* and the *Primer* continued in use; Henry Houghton gave first communicants a copy of the 'half-manual'. Other prayer books included the *Key of Heaven*, which was published in 1755 in Liverpool by John Sadler for

> mariners and others whose business will not allow them to attend the public service of Mass.

The book included prayers at Mass in two columns, Latin and English, and prayers for Benediction. (The use of the word 'public' is revealing.)[16] By the end of the century both Preston and Wolverhampton had their 'own' published collections of prayers. The move to encourage the laity to participate more actively in the prayers of the Mass demonstrates yet again that English Catholics were not isolated from the developments taking place in the rest of the Church.

These books were written for those who could read; but we should not underestimate the extent of literacy even in the countryside. In 1747 a papist book was in the pocket of a poor woman found dead at Derwent Bridge, Walton, Lancashire. It was entitled *A short abridgement of Christian doctrine* and endorsed 'Mary Arrowsmith her book'. The household accounts of the Weld family (1764-1768) at East Lulworth show that many of the men and women servants could sign for their wages. The accounts were written by the housekeeper, Richard Champ, who had made his mark when he was first taken on as a day labourer, but after seven years when he became 'underservant to Thomas Win' he signed his name in full. Similar teaching was available in a Catholic household in Durham. The hornbooks and ABCs with which children started to read used the Lord's prayer and the Doxology as their texts, and they continued to learn by reading parts of the Old and New Testaments.[17]

Catholics and Marriage

Marriages recorded in the Catholic registers follow the instructions of the Council of Trent, taking place before a priest and at least two witnesses. A marriage between Catholics taking place outside the Anglican church and not according to the tenets of the Church of England had been illegal since 1606 (3 James I. c.5). Husbands convicted of a popish marriage lost all their estate and the wife her dowry.[18] In the moral crusade of the late seventeenth century there was a flurry of prosecutions before the church courts for 'fornication' or for 'clandestine marriage' which could sometimes refer to Catholic couples married before their own priests. Although such prosecutions continued sporadically in the early eighteenth century they never affected more than a few Catholic couples. Catholic marriages were challenged in the courts from time to time, usually when there was a disputed inheritance, but such cases were few and often settled out of court. The mixed motives are neatly illustrated in the letter concerning a couple at Dilhorne, Staffordshire,

> who have cohabited together for about three years and have had two children together without being married according to our laws. Popery in this case is made a cloak to defraud my wife of an estate left her by her brother. Whether these persons are to be suffered to go in this way in defiance of our laws... and to the scandal of the whole parish without being punished in the ecclesiastical courts, I submit to your lordship's better judgement.

In this and other cases the couple were in the event 'suffered to go on', and the overwhelming majority of Catholic marriages were accepted in practice by their neighbours as legitimate.[19]

In a letter to his daughter to be opened after his death, William Statham was concerned not only that she should marry a Catholic and bring up her children as Catholics but also that the marriage should not take place anywhere but in a Catholic chapel.[20] Both the State and the Catholic Church recognised the essential validity of the sacrament as depending upon mutual vows and consent of the couple, but were concerned to prevent the social evils of clandestine marriages. The response of Catholic priests and of lay people to the Hardwicke Act of 1754 varied.[21] Some priests exhorted the people to ensure that at the least the Catholic marriage should precede the Anglican ceremony and that the Anglican ceremony should be abbreviated. Nevertheless, Bishop Challoner in 1760 wrote that

> Many of the inferior sort have ventured to marry without going to church at all and others have gone to church and have gone through the whole ceremony of the Common Prayer Book, either for want of instruction, too many of the priests themselves favouring these marriages, or for want of resolution.

He went on to say that it had been impossible to prevent irregularities when the people insisted it was permissible to go to the Protestant church first, and he recognised that it was impossible to oppose the civil law and the practice of the majority of Catholics.[22]

Some Catholic priests discontinued registration for some ten years. At Edgbaston registration of marriages ceased after 25 March 1754 until 1764. At Liverpool the priest discontinued entering marriages after the end of 1754.[23] On the other hand at Brindle, Lancashire, the priest continued to register marriages after the Hardwicke Act, 52 before 1754 and 42 after 1754. Out of a total of 94 Brindle marriages in the Catholic register 1722-1769 only 19 were registered in both the Catholic and in the Anglican register of Brindle, the two ceremonies taking place on successive days. Some of the Catholic couples of Brindle may have registered their marriages in another Anglican parish but most of the Catholics of Brindle in the heart of Catholic Lancashire regarded Hardwicke's Marriage Act as something to be ignored.[24] In contrast, the Catholic register of Cheam, Surrey, included the date and place of the Anglican ceremony and the calling of banns in the parish church, suggesting that in that mission both the priest and the couples saw the two procedures as complementary.[25] In 1764 the Vicars Apostolic instructed the priests that they must resume registering marriages. Any consideration of the numbers of Catholics based on Catholic or Anglican registers has to take account of all these factors.

In addition to the problem of where the marriage should take place there was the question of mixed faith marriages. Marriage with a heretic or schismatic was a mortal sin and priests were told not to countenance a mixed marriage by their presence. Dispensations had to be referred to the Vicars Apostolic, and Bishop Witham urged his priests to exercise 'great caution in marrying together persons of different religion'.[26] From their side the Anglican clergy were also opposed to mixed-faith marriages believing that such marriages were likely to lead to the 'seducing' and 'perverting' of the partner and the children to popery. The Visitation returns quite frequently include complaints about the harmful effect of marriage with Catholics, but also record cases of Catholics marrying Protestants and transferring allegiance to the Church of England.[27]

Nevertheless, mixed marriages were not uncommon. Lesourd, using the 1767 return produced a national figure of 10-12% of husbands and 20% of wives who had non-Catholic spouses. He also examined 19 Catholic registers of various dates between 1735 and 1792 and found in the aggregate similar proportions of mixed marriages.[28] Such generalisations are deceptive, since the proportion of mixed marriages varied widely from mission to mission. Dr Gooch has demonstrated that mixed marriages were frequent in Durham County. High proportions of mixed marriages are found at Stonecroft and Hexham (1715-1773) and the registers show the same for the mission based at Cowdray Park, Sussex. The former was a relatively independent mission the latter a seignorial mission, which makes it difficult to offer dependency as 'an explanation' of the difference in practice. Bossy believed that mixed marriage was an indication or even a cause of growth and expansion[29] but Kinoulty found a high number of mixed marriages in Sussex, where the Catholics were dwindling in numbers and importance.

Figure 8: Marriage Horizons amongst West Sussex Catholics

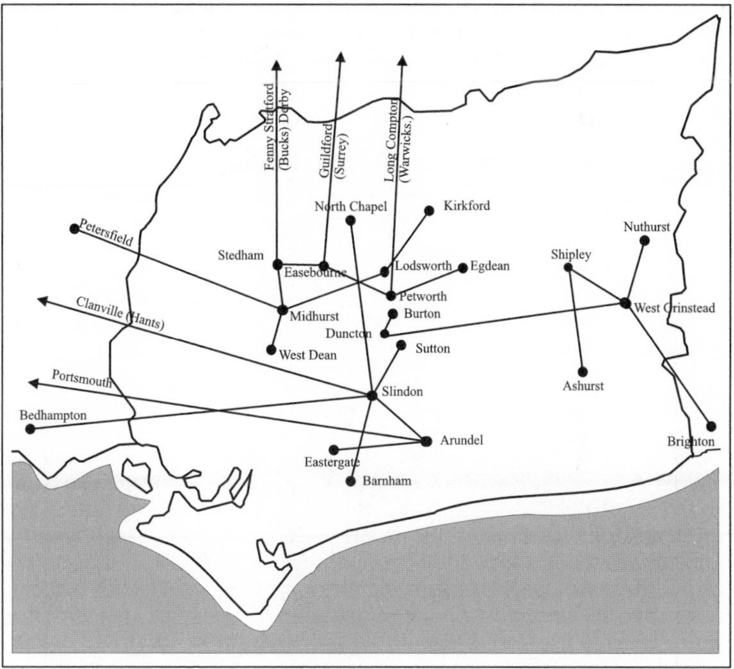

Catholic couples usually found partners within the area of the missions in which they lived, but in Sussex Kinoulty found that more marriage partners came from a distance. She also found evidence of a late age of marriage in this area. Both features may suggest that Catholics found it harder here to find Catholic partners than they would have done in, say, Liverpool, London or some parts of rural Lancashire.[30] The majority of marriage partners in Brindle register came from townships in Brindle and

Blackburn parishes. Although a total of 89 different townships were mentioned, most lay within twenty miles of Brindle.[31]

Trying to convert people to popery was still a serious offence at law, but conversions to Catholicism did occur. In the 1767 return 86 women and 54 men are specifically mentioned as having been 'perverted to popery', while the Catholic registers also record conversions: for example at Brindle, Lancashire, there were 213 between 1711 and 1767. At Edgbaston, Warwickshire, Lawrence Loraine alias Thomas Hall reported 43 converts in the area around Solihull between 1725 and 1737.[32] The Jesuits during the Jubilee of 1750 reported converts in many places, notably thirty persons at Newcastle upon Tyne. Among these were Alice Moss, wife of John, who was received after 19 years of marriage to a Catholic, and Alice Chatham, who was reconciled after 17 years.[33]

Figure 9: Marriages from the Brindle Register

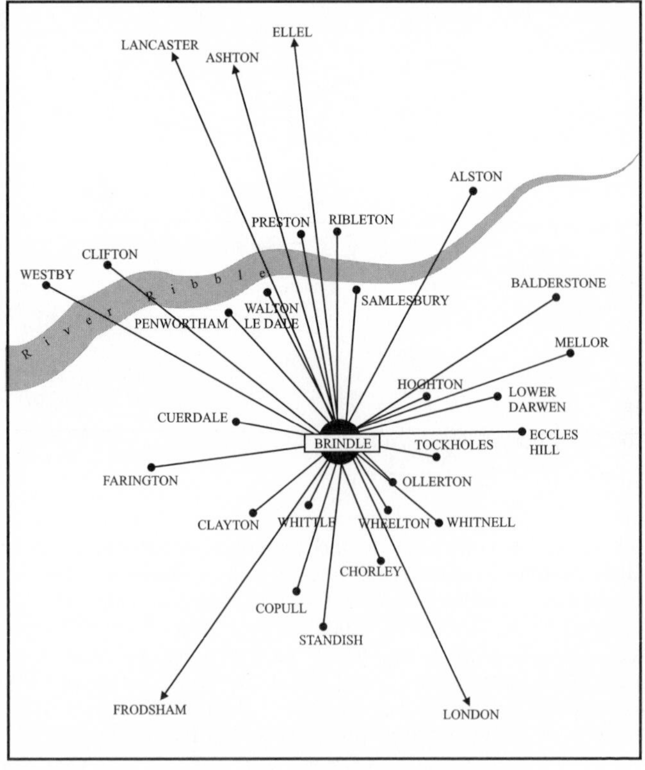

Some of the Jesuits referred to the converts as 'reclaimed', which was probably the more correct word in many cases. At Egton, Yorkshire, many of the *reconciliati* were members of Catholic families, who, one assumes, had been away from the sacraments for some time, rather than 'converts' in the modern sense. Aveling provides a list of converts among intellectuals and artists but some of these were individuals whose association with Catholicism was not long lived.[34]

The procedure for reconciliation could be quite formal. In Oxfordshire on 14 December, 1729 Sarah Hopkins 'was reconciled to the church.....before the whole congregation' of Old Heythrop.[35] One of the few converts to have given us some account of his approach to the church was William Statham, who as a young man worked for an English wine-merchant in Lisbon. He was impressed by the services and by the confidence of Catholics as he saw them in Lisbon, especially the Corpus Christi processions, and he compared them favourably with the Anglican services he attended at the English Embassy. At the age of 21 he began to spend his spare time reading the scriptures and in meditation on the passion of Christ. This continued over a period of four years, during which he saw himself as 'casting off the prejudices of education'. The outcome was that he felt 'forced into the secure bosom of the Church'. He is writing to edify his daughter fourteen years after the event, but his description of his self-consciousness at his First Communion rings true. He says that

> Some things [of] which I had yet but imperfect knowledge appeared strange at the first view, which gave me a secret desire of inquiry, and when I had penetrated into them I was ready to proclaim with joy. Man seemed to be the contriver, the Holy Ghost was the only director of great wisdom.

By this time he had returned to England, where he became part of the congregation of the Jesuits at Spinkhill, and he was confirmed at Sheffield, although he had earlier been confirmed in the Church of England. His conversion alienated him from all his relations and, he believed, cost him an inheritance. After unsuccessful attempts at farming he became an assistant to one of the Duke of Norfolk's agents. His wife never became a Catholic and he clung to a small group of Catholic friends.[36]

The Baptisms of Catholics

The Catholic registers are at their most complete and consistent in the registration of baptisms. The frequency with which a priest was called upon to baptise children is some guide to the size of the Catholic congregation and the work of the priest for comparison with other Catholic missions. For example, at Brockhampton, Havant, Hampshire, the priest between 1733 and 1775 baptised six or seven children a year.[37] At Wigan, Lancashire, during the period 1757-1767 the baptisms averaged 32 a year.[38] In the mission of Brindle, Lancashire, there were 418 baptisms between 1721 and 1769 of children of families resident in Brindle parish, and 976 from families resident in other parishes.[39] Catholics in areas where there were several missions did not necessarily choose to attend the one in their (Anglican) parish.

In Sussex many Catholic children were apparently baptised in their own homes but elsewhere practice seems to have been different. At Chillington, Staffordshire, (1723-7) the children were baptised in the chapel unless the priest stated otherwise.[40] At Walton le Dale, Lancashire, the parish registers recorded 72 baptisms of Catholics between December 1717 and February 1766, and also the birth date.[41] These families were probably associated with the Catholic mission of Brindle or Samlesbury.

It is worth noting that with a few exceptions children were baptised by Catholic priests within two days of birth, especially in rural missions. By the mid-eighteenth century this was an old-fashioned practice, and in the country as a whole the gap between baptism and birth was widening to become on average 30 days by 1800.[42] In the case of Liverpool, the necessary information is provided in the case of 99 baptisms, between 1734 and 1770. Of these 51 took place within five days of the birth of the child. In the case of a woman dying in childbirth the child was to be extracted if possible and to receive baptism if alive. Illegitimate children appear occasionally in Catholic baptism registers, but in the rural congregations they were fewer than would be expected from contemporary national norms.[43]

A distinctive feature of Catholic registers is the care with which the child's godparents are recorded, for this spiritual relationship was regarded as sufficiently close to be a bar to marriage. In ninety-five baptisms registered at Chillington (Fig. 11, p. 279), between 1720 and 1731, 44 of the godmothers can be shown to have been related to the child, and 31 of the godfathers, but there may well have been more cases which have not been established. Many of the men who stood godfather sponsored more than one child. At Brockhampton, for example, between 1733 and 1767 there were 115 godfathers for 267 children but only 15 babies who had no recorded godfather. John Biggs sponsored no less than 14 children. Richard Knapp senior and Richard Knapp junior between them stood godfather to 13 and John Stone to 7.

Figure 10: West Sussex Catholic Godparents

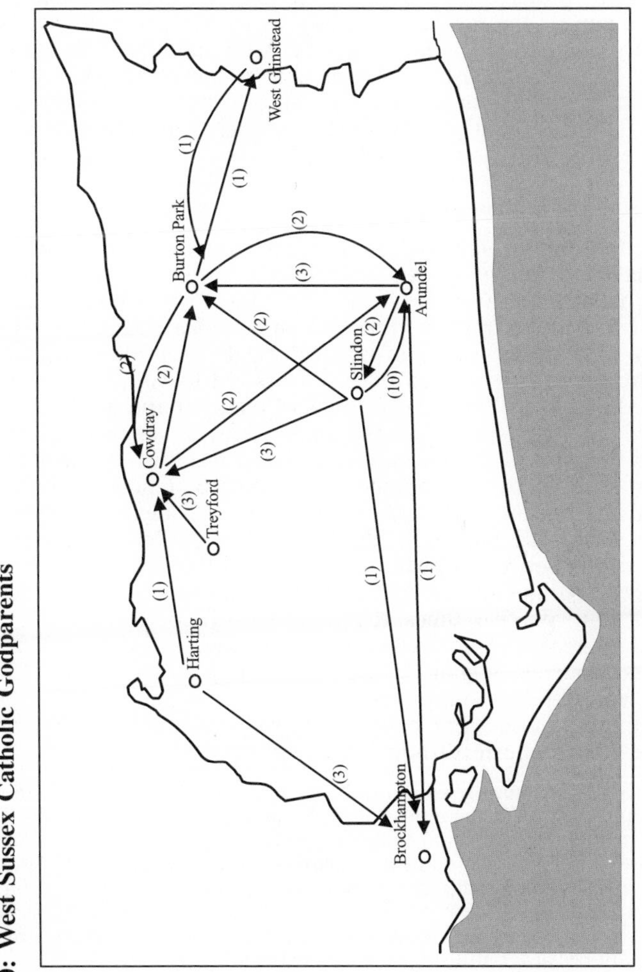

The connections between missions forged by the choice of godparents from other congregations.

In respect of the same 267 baptisms there were 112 godmothers and thirteen children who had no recorded godmother. Mrs Elizabeth Champ senior and Mrs Elizabeth Champ junior had 13 godchildren between them, Mary Knapp had five and Catherine Knapp two godchildren. In this case the register supplies the maiden name of the mother, enabling us to see more clearly the constantly reiterated connections between families. In most Catholic baptismal registers persons can be identified who stood godparent regularly for babies not so provided: at Chillington Thomas Dodd the butler acted in this capacity; at Brindle it was Mrs Leverson, the priest's housekeeper.[44]

Catholics and Confirmation.

Confirmation was received as a completion of baptism and a preliminary to receiving the sacraments of Communion and Confession. Although seven to ten years of age was recommended for receiving the sacrament, the ages in practice showed a wide span. In 1735 there were confirmed at Edgbaston 34 adults and 80 children. The ages ranged from 4 years old to 50, of whom 65 were aged between 12 and 21. Groups of children and adults were presented by their priest at the main centres; smaller groups travelled in from neighbouring missions and were listed under the names of their priest. The numbers confirmed by Challoner in the south of England in 1741 varied from three at Dagenham, Essex, to 116 at Cowdray, Sussex. In the North, Bishop Petre confirmed at 35 missions between 13 May and 10 July 1756 and at a further 35 between 15 June and 18 August in the following year. On each occasion four or five times the numbers of confirmandi were recorded as receiving communion. The largest gathering of this tour was that at Wigan, where 70 were confirmed but 350 persons were listed as communicants.[45]

The stir these occasions caused was well captured in 1709 by the vicar of Blackburn. Bishop Smith, he reported,

> came to Mr Walmesley's of Lower Hall in Samlesbury within my parish and confirmed there on Friday, Saturday and Sunday viz. the 8, 9 and 10 July. I cannot find that there were any persons of note there or any Protestants. The number of papists there were great; Mr Hull, my curate, at Samlesbury chapel tells me he saw multitudes go that way past his house, some on foot, some on horseback most of them with little children in their arms, but the great concourse of people was on Sunday because the Bishop was to preach that day.

The vicar is anxious to point out that there were no 'persons of note' present. In many of the confirmation lists the gentry are conspicuous by their absence, some of them perhaps having been confirmed abroad at school.[46]

Figure 11: Catholic Linkages by Godparents, Chillington Hall, Brewood, Staffordshire

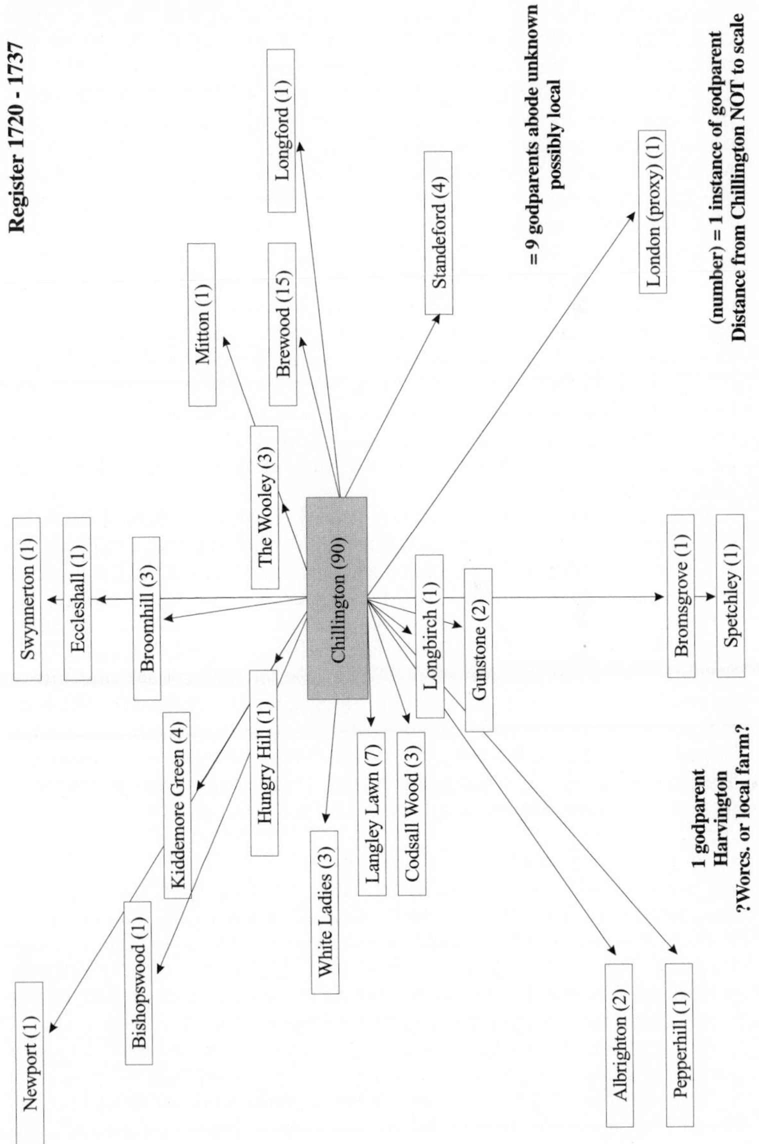

Catholic Burials

The great majority of Catholics were buried in the parish graveyards, and the minister and churchwardens for the most part averted their gaze from Catholic burials, Catholics being left to carry them out themselves, often at night. Fewer and fewer Catholics were officially excommunicate, so there was less of a problem than in the previous century. Catholic registers do not, on the whole, record burials, though at Holme-upon-Spalding-Moor the Catholic priest recorded those to whom he had given the last sacraments using the formula 'William Smith at Hayrick Mill in the parish of Skerkenbreck [Skirpenbeck] died, was assisted by me and has been buried. He died 28 January 1758'.[47] At Egton, Yorkshire, where there was one of the largest groups of papists in England, they had a particular part of the churchyard assigned to them and they were married, baptised and interred without the incumbent 'knowing anything of the matter till afterwards that they come to pay his fees'.[48]

Nevertheless, Catholics were never secure that the tolerance of their neighbours would continue; and from time to time a personal grudge or a new and zealous incumbent could lead to distressing situations.

The importance of Catholic burial grounds should not be exaggerated. There were 131 burials at the ground endowed in 1613 by the Blundells at Hawkirk, Lancashire, but after 1629 it was used mainly for the burial of priests.[49] At Windleshaw, St. Helens, the Catholics used the grounds of a former chantry chapel[50] and White Ladies, Shropshire, similarly used, was formerly a mediaeval nunnery.[51] Winchester had a Catholic burial ground at the medieval chapel of St James from the reign of Elizabeth. Recent research suggests that there may have been a burial ground adjacent to the Mass centre at Sedgley, Staffordshire. Even if Catholic burial grounds or plots were more numerous than is presently known, and even if they were used regularly, they could never have provided a resting place for more than a small proportion of Catholics.

Catholics were presented from time to time with questions of conscience as to whether they should attend the marriage or burial services of their neighbours, 'participating in the rites of heretics'. By 1803 Milner noted that Catholics were routinely attending the burials of their friends in Anglican churches but it is not clear how long-standing this practice was.[52]

As on the Continent, Catholics were encouraged to join confraternities and religious associations, especially in missions served by the regulars. They were encouraged to prepare for death by joining Bona Mors societies. This committed the individual to monthly confession and communion and to saying daily three Paters, three Ave Marias and three Glorias and meditating on the Crucifixion. On leaving the church or chapel, the member was to say five Paters in honour of the five precious wounds of Christ. At Hopcar, Lancashire, there were 122 members of the confraternity, men and women, which can be compared with 128 making their Easter communion. The regular clergy enrolled members in the Third Orders and other devotions included those of the Sacred Heart, the Stations of the Cross, and the Five Wounds.[53]

The Jubilee of 1750 was an opportunity for special devotions in all the Jesuit missions. In Durham during a special period of 52 days there were prayers morning and afternoon with meditations and instructions, and 200 came to Mass, as many daily as normally came on holydays; some made a general confession of their whole life.[54]

Great importance was attached to regular formal teaching by the priest, and this was by no means confined to the sermon. Shorter catechisms were published for the laity

> according to the nature of their circumstances, trade or employment, as of merchants and such like in those places where they have meetings, and care should also be taken for those in hospitals and distressed and abandoned poor.

Large numbers of catechisms were bought both by Jesuits and secular clergy 'for the poor' and catechising was a normal part of pastoral care, with individual teaching of converts. Challoner's *Abridgement of Christian Doctrine* and *The Catholic Christian Instructed* (1737) offered a series of clear and unequivocal directions covering Doctrine, the Sacraments, the Mass and the Christian life. All teaching was based upon the authority of the teaching Church mediated through her ordained ministers, but at the same time every individual Catholic rich or poor, man or woman, old or young, was responsible for his or her own individual knowledge of religion, religious practice and moral living. The tone was uncompromising and fear of God's punishment was the main sanction. His *Meditations* were more in the manner of the sermons of the time, rhetorical and hortatory and seeking to encourage the individual to the practice of religion by stirring up emotions whether of compassion for the sufferings of Christ, fear of Hell, or a sense of guilt. Nevertheless Challoner's work was rooted in the problems and limitations of everyday life.[55]

It was recognised by the Vicars Apostolic and by priests that the precepts of best Catholic practice could present working people with special difficulties. Even the much-stressed prohibition on Catholics attending the parish church could conflict with the need to earn a living. Much earlier, in 1662, a London priest had written with insight of the difficulties in this respect experienced by a Catholic woman whose sole support for herself and her family was her work as a midwife. Her problem was that the (non-Catholic) families who employed her expected her, as was customary, to go to the parish church with the mother and baby for the churching. Her refusal to do so on religious grounds caused offence and so lost her much-needed employment. The unknown author pointed out that although she, a poor woman, was censured by her priest, Catholics at court were not censured for going to Church of England services, and he argued for a relaxation of the rules in the case of working people.[56] Another issue was the loan of money at interest. The prohibition of usury was occasionally raised by 'hard-line' priests. In the early Middle Ages to lend at interest was to take unchristian advantage of a person's poverty, but in the capitalising society of England of the seventeenth and eighteenth centuries every villager and townsman who had any surplus put it out at interest to friends and neighbours. The Vicars Apostolic and the heads of the regulars issued clear directions that putting out money at 4-6% interest with the right to recover the principal was lawful, and most clergy money was invested in public funds.[57]

An increasing number of Catholics worked in manufacture, in the extraction industries and in the service trades, following hours and patterns of work that had nothing to do with the agricultural year, or the corresponding liturgical year. The traditional holidays and fasts had been integrally connected with the farming year, and the prohibition of servile work enabled the poor to carry out their religious duties without being forced by their lords to labour. In industrial societies periods of intensive work were often followed by comparative idleness depending upon the fluctuating demands of distant markets. In an increasingly capitalist society abstaining from servile work disadvantaged rather than protected the poor. Hours of work were becoming more formal and some persons were employed on a legally binding contractual basis which in its standard form required the employee to work for stated hours on all days of the week except Sunday. Other Catholics were working in places such as breweries or iron furnaces where production had to be continuous. In such circumstances those employed by non-Catholics, whether as servants or as tradesmen, could not expect time off to go to Mass on holydays, and fasting and abstaining might also present special difficulties.

What is striking is not the peculiarities of the practice of religion by English Catholics but how closely it compared with that of the Continent, and the lack of indication of any distinctively English practices.

NOTES

[1] Lesourd, p. 10.

[2] Worrall 1, p. 66.

[3] L.J.R.O. Visitation 1751 B/V/5; Worrall 2, p. 93; Bellenger, *Priests*, p. 123; Anstruther 4, pp. 205-14, 221, 305; Rosamund Meredith, *Farms and Families of Hathersage Outseats* (1991).

[4] John H. Whyte, 'The Vicars Apostolics' Returns of 1773', *Recusant History* 9, no. 4 (1968), pp. 205-14; Geoffrey Holt, 'A Note on Some Eighteenth-Century Statistics', *Recusant History* 10, no. 1 (January 1969), p. 3; see also pp. 239, 256n.2 above.

[5] Edward Lloyd Jukes ed., *Visitation Returns 1738 and 1761* (Oxfordshire Record Society, 1957); John S. Hansom ed., 'Catholic Registers of Rev. Monox Hervey 1729-1756', *Miscellanea* (C.R.S. 14, 1914), hereafter referred to as *Monox Hervey Registers.*

[6] Bernard Foley, 'Some Papers of a Riding Priest: Thomas Roydon 1662-1741', *Recusant History* 19, no. 4 (1989), pp. 460-9; Joy Rowe, 'The 1767 Census of Papists' in D. Chadd ed., *Religious Dissent in East Anglia 3* (1996), pp. 197, 201.

[7] Farm St., Galloway MSS., Accounts 1761, pp. 19-20, 52.

[8] W.A.A. vol. 38, f. 30 (n.d.); Old Brotherhood MSS., p. 172.

[9] Farm St., Residence of St. George, District Book, 1695-1760; Holt, *Jesuits,* p. 24.

[10] Jukes, p. 68.

[11] Worrall 1, p. 176.

[12] Worrall 2, p. 116; Jukes, *Visitation Returns*.

[13] R.Cole ed., *Speculum Dioeceseos 1705-1723* (Lincolnshire Record Society 4, 1913), p. 32; J. Anthony Williams, C.R.S. 65 (1975), p. 37.

[14] B.A.A. A 532a, List headed 'Goods which Daniel Fitter had of his own' in the chapel and sacristy at St. Thomas, Oscott, Staffordshire; B.A.A. A 158a & 416; Farm St., List of benefactions of Bryn alias Aston, College of St. Aloysius Lancashire; List headed 'Goods of John Perrott priest', W.A.A. 39, pp. 28-9.

[15] *The Abridgement of the Douai Catechism* (1715 edition), p. 146; Statham, p. 125; James D. Crichton, *Worship in a Hidden Church* (Ireland, 1988); James D. Crichton, 'Recusants and the Mass', *Worcs. Rec.* 52 (December 1988), pp. 17-27; George Every, 'The Laity and the Liturgy 1600-1800', *Worcs. Rec.* 43 (June 1984), pp. 3-12; *The Office of the B.V.M. and the Manner of Serving Mass* (1770); Bellenger, *Scrolls*, pp. 106-10; *The poor man's posey of prayers; or The Key of Heaven* (Liverpool, 1755).

[16] *Manual of Prayers for all Persons and Occasions* (Preston, 1777).

[17] Dor. R.O. D/WLC/R14 (I am grateful to Mrs Liz Adams for this information); Spufford, pp. 70-5; R.B. Houston, 'The Development of Literacy in Northern England 1640-1750', *Economic History Review* Second Series 35 (1982), pp. 119-216; R.O. Malcolmson, *Life and Labour in England 1700-1780* (1981), pp. 95-7; Lancashire R.O. Hoghton deposit (uncalendared): information from M. Panikkar.

[18] J. Hugh Aveling, 'Marriages of Catholic Recusants', *Journal of Ecclesiastical History* 16 (1963), pp. 68-83.

[19] Worrall 2, p. 78; Marie B. Rowlands, 'Staffordshire Papists in 1767', *Staffs. C.H.* 6 (Summer 1965), p. 24.

[20] Statham, p. 156.

21 John Bossy, 'Challoner and the Marriage Act' in Duffy, pp. 126-37; Steel & Samuels, p. 856-61; Hardwicke's Marriage Act 26 George II c. 33.
22 Ushaw MSS 2/93; 7/2.
23 B.A.A. C88; *Edgbaston Register*; *Liverpool Registers*, pp. 178-253.
24 John P. Smith ed., 'Registers of Brindle 1721-1840' & George Woods ed., 'Samlesbury Register 1732-1834', *Lancashire Registers 4* (C.R.S. 23, 1922), pp. 1-305, 306-82. Hereafter *Brindle Register* and *Samlesbury Registers*. Analysis of period 1721-1740 carried out by Catherine Coleman.
25 John Hanson ed., *Catholic Registers of Cheam, Surrey, 1757-1788* (C.R.S. 2, 1906), pp. 314-338.
26 W.A.A. VA 2, p. 29; VA 38, item 30.
27 For example Stone, Staffordshire: *Staffs. C.H.* 17 (1977) p. 40.
28 Lesourd 1, pp. 313-4, tables 27 & 28; 315, table 29; Mary D.R. Leys, *Catholics in England* (1961), p. 190; John R. Baterden ed., *Catholic Registers of the Secular Mission at Hexham at Cockshaw* (C.R.S. 26, 1926).
29 John Bossy, *Rural*, pp. 88-119; Bossy, *Northumbria*, pp. 11-34; Steel & Samuels, pp. 870-2.
30 Kinoulty, pp. 163-4.
31 *Brindle Register*.
32 Father Thaddeus [Hermans], *The Franciscans in England* (1898), pp. 2-3.
33 Holt, *Jesuits*, pp. 22-3.
34 Aveling, *Handle*, pp. 290-2.
35 *Monox Hervey Registers*, pp. 373-5.
36 Statham, p. 116.
37 R.E. Scantlebury ed., *Registers of Brockhampton (Havant Hampshire) 1733-1855* (C.R.S. 44). Analysis by S. Watts.
38 P.S. Fairclough ed., *The Catholic Registers of St John's, Wigan 1732-1786* (privately printed, n.d.).
39 *Brindle Register*, passim.
40 Chapter 1 above; Worrall 2, pp. 84-6.
41 Register of Walton le Dale, I.G.I. Index.
42 E.A. Wrigley & R.S. Schofield, *The Population History of England, 1541-1871: A Reconstruction* (1981), p. 111.
43 Illegitimacy rates at this date were about 3% of live births: David Hey, *The Oxford Companion to Local and Family History* (1996), p. 228.
44 Chillington Registers, pp. 9, 243-7.
45 *Abridgement of the Douai Catechism* (1715); W.A.A. 40/117, Confirmations Richard Challoner; Pres. R.O. RCLV 60, Petre; Lesourd, pp. 243-7. Most of the Catholic registers include confirmation lists, but the ones which have been mainly used are: J.S. Spedding & J.R. Baterden, 'Catholic Registers of Capheaton, Northumberland 1769-1785' and J.S. Hansom , 'Catholic Registers of Biddlestone Hall, Northumberland 1769-1840', *Miscellanea* (C.R.S. 14, 1914); *Edgbaston Registers*; Rowlands; *Brockhampton Registers*; *Brindle Registers*; *Samlesbury Register*; *Liverpool Registers*.
46 Anstruther 3, pp. 206-7.
47 *Catholic Registers of Holme-on-Spalding-Moor, East Riding of Yorkshire* (C.R.S. 4, 1907), p. 306.
48 Information from Dr. Sheils.
49 F.O. Blundell, *Old Catholic Lancashire* 1 (1915), pp. 35-7; T.E. Gibson ed., *Crosby Records* (Chetham Society N.S. 12, 1887).
50 *Monumental Inscriptions at Windlesham Chantry* (St. Helens Family History Society, 1985).
51 Steel & Samuels, pp. 888-9.
52 B.A.A. A968.
53 W.A.A. vol. 37, no. 31; vol. 40, p. 117; *Brindle Registers*; *Samlesbury Registers*; 'Rosary Confraternity Lists', *Miscellanea* (C.R.S. 14, 1914), p. 217; Kinoulty, pp. 86, 89; L. Whickham Legge, *Tusmore Papers* (Oxford Record Series, 1939), p. 29;

J.S. Hansom ed., 'Catholic Records of Crondon Park, Essex, with notes about Hopcar, Lancashire 1759-1831', (C.R.S. 9, 1909); J.R. Baterden ed., 'Registers of Stone Croft Northumberland 1757-1821 (C.R.S. 26, 1926), pp. 151-85; Statham, p. 116; Farm St., Sacred Heart Devotions Galloway MSS. 1767, p. 14; G. Corr, *Devotion to Our Lady among English Catholics in the Seventeenth and Eighteenth Centuries* (1992).

[54] Holt, *Jesuits*, pp. 20-4, for details about the Jubilee in the Durham and Lancashire districts.

[55] James D. Crichton, 'Challoner and the Penny Catechism', *Recusant History* 15, no. 6 (October 1981), pp. 425-33; R. Challoner, *Meditations for Every Day of the Year* (1754) and *The Catholic Christian Instructed* (1737); *The Abridgement in the Catholic Council of Trent* (many editions from 1582, 1686 edition used here); R. Luckett, 'Bishop Challoner the Devotionary Writer', in Duffy, pp. 71-89. See now also Blom, Blom, Korsten and Scott, *English Catholic Books, 1701-1800* (Aldershot, 1996).

[56] Ushaw MSS D6 21 1663.

[57] W.A.A. Old Brotherhood Archives 4, p. 145; B.A.A., A.382x.

14

1767—THE NEW PEOPLE

The Returns of 1767 provided different kinds of information from the Compton Census of 1676 and the geographical coverage is different. Nevertheless, it is possible to use them to show the dramatic transformation which had taken place within the Catholic body in England by organising the information on the same basis: from rural places, from towns and from industrialising areas. As in Chapter 5, the towns are subdivided into London, county towns, market towns, ports and leisure towns.

CATHOLICS IN THE COUNTRYSIDE

About 55% of the labour force of England was engaged in agriculture and related occupations in the 1760s. The majority of Catholic missions were in the countryside and we would expect to find that the majority of Catholics were yeomen, husbandmen and labourers. Yet Lesourd counts only 3,511 men identified in the return as engaged in agricultural employment out of the 18,079 to whom a specific trade is ascribed. He then makes adjustments for the wives and dependants of such men and offers a figure of 16% of the identifiable workforce.[1] This calculation is clearly open to criticism, not least in that it includes many yeomen and husbandmen living in or adjacent to towns and in parishes where manufacture was carried on. Another approach is to identify the number of rural parishes returning Catholics and to consider the numbers of Catholics returned from those parishes. Two thirds of all such parishes were in rural areas where all the Catholics with named occupations were engaged in agriculture. However, the numbers in such parishes were for the most part small, only very rarely rising above 20 and often comprising only three or four families. Not more than a quarter of the Catholics returned lived in the rural seclusion described by nineteenth-century writers.

Catholic Gentlemen and the Catholic Body

Bossy, Aveling and others have charted the 'death of the Catholic aristocracy' by conformity, by mixed marriages, by extinction of the line or by extravagant living and (more respectably) by the ordination of numerous sons to the priesthood. There is no need to rehearse this *in extenso* since it is a well-established and general feature of the period 1740-1830.[2]

The traditional household had not died out completely. In the nineteen dioceses for which information is sufficiently detailed, the returns of 1767 record 62 households with a resident Catholic squire, his family, five or more Catholic servants and a priest.

Table 27: Gentry Households with Five or More Catholic Servants and a Resident Priest, 1767

County	Place	Servants	County	Place	Servants
Berks.	Sonning	7	N'land	Ellingham	10
Berks.	Woolhampton	18	N'land	Whelpington	5
Berks.	Ufton	8	N'land	Wycliffe	5
Cumb.	Greystoke	13	Norfolk	Costessy	9
Cumb.	Warwick	6	Oxon.	Heythrop	13
Cumb.	Wetheral	10	Oxon.	Mapledurham	7
Derbys.	Buxton	12	Oxon.	Newington	12
Derbys.	Wingerworth	14	Oxon.	Pirton	9
Devon	Chudleigh	11	Salop.	Acton Burnell	10
Devon	Tormorham*	10	Salop.	Lydbury North	6
Dorset	Lulworth	20	Salop.	Worfield	8
Durham	Monk Hesledon	5	Staffs.	Swynnerton	10
Durham	Croxdale	11	Staffs.	Tixall	12
Essex	Kelvedon Hatch	6	Suffolk	Bury St Mary	5
Essex	South Weald	10	Suffolk	Stanningfield	18
Essex	Walthamstow	18	Suffolk	Stoke-by-Nayland	12
Hants.	Crawley	11	Sussex	Harting	12
Hants.	Petersfield	5	Sussex	Bodecton	10
Heref.	Sarnesfield	5	Wilts.	Donhead St Andrew	25
Kent	Canterbury	14	Yorks.	Aberford	9
Kent	Lynstead	7	Yorks.	Brandsby	6
Lancs.	Croston	9	Yorks.	Broughton	9
Lancs.	Kirkham	5	Yorks.	Carlton	7
Lancs.	Lytham	29	Yorks.	Catterick	15
Lancs	Prescot	6	Yorks	Gilling	15
Lancs.	Sefton	7	Yorks.	Holme-on-Spalding Moor	9
Lancs.	Wharton	8	Yorks.	Hovingham	7
Lancs.	Winwick	13	Yorks.	Manfield	16
M'sex	Chiswick	6	Yorks.	Nidd	6
M'sex	Isleworth	6	Yorks.	Romaldkirk	9
N'land	Chollerton	13	Yorks.	Swine	15

*near modern Torquay

No such households in Huntingdonshire, Rutland or Cambridgeshire. There is insufficient information from Leicestershire, Lincolnshire, and Worcestershire.

In some of these households weekly and daily patterns of worship continued, but actual practice over time varied according to the circumstances and commitment of the squire and his lady. At Linley, Shropshire, the wife of Sir Richard Lacon was delighted with the large numbers of people attending Mass there, but after her death Sir Richard admitted that he was less enthusiastic, and deplored the large numbers of dinners and stabling for horses he was expected to provide.[3] A considerable number of long-standing Catholic family centres were by this time headed by the steward rather than the land-owner. The steward maintained a Catholic household for his master but on a smaller scale, as at Lawshall, Suffolk, and Little Crabbitts, Crawley, Sussex.[4]

We cannot assume that all gentry households were the focus of a Catholic congregation of commoners. In some cases the rural mission was little more than a great house and its park. At Buckenham, Norfolk, the great house was the only house in the parish, and there were no Catholics in the surrounding parishes. Mrs Howard, sister to the Duchess of Norfolk sometimes resided there 'but not generally'.[5] At Sixhills, Lincolnshire, under the patronage of the Heneage family there were six Catholics among 17 families and the priest came once a month to the 'papist conventicle'. The Sixhills priests also rode a large circuit.[6] At Sawston, Cambridge, John Champion, chaplain of the Huddlestone family, was preoccupied with family matters in his letters and occupied at least some of his time with his reflecting telescope, literature and sport. Although for seventeen years rector of the East Anglian Jesuits, he was remembered as living at home in solitude and retirement as a worthy and humble priest. The impression given by his letters is confirmed by the few returns of papists listed from the parishes near Sawston Hall.[7]

However the loss of gentry leadership did not always mean that rural Catholics no longer had the opportunity for Mass and pastoral care. In a detailed study Joy Rowe has shown how the focus of Catholic life shifted from the gentry houses in Norfolk and Suffolk in the course of the period 1740-1767 and was re-aligned around the places where the priest said Mass, forming 'a cluster delineated by distance' with the priest serving a 'neighbourhood community'.[8] Similarly, in western Sussex all the missions had been gentry missions in the early eighteenth century and the six families of Catholic gentry between them owned much of the land of the county. Four of those centres were lost by 1767; in two cases the mission continued and in two other cases it faded out. In West Grinstead the Catholic hall was sold in 1758, but the mission continued from Harting where another gentleman maintained the priest.[9] In Oxfordshire the Noke estate had been in Catholic hands in the reign of Elizabeth and was formerly a Mass centre. It was leased to a farmer by 1706 and later sold and demolished but the priest continued to visit the remaining three yeoman families.[10] There were two chapels at Painsley, Staffordshire, one at the hall and another for the tenants, but when the last of the Draycotts died the tenants' mission at Lees Houses continued.[11] At Thropton, Northumberland, the Widdrington family sold their estate but the mission was provided with an endowment and the priest lived in the house with his own servants.[12]

The Relations of Catholic Squires and Commoners

The social distance between squires and people was widening. Catholic gentry, like their peers, rebuilt their houses not, as formerly, to be semi-public places, but as private homes surrounded by great parks which placed a distance between the gentry and other people. As at Sandon and Chillington, Staffordshire, and Everingham, Yorkshire, this often involved moving whole villages and relocating the tenant and cottage population out of sight from the pillared portico of the Hall. Gentry were frequently absent from home, travelling abroad or staying in London. Their relations with their tenant farmers became increasingly impersonal and the labourers and cottagers saw little of them.

The Servants of the Hall

One significant group of 'commoner' Catholics was an exception. The number of residential servants in great houses, though still large, was declining. The numbers in the households in the 1767 return vary between four and 47, with women outnumbering men. Inferior servants were often unmarried and women servants left on marriage. In these smaller households servants depended more than ever on the Family whom they served for their self-esteem and economic advancement.

At Ladyholt, Sussex, even when the Caryll family were away, the servants were required to attend daily Mass and vespers (1740-1780). In all Catholic households the Friday abstinence and Lenten fasts were required. There are examples of individual servants becoming Catholics when entering service in a great house, and at Lytham, Lancashire, according to the Anglican minister it was a condition of employment.[13]

Catholic servants working in Protestant households might find it difficult to get to Mass. Two servants from Higham, Suffolk, attended Mass at Gifford's Hall.[14] Occasionally priests referred to their people encountering difficulties in obtaining leave to abstain from work on holydays.[15]

Property and Tenurial Relations

The Church of England clergy frequently complained about the common people being perverted to popery or maintained in popery because of favourable treatment by the squires as tenants. Due weight must be given to this evidence. There are certainly cases where the arrival of a vigorous Catholic squire can be shown to have increased the numbers of Catholics. Mr Edmund Plowden, it was said in 1767,

> leaves no stones unturned to gain over as many as he can... Then he settles them in some of his farms or cottages and for the most part maintains them afterwards.[16]

Thomas Clifton at Lytham, Lancashire, was said to be granting tenancies to Catholic strangers when they fell into his hands. Sir Thomas Gage at Stanningfield, Suffolk, had five Catholic tenant farmers.[17] However, detailed studies do not always support these complaints. In West Sussex, Kinoulty was able to trace few Catholic tenants and the number of Protestant tenants was far greater at all times.[18] Tiller in a similar study of Wiltshire came to the same conclusion that there is no evidence of favouring of Catholic tenants either in rents or in grants of tenancies. It has not proved possible to identify a bias towards Catholic tenants on the Giffard or Fitzherbert estates in Staffordshire. In Northumberland the majority of the tenants were Catholics, but the proportion varied on different Catholic estates.[19]

There were certainly close links for many generations between some tenant farmers and some Catholic landlords especially in the North of England, but here as everywhere many Catholics sublet land from other tenants. The number of tenants was falling on many estates and the majority of the inhabitants were sub-tenants or had no formal link with the landlord.

Some Catholic farmers were able to prosper and make the transition from tenant farmers to 'gentlemen'. Many of them were by the time of the Return becoming more independent of their landlords as they consolidated and enclosed their holdings, diversified their farming and extended their markets. Courts baron, once the expression of the landlord's social and economic control, were obsolescent and parish élites governed through the vestry or court leet, or often an amalgam of the two, and were solely responsible for administration, law enforcement, tax listing and collection, and also therefore for matters concerning their neighbours who were papists.

Lancashire Catholic Congregations 1: The Fylde

Lancashire contained more than two-fifths of all the Catholics listed in 1767. There were in Lancashire before the Relief Act of 1778 about 70 Mass centres with resident priests in 26 parishes, and at least 24 of them have survived to the present. Local Catholic traditions have been lovingly preserved and venerated and there is a wealth of printed material available.[20] What follows is an attempt to penetrate a little deeper into six Catholic communities of Lancashire, using mainly non-Catholic sources in conjunction with the 1767 return.

First, however, a general point: were there parishes in Lancashire where Catholics were in a majority? The Anglican ministers' replies to Visitation articles suggest this to be very unusual. Even in the 'most Catholic' parishes Catholics were almost always in a minority. (See Appendix 1.) However the incumbents may well have been concerned to minimise what was after all a slur on their efficiency.

The **Fylde of Lancashire**, that is the mainly rural district between Preston and modern Blackpool, probably had more Mass centres than any other part of England. Apart from Preston itself it was a mainly rural area with some small market towns and a few traditional industries. It has always been at the heart of Catholic Lancashire's cultural tradition; yet even here a close look at four of the Fylde parishes shows that even here Catholics' circumstances could differ greatly within a few miles.

Kirkham parish comprised many scattered settlements, large and small, urban, rural and industrial. It had 23 townships, some of which were themselves made up of two or three hamlets. The Visitation return of 1778 suggests a population of 1,996 families, of which 386 were in the chapelries. The small market town of Kirkham had an area of about 840 acres and the parish as a whole 48,500 acres. The strength of Catholicism was not the result of any weakness of the Church of England. On the contrary, the parish church was supported by three parochial chapels with curates, and three new Church of England chapels had been established in the 1720s at Rigby, Marton and Threlfall. There were five schools for boys, and the headmasters, all Church of England clergymen of course, helped as ministers at the chapels.

Local government in Kirkham town was in the hands of a body called the 'Thirty Sworn Men'; elsewhere the parish was governed by the court leet and the vestry. The major landowners throughout the area were branches of the recusant Clifton family, whose forebears had been banished in the Commonwealth and imprisoned during the Oates Plot. In the eighteenth century the

Figure 12: The Boundaries of the Parishes and Townships of the Fylde

1 Goosnargh
2 Layton with Warbeck
3 Bispham with Warbeck
4 Thornton
5 Great and Little Carleton
6 Great and Little Poulton
7 Hardthorn with Newton
8 Great and Little Marton
9 Hambleton
10 Great and Little Singleton
11 Little Eccleston and Larbreck
12 Weeton with Preese
13 Greenhalgh cum Thisleton
14 Medlar with Wesham
15 Treales, Roseacre, and Wharles
16 Clifton with Salwick
17 Newton with Scales
18 Freckleton
19 Kirkham
20 Ribby with Wrea
21 Bryning with Kellamergh
22 Warton
23 Westby with Great and Little Plumpton
24 Lytham
25 Out Rawcliffe
26 Upper Rawcliffe with....
27 ....Tarnacre
28 Great Eccleston
29 Elswick
30 Inskip with Sowerby
31 Eaves, Catford, and Bartle

= Township
= Parish

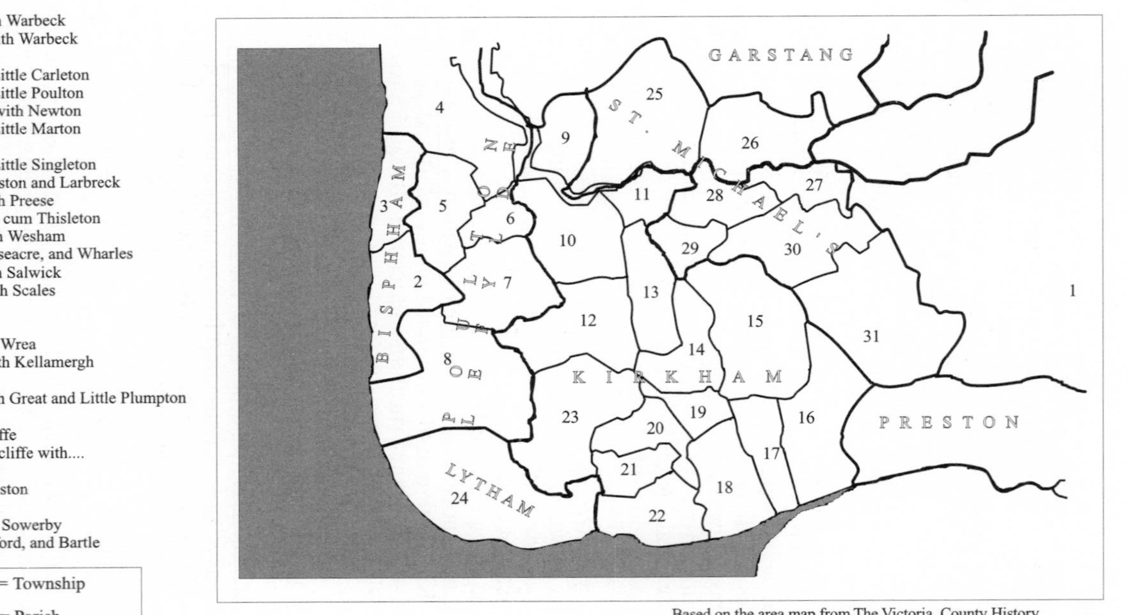

Based on the area map from The Victoria County History

senior branch was resident at Clifton Hall in Lytham the neighbouring parish to Kirkham; Sir Thomas Clifton held Kirkham manor by lease. Several of the other Roman Catholic gentry in Kirkham and Goosnargh had forfeited their estates after the '15 or the '45 and their houses were in the possession of tenant farmers.[21]

The total number of papists, men, women and children, reported by this parish in 1767 was exceptionally high, for it showed 1,275 persons distributed through the townships, less only than London and the towns of Preston, Liverpool and Wigan. The Mass centres and priests were not in the market town of Kirkham, but in halls and townships of the rest of the parish. A priest was resident at each of Westby, Salwick and Mowbreck. At Medlar, a little further west, lived John Jones, a secular priest, while yet another secular priest, William Blackow, was apparently living with his brother Thomas Blackow, yeoman, and his wife, four daughters and three sons at Great Plumpton.[22]

At Westby Hall there was a succession of Jesuits from at least 1700 and Mass was said in a chapel at the west end of the hall. Thomas Cuerden the Jesuit headed the 1767 list. Westby Hall was let to tenants and the chapel in the Hall had been 'opened for the use of the Catholics in the neighbourhood' in 1742.[23] The Catholic register for Westby, which dates from 1763, records 38 families between 1763 and 1770 coming from Weeton, Ballam, Moss Side, Brown Moss and Westby Mills. Between 1763 and 1770 38 families appear in the register.[24] Mass was also said occasionally at two houses in Little Plumpton, in one of which the priest William Hodgson used to live in one room containing his theological books, a room which was always kept locked.[25]

Goosnargh was a detached portion of Kirkham parish ten miles from the parish church, a chapelry virtually independent and itself including a second Anglican chapelry. Three Catholic priests were listed in Goosnargh in 1767. These were Charles Tootell, aged 70, (probably the Charles Tootell O.F.M. who died in 1771), John Carter, aged 55, at Newhouse, and with him his nephew John Maudsley (vere Carter), aged 25. John Carter had served the chapel at Newhouse from 1736 and was to continue to do so until his death in 1789. John Maudsley remained with his uncle and succeeded him in the care of Goosnargh until 1814, when he in turn was succeeded by his nephew Henry Carter. The Catholic register of Goosnargh which started in 1770 included people from Dilworth, Alston, Whittingham, Inglethwaite, Bleasdale and Chipping Thorney.[26]

Thus in Kirkham parish there were seculars, Jesuits and Franciscans, each offering their distinctive spirituality derived from the faith common to them all. They all brought groups from their congregations to confirmation, showing that they had regular care of souls. Their people were drawn from overlapping areas; Catholic families under these circumstances had some choice of Mass centre. By 1767 only two priests were in any sense chaplains, and the great houses with two exceptions were either let or empty. The missions were financed in part from endowments, in part from the personal income of the priests, in part from clergy common funds, and only to a limited extent by individual patrons. Of the nine priests in Kirkham and Goosnargh in 1767, five lived in the houses of yeomen or in their own house with a housekeeper or servant, four lived in a Hall but nevertheless may have been living independently, and two may not have been permanent residents.

The parish of Kirkham contained a small town, which had been distinguished for its Protestantism in the seventeenth century. It was a well known centre of the linen trade and produced sail cloth in particular. Among the Catholics there were three hatchellors, who worked in preparing flax for weaving, and one weaver. Otherwise the few Catholics of Kirkham town followed the usual urban trades. Mr Thomas Swartbeck the apothecary and his family and perhaps the innkeeper Robert Gibson enjoyed the highest status in the congregation. There was a butcher, maltster and several servants, a glover and his apprentice and a joiner and his apprentice.

In the agricultural townships of the parish the land was predominantly arable, divided into many small-holdings, and few families were conspicuously richer than their neighbours. Fifty-four Catholic families were yeomen and 91 husbandmen with 61 labourers. There was a Catholic innkeeper at each of Little Plumpton, Weeton, and Greenhalgh, and a miller at Little Plumpton, Riby, Medlar, Greenhall and Freckleton. In Freckleton the miller and his family of nine were all the papists reported. In the hamlet of Salwick all but one of the adults reported were husbandmen or labourers.

In this part of the Fylde there had been little change during the last hundred years in the way Catholic families earned their livings. The Catholics who had been presented to Quarter Sessions in 1679 had been following similar occupations to those of 1767. At that time more than a quarter had been husbandmen; there had been a few yeomen, labourers, and servants. In 1679, as in 1767, seven millers were included in the same locations, and there was a group of linen-weavers.[27]

The Catholics of Kirkham had many co-religionists in surrounding parishes. Between Kirkham and the coast, and to the immediate north of Lytham, lay the parish of **Poulton le Fylde**, which included an old market town and river port with five townships. It covered 15,813 acres and included two chapelries, Singleton and Marton. The people were engaged mainly in pastoral farming. There had been a succession of Catholic priests there and in 1715 the chapel and house was handed over for the sole use of the priest. Six of the male heads of Catholic households of Poulton were described as husbandmen. There were two innkeepers, who, with John Hodgson, ironmonger, and Thomas Tomlinson, farmer, were probably the most substantial of the Catholics.[28] Along the coast lay the parish of Bispham, a narrow strip of relatively poor land. Despite several Catholic landowners, there was no resident priest and only two Catholic labourers, a house carpenter and a blacksmith, none of whom had been born in the parish. These Catholics were within reach of the missions of Kirkham parish, and appear in the Catholic registers of missions in that parish.[29]

To the south of Kirkham on the coast was the small parish of **Lytham,** a very different community. In 1778 the whole parish comprised 187 families, indicating a population of about 900 people. In 1767 384 individual papists were returned. Only 130 persons made their Easter communion in the parish church in 1784, in which year 384 Catholics made their Easter communions in the Catholic chapel, but it must not be forgotten that these would include some Catholics from surrounding parishes.

The reason for this was not far to seek. Thomas Clifton, esquire, was the principal landowner, he was resident and with his wife, Lady Jane, most active in encouraging Catholics. His grand Hall was rebuilt between 1757 and 1764, fronting east with a great pediment supported on Corinthian columns, and the chapel was in the house. Forty-seven indoor and outdoor servants and their families were maintained, making it the largest Catholic household recorded in the 1767 return. As well as maids and menservants, there were gardeners, a dog-man, grooms, a postilion and an under-jockey, all Catholics. The high number of seventy-four adults had been born in the parish. These included six yeomen, 19 husbandmen, and five labourers. Several Catholics in the parish were concerned with the building trades, perhaps reflecting the recent work at the Hall.[30]

Other parishes in west Lancashire which had large numbers of Catholics included Sefton, Winwick and St Michael on Wyre, though none were so numerous as Kirkham or as high a proportion of the population as Lytham. The variations of culture within a generally 'Catholic area' bring to mind the similar variations charted by Bossy in twelve Northumbrian congregations in 1978 and 1979.[31]

Figure 13: Map of Claughton, near Lancaster, and Surrounding Parishes

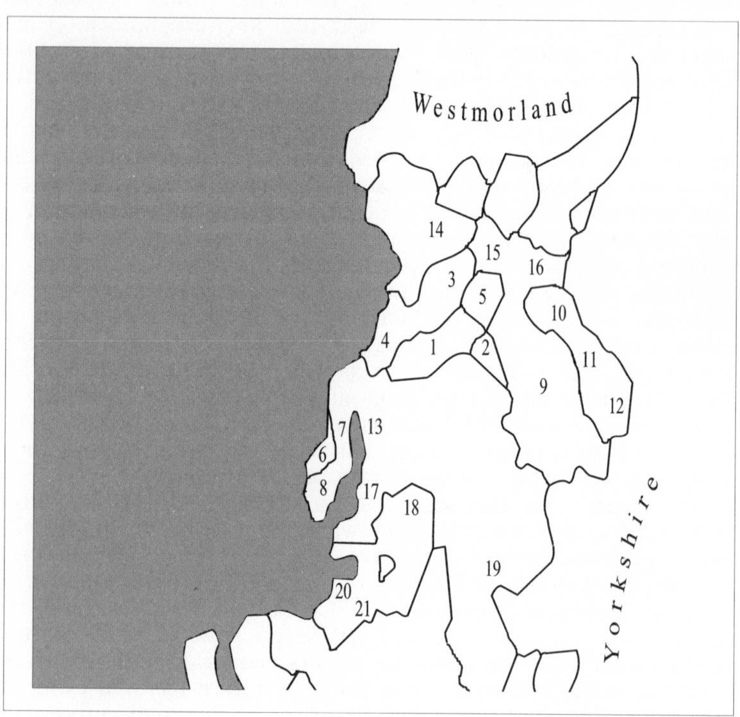

1 Halton	8 Overton	15 Arkholme
2 Claughton	9 Hornby	16 Melling
3 Over Kellett	10 Tathom	17 Admarsh
4 Bouton le Sands	11 Bentham	18 Ellel
5 Gressingham	12 Tathom Fell	19 Wyresdale
6 Heysham	13 Lancaster	20 Thurnham
7 Poulton le Sands	14 Warton	21 Cockerham

Lancashire Catholic Congregations 2: Claughton, near Lancaster

Further north, around Lancaster, there was a group of Catholic centres at Claughton, Melling and Tatham. **Claughton** in Lonsdale by the River Lune was a wholly rural parish and was exceptional in Lancashire in that it was small both in extent and in population. It comprised only 1,581 acres and was not even treated as a separate township for local government purposes but was combined with Caton. The little village was about one-fifth part of the township of Caton with Claughton. The parish had two churchwardens but the vicar was non-resident and the parish church in disrepair. The manor was held by the recusant family of Croft until they joined in the rebellion of 1715 and their estate was sequestered and sold by 1718. The manorial rights had been transferred in 1712 to the Fenwick family. The village returned only 13 Catholics in 1767, of whom only three men and four women were aged over 20. In 1722 there had been only 20 families in the whole parish, of which three were Catholic. Thomas Sweetlove, yeoman, left money for building a chapel in 1734, but much of his bequest was used for a law suit and it was not until about 1770 that a stone church was built near the parish church, of which Mrs Ann Fenwick was the main provider. In 1778 it was reported that a priest came monthly.[32]

On the evidence so far and in statistical terms, Claughton with Caton was insignificant in the life of the Catholic church, but more intensive reconstitution reveals several points of interest. In the first place, the yeomen families were outstanding in their Catholic activity. In all there were 22 Catholic Layfields in the Lune Valley in 1767, eight in Hornby, five in Claughton and nine in Caton, each with a further set of links with co-religionists and Protestants. Caton provided the church with two priests, sons of Richard and Elizabeth (Atkinson), namely James (born 1701) and his younger brother Christopher Layfield (born 1701). They learnt Latin in England, then went abroad and studied at Douai and Rome respectively. This argues a sufficient level of patronage or family wealth to pay the fares, fees and maintenance and the ability to do without the services on the farm of the sons of the family.

In the second place, Claughton provides evidence of committed Catholics participating in local government. In every parish in England the vestry had to be appointed to carry out the multitude of duties required of them by the State and the Church. Protestant Dissenters commonly served in local office but Catholics normally were excluded by the requirement to take the oath and the sacrament for the more senior offices. In Claughton there were few men from whom to appoint every year two constables, two overseers of the poor, five highway surveyors and two tax collectors. Inevitably in such a small parish, the Catholic householders had to be drawn into the process of parish government. In 1725 William Foxcroft, a Catholic, was announced in the church as overseer of the poor, but did not act. In parishes everywhere such duties were often associated with particular landholdings and the person who was required to do the duty not infrequently passed it on to others. The parish might or might not require a fine for such a transfer and it was not unprecedented for a person known to be unable to serve, even a woman, to be appointed in order to swell the parish income. However, Robert Layfield, undoubtedly a committed Catholic, certainly served in office. He was a yeoman in his forties, and although a Catholic he was appointed constable in 1744, overseer 1745, tax collector 1749, 1753 and 1755, and churchwarden in 1764. He should have taken the oath of allegiance and the sacrament in the Church of England, but it appears that he was not sworn. In view of the shortage of suitable men in Claughton it seems probable that the parish colluded at his failure to take the oath and the sacrament. Other examples have been brought to light, not necessarily in places with tiny populations. There was a Catholic headborough and a Catholic tax-collector at Brewood but these offices did not require the holder to take the oath and the sacrament.[33] The incumbent of Chipping Norton wrote angrily to Bishop Secker in 1741/2 about Anabaptists, Dissenters and Papists in his parish, who dominated the elections for the vestry and even became churchwardens.[34] Such indications are, however, few in number and it was probably uncommon for Catholics to hold parish office.

Large Catholic Congregations in Derbyshire and Yorkshire

In no other part of England was there such a concentration of priests and Mass centres as in western Lancashire, but there were more than a hundred other areas where several rural Catholic missions overlapped and interacted with each other. Two of the largest of these clusters of Catholics, Hathersage in the Peak District and Egton in the arable North Riding of Yorkshire, have been examined in some detail, combining the 1767 return with other evidence.

The group of missions in the Peak District of Derbyshire was vigorous and independent. We have seen that the parish of **Hathersage**, Derbyshire, made one of the largest returns of papists in 1676, and it continued to be one of the largest of the rural missions. In 1751 the return to the Church of England Bishop noted 34 families of papists out of a total of 193 families

Figure 14: Catholics along the Derbyshire - Yorkshire Border, 1767

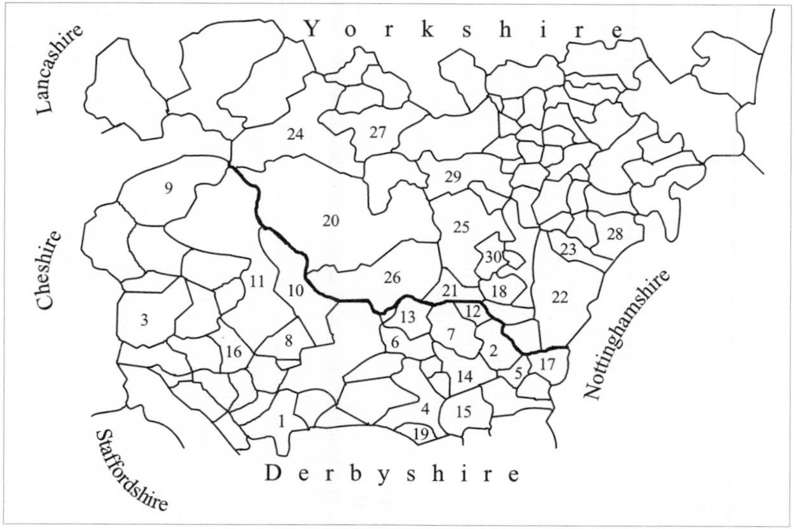

Derbyshire

1	Bakewell	40
2	Barlborough	65
3	Chapel en le Frith	3
4	Chesterfield	6
5	Clowne	6
6	Dronfield	16
7	Eckington	62
8	Eyam	9
9	Glossop	19
10	Hathersage	115
11	Hope	17
12	Killamarsh	23
13	Norton	2
14	Staveley	9
15	Sutton cum Duckmanton	12
16	Tideswell	43
17	Whitwell	8

West Riding

18	Aston	4
19	Doncaster	8
20	Ecclesfield	49
21	Handsworth	5
22	Laughton	5
23	Maltby	3
24	Penistone	11
25	Rotherham	39
26	Sheffield	361
27	Silkstone	7
28	Tickhill	3
29	Wath	2
30	Whiston	16

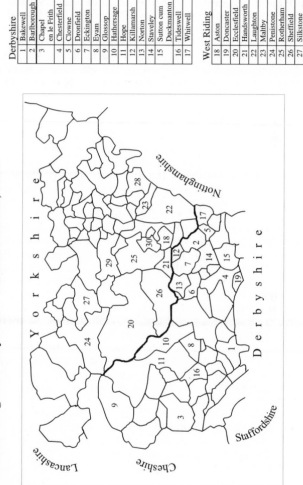

This map should be compared with Fig. 3, p. 95. Two of the largest of these clusters of Catholics, Hathersage in the Peak District, and Egton in the arable North Riding of Yorkshire have been examined in some detail, combining the 1767 Return with other evidence.

in the parish. This figure is consonant with the 27 families and three individuals of the 1767 return and the 25 masters of families reported in 1771.[35] Nearby Bakewell, Tideswell and Eckington, also in the High Peak district of Derbyshire and South Yorkshire, had large numbers of papists both in 1676 and 1767[36] and there were Mass centres at Eckington and Bakewell. The neighbouring parish of Tideswell did not have a resident priest, so the 33 Catholics listed there were presumably part of one of these congregations. In these Peak parishes by this time there were no resident gentry except Mr Crooke, steward to Rowland Eyre, esquire.

The ruins of the chapel destroyed in 1688 remained for William Statham to see in 1727. He also saw priests' vestments and marble images, 'not much defaced', that had been taken out of the house of Thomas Eyre at Thorpe, a yeoman in whose house the papists met privately for Mass.[37] This Thomas Eyre was not a member of the gentry family of the Eyres of Hassop; the name was a common one in this area. They were still worshipping in the upper room of a private house in 1772. There was a succession of priests residing in Hathersage from at least 1700 as boarders with Thomas Eyre. Most of the Catholics in 1767 were farmers, but there were also two mill-stone makers, a wire-sieve maker, a button-maker and an innkeeper. The population here was largely indigenous, and this meant that there were many families with the same surnames, making it difficult to distinguish between Catholics and Protestants. Probate documents provide a basis to show that, as in the other parishes considered, the Catholics had a close family and confessional network of friends and relations. But what is more unexpected is that in this old Catholic centre these same families also had many links of relationship with Protestants. They quite frequently asked non-Catholics to witness their wills and appraise their goods, and Catholics also witnessed the wills of non-Catholics. Some of the churchwardens may have been Catholics, and Catholics certainly attended the annual vestry meetings. The Catholic craftsmen had no objection to being employed by the churchwardens on carpentry or mason work in the parish church and William Walkeden, grocer, who was listed as a Catholic in 1705, supplied the parish church with lubricating oil for the clock for many years.[38]

Egton in the North Riding had made the largest rural return in 1676 (pp. 86, 92 above). It was one of a group of parishes making a high return, including Stokesley. However, although it remained an important centre, it was growing only slowly. Egton Catholics found themselves in 1758 confronting the opposition of a new landlord, Cary Elwes, who pursued an active policy of discouraging Catholics as tenants, and sought to discourage mixed marriages. Numbers had probably declined a little in the early eighteenth century and there was perhaps also some decline in social status, but by 1767 the return listed 213 individuals of whom 65 were under 18. Nine were weavers, and three were coopers. There were eight farmers and the remainder were described as poor. There was a Masshouse by the 1670s but later priests lived with a gentry family at Bridge House and there was a chapel on the side of the house by 1743. Protestants were roughly equal in number to the Catholics and there was also a small group of Quakers who attended Meetings in the next parish. The return of 1767 describes 102 of the 125 adults as native to the parish, a high proportion indeed. Even so, correlation of a wide range of sources shows that there were frequent cases of individuals lapsing and of new names appearing on the lists

Like the Catholics of Hathersage, the Catholics of Egton formed a close network, and had a long history in the parish, but this was not incompatible with openness to others. Many of the Catholics of Egton had non-Catholic relatives and asked their non-Catholic friends to witness their wills and record their goods and chattels for the probate courts. This was in part a precaution to strengthen the presentation in the probate court, but also demonstrated their integration with the wider community.[39]

Diversity is perhaps the most important element in the overall picture of English rural Catholicism, but certain generalisations may be possible. The return of 1767 suggests that rural missions were on the whole stable and persistent, although there was decline in the Welsh Marches and in the South. The numbers of Catholics in each mission were usually small, but the clergy were committed to maintaining old missions, however small the numbers of communicants. Many of the original trusts were made in the name of a layman but had been immediately passed over to the clergy. The original terms were held to be binding and unalterable and were still causing headaches for diocesan treasurers in the late nineteenth century.

Rural congregations were a combination of a few yeoman families rooted in the parish by their land with a larger number of persons who had been born elsewhere, and who might move on again. They did not usually form an exclusive group, although there were strong ties between them of family and godparents. Priests often remained in the same rural mission for the greater part of their lives, which reinforced the continuity and stability of the mission despite the mobility of the congregation. By 1767 a considerable number of the priests lived in separate accommodation and some chapels were located outside the Hall. In the countryside, the role of the gentry might on the one hand be direct and immediate in the case of active resident Catholic gentry, or it might be historic in the sense that mission centres which had been established in the seventeenth century continued independently. The decline of Catholicism in some parts of the south and west may also have been linked with the relative failure of those areas to urbanise and industrialise. It was certainly the case that the most dynamic developments in both the general population and in the Catholic population were taking place in towns and industrial areas and it is to these we now turn.

CATHOLICS IN THE TOWNS AND PORTS

The growth of commercial activity in England in the eighteenth century was accompanied by a corresponding growth in the proportion of the population living in towns, estimated as being about 30% of the population by 1770. London continued to grow in size, wealth and international importance; some great provincial cities and industrial towns by this time had populations of over 20,000 even though that of some small country towns were still as small as 200.[40] Correspondingly existing urban Catholic missions were growing in size, some new urban missions were being established and some rural missions were relocated to a town. .

Catholics in London

By 1750 about 11% of the population of England inhabited the conurbation known as **London**, a metropolitan city of over 700,000.[41] The City, Westminster and Southwark were surrounded by rural parishes, which were also rapidly becoming built-up suburbs, and for the present purposes these parishes have been included.

The total number of population and of papists becomes harder to establish, as the social unit called London spread into parts of many jurisdictions and the built-up area bore less and less relation to ecclesiastical boundaries. Catholics were reported in sixty City parishes, although the numbers remained very small in relation to parish populations. Penelope Corfield dismisses the Catholics in a sentence as 'mainly Irish in origin and settled chiefly in St Giles and Holborn'.[42] This is misleading. Catholics were diffused throughout the London in both poor and prosperous parishes, and persons described as Irish were concentrated in certain parishes mainly Christchurch, Spitalfields, Shadwell and St Giles in the Fields.

The 1767 returns for London as we have them in the House of Lords MSS. are supplemented by additional detail from the original returns for many parishes of London diocese. There was some clustering in the north-east and in the larger parishes outside the City wall, notably St Giles Cripplegate (156), where Mass was performed every Sunday 'on the Lord's Day from time immemorial', and also St Luke Old St (234), and St Botolph without Bishopgate (101). In the parish of St Michael Wood Street in the City, Thomas Hunt, his wife, family and lodgers were included as refusing to give an account of themselves. Thomas Hunt and his wife Ann had four children baptised by Fr. Arthur Pacificus Baker. In all there were 1,492 Catholics in the City. There were 173 named individuals in the original returns for Christchurch, Spitalfields, almost all weavers with a few market traders and a mathematical-instrument maker believed to be a priest. Between the City and Westminster, Catholics were, as ever, most numerous in St Andrew's, Holborn, St Giles' in the Fields and St Martin's in the Fields. The Westminster return totalled 7,724 Catholics in 13 parishes with especial concentration in St James and at St Giles in the Fields, both well in excess of 200. Eleven original returns survive for Westminster, five of which include named individuals and heads of families. The parish of St George Hanover Square listed 314 papists and included their addresses by street. They included a Benedictine priest living in Mount Street. The parish of St Paul's Covent Garden had for several generations been the place of business of a Catholic family of bankers, the Wrights, at The Golden Cup, Henrietta Street. Anthony Wright in 1767 resided at South Weald, Essex, where he kept a large establishment of Catholic servants and maintained a chaplain. The parish of St Giles had been the town residence of the Catholic Digby family; the Arundel family had property and the Weld family continued exercise influence in the area which they left when they made the transition from drapers to gentry.

The twelve Middlesex out-parishes listed more than 2,000 papists. To the north-west of the City in Marylebone, a relatively wealthy parish, there were 295 men, women and children and 59 lodgers, and Catholics were numerous in St James, Piccadilly, and Bloomsbury. In contrast, Wapping, Stepney, Poplar, Shoreditch and other parishes to the east of the City and around the docks were home to thousands of labourers, casual workers and persons on the move. Of the 367 adults listed for Wapping, 30 were labourers, and so were 185 out of 293 adult Catholics at St

George in the East. They were served by a chapel in Virginia Street located between the Tower and the Docks.

South of the River Thames, Southwark was linked with the City by London Bridge and had from earliest times been part of the metropolis, supplying labour and services. Six riverside parishes in the Southwark Deanery made a combined return, namely, St George (42), St Thomas (18), St John (105), St Olave (47), St Saviour (19), Christchurch (26), giving a total of 257. In addition there were Bermondsey (199) and Rotherhithe (39).

Catholics were greatly exceeded in number by Protestant Dissenters (who by this date included Methodists), and were roughly equal in number to London Jews.[43] Although a small minority in London, Catholics amounted to about a fifth of the total of Catholics listed in the 1767 return for England as a whole. However, these figures cannot have represented the whole numbers of Catholics in London. In a capital city there was a much greater degree of anonymity and lodgers were very numerous. In St Sepulchre there were said to be 45 lodgers, of whom nothing was known. In St Andrew's by the Wardrobe, it was said that there were 'no native lodgers', which presumably implied that there were other lodgers not included. In St Paul's Shadwell there were 300 Irish labourers plus 25 English labourers. In Stepney there were 80 persons who refused to give accounts of themselves.

The occupations of Londoners in general were so multifarious that it is impossible to encapsulate them in a few sentences. Few gentlemen and gentlewomen were listed and those mainly in St Ann's Soho, St Margaret's Westminster, St George's Hanover Square and one each in St Dunstan in the East and in the West. The largest groups were manual workers and domestic servants.

The London shops were famous and one third of the shopkeepers had an income of over £75 a year. Among them were many Catholic shopkeepers and some of these were men of substance, notably Thomas Mawhood, draper. However, although his diary shows that he was actively concerned with his shop in the city, he was recorded in the 1767 return at his country home at Finchley, and this may have been the case with other Londoners. There was a large sector of small family businesses engaged in manufacture of every conceivable kind of consumer durable, many of them making relatively cheap luxuries for a mass market, such as watchmakers and toymakers. There were those who served those above them: tailors, engravers, cabinet- and coach-makers. There were others who earned their living in the traditional urban retail trades, including bakers, victuallers and greengrocers. Surprisingly, there were only two publicans. Builders, plasterers, brickmakers, carpenters were fewer in number than might be expected. There were the intermediaries: the porters, the messengers, and sedan-chair carriers.

Catholic women's trades were not distinctive. The largest number were domestic servants and washerwomen; the remainder got their livings by their needle as stay-stitchers, milliners, and quilters, while slightly lower in the social scale were those who hawked their wares on the streets, milk-women and pedlars. In the dock side area there were women labourers and oyster-catchers. Working women were far more numerous than the resident gentlewomen. Many of the people who employed these Catholics, or bought from them, probably did not know they were Catholics, and the Catholics had no need to obtrude the fact.

The incumbents of 25 parishes did not give the length of residence, or did so in a generalised form, and in other parishes it was given for only some of the Catholics. This in itself is an indication of the mobility of the population. The short term residents would comprise both those recently arrived in the metropolis and those who had moved from one parish to another within London.

Table 28: London Catholics, Length of Residence, 1767

	Persons	<1	1-5	6-10	11-20	>20
City Parishes	464	41	228	77	85	31
Middlesex	222	31	85	66	29	10
Westminster	98	8	37	23	26	4
South of Thames*	276	14	105	70	59	26

(*The six parishes of Southwark plus Lambeth, Bermondsey and Rotherhithe.)

Only five adults were described as native. To this handful can be added the banker aged 83 who, having been resident in his City parish since 1707, was hardly a transient.[44]

The Pastoral Care of London Catholics

To an even greater extent than elsewhere in England, continued religious commitment was a matter of individual choice, subject, of course, to many influences and to opportunity. Mass centres and priests were available to them but London Catholics in moving from place to place had to be responsible for their own attachment to a Mass centre, otherwise they could easily slip out of pastoral care. They did not depend on one priest or one Mass centre but went to whatever Mass centre was convenient or congenial to them, and, although the Mass was the same, the context, the liturgical elaboration and social relations with fellow worshippers were very different. Educated Catholics in London had independent access to Catholic booksellers and so to printed books, including Catholic books and prayer books, and they could if they chose inform themselves of controversial opinions within the Church. On the other hand anti-Catholicism remained stronger in London than elsewhere, especially among the poorer classes, even though such attitudes were unfashionable at Court and among the upper classes.

The priests included secular priests, Jesuits, Franciscans and Benedictines. The Embassy chapels at this date were five in number. They provided an opportunity to worship publicly with grand music and lavish decorations. The Portuguese Embassy chapel was in South Street, where there were two priests, both Englishmen, on the Embassy staff and where the chapel was open to the public. The Bavarian Embassy was in Great Wild Street, the Sardinian Embassy was in Duke Street, Lincoln's Inn Fields, and the Venetian chapel in Suffolk Street. The Embassy chapels played a major part in providing pastoral care, especially for the gentry and the wealthier Catholics, and, as their registers show, they were also much used by Catholics visiting London.

Table 29: Resident London Priests in the Return of 1767

Parish	Resident Priests
Christchurch, Middlesex	1
Poplar & Blackwall	1
St Anne, Soho	2
St George, Hanover Square	11
St Giles, Cripplegate	4
St George the Martyr	4

Source: Worrall 2, pp. 134-41, and 149-51.

It is clear that, to a much greater extent than elsewhere, London priests were omitted from the returns. The return of the Vicars Apostolic to Rome of 1773 gives 48 priests living in London. There were said to be 11 Franciscans in London in 1758, three at the Portuguese Embassy chapel, one at the Bavarian Embassy and one each with Lady Howard, Mrs Eyre and Mr Bird. Father Baker OSF had an 'elegant chapel' at Wild Street by 1763. There were 18 Jesuits, five at Great Wild Street, five at Great Queen Street and one each at Drury Lane, Gloucester Street, and Little Street. There was a Masshouse at Moorfields in Ropemakers alley, where Mass had been performed every Lord's day 'from time immemorial', a large building with three named priests. and another at Butler's Alley, Grub Street. There were probably three Mass centres in Southwark. There was, at least for a time, a chaplaincy to Newgate prison. In view of the many prosecutions of priests in 1766-7 it is not surprising that there was greater caution and some of the priests may have withdrawn to safer places.[45]

Bishop Richard Challoner lived at King Street, Golden Square, near Lincoln's Inn Fields. His notebook (1736-47) gives a vivid insight into his day-to-day work with people in London. It consists mainly of long lists of names and notes to jog his memory, and is clearly his way of keeping track of all his people. There are lists of Easter communicants, including Baker's boy, Mrs Chevy, Mr Massey's friend and Noble's lodger, young Bowman and Mrs Kenny's maid. There are lists of confirmations and many lists of persons being catechised. He notes down Mass offerings and requests for prayers. He records the names of three boys setting out for Leghorn, sent by the Bishops of the Midlands and of the North. He was working day in, day out, going from house to house catechising, preparing people for the sacraments, administering them and distributing books of instruction. In all he did and wrote, his objective was clearly to bring persons to individual conversion, irrespective of their social status or age.

In view of the many immigrants and unmarried young men, the distribution in small numbers throughout the metropolis and the extreme variety of social and economic circumstances among Catholics, it seems probable that Catholics in London were less closely bonded with each other than elsewhere, and even the priests and Mass centres had less continuity in any one place. It is significant that a general register of baptisms by the secular clergy of London was kept.[46] The Catholic people of London owed little to the past, but were, as Challoner well knew, a new people, both at the time and as a portent of future developments.

The County Towns

There was a marked increase in the numbers of Catholics and missions in county towns. By 1767, of the 37 English county towns 12 had public Masshouses, and a further nine had resident priests who said Mass in their homes.

Table 30: Priests and Masshouses in County Towns, 1767

County Town	Population	Masshouse	Priest	Papists
York	11,000	Y	Y	633
Norwich	37,000	Y	Y	441
Durham	6,000	Y	Y	420
Lancaster	7,000	Y	Y	236
Worcester	12,000	Y	Y	147
Chester	14,000		Y	129
Winchester	4,500	Y	Y	125
Stafford	3,000	Y	Y	84
Alnwick		Y	Y	72
Nottingham	17,000		Y	43
Lincoln	5,000	Y	Y	34
Shrewsbury		Y	Y	32 adults
Exeter	15,000		Y	26
Oxford	10,000	Y	Y	23
Derby	7,000		Y	19
Hereford	5,500	Y	Y	18
Reading	8,000		Y	13
Ipswich	12,000		Y	12
Berwick on Tweed	5,000		Y	12
Salisbury	7,000		Y	11
Gloucester			Y	10

The population figures are based on contemporary estimates and are intended only as a guide. Source: J. West, *Town Records*.

The largest returns from towns included those for York, Durham, Worcester, Norwich and Winchester. These were usually increased by Catholics from surrounding parishes. As with the rural parishes, what is striking is the variety in the social composition of these Catholic congregations, reflecting both differing traditions and local secular circumstances. That of **York** reflected that city's gentility even though many of the Catholics were poor. The Catholic population of York was the largest in any county town. Among them were five families headed by esquires and two gentlemen with their households and servants. The gentry were increasingly concentrated around the Bar Convent in Micklegate and they shared in the intellectual social and artistic life of the city. They were not necessarily in continuous residence.

Figure 15: The Bar Convent, York, in the Eighteenth Century

From a drawing in the Convent Archive.

There were about 30 families of substantial tradesmen, some of whom are given the courtesy title of Mr., as for example Mr R.D., coal-owner. Catholics were to be found in almost every trade: clothing, luxury trades, food, building and a great variety of crafts. They followed in all 73 trades little different from the pattern of trades in the city as a whole, and ranged from men of real substance to the poor. Seventy-six were servants of the gentry, of priests or of other tradesmen. Aveling estimates that about half the 262 adult citizens were probably poor, 50 were substantial and the rest small tradesmen. There were a few, a very few, professionals including two surgeons, one apothecary, a schoolmaster and a French master. There were nine priests in the city with various ministries, six of whom are included in the return. The chaplain of Bar Convent was responsible for the 49 girls at the school, the sisters and their servants, but took no active part in the care of souls in the town. Although the majority of the Catholics had moved into the city from elsewhere, it was not a youthful congregation and over a quarter of the adults were more than fifty years old. The genteel profile of the York Catholic congregation was enhanced by the Bar Convent where most, though not all, of the sisters and the pupils were ladies. Two of the seven gentry resident in the city had private chapels, where the chaplain said Mass for the servants and family. York was, from 1770, the residence of the Catholic bishop with his chaplain and household. Each of these chapels had a small number of attenders who preferred them to the secular chapel at Lop Lane which was the main Mass centre for the city. It had originated as an annexe to the priest's house, but this had been replaced by a purpose built chapel in 1760.[47]

Although historically a major city, **Durham** was smaller and less wealthy than York. The Catholic population, although smaller in the aggregate, was larger as a percentage of the whole. In 1767 the city had two chapels, 'ample and elegant'. There had been a fund to support a secular priest at Durham from about 1700 and there was a public Mass house by 1706. Less than a quarter of the Catholic adults were native to the city and both natives and immigrants were distributed throughout the ten parishes and liberties. It was a younger congregation than that of York, but there was a marked discrepancy between Gillygate and the City. There were 102 Catholics in Gillygate, of whom only 16 were over 50 years of age, whereas 68 out of 305 were over 50 in Durham city. It was also a noticeably poor congregation especially in Gillygate and St Nicholas parish, including one Catholic in the House of Correction and one in the poorhouse. Just outside the city in Brome chapelry and in Fencola there were two Catholic farmers. Three priests were reported in Durham: one living with Mr Ward, the woollen draper, one in Old Street and one in Old Elvet. There were two chapels, one in the city in the care of the Jesuits and one in Old Elvet belonging to the secular clergy. Confirmation lists show Catholics coming for the sacrament from as much as six miles away and a particularly strong group from Sunderland and Belper. Although the congregation had always included a few substantial tradesmen and widows who were comfortably off, it was a more 'plebeian' Catholic group than York.[48]

Worcester also had a tradition of being a Catholic centre, but details of its history before 1700 remain obscure. At least one Jesuit priest lived in the city, but it is not clear when the Jesuits began to occupy the Sansome Street house which was eventually registered as a place of worship in 1791. The great cathedral dominated the city and there were eight parish churches, four of which were rebuilt or restored before 1767. Nevertheless, Dissent was also well established; the Quakers had a meeting house from 1701, the Congregationalists from 1708 and the Baptists in the early eighteenth century. Worcester was famous for its elegant entertainment and as the occasional residence of many gentry families. There were fashionable race meetings and a choir festival, as well as concerts, coffee houses, baths and academies, and it produced one of the earliest provincial newspapers. The Catholic congregation included not only several resident gentlemen but also several substantial tradesmen. In 1749 the porcelain works had been established in the city and the Delabore family, who appear prominent in the listings and registers of Catholics, were one of the group of French porcelain painters brought in at this time. The Worcester congregation was augmented by the Catholics from the surrounding parishes of Claines (36) where there was a Catholic schoolmaster, and Powick (7), where lived the most outstanding member of the Worcester congregation, Dr. Thomas Attwood.

Light can be thrown on the residential distribution of Catholics in Worcester from the Catholic register and the incumbent's original returns, and this exercise demonstrates how closely the Catholics were immersed in the local economy and social organisation. Seventy of them lived in the parish of St Nicholas, ten of whom followed Worcester's predominant trade as glovers, while nine were domestic servants in modest households, one was a nurse and one a washerwoman. The Catholics in St Swithin's parish were tradesmen: three tailors, one cabinet-maker and two butchers (one a widow aged 90). In the small parish of St Andrew lived John Halles, a potter, and Ann Steward, who was the wife of John, a victualler: he was not a papist, but their son Charles aged 14 is so described. In the parishes of All Saints and St Clement the Catholics were noticeably young people. In All Saints there were 9 adults and five persons under the age of 20; only one couple were elderly. In the parish of St Clement there were only two couples, both day labourers but there were several single people, apprentices and servants, a governess aged 21 and a journeyman barber, all young people not yet settled in life. In the parish of St Peter's in contrast there were two families of gentry, a porcelain manufacturer and his family and a glover and his apprentice, all substantial and independent families. St Helen's reported 32 papists over 20 and 21 papists under 21, most of them recent arrivals in the city. To a greater extent than either York or Durham, the majority of Worcester Catholics were incomers, including young people coming to the city as apprentices and servants and two schoolgirls at Mr Spencer's school. Among the Catholic adults of Worcester there was a marked preponderance of men and women in their forties, implying an increment of population in the 1720s, a period when population was growing rapidly in Worcestershire parishes.[49]

Winchester had been a notorious centre of popery since Elizabethan times. In 1740 a congregation of 233 had gathered on the occasion of Challoner's Visitation, of whom 82 were on that occasion confirmed, and by 1779 there was a Catholic chapel in the city. In the city itself, only 17 papists had been born in Winchester Soke; 111 were over 21 and of these only 13 were natives. There were over 200 more Catholics in parishes adjacent to Winchester, but the mission of Winchester City was distinct from the nearby missions derived from old Catholic families.

They were dispersed all over the city. There were five families earning their livings as, respectively, a whipmaker, staymakers, a painter and a cabinet-maker. In the Soke there were staymakers and some retailers, a grocer, a brewer, a baker, a confectioner and a greengrocer. The bulk of the Catholics resident in the Soke were six households of gentlemen, gentlewomen and their servants. There were also some labourers and a schoolmistress aged 35, who had been in the parish of St Thomas for 7 years. In Winchester it seems clear that the urban Catholic population was composed of persons in service trades and more dependent upon the gentry than in other cities.[50]

Norwich was still in 1767 one of the largest cities in England. The chaplain of Costessy Hall had taken up residence there about 1722 and a chapel was built in 1764 in St Swithin's parish. By 1767 there were two priests, one at Shoulder of Mutton Yard, where a Mass house was built about 1760, and one at the Old Palace chapel. The Catholic chapels were part of a city landscape, which included on the one hand the magnificence of the Anglican cathedral and on the other hand meeting houses of Dissenters. Although the city itself was in the process of being overtaken in numbers and wealth by the new industrial towns, the Catholic congregation was growing and comprised both native and incoming Catholics. Thirty-seven adult men and women are reported as natives, but three parishes did not supply this information. Native Catholics were most numerous in the two parishes of St Lawrence and St Swithin. More than a third of the Catholics were under 21 years of age and in general were most numerous in the parishes of St John's Maddermarket and St Peter's Mountergate. The occupations of Norwich Catholics as elsewhere were diverse including the building industry, retailing and the service sector. Textiles were, as we would expect, the most predominant, with 55 weavers, 10 worsted weavers and some cord spinners and lace makers. Like Worcester, there were some Catholics of the middle class, namely a wine merchant, a bookbinder and a surgeon and two resident gentlemen and a gentlewoman. Mrs Mary Suffield and her two adult sons, both merchants, should probably also be included.[51]

Figure 16: Age Structure of the Catholic Population of Norwich

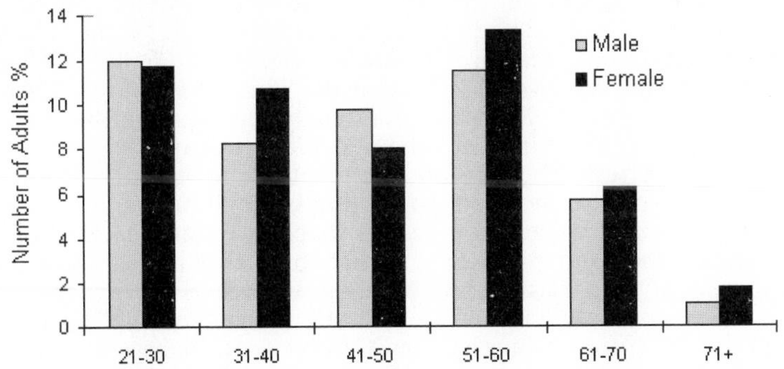

Total Number of Adults (20+) = 224

		Men	Women
Native:		26	25
Resident:	51+ years	6	1
	41-50 years	12	1
	31-40 years	13	5
	21-30 years	38	8
	Less than 20 years	13	76

These five cities had long been important centres of urban Catholicism, but they were renewing their Catholic population more by immigration than natural increase. The very few described as natives imply that there was emigration as well as immigration. The local Catholic gentry played their part in visiting the cities and maintaining houses and in some cases chaplains, but they had little to do with the Catholic commoners of the city and usually lived in the surrounding rural areas.

New Missions in County Towns

County towns which had not previously had regular missions acquired small Catholic centres in the period immediately before the Relief Act. In several cases these were established by a deliberate shift from the traditional seigniorial centres to the towns on the initiative of the clergy and by means of money provided by individual priests. This move seems to have been made on the grounds of convenience rather than on numbers of resident Catholics.

Just outside **Stafford** was the seat of the Fowler family at St Thomas (Baswich), a Catholic centre since Elizabethan times. The Fowlers died out in 1717, but the mission continued until the 1730s. A chapel then seems to have been opened in the town under the auspices of the Stafford-Howards. Possibly it was served from Tixall, 3½ miles east: certainly in 1754 the Tixall priest moved into Stafford, where he died in 1766. By 1769 a fund had been established by one of the Stafford-Howards. There was a priest about 1780, who traditionally said Mass in the garret of a house on The Green; in the mid-1780s a chapel was opened in Tipping Street. The mission was not the outcome of a sudden growth of Stafford itself. Its population was still only about 3,000 at this time and it had little besides its county status to maintain its importance and prosperity. It had only two parish churches and few if any Dissenters' Meeting houses. The number of Catholics was only 84 in 1767, with 41 in neighbouring Baswich, and 21 in Castle Church. The Catholics of highest status in Stafford included a doctor of medicine but otherwise they pursued the trades usual in small towns.

The Catholic congregation of Stafford included only seven adults native to the place, four in Stafford and three in Baswich. This profile is especially noteworthy in a town which was growing only slowly and where there were few new opportunities for employment. Even so, the proportion of young people was high, for there were 38 Catholics under 21 in the town, 18 in Baswich, and 17 in Castle Church who were aged less than 21.[52]

A similar move took place at **Shrewsbury**, Shropshire. The main focus of mission was shifted, probably by September 1731, from the estates of the Berington family at Mote Hall, just outside the town, to Berington House in the main square of Shrewsbury, St Alkmund's.[53]

A new Catholic mission developed rapidly in **Lancaster** from the mid-eighteenth century. The town of Lancaster must be distinguished from the extensive parish of Lancaster, which included a number of important Catholic houses. Traditionally the city had been hostile to Catholics and a priest died in Lancaster gaol as late as 1718. By the middle of the eighteenth century a priest and Mass centre were established in Leonardgate.

Comparison of the numbers of baptisms in the Anglican register of Lancaster with the number of children under five in the 1767 return gives some indication that one in twenty of the town's children were Catholics. The congregation was well balanced in terms of age; of the 168 adults living in the city 57 were aged between the ages of 13 and 25, and 71 between 26 and 50, while there were forty over 50.

Only 45 Lancaster Catholics are found as prime occupiers of the 944 houses paying window tax and there was a slight, though not marked, tendency for Catholics to occupy the smaller houses. These 45 Catholic ratepayers followed 22 different trades and professions and 34 of them were enrolled as freemen of Lancaster. Among them were some thirteen Catholic cabinet-makers. Robert Gillow, cabinet-maker, had established himself in trade in Lancaster in 1751, founding what was to become a prestigious firm in the nineteenth century. He took as apprentice a fellow Catholic, William Forrest of Hornby. Ten years later William himself became a freeman of Lancaster.

The thirteen Catholic cabinet-makers had between them eight Catholic apprentices. Apprenticeship was an important link between Catholic families, especially in towns, and the priests encouraged the apprenticeship of poor Catholic boys, sometimes providing endowments. John and Thomas Caton of Lancaster were both barbers in Lancaster and had lived there all their lives. John Caton became a freeman in 1742, took on a Catholic apprentice from Kendal and some time later married Ann Gregson of Broughton. They had sons and a daughter by 1767, of whom the eldest Thomas was later ordained. The household included five apprentices, two of whom were Gregsons. In Lancaster the Catholic apprenticeship fund set up by Hawkesley of Caton was especially well managed and effective. In all, there are 20 apprentices listed for Lancaster.[54]

Chester might be thought to have much in common with York, since both were regional capitals, diocesan centres, declining ports, markets for a rural hinterland and strategically important. The Catholic groups in the two cities were nonetheless very different. One third of the papists listed in Chester were men and women over 50 years of age and, unusually, there were few children. The largest occupational group of Catholics were the labourers. The occupations of the remainder were mainly in the leather industry, textile trades, and as craftsmen in wood. Most of them lived on the outskirts of the city beyond Northgate and Foregate Street. Only six Catholics can be described as of middling rank and two of these were surgeons with a foreign name. Three families had persisted through the eighteenth century: those of Keay, cobbler, Williams, labourer, and Waring, gardener. Otherwise, all of the Catholics were immigrants, mostly of less than ten years' standing. Both Welsh and Irish origins are suggested by their surnames. Immigrants outnumbered Catholics born there by four to one, male Catholics greatly outnumbered

Figure 17: Age Structure of the Catholic Community of Chester, 1767

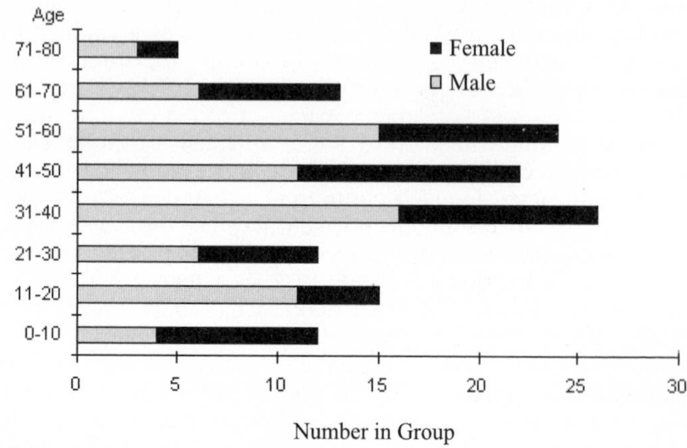

Total in Group = 129
Male = 72
Female = 57

Figure 18: Distribution of Catholics in Chester, 1767

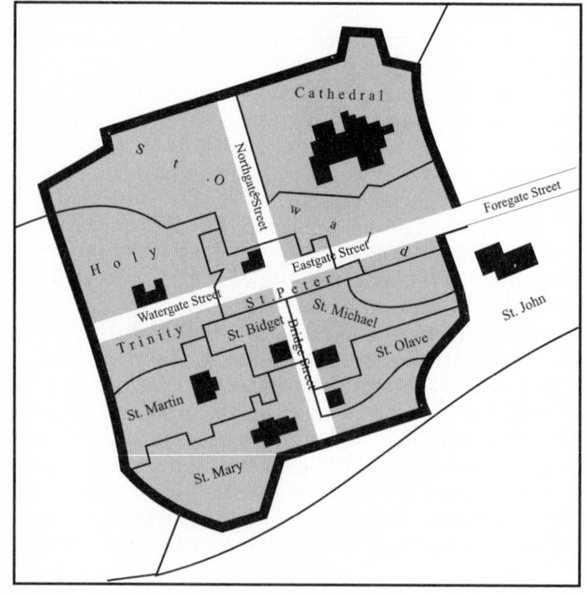

Cathedral	1
St. Oswald	46
Holy Trinity	1
St. Peter	9
St. Bridget	3
St. Martin	9
St. Mary	13
St. Michael	1
St. Olave	3
St. John	43

female, and there were twice as many unmarried as married men. Since 1758 there had been a resident priest but there was no Masshouse, and he lived in one of the poorest parts of the City.[55]

Alnwick, the county town of Northumberland, to some extent combined the gentrified and the plebeian. It was a small and old market town at the Castle gate but it was growing rapidly, and developing a new importance with the turnpiking of roads and the growth of great ports nearby which needed to be supplied with grain. The great four-and-a-half-acre market-place was surrounded by new stone buildings, shops and assembly rooms, and this is reflected in the occupations of the Catholics as building workers, servants, and lodgers. The mission in the county town of Northumberland owed much to the influence of the Claverings, but the earliest known chapel was in the house of the Widow Coles in Bondgate. There were 72 Catholics listed, headed by the priest and Francis Clavering but no other Clavering family members. The rest of the congregation consisted largely of immigrants of less than five years standing and there were only two Catholics who had been born in the town. There were Catholics in the surrounding parishes of Edlingham, Felton Longframlingham, Longhoughton and Embleton.[56]

Of the other county towns less need be said. The Jesuits were active in Lincoln, and there was a chapel first in the Thornbridge area and, from about 1750, in Bank Street. There were also congregations with resident priests at Berwick on Tweed, Canterbury, Chichester, Derby, Hereford and Warwick and at Leicester from 1774. The county towns without a resident priest were mainly those of eastern England, but Norwich, Canterbury and Lincoln show that this generalisation must not be pushed too far.[57]

At **Lichfield** in Staffordshire, there were 25 Catholics in 1767 in and around a cathedral city of about 3,000 people. They included a sausage-seller (a native), a chairmaker, a quilter, a shoemaker, two farmers and their families, several servants, a labourer's wife, a pauper widow on parish relief, and the wife of a Protestant. There were also Miss Teresa Wakeman, described as a young lady of fortune, and her resident priest, the Franciscan Lawrence Loraine alias Thomas Hall. The Mass-centre was at Pipe Hall to the west of the city and was served by Fr Loraine. The Hall had passed to the Catholic Heveninghams early in the reign of Elizabeth and to the Catholic Simeons in 1691. In 1768 it came into the hands of the Catholic Welds, who rebuilt it and made provision for a resident priest. After the sale of Pipe Hall in 1800, a chapel was opened in Lichfield itself.[58]

The population of **Canterbury** in 1770 was about 9,000. There were 123 Catholics reported in nine parishes of Canterbury, including 'a person supposed to be a priest' and a reputed priest. The most prestigious family was that of the steward of Sir Edward Hales, who was reported to be going away. Most of the Catholics in Canterbury were employed in the service trades and there was a French boy at the inn, a French tailor, a Frenchwoman come to learn English, a Prussian teacher of languages, and several Irish people. Clearly we have here a very heterogeneous congregation brought together by the growth of commerce.[59]

The wealthier Catholic tradesmen played no part in the government of any of these cities, an exclusion at least as significant for them as for the gentry at county level. In every case, Catholics lived in many parts of the cities, and were not concentrated to any notable extent in any one part, even particularly near their chapels. The finance for the early stages of these new missions and the building of the new chapels came for the most part from clergy funds and a very few local people, while the gentry were called upon to contribute to chapels in general, not only to those in their own sphere of influence.

Rural Market Towns

We can now turn from Catholics in the county and cathedral towns to those in rural market towns. About one third of the 700 market towns made at least some return of papists in 1767, but 36 returned more than 40 Catholics. On the face of it there is a remarkable increase in Catholic centres in market towns since the seventeenth century and some groups were significantly large. However, the problem is to distinguish those Catholics who lived within the town itself from those who lived in the surrounding rural area. Many of the smaller market towns had never become completely separated in administrative terms from the parishes within which they were founded. In most cases the name of the parish and the name of the town were the same, making separate identification in the lists difficult. Some of the Lancashire returns distinguish between the town and the parish. Burnley for example returned 35 papists in the parish of Whalley, which had 118. Garstang town had 46, but the parish 837.[60] Brewood and Stone, both in Staffordshire, are striking examples of the dangers of identifying missions as urban by the name of the parish only.

Brewood parish contained three Mass centres and the estate of one of the most influential Catholic squires the Giffards of Chillington, but the Catholic registers show that few of the papists lived in Brewood, the small town of the parish.

Table 31: Parishes containing Market Towns and reporting 40 Papists or over, 1767

County	Parish	Town	Town Area	Parish Area	Papists in Parish	Papists in Town	
Lancs.	Kirkham	Kirkham	840	48,530	939	66	Priest
Lancs.	Garstang	Garstang	500	31,403	837	46	Priest
Staffs.	Brewood	Brewood		11,839	389		Priest
N'land	Hexham		4,775	55,229	287		Priest
Notts.	Worksop			18,220	233		Priest
Warw.	Brailes				190		Priest
W'land	Kendal			10,968	165	45	Priest
Suffolk	Bury St Edmunds			7,000	158		Priest
Durham	Stockton-on-Tees		3,032	5,160	144	63	Priest
Staffs.	Stone			20,030	132		
Yorks.	Spofforth	Wetherby	3,032	12,958	121		Priest
Sussex	Midhurst			671	120		Priest
Lancs.	Whalley	Burnley	1,839	104,689	118	51	Priest
Worcs.	Bromsgrove			10,968	118		Priest
Sussex	Winchelsea			1,510	114		
Warw.	Solihull			11,296	111		Priest
Cumb.	St Bees	Whitehaven	26,907	71,332	90		Mass
Sussex	Arundel			1,968	87		Priest
Durham	Morpeth		537	8,177	86		
Durham	Darlington		3,569	7,856	84	63	Priest
N'land	Haltwhistle				79		
Yorks.	Sherburn		3,500	11,896	78		
N'land	Rothbury		4,923	34,798	64	9	Priest
Dorset	Shaftesbury			2,400	68		
N'land	Corbridge		4,499	13,130	63		Priest
Lancs.	Romaldkirk				52		
Warw.	Wootton Wawen	Henley-in-Arden		8,700	51		Priest
Yorks.	Aldbrough		1,890	9,323	50		Priest
Staffs.	Eccleshall			21,460	47		Priest
Staffs.	Tamworth		6,450	12,420	46		Visits
Herts.	Baldock			200	45		
Yorks.	Helmsley		8,200	44,382	44		
Yorks.	Hovingham				44		Priest
Herts.	Standon			7,520	43		
Derbys.	Bakewell			43,020	40		Priest
Gloucs.	Horton				40		

Source: Worrall 1 & 2; Clark, *Population*, passim. The population figures are taken from contemporary estimates and provide an estimate only.

The market-town of Stone was part of a parish of 20,030 acres in Staffordshire where there had been many Catholic gentry families, but they had for the most part died out or left the district. Most of the 132 reported papists lived in the rural part of the parish, pursuing rural trades, and there was no reported priest, although there were Mass centres at Stafford and Tixall nearby and a priest resident in neighbouring Eccleshall parish. In the town of Stone there were only 18 families of Catholics. Only four of the adults were born in the parish. The Catholics of Stone were notably poor, five paupers, seven labourers, nine servants. Stone's Catholics are revealed as a residual population from former gentry missions.[61]

In most of the towns in Table 31 the influence of Catholic landowners was of long standing, for example, Worksop and Midhurst. **Worksop**, Nottinghamshire, in the Dukeries belonged to the Duke of Norfolk, and he and his wife headed the list of papists. There were his bailiff, his steward and other workers dependent upon the estate, down to the humble weeders. The priest was 'at the Duke of Norfolk's'. Most of the Catholics were long-term residents and 27 of them had lived in Worksop parish all their lives, but it was not an ageing congregation, for almost half were under 18. There is no clear indication who lived in the town itself, but they may well have included the attorney's clerk, the innkeeper, the waiter at the inn and the apothecary.[62]

Midhurst, Sussex, was still under the influence of the Browne family at Cowdray House in neighbouring Easebourne, where the priest lived. The Catholic register shows that the congregation consisted of the family and dependents of Cowdray House and the townspeople of Midhurst. The townspeople followed a variety of occupations: such as shopkeeper, brazier, cabinet-maker, watchmaker and staymaker. Confirmations were held in the chapel at Easebourne. This was one of the more genuinely urban Catholic congregations but it was small. When confirmations were held in 1761, 21 persons received the sacrament, and 26 in 1770.[63]

Although the influence of the gentry continued in some town missions, others were becoming more independent. Two examples of this trend are provided by Solihull and Hexham. **Solihull**, Warwickshire, notable in 1676, no longer had resident gentry, and Solihull Catholics were no longer numerous in the Edgbaston register. By 1767 Solihull had a resident priest of its own, namely Henry Dixon, aged 40, resident 12 years. The mission had an endowment of £30 a year, but the priests had to supplement the charge of their board and keep a horse from their own resources. Solihull was a very small town in a parish of over 11,000 acres. Even in 1811, the population of town and parish combined was still only 2,500. More than half the adult Catholics were described in 1767 as having lived in Solihull all their lives. However, most of the Solihull Catholics were farmers and labourers and few of them lived in the little town. Two who did have a town house were Hugford Hassal, a scrivener, and his clerk Caesar Johnson, aged 21. Hugford Hassal came of a family of minor gentry and had several priests among his relatives. Both he and Caesar Johnson were frequently employed by the clergy and the Vicars Apostolic in their legal and financial dealings, and it was Hugford Hassal who gave land for the building of the Catholic chapel and priest's house about 1760 in Solihull.[64]

Hexham, Northumberland, was another small rural town with a long Catholic history, but relatively independent missions. The town covered 4,755 acres in a parish of 27,973 acres. Although the congregation included two Catholic farmers, the trades of the 267 Catholics included an innholder, a surgeon and two conveyancers. There were two priests, both of whom were included in the return. There were two missions, each using a small ancient chapel outside the town itself. Battle Hill was in the care of the Dominicans and a secular priest said Mass in the house of a tanner at Cockshaw. At Easter 1757 166 persons made their Easter Communion.[65]

There were several market towns where a priest had recently taken up residence, namely in Banbury and Chipping Norton, Oxfordshire; Tiverton, Devon; Leominster, Herefordshire: and Marlborough, Wiltshire.[66] The Catholic register of Bury St Edmunds, Suffolk, began in 1765. Other market towns were served on an increasingly regular basis from rural missions, as, for example, Tamworth, Warwickshire; Morpeth, Northumberland; Bishop's Auckland, Durham; and Nantwich, Cheshire.[67]

The Ports

To enumerate the total number of ports, large and small, where some commercial activity was going on in 1767 would be an impossible task, especially as to the coastal ports must be added the river ports and the ports of the new artificial waterways. There were very few of them which had a long Catholic tradition, but in some there were new and vigorous Catholic congregations. The greatest port of all, London, has already been considered and some smaller ports, such as Christchurch, Hampshire, have been considered elsewhere, since sea trade was not their most significant function. Of the larger ports, Liverpool, Newcastle and Bristol each have features of special interest. Liverpool had the largest and most rapidly expanding Catholic population in England and for that reason merits detailed consideration. The second largest Catholic congregation in a port was at Newcastle-upon-Tyne with its associated ports of Tynemouth and Gateshead. In contrast with Liverpool, Newcastle had a long Catholic tradition. The third example of the larger ports was

Bristol, where the Catholic congregation was notably impoverished in a great port dominated by wealthy Protestant and Quaker merchants and industrialists. Few of the small ports reported a resident priest and congregation. Of these Havant, Hampshire, has particularly good documentation, making it possible to investigate it in some detail and provide a counterpoise to the study of Liverpool.

By 1767 **Liverpool** had a larger Catholic population than any provincial town, even Preston and Wigan. It had overtaken Bristol as the major port for the New World and by 1750 it stood second only to London in the volume and value of its Anglo-American trade. Its trade with Dublin and Drogheda also greatly increased and spread to include the smaller ports of Northern Ireland. The trade in African slaves became of major significance in the mid-eighteenth century; Liverpool dominated the three-cornered trade, taking manufactured goods to Africa and African slaves to the New World and bringing back sugar and tobacco. Large-scale international businesses grew alongside a great multiplication of small workshops and commercial enterprises. By 1773 it was a town of 34,407 inhabitants, almost all of whom lived in the streets and alleys of the built-up town. It was an independent chapel of Walton parish, and was a manorial borough governed with efficiency and sophistication by the Leet court and the Vestry. The parish, and therefore the 1767 return, covered very little territory outside the town.

The need to establish a priest there had been recognised by Nicholas Blundell of Crosby Hall (Sefton parish, Lancashire) and a priest began to 'help' there on a regular basis in 1701. The third priest of the mission wrote that he received 'one year with another about two and twenty pounds for my maintenance' and he raised the money for building a chapel in Edmund Street, then on the edge of the town 'from friends in other places'.

By 1767, 1,743 Catholics were listed but there was some double registration and the number should be 1,641, of whom 693 (42%) were under the age of 20. Of 899 persons over 20 years of age, only 78 were born in the town. Over a third of both men and women had arrived between 1762 and 1767. Two thirds of the adult immigrants were below the age of 35, as one would expect, but one third had come to Liverpool aged over 35, many of them with their families. Half the Catholics described as labourers were over 49 years of age. Liverpool did not only attract young single people. The Catholic marriage and baptism registers rarely indicate parish of origin, but when they do so they suggest that the immigrants were coming mainly from south-west Lancashire and from just across the Mersey in Cheshire. The evidence of

Figure 19: Locations of Catholics Migrating to Liverpool, 1771-1774

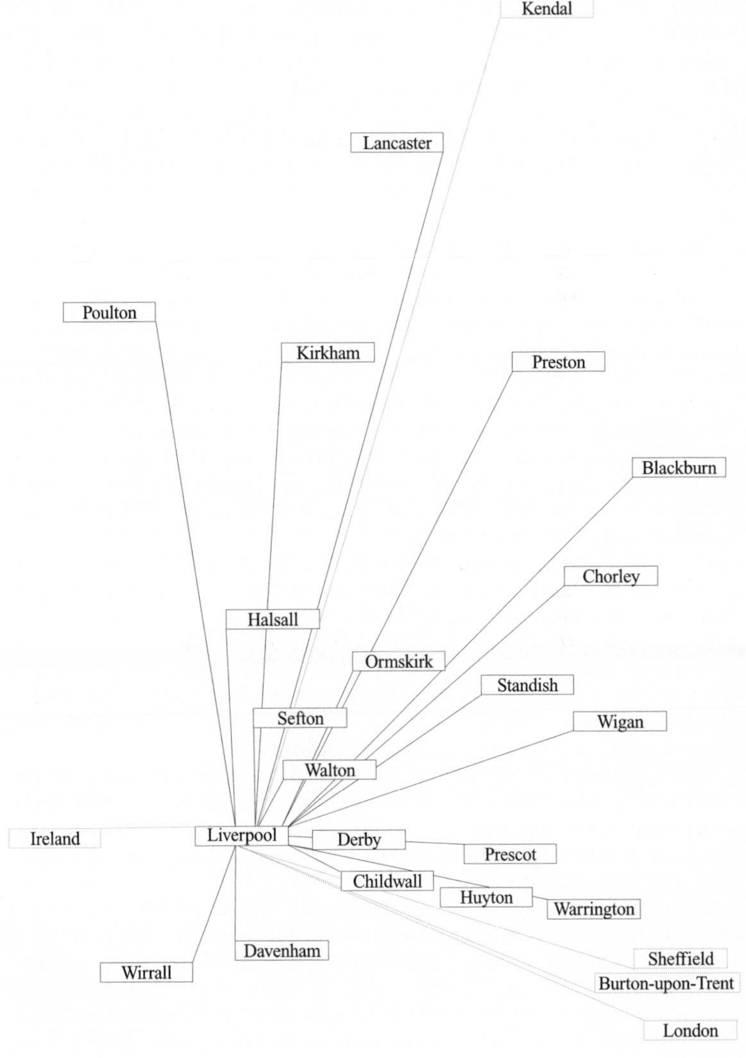

surnames indicates the importance of Irish immigration. In the 1740s many of these were registered merely as 'an Irishman', suggesting that the priest scarcely knew them. Some of them settled down, their names and families appear regularly in the Catholic registers, and anonymous entries become infrequent. The volatility of the Liverpool congregation is further illustrated by the low level of correlation between the return and the registers. A total of 297 men over the age of 20 appear in the Liverpool return and of these only 104 also appear in the Catholic registers between the years 1757 and 1771 as father or groom. However, there are a much larger number who appear in the register but not in the return.

The number of Catholic registrations of baptism in the decade 1741-50 was 386, when the number of Church of England registrations was 6,001. Twenty years later in the decade 1761-1770, Catholic baptisms numbered 1,234 and the corresponding Church of England figure was 9,656. These crude figures need to be adjusted to take into account many factors, including under-registration and nonconformity. Even as they are, they suggest that Catholic numbers were increasing as a proportion of the whole population and perhaps at a faster rate. It is instructive to contrast the work of the Jesuit priests in Liverpool with 300-400 baptisms a year with that of the chaplains of Plowden and Sawston (pp. 224, 288 above).

The occupations of the male adults covered a wide spectrum of activity and social standing. The largest group were the 70 men described as labourers and 56 men whose work was associated with the sea and the port. The occupations of the female adults were more limited, and the occupations of Catholic women rarely fall outside those conventionally occupied by women earning a discrete living. There were 40 servants, washerwomen, shopkeepers, seamsters, and one schoolmistress.

The Catholics lived in both the old and the newer parts of the town and in the 'superior' as well as the poorer parts, with some concentration around the docks and Dale Street, Frog Lane and the area around the chapel, but these were in any case the most crowded parts of town.

Both on the evidence of occupation and the evidence of place of residence it would be erroneous to characterise the Liverpool Catholics as poor and ignorant, but they are very under-represented in the professions. As we have seen in the case of Lancaster, apprenticeship was a means of strengthening Catholic ties and protecting the transmission of religion, and 22 Catholic households had Catholic apprentices. However, this was not exclusive. Ten Catholic apprentices had non-Catholic masters, including one boy whose master was a churchwarden.[68]

On the eastern coast, **Newcastle-upon-Tyne** was a great port which for centuries had been closely linked with London, exporting coal from the extensively developed coalfields in its hinterland. By mid-century its population reached 29,000 and its ships were travelling throughout the world. In contrast with Liverpool it had a long Catholic tradition and 123 persons had been confirmed there in 1705, yet none of the 199 Catholics listed in 1767 were described as born in the parish. This is a congregation constantly renewing itself. There were two secular priests catering for the town and parts adjacent. Associated with Newcastle were the ports of Gateshead and Tynemouth, each with Catholic congregations and resident priests living at the expense of the Jesuit college; though it is not clear whether either had a chapel at this date, they certainly had both had one earlier.[69]

The second greatest port in England was **Bristol,** but there the Catholic population was much smaller and poorer than in Liverpool. The city was a long standing centre of Protestant nonconformity, and Quakers were responsible for major commercial and industrial enterprises in and near the city. A Jesuit was living in Earl Street, Jobbing's Lays, in 1724 and John Scudamore S.J. was saying Mass in an upper room at Hook's Mills, about a mile from Bristol, for the brassworkers, many of whom were foreigners. In 1743 Mass began to be said regularly in a chapel in St James' Back. In 1767 Bristol returned 487 people as papists, of whom 124 were children, a small minority of the whole population of Bristol. Bristol mission was only half the size of that of Liverpool and there does not appear to have been a permanent chapel until 1787. According to the returns there were no Catholic men native to Bristol, and more than two thirds of Bristol Catholics had arrived in the city in the previous ten years.

The Catholic group in Bristol included four gentlemen, eight gentlewomen and four servants, but in a city of rich merchants there was only one Catholic merchant and a Spanish merchant's clerk. The largest occupational group were the 102 mariners. Other Catholics associated with the work of the port included two shipwrights and two saddlecloth-makers and a ships' scraper. Seven men and five women were employed in the Bristol brass trade, probably for one of the great Quaker firms. Most Catholics in Bristol earned their livings in a variety of service and retailing trades, while 26 men and two women were described as labourers. The majority of the women were characterised as wife or widow, but in this busy port 42 women were earning their own living in the characteristically women's trades of mantua-maker, bonnet-maker, china-seller and staymaker. Eight were described as hucksters and eight as victuallers. At the bottom of the social pile were the three women who earned a painful living as oakum pickers. Apart from the brassworkers at Hook's Mills and Baptist Mills, there were few Catholics in the parishes surrounding the city. Even though Catholics in the city numbered almost 500, the contrast between the poverty of this Catholic congregation, lacking even a chapel, with the wealth and influence of other Bristol Dissenters is marked.[70]

It was not only in the major ports that Catholic missions were growing; there were also new missions in some small ports. At Workington and Whitehaven, Cumberland, immigrants, including Irishmen, combined with a small number of local Catholics. They were a pathetic group and included the Murray family who 'pick oakum or do anything they can towards their support', and eight apprentices to the sea aged 15-18 'picked up in Ireland by masters of ships'. There were only four small ports which reported a resident priest and congregation, namely Whitby and Yarm, Yorkshire, Fowey, Cornwall, and Havant, Hampshire.[71]

A study of the Catholic register of **Havant** reveals a congregation drawn from parishes along the south coast road from Southampton to Chichester. Children were baptised whose Catholic fathers lived in Emsworth, Westbourne, Hayling, Warblington, Nutbourne, Bedhampton, Langstone and Chichester. It was an exceptionally mixed congregation in terms of social standing, occupations, residence and age. The secular networks of the people of Havant were wide-ranging. Havant was not only a port, but also a market centre for the many diverse food crops of the region shipped from Havant, Chichester and the smaller ports to London and the Continent. The surrounding parishes were Portsmouth, Hayling, Portsea, Gosport, Ferham and Bedhampton. The small ports along the Hampshire coast had been noted in the reign of Elizabeth for the landing of priests, and even in the eighteenth century the local vicar suspected that the Catholics sent intelligence abroad to enemy France. The main centre had been at Warblington, where the Pound family had maintained a priest and where there had been a burial place for Catholics. The mission was established financially from 1715 by Philip Caryll of North House, Catherington, but the centre had been visited by a riding priest from West Grinstead from at least 1671 and the surviving registers run from 1733. Mass was said at first in the cottage of Mr West at the corner of Brockhampton Lane at Langstone and the priest lived in one of the cottages. A chapel was built in full public view in 1752. Bishop Hoadley wrote in 1759:

> A house with a large chapel was built a few years ago by one Morgan, a popish priest, opposite Langstone harbour, and is a building which cost 12 or 14 hundred pounds All the papists in and about Portsmouth and all who come from abroad and go abroad from thence make no secret of going to this chapel.

In 1725 50 reputed papists were reported in Havant who met frequently at Middle Leigh with others, and there were another 69 papists at Bedhampton. By 1759 there were two Jesuit priests at Brockhampton. Confirmations were held there in 1761, 1763, 1764, 1765 and 1770.

The 1767 return included four gentlemen, one at Bedhampton and three at Havant, and their servants, four masters of vessels, one sailor, a saltboiler, a cidermaker, and two millers. There are, unusually, no husbandmen or yeomen. No Catholics worked in the Portsmouth royal dockyards but the two victuallers, the watchmaker, and even the musician may have had customers there. There was a Catholic schoolmaster in Portsmouth, aged 34, who had been there three years.[72]

In the ports the priest lived independently and served a mixed congregation of residents and transients busy earning their livings in commerce and manufacture and as labourers and retailers.

The Leisure Towns

There were a number of towns whose business was to attract the wealthy to spend money on entertainment and in the pursuit of health, social opportunities and elegance, among them the Catholic gentry. By 1767 there were resident priests at Bath, Tunbridge Wells, Richmond and Bakewell. A priest visited **Scarborough** and by 1767 there was a resident priest and 39 resident Catholics were reported there, 18 of whom were under 20 years of age. The adults included a stationer, a coffee man, a confectioner, a clothes-scourer, and one fisherman. Only four adults out of 21 were natives of the port.

Commercial development of the leisure industry and building got under way in the town of **Bath** from the 1720s, but leading Catholic families had been visiting the town for many years before that, and a series of Benedictine missionaries had been maintained on a stipend of £24 produced by the interest on money given 'by several benefactors' since the seventeenth century. Catholic visitors lodged at the Bell Tree House and brought with them their personal servants. The Bell Tree House was held in the name of the Husseys of Marnhull but on the second floor was a chapel and accommodation for the priest. The house had its own housekeepers and servants. It stood at the corner of Binbury or Bilbury Lane and Beau Street near the Cross. The chapel, which by 1725 was freely accessible to Catholics, had rich vestments and chapel decorations. Altar wine was bought by the gallon and there were elaborate flower decorations at Easter.

As there was no return for the parish of St Michael's, Bath, the exact number resident in the town is uncertain. In the parish of St Peter and Paul there were 29 adult papists in a parish with 319 ratepayers in 1766 and in St James 52 out of 418. In the parish of Walcot, which lay partly in and partly outside the city, there were 40 papists among the 560 ratepayers. This was in the context of a total town population of 13,000 in 1766. Surprisingly there were no resident Catholic gentry. The more skilled trades were monopolised by the city council and the Catholics were almost all servants, hairdressers, starchers and similar occupations, which reflected the leading trade of the city at a humble level. In St Peter and Paul there was one servant out of place, a ribbon-weaver, a perfumer and a linen-draper. In St James's there were fifteen 'of no business', alongside a hair-weaver, clear-starchers, seamstresses and washers. In Walcot parish there were four gentlemen and -women, a physician and a musician. All the Catholics were incomers. Catholic gentry who visited Bath brought with them their own domestic servants and the city provided a marriage market for servants as well as for the gentry. Four years after the 1767 return, in 1771, a new chapel was built by subscription, the Bell Tree House chapel being by then too small. It is clear that the congregation there consisted mainly of visitors rather than residents.[73]

Holywell, Flintshire, was frequented by English Catholics throughout the period and was a centre of mission for parishes in Shropshire as well as Wales. William Statham of Hathersage, Derbyshire, left a detailed account of his pilgrimage there. There were two Mass centres both located in inns, continuing a long standing tradition. The Jesuits had long been established in the town at The Star and recorded miraculous cures of the sick and conversions as a result of the intercession of St Winifred. The secular priests, who maintained a chapel at the Cross Keys, lived independently and paid their rent to the innkeeper. The Holywell missions represented an old tradition of Mass centres in inns catering for both resident and transient Catholics, and, like Bath, the resident Catholics were in the service sector.[74]

Catholics in the county towns, the ports and leisure towns were almost all members of independent missions, and Mass was said in chapels, in priests' houses or in inns. The impetus of commercial development encouraged urbanisation and within this framework the growth of independent town missions owed as much to secular change as to ecclesiastical factors. This is dramatically evident in the industrialising areas.

CATHOLICS IN INDUSTRIALISING AREAS

In 1974 Lesourd, and in 1975 John Bossy, drew attention to the transformation of the English Catholic community from a predominantly rural way of life to one which was a predominantly industrial and urban, and further claimed that Catholics were not only participating in the changes of English society at large but were shifting 'more rapidly than other Englishmen out of the ways of their forefathers'. In the years since these studies were published historians have revised upwards their estimate of the proportion of the population engaged in trade and manufacture, recent suggestions ranging from 30-40% up to nearly 52%. Catholics were evidently less distinctive in this respect than Lesourd and Bossy originally believed.[75] This does not lessen the significance of the social transformation of the Catholic body itself between the late seventeenth and the late eighteenth centuries.

Table 32: Industrial Parishes with 200 Papists or more, 1767

		Population		Papists
Lancs.	Prescot	2,689	houses	1,497
Lancs.	Wigan	4,500		1,194
Lancs.	Preston	5,000		1,043
Staffs.	Wolverhampton	10,500		496
Lancs.	Warrington	2,150		458
Durham	Ryton	600	families	447
Lancs.	Brindle	130	families	364
Yorks.	Sheffield	12,900		361
Lancs.	Blackburn	1,800	families	294
Lancs.	Manchester	22,500		287
Durham	Lanchester			284
Lancs.	Ormskirk	3,000		230
Warw.	Birmingham	51,000		222
Lancs.	Chorley	4,000		202
N'land	Newcastle	29,000		199

(The population estimates are taken from contemporary sources and are provided as a rough guide only: J. West, *Town Records*; Clark, *Population*; J. Aikin, *Description of the Country... round Manchester* (1795); Visitation returns.)

Table 33: Industrial Parishes with Priests, 1767

County	Parish	Masshouse	Priest
Durham	Ryton		Priest
Durham	Lanchester	Chapel	Priest
Durham	Gateshead	Masshouse	
Lancs.	Prescot	4 chapels	4 priests
Lancs.	Wigan	2 Masshouses	3 priests
Lancs.	Preston	Masshouse	Priest
Lancs.	Manchester		Priest
Lancs.	Warrington	3 Mass centres	Priest
Lancs.	Brindle	Masshouse	Priest
Staffs.	Wolverhampton	Masshouse	Priest
Staffs.	Stoke-upon-Trent	Chapel	Priest
Warw.	Birmingham	Franciscan House	Priest
Warw.	Coventry		Priest
Yorks.	Sheffield	Masshouse	Priest

Chapel = Chapel in private house
Masshouse = purpose built as a Catholic chapel

The most dynamic areas of economic growth and rising populations were to be found in the north of England and there too were the most rapidly growing and dynamic Catholic congregations outside London. Nine of the towns and parishes which returned more than two hundred papists were in industrial areas, particularly on the coal-fields, but industrialisation involved a change of balance of population not only from rural to urban and industrial, but also from south to north.

There had been a great increase in the number of priests and Masshouses in industrial settings, some as the result of industrialisation in old Catholic centres, and some by the development of new centres.

The Occupations of Catholics

The fifteen places in Table 32 between them reported more than a tenth of all the Catholics listed. With the Catholics of London, Liverpool and the larger cities and towns, it is clear that a very large proportion of English Catholics lived in urban and industrial settings. This is borne out by a study of their occupations. Lesourd calculated the proportions of Catholics engaged in various sectors of the economy from the occupations given in the 1767 return, omitting those for whom there is no indication of occupation or status and the children. Information about occupation is specified for 18,000 persons, and of these, according to Lesourd, 17.5% were in commercial occupations, 2.2% '*métiers tertiaires*', and 51.8% were workers and artisans. However, any attempt to quantify so precisely must involve such a large number of adjustments and of attributions record by record, based on assumptions rather than evidence, as to render the figures, as such, fragile. What is important, and all that is necessary for our purpose, is the clear signal verified by much other evidence that at least half the Catholics in the return were working in industry and commerce rather than agriculture.[76]

The largest aggregation of Catholics in this group was presented by **Prescot**, Lancashire, a parish of 37, 221 acres with fifteen townships and three chapelries. The parish included the borough of St Helens. The population was well over 10,000, of which about half was in Prescot township. In 1767 there were priests in Parr and Windle and two in Eccleston. The main landowners were for the most part Catholics, but only ten were listed in the parish: the Orell family, Mr and Mrs Lancaster, 'esquire Ecclestone' and some Catholic gentlewomen living in small households with their servants. Mass was said at Eccleston Hall, Blackbrook House and Hordshaw Hall, and Scholes House was rented for a chapel from 1728. In 1769 the landlord conformed but the resident Benedictine priest converted a farm building for a chapel. In 1743 the widowed Mrs Ecclestone, née Lowe, converted the largest rooms in her house to provide a chapel, which was known as Lowe House.

The return is presented in ten separate lists with the largest numbers in Ecclestone, Sutton, Prescot, Windle and Parr. Less than a quarter of the Catholics lived in the other ten townships. Prescot was a parish of very mixed economy and Catholics earned their livings in a wide variety of ways, skilled and unskilled. The largest single occupation group were the husbandmen, 89 in all, mainly in the townships of Windle, Rainford and Farnworth. There were also 27 farmers. However, Prescot also supported an exceptionally varied range of trades. There were 29 coalminers; clay pots mainly for the sugar industry were a specialism of the parish and there were two potters. The parish was outstanding for the skill and innovations of its watchmakers, watchtool-makers and instrument-makers. Skilled men in these trades commanded respect and high remuneration in busy times, and the patronage they looked for was an order for work.[77]

In general tradesmen provided and controlled their own family workshops, and depended not on the local gentry but upon the commercial capitalists who obtained orders and distributed their products at home and overseas. The heads of households employed journeymen and apprentices and organised the work and education of their families. Such conditions have been cited to 'explain' the incidence of Dissent and Methodism. It is evident that they could also be equally conducive to Catholicism, and that capitalism was not necessarily Protestant.

A study of some of the congregations in the industrialising areas shows new congregations emerging and old ones changing in size, composition and ethos. Change was rapid in the textile, metalworking, coalmining and pottery industries, and so correspondingly was the social transformation of the Catholic congregations.

Catholic Textile-Workers

For hundreds of years textiles had been Britain's major industry and until the middle of the seventeenth century her principal export.

Table 34: Places returning Catholic Weavers, 1767

County	Places	Number	County	Places	Number
Cheshire	3	4	Nottinghamshire	5	7
Cumberland	1	4	Oxfordshire	3	4
Derbyshire	4	10	Shropshire	3	3
Devon	1	1	Somerset	2	3
Dorset	3	11	Staffordshire	8	19
Essex	1	1	Suffolk	1	2
Hampshire	1	1	Warwickshire	5	7
Lancashire	38	1,186	Wiltshire	2	6
Norfolk	7	47	Worcestershire	5	6
Northamptonshire	3	4	Yorkshire	25	85
Northumberland	12	24			
			Totals	133	1435

Source: Worrall vols. 1 and 2. Places = Parish, Chapelry or as the returns were made

By 1767 there were few Catholic weavers in the parishes engaged in the old woollen manufacture in Devon, East Anglia, Essex and the Cotswolds. The whole diocese of Exeter reported only one Catholic weaver, although in Totnes there were five Catholic clothworkers, and three in Kingsteignton. There were two groups of Catholic cambric weavers at Faversham, Kent, and in the small port of Winchelsea, Sussex, on the south coast; in both cases they seem to have been isolated from the rest of the seignorial Catholics of Sussex and Kent. Even in Yorkshire the numbers were not remarkable.[78]

The contrast with the textile regions of Lancashire could hardly be greater. Catholic weavers were numerous in the parishes of Billinge, Cuerden, Euston, Heapy, Oldham, Preston, Salford, Samlesbury, and Wigan. Yarn was supplied by large number of spinsters, particularly notable in Altcar, Formby, Lydiate, Maghull, Standish and Westleigh, but most notably of all in Blackburn, Leyland and Brindle. Some incumbents indicated the diverse types of cloth being produced. In Harwood in Blackburn parish the Catholics were plod-weavers (plaid weavers) and jersey-spinners, and in Oldham, Prescot and Blackburn cotton spinners, while in the Fylde the older trade of linenweaving still predominated. There were plush-weavers in Cheshire, shag-weavers in Stockport, and flax-spinners in Dalton. Both weaving and spinning cotton was spreading rapidly in the North-West and Catholics were well represented in this comparatively new trade.[79]

Table 35: Lancashire Catholic Weavers by Parish, 1767

Blackburn	287	Ribchester	18	Dean	4
Wigan	169	St Michael on Wyre	13	Windle	3
Leyland	91	Eccleston	9	Huyton	3
Preston	78	Penwortham	8	Eccles	3
Brindle	58	Ormskirk	8	Chipping	3
Prescot	42	Oldham	8	Lytham	2
Leigh	38	Garstang	8	Liverpool	2
Winwick	33	Bolton	6	Sefton	1
Kirkham	33	Walton	5	Poulton le Fylde	1
Manchester	30	Standish	5	Childwall	1
Whalley	24	Cockerham	5	Aughton	1
Lancaster	22	Rochdale	4	Altcar	1
Croston	21				

Total = 1,052

There were in addition 6 silk weavers, 16 fustian weavers, 106 linen-weavers and 6 plod-weavers:1,186 in all.

Catholic Congregations in the Textile Regions

In 1975 Bossy demonstrated the growth of Catholicism in industrial areas citing in particular Preston, Wigan, Liverpool and Manchester, and so it is appropriate to look more closely at these places to investigate the dynamics of that change. Liverpool has already been considered as a great port. Wigan and Manchester were primarily, though not exclusively, textile towns, and Preston also had a strong reliance on textiles among other sources of income and influence. In addition it is important to examine the development of Catholicism in the industrialising parishes and Hindley and Brindle were selected on the basis of their relatively good documentation. There were other branches of the textile industry and the growth of the silk industry in Coventry also provided the trigger for the establishment of a new congregation in that city.

The town of **Preston**, Lancashire, had an especially strong and independent Catholic tradition. In 1714 it was said that there were five or six houses in the towns where Mass was celebrated and that a number of Catholic priests met in the town on market days. In the surrounding country there were numerous papist landowners. Just outside the town, in the chapelry of Broughton, there was the pilgrimage centre of Fernyhalgh with a permanent chapel, a resident priest and a Catholic school. Preston Catholics had suffered sequestrations of property after the '15 and '45, but the priests had managed to retain the house and chapel at Greystocks in the Friar Gate near the White Bull, where Mass was said, because various gentlemen held it in trust for them. Over a thousand Catholics were listed in 1767 in the town and parish, and 47 different trades. Sixteen men pursued much more prestigious trades than were commonly found among town Catholics. These included a grocer, a hosier, and a linendraper. There were six superior textile tradesmen, a silk-dealer, a silk-comber, a cotton-spinner and a flax-dresser.

Forty-one Catholics of Preston were weavers, more than half of whom had arrived in the town since 1757, and 20 since 1765. There were also Catholic weavers in two of the four townships of Preston parish, ten in Broughton, and 29 in Fishwick. There were 14 farmers, of whom nine were native to the parish, the characteristic stable core, through whom continuity of tradition was maintained, but the husbandmen and labourers they employed were incomers. Even in Preston the majority of the adult Catholics were immigrants.[80]

Wigan was second only to Preston and Liverpool in the number of papists returned. Like so many other towns in the Midlands and North, Wigan was a borough with some self-government set in a parish of numerous townships, and the Catholics listed for the parish included some who lived in the town and some in the rural area of the out-hamlets. There were two missions in Wigan, the Jesuits using a chapel built by a priest about 1740, and the seculars a chapel a short distance away at

Standish Gate. There was also a Dissenters' meeting house, a Methodist meeting and an Independent meeting.

In 1767 of the adult Catholics, 29 men and 33 women had lived in Wigan for only one or two years when the census was taken. Half the men and half the women had lived in the town less than six years. Fifty-three men and 59 women had lived in the parish for between ten and three years. Only seven men and 14 women had lived in the town for more than 20 years. As one would expect, most of the immigrants arrived there in their twenties. Forty couples arrived in the town married, and nineteen found marriage partners after arrival. The position in the out-hamlets was similar. The age of coming to residence was between 20 and 30, although in Wigan there were relatively more who arrived at a slightly higher age. It may be that this indicates a two-stage process.

There were a total of 166 adults described as weavers in the Wigan Catholic congregation in 1767, 70 in the town and 95 in the townships, few of whom had been born and brought up in the parish. Only in the townships of Pendleton and Haigh were there any persons native to the place.[81]

The production of textiles was developing rapidly in rural as well as urban parishes. **Brindle** was one such parish and its detailed Catholic register makes it possible to provide a context for the 1767 return. It was small by Lancashire standards, two and half miles by two miles with no villages or hamlets. It was a long standing mission served by a succession of Benedictines. The manorial family were the Gerards, but they had sold the manor in 1582. Lesser branches held land in the area and the Gerards continued to live nearby where there was a chapel, but had ceased to have any direct influence in the parish by 1767. The editor of the Catholic registers says (without providing any evidence), that, although there was no resident priest, this was the principal place where Mass was said in the district. The Jesuits had an endowed chapel in Brindle, which was confiscated in 1715, after which the Jesuits 'worked from a succession of centres' but moved to Slate Delph in the 1740s. The Benedictines lived in the parish and had a chapel at Newhouse, a seventeenth century endowment. In 1735 they acquired a house and five acres of land on which a new chapel was built, and the registers begin in that year.

There were 364 Catholics listed in 1767, of whom 205 were adults, 64 of whom were born in the parish. In 1779 the churchwardens reported to the Church of England Bishop that there were 129 households of communicant families, 280 papists with a Masshouse, but no Dissenter families. Fifty years before, a

Visitation return had given 100 Anglican families and 50 Catholics. It would seem that the Catholic population of Brindle was growing at a much faster rate than that of the parish as a whole. Of the 103 adult Catholics with named trades, 49 were weavers, and 20 husbandmen. There was a noteworthy absence of persons described as servants and labourers.

Brindle was one of several missions in the area and Catholics did not take notice of Anglican parish boundaries. The Benedictines registered baptisms not only from Brindle parish itself, but also from Balderstone, Cuerdale, Salesbury, Samlesbury and Walton le Dale, all townships in Blackburn parish to the north of Brindle. The remainder with a few exceptions came from places within a ten mile radius especially from the west and east of Brindle. There were even 79 references in the Brindle register to Preston on the other side of the River Ribble. Many Samlesbury people were also part of the Brindle congregation, even though there was an equally vigorous mission there run by the Jesuits at the Lower Hall.[82]

The people of the Jesuit mission at Samlesbury conversely included some from Brindle. Where there were several contiguous missions Catholics had a choice of congregations, and the Catholic registers show that their adherence was not determined solely by their place of abode. Catholic registers show similar overlapping of missions in the Fylde, in Northumberland, in the Severn valley and south Staffordshire.[83]

In **Hindley**, a rural/industrial parish south-east of Wigan, there were 108 papists, 75 of whom were immigrants. The average age on arrival of 50 males was nineteen, much younger than in Wigan or Preston. In such parishes the probability is that young men moved first into the industrial villages and then later into the towns, where there were opportunities for more remunerative work as they became established in their trades. By 1778 there were in all 182 houses in Hindley, so that Catholics comprised about one fifth of the inhabitants. Hindley lay on the coalfield but the most notable trade among Catholics was cotton spinning carried on by thirty-one women, while the men wove cotton, linen and fustian. The Benedictines had long been established in the chapelry of Hindley, and also served Standish and Charnock Richard; the latter was ten miles distant. In 1778 it was said that Catholics assembled for worship at Strangeways, Manchester.[84]

The industrial towns and parishes considered so far all had a background of Catholic gentry families in earlier times and in many cases there were associations with local martyrs and cults. **Manchester** was different in history, organisation and commercial importance. The town had been prominent in supporting

Protestantism, and the Collegiate Church, the Grammar School, and from 1653 the Chetham Library and School, provided employment and opportunities for outstanding Church of England preachers and ministers, and many No-Popery sermons were preached in the collegiate church. The Court Leet ruled the town effectively and vigorously, but exercised no power in the Foreign. The main business of the town had long been the manufacture and distribution of linens, fustians and all kinds of small wares. It had overtaken Norwich to become the third largest town in the provinces, and by 1770 its population was approaching 30,000. This included 287 Catholics, a small number compared with Liverpool, Preston or Wigan, but a substantial congregation nevertheless and as large as the largest rural congregations. No resident priest was specified in the return, but the entry for Macclesfield mentions that 'the priest Mr Hulme resides chiefly at Manchester' and in the Manchester return an entry added at the end in another hand reads 'Edward Hulme, aged 45, gentleman, resident for 15 years'. This is presumably Edward Hulme of Helme, a secular priest, who was born in 1725 and ordained in 1748.

Manchester Catholics included J. Scarisbrook esq., and his household, three other gentlewomen and the wife of the Duke of Norfolk's steward, but otherwise the congregation was composed of tradesmen, labourers and servants. Many of the Catholics were involved in the textile trades, not only as weavers and spinners, but also as quilters, cloth-workers, wool-combers and there was a tape-weaver, a winder of yarn, and a flax-dresser. Small metalwares were also represented by a pin-maker, a watchmaker and two whitesmiths. The commercial development of the town is indicated at different social levels by a merchant, Michael Walton, Mr Langdale, a merchant's rider, and John Hesketh, a servant in a warehouse. The majority of the congregation were young, 200 being between the ages of 14 and 40. Most were immigrants, but there were five heads of households and seven individuals who were natives. Here was a congregation growing almost entirely from the aggregration of persons following their economic interests, but carrying their Catholicism with them into a new place of residence and a new society.[85]

Silk-working is traditionally associated with the Huguenots in London but in the late seventeenth century there was a great expansion of the provincial trade, mainly around Coventry, Macclesfield, Stockport and Leek. Catholics were not especially prominent in the trade but they were not excluded from it, nor from the manufacture of tape and ribbons, which also contributed to the growth of **Coventry**. By 1767 there was a

Catholic mission in that city, a remarkable development, for not only were there no Catholic gentry in the area, but the city had a strong tradition of active Protestantism stretching back to link with the mediaeval Lollards. Even so, there were by 1767 86 Catholics, forty-three of whom were under 21 years of age, and a priest. The Catholics included four silk-weavers, a silk-winder and a silk-man. Coventry's population began to grow rapidly from the 1710s, and although Catholics were a small group among a total population which reached over 14,000 by 1775, they were sufficient to sustain a mission.[86]

Catholic Congregations in Metalworking Districts

Catholic congregations were also developing rapidly in the metalworking districts, as for example in Wolverhampton, Birmingham and Sheffield. Metalworking during this period became a major commercial contribution to England's wealth. There was a great increase in the production of iron, copper, zinc and lead at sites determined by those of the raw materials, fuel and water-power, which were often in otherwise rural areas. Iron forges were mainly concentrated in Furness, the Pennines, north Wales, the Welsh Marches and the Forest of Dean, the Midlands and to a less extent in the Weald. Catholics were to be found among those employed by the family partnerships, who controlled these works, including some who were highly skilled and commanded high remuneration, but they do not stand out in the Catholic congregations since they worked in isolated places, and moved not infrequently to works in different parts of the country.

The manufacture of metals into goods for world-wide export and a growing domestic consumption was comparable in diffusion and organisation to the textile industry and was carried on in small workshops and marketed by commercial partnerships. Metalworking had long been an important part of the parish economy in parishes in south-west Lancashire, Sheffield and Hallamshire, Rotherham and Barnsley, and in north-east Durham, in the hinterland of Newcastle-upon-Tyne and in the West Midlands. In all these areas there were concentrations of Catholics and missions.[87]

The metalworking town of **Wolverhampton** had a Catholic tradition traceable from the Reformation, but was a thoroughly urbanised and industrialised Catholic community in 1767. The Wolverhampton congregation consisted of 496 persons in a town of about 10,500 inhabitants. The Catholics included 64 heads of families in the older part of town, but of these 16 had been there less than ten years and only twenty had been born in the parish.

Twenty heads of household had settled in the town before the age of 20, perhaps as apprentices. In the new housing development around St Johns' Chapel almost all the inhabitants had come in the previous 6 years. Of all the Catholic families, there were only three cases in which both husband and wife had been born in Wolverhampton. Groups of Catholics in Sedgley, Bilston and Bloxwich had been served by the Wolverhampton 'outpriest' since about 1700, but were soon to have their own settled priest.

The public Masshouse in Goat Street (North Street) was 'openly resorted to', so much so that an errant apprentice could run in off the street during Mass to see what was going on. It was built between 1723 and 1733 on the site of an earlier house used regularly for Mass from at least 1690 at a total cost of £1069.2s.2d. Mrs Elizabeth Giffard who had lived there as 'housekeeper' gave the house to the Midland District. She was a niece of Bishop Bonaventure Giffard, who, although by 1723 Bishop in London, played a large part in the building project and the money came mainly from him and from the clergy. The subcontractors for the priest's house included Edward Collins, lockmaker, and Thomas Marson, innkeeper, both prominent Wolverhampton Catholics.[88] It was a dignified and stylish town house with a fine staircase and quality furnishings, and the chapel was in the rear of the house on the ground floor and directly accessible from the front door. The house was inhabited by two priests and a housekeeper. It was very similar to another house nearby built about the same time for the wealthy merchant Benjamin Molineux, who had made his wealth in the West Indies and who now spent it on a large house and a superb garden. These two houses, so alike in appearance, yet inhabited by such different residents, were probably designed by the same architect and symbolise the way in which Catholics could be both part of their local society and at the same time separate from it.

Birmingham reported 222 Catholics, a small group in a town which had grown to 30,000 inhabitants, almost all urban dwellers. Industrialisation brought together a substantial numbers of Catholics, and the mission owed much to the active missionary work of the Franciscans. In the town there were two Church of England churches, three Church of England chapels, seven Dissenters' chapels and a Jewish synagogue in a private house, but there was no Catholic priest. Birmingham Catholics were by 1767 the main core of the Franciscan mission, located in Pritchatt's Lane, Edgbaston, only two miles from Birmingham.[89]

It was said that there were only two Catholics in **Sheffield** in 1713, despite the influence of the Duke of Norfolk in the town, but a Visitation return of 1735 named 46 Catholics, of whom

Figure 20: Eighteenth-Century Masshouses

By the second half of the eighteenth century Mass was said on a regular basis in houses of the lesser gentry, town houses and in a number of purpose-built houses which provided a chapel and a house for a priest.

Lane End House, Mawdesley, near Ormskirk, Lancashire

The home of the Finch family, it was built in the sixteenth century and used for Catholic worship until 1831. The large chapel was at the top of the house. After 1715 it was the only Catholic chapel in the area.

Drawing based on an illustration in F.O. Blundell, *Old Catholic Lancashire*, vol.3 (1941).

Giffard House, North Street, Wolverhampton

Built between 1723 and 1730 as a public chapel and priests' house. It was built on the site of an earlier Mass centre in the house of Mrs Elizabeth Giffard. The cost of building was met by subscription mainly from Bishop Bonaventure Giffard and the Midland clergy funds. The chapel was at the back of the house on the ground floor.

Drawing based on photographs in the possession of M.B. Rowlands.

Alnwick chapel, Bondgate Without

This was next door to the Plough Inn, and was the home of the Cotes family. Mass was said here in the early part of the eighteenth century.

Drawing based on an illustration in A. Chadwick, *St Mary's Church: a Centenary History* (1936).

Brackenlea, Lancashire

The home of the priest and Mass centre.

Drawing from a nineteenth-century photograph supplied by Mr & Mrs Ackers of Thimble Hall, Scorton, Lancashire.

Figure 21: Places where Mass was said in Sedgley, Staffordshire

In 1651 in this house in Woodsetton, Sedgley, relics of St. Chad were found in the upper part of the bed of the dying Henry Hodgetts. They had been given into his care by two ladies named Dudley, who had received them from a priest of the same name. He had removed them from Lichfield Cathedral in 1538.

This window was removed from St. George's chapel on its demolition. It still retains its coloured glass and is installed in one of the three cottages facing Himley church. Another window of the same design but with plain glass is in one of the outbuildings.

At the gable end of these three cottages is the site of St. George's chapel, built in 1789. It had dimensions of 31 ft. long, 21 feet wide and 11 ½ ft. high.

Mass had previously been said in houses in neighbouring villages. The site of the chapel is in the secluded hamlet of Sandyfields, about a mile from Sedgley village. The small group of cottages and farms of the hamlet together with Wood Farm, Brownswall Farm, and Cotwall End Farm which were linked by a footpath, were almost all occupied by a flourishing Catholic community of farmers and farm-workers. St. George's was demolished in 1819 and replaced by a larger church, built on the main road in Sedgley in 1823.

eight families worked in the toy and cutlery trades, and there were also some husbandmen and a labourer. Four were directly employed by the Duke in various capacities and the annual rent collection day, to which the Duke came in person, was made a great day with not only a feast but Mass for the tenants. They were joined on these occasions by Catholics from Rotherham and Prescot. There was a succession of Jesuit priests and Mass was said at the agent's house every Sunday. The Sheffield congregation in 1767 included an innkeeper, shoemakers and a breeches-maker, but was one of the most industrial in the country. Sheffield at this time had a population of over 12,000, so the 319 Catholics were a small group, but nonetheless were more numerous than the Dissenters and Quakers.[90]

The Coalfields and the Potteries

Catholics made a living in all the coalfields then worked, that is in Shropshire, Staffordshire, Warwickshire, Yorkshire, Lancashire and Durham. On the south bank of the River Tyne in 1767, Jarrow returned 40 Catholics and South Shields 29 out of a population of 28,000. Ryton parish returned 457 names, including wherrymen, staithemen, colliers and railwaymen. The neighbouring parish of Whickham was surprisingly free from Catholics, and only three were employed in the Crowley works at Swalwell.[91]

On the North Staffordshire coalfield there were Catholic coal-miners, metal-workers, and ironmakers, but by 1700 it was the pottery industry which was becoming the leading sector of the local economy with a national and international market. A group of about ten families of master potters had emerged, of which three were Catholics. The large parish of **Stoke-upon-Trent** covered about 12,500 acres of uplands and had a population of about 15,000. It contained 11 townships of which the chapelry of Burslem was the largest in population with about 3,000 persons in 1778. The leading families of the Catholic congregation were the Bagnalls, Bucknalls and the Warburtons and there were many links of marriage and business between them. These men, far from being ignorant peasants as characterised by their business rival Josiah Wedgwood, were men of wealth and sophistication. John Warburton, who appears in the return of 1767, was one of the most intellectual potters of his day. He travelled on the Continent in the course of his business, spoke French, Dutch and German, and at the time of his death was learning Italian. Like most of the master potters he associated with artists and scientists. His father, who had died in 1761, had been an innovator at his Hot Lane works, improving the manufacture of salt-glazed ware. Two of his daughters went to the York Bar Convent school. The Bagnalls, with potteries in Burslem, lived at Biddulph Lodge and at Rushton Grange as farmers.

This mission neatly illustrates the transformation of the leadership of the Catholic community from gentry to manufacturers. The old Catholic gentry family were the Biddulphs, but they had gone to live in Berkshire. In the 1750s, a secular priest, George Hardwick, occasionally said Mass at Chesterton Hall, three miles west of Burslem. An Irish priest, Thomas Flynn, was at Rushton Grange from 1760 to 1779. In 1780 or 1781, his successor, John Corne, built a chapel and house at Cobridge. Catholics here were few in comparison with Anglicans, Dissenters and Methodists. Nevertheless this became the mother church of many of the Catholic missions and chapels in north Staffordshire.[92]

The Nature of Catholic Congregations

The Catholic congregations of the large towns and industrial areas with their numbers and their predominance of working people were a far cry from the tiny groups of Catholics which still formed missions in the backwaters of Sussex and Herefordshire or from the congregations in and around towns. The Catholic chapel in such places was one of several non-Church of England places of worship: Dissenting, Methodist, Quaker and perhaps Jewish, and new Church of England chapels were being built by subscription. The parish church as such ceased to be a significant focus of religious unity; it was too small to hold the whole population, and large numbers of people had little contact with any church except for burial. Catholics lived among people of different faiths and no faith, as a matter of course and daily experience. They lived alongside and in a state of insecure truce with the Dissenting congregations, and maintained a conciliatory attitude to the Church of England and secular authorities. They were predominantly literate and independent, with their assets in goods rather than land. They were beginning to set up Catholic friendly societies to look after their needs. The new Catholic school at Sedgley Park, near Wolverhampton, expressly catered for the education of Catholic boys who would later earn their livings in business.

Such urban congregations were often dismissed by the Church of England clergy as 'poor', a word that covered a wider spectrum of people than it does today. Even so, Lesourd found only 2,414 persons male and female described as poor in the returns, that is 3.5% of the Catholics listed.[93] It is clear, however, that the Catholic Church in England was predominantly 'working class' well before the population explosion of the early nineteenth century or the Irish immigration of the 1840s.

Middle-Class Catholics

The number and influence of Catholic leaders in industry and commerce before 1780 was, however, surprisingly small. Aveling adduces the Catholic master potters of Burslem, Liverpool and Chelsea, a glassmaker at St Helen's, William Mawhood the draper and Langdale's gin distillery in London and the Gillows of Lancaster, cabinet-makers, all of whom were large-scale masters and influential Catholics.[94] However, these men were exceptions. Catholics did not build up national and international networks of commerce and credit based on the mutual trust and opportunities of being co-religionists which were characteristic of the Quaker Lloyds, Barclays, Darbys, Champions and Frys. Leeds, a town of rich merchants and over 12,000 inhabitants, had only a handful of Catholics and none of them were merchants. In wealthy thriving Liverpool there were perhaps only two or three Catholics who had become rich from commerce. In the Midlands the leading industrialists were members of the Church of England, Dissenters or Quakers. The only Catholic entrepreneurs were the Gibbons family of Sedgley, Staffordshire, who were innovators in coal and iron and subsequently in banking. Manchester, another great centre of industrial development, had some Catholics of many different trades but the Catholics were workers rather than masters.

Although the more prosperous members of the medical and legal professions merchants, bankers, some brewers and other employers of large numbers of workers could all aspire to be called gentlemen, they were also more properly a 'middle class'. As we have seen, this group is also under-represented in the return of Papists.[95] At Liverpool 34 were so described but this was the largest number outside London. Lesourd counted the professionals and persons of the related trades in 1767 as follows:

Apothecaries	29	Schoolmasters	37
Surgeons	31	Schoolmistresses	27
Physicians	15	Midwives	37

Source: Lesourd, Table 15, p. 121.

Although small in numbers, many of them contributed to the growth of Catholicism to a marked extent: some were the fathers of outstanding priests, some worked closely with the clergy in holding secret trusts and managing accounts, and some were active in chapel building. There were some school teachers, both men and women, but in some known cases they were not keeping schools for Catholics or for religious instruction, but general day schools attended by children of all denominations. For all but the youngest children, education in religion was, wherever possible, in the hands of priests and nuns. Boys were educated either abroad or in England at Sedgley Park, Staffordshire, and Edgbaston, Warwickshire, and girls abroad or at the convent schools at Hammersmith, Middlesex, and York. There was an increasing number of middle-class children in these schools.[96]

A noteworthy group among the middle class were the stewards of the great Catholic estates, who in a number of places both rural and urban were responsible for lodging the priests by the 1760s. Another important group who await further study are the Catholic conveyancers, mainly resident in London, who were skilled in drawing up documents which would protect the interests of Catholic clergy and Catholic laity, making property illegally held for religious purposes as secure as possible. They were called in to arbitrate between the competing claims of the clergy and of Protestant relatives, and to rescue investments from the often amateur supervision of the secret trustees of money left for what were regarded by the law as 'superstitious uses'. Some were the younger sons or cousins of Catholic gentry families and the fathers or brothers of prominent priests. Such Catholics were few in number, but a very necessary element in the organisation of a church which was still entangled in a net of legislation hindering its ownership and transmission of property.

The Mobility of Catholics

Lesourd estimated that 69% of the Catholics had lived less than ten years in the parish in which they were listed, and that nearly half of these had been there for five years or less. Less than one third had lived in the same parish for 20 years or more. He does not correlate length of residence with the age of the individual, and it would seem appropriate to consider only adults for this purpose.[97] When this is done, it emerges that the number of Catholics who lived in the parish in which they had been born was even smaller than his figures suggest. The few parishes with numerous native Catholics were located in the south as well as the north of England and include rural, urban and industrial parishes.

Only eleven parishes out of 101 returns for Worcestershire have any described as natives, and in the county of Norfolk only three parishes out of 57. In some places which did report native Catholics they were insignificant in numerical terms, as for example Shaw (Oldham, Lancashire), which contained only one Catholic individual, or Gislingham, Suffolk, one Catholic family of four. The parishes which did report more than ten adult Catholics of whom more than half were natives included both rural and industrialising parishes. We have already noticed the rural parishes of Egton and Hathersage with a high proportion of native Catholics. Other rural parishes with a high proportion included Solihull, Warwickshire, and the Lancashire parishes of Sefton and Ribchester. It is difficult to link the numbers of Catholics born in the parish consistently with any other factor. Lesourd suggested that industrialisation encouraged displacement and so loss of faith. However, this is not supported by detailed study. Samlesbury, Lancashire, had one of the largest native Catholic populations, many of them weavers and spinners. Similarly, there were larger numbers of native Catholics in the parishes of Ryton, Durham, especially in the township of Winlaton, and in Brancepeth and Tudhoe, Durham, and in Sedgley, Staffordshire, where out of 70 adults 42 were native. Parishes where a combination of agriculture and coalmining predominated could support an increasing population, and while they provided incentives for immigration there was less need for emigration. There was, therefore, a larger core of stable families, non-Catholic and Catholic. It is tempting to speculate that in such circumstances some Catholic families may also have been motivated by the availability of the sacraments to stay in the same place of residence.[98]

Persons described as having shorter periods of residence were not necessarily strangers, for family reconstitutions show family members living in neighbouring parishes and towns rather than concentrated in a single parish, and, as we have seen, Catholic congregations were drawn from several parishes.

The Catholic local population was stable in that traditional Catholic centres were maintained and Catholic family names do persist, but there has been too much emphasis on continuity. The presence of a ‘Catholic name’ in a return cannot be automatically linked with the same name in earlier lists. The marriage and remarriage of females was central to the transmission of beliefs and practices, but could also lead to a change of religion. In most villages there were a number of families bearing the same surname but not necessarily closely related to each other, and the number of Christian names in use was very limited. The surname of the landowner was often shared by many quite unrelated commoners in the same area. When families are reconstructed in depth, it is their mobility and their varying commitment to Catholicism over a lifetime which become evident.

CONCLUSION

The laws penalising Catholics had been drafted in a society in which tenurial relations and parochial administration provided the framework for order and social discipline. Their impact was much less on those who by 1767 formed the great majority of Catholics, people who had little or no landed property, who lived in parishes of tens of thousands, and who sought economic betterment by moving from place to place.

In the years after the first Relief Act (17&18 Geo. III. c. 49) the gap, which had been widening for many years, between the upper-class Catholics and the great majority, became even more apparent. The gentry and the aristocracy in their much depleted numbers expected to maintain leadership at the centre. The Court Catholics such as the Jerninghams and the gentlemen of the Catholic Committee, as described in the sympathetic narrative of Charles Butler, appear to be champions of lay leadership and of an enlightened, even ecumenical, outlook. This image was attractive to Victorian Whigs and later to twentieth-century Liberals. However, in the light of this study from the standpoint of the common people, the Cisalpines and their associates appear to be an eddy on the surface, irrelevant to the powerful undertow of Catholic life. Dr Gooch has written recently:

> Their willingness to surrender various ecclesiastical prerogatives and their attempts to elect successor Bishops were given challenges to episcopal jurisdiction. The rupture was the immediate cause of the uncoupling of the mission from the country houses of the gentry.[99]

The familiar and only too useful phrase the 'English Catholic Community' does not seem entirely appropriate for the Catholics we have been studying. Were they a community? The congregations were extremely varied in size, composition and experience, and there is no known evidence of association or co-operation between them as congregations. Was there a distinctive 'English Catholic' culture, which was, in some important way, different from the rest of the Catholic church? But Catholic registers produce no indications of national practices and, although there were particular cults of local martyrs, this was the case throughout the Church.

The stereotype of Catholics as a *gens lucifuga* is derived from the pious distortions of the nineteenth century and a folk memory of earlier times, and bears no relation to the real circumstances of Catholics on the eve of the Relief Acts. English Catholics, and more particularly English priests, were in touch with Catholic issues, personalities and the devotions of their Continental contemporaries. Priests spent their formative years in colleges and monasteries abroad and saw life there as a model to be followed as far as possible in England. Some of the Jesuit priests had previously worked in the New World, and Catholic seamen and overseas traders had experience of the Church in foreign lands. The things which bound Catholics together were precisely those which they shared with the rest of the Catholic Church. The experience of persecution and exclusion provided English Catholics with a powerful collective myth and perhaps a certain rigour of practice but does not seem to have made them turn in upon themselves; rather they valued the links with the whole Church which they had maintained with such difficulty. In this, as in so much else, the attempt to derive academic categorisations and generalisations from the evidence has created artificial dichotomies. In reality, there was both tradition *and* change, prejudice *and* toleration, separation *and* integration, danger *and* security, and individuals managed these contradictions as best they could, responding to changing pressures in different ways from day to day.

NOTES

1 Lesourd, pp 116-120.

2 Aveling, *Handle,* pp. 253 - 283. In the North Riding 28 Catholic gentry families ceased to be influential and in the East Riding a further 22 families: Bossy, *Catholics*, pp. 324- 6.

3 B.A.A., A256a, A258.

4 Worrall, 2. pp. 125, 153; P.J. Doyle, 'The Catholic Land Agent', *London Recusant* 1, no. 1 (1974), pp. 38-41.

5 Worrall, 2 p. 122.

6 Farm St, Sixhills file 4/4/3.

7 Geoffrey Holt. 'An Eighteenth-Century chaplain: John Champion at Sawston Hall' *Recusant History* 17, no. 2 (October 1984), pp. 181-8.

8 Joy Rowe 'The 1767 return of papists in the Diocese of Norwich: the social compostion of the Roman Catholic Community' in David Chadd ed., *Religous Dissent in East Anglia 3* (1980), pp.202-234.

9 Kinoulty, p. 44.

10 Timothy Hadland, *Thames Valley papists: from Reformation to Emancipation* (privately published, 1992), p. 114.

11 M.B. Rowlands, *Catholics in Staffordshire: from the Revolution to the Relief Act* (M.A. University of Birmingham, 1965), pp. 170-7.

12 Bossy, *Rural*, p. 66.

13 Kinoulty, pp. 45-9; Ches. R.O. ED/V/1 Visitation Return.

14 Worrall, p. 124.

15 The problem of whether servants could be allowed by the priest to attend their masters to church was raised from time to time by the clergy., e.g. Ushaw, Old Series MS XVIII, D.621.

16 W. Price, 'Three Jesuits at Plowden Hall in Shropshire in the eighteenth century', *Recusant History* 10, (1969-70), p. 169.

17 Ches.R.O. Visitation Return 1778 ED/V/1; Rowe, 'The 1767 Census of Papists', p. 192.

18 Kinoulty, p. 50.

[19] Wiltshire estates studied by Dr C.F.R. Tiller; Rowlands, 'Catholics in Staffordshire';. Bossy, *Rural*, , p. 66-77. ; V.C.H. *Staffordshire* 6, pp. 84-6.

[20] John A.Hilton, *Catholic Lancashire* (1994) (with bibliography) *N..W.C.H.* (1971-1997), passim.

[21] Chester R.O. EDV/10; H.Fishwick, *The History of the parish of Kirkham in the county of Lancashire* (Chetham Society, Old Series, 1884); V.C.H *Lancashire*, 7, p. 143-233. 174-6; F.J.Singleton 'Recusancy in the Fylde' *N.W.C.H.* 13 (1976), pp. 31-35.

[22] Worrall 2, pp. 111-24.

[23] In 1702 the parish Registers of Kirkham had recorded Catholics from Bryning, Clifton, Mowbreck, Plumpton, Ribby, Salwick, Singleton, Warton, Westby and Weston (ex inf. Mrs C. Coleman).

[24] V.C.H., *Lancashire* 7, pp. 245-51; J.P. Smith ed., 'The Catholic Register of Westby Hall' (C.R.S. 15, 1913), pp. 1-8.

[25] Holt, *Biog.*, pp. 73, 147, 262.

[26] Worrall 1, 118-22; F. R. Raines, *Notitia Cestriensis* 2 part 3 (1850), p. 420.

[27] Worrall 1, pp. 118-22; Lancashire Record Office Quarter Sessions 1678/79 QSV/V/1.

[28] V.C.H. *Lancashire* 7, pp. 219-42; Worrall 1, pp. 36-7; J. O'Reilly, 'Lytham 1753-1803' & J. Gillow, 'Introduction to the register of Poulton', *Lancashire Registers 2* (C.R.S., 16, 1914), pp. 562-606; J. Fishwick, *History of Poulton-le-Fylde* (Chetham Society New Series 8, 1885), p. 456

[29] Worrall 1, p. 104; Raines, *Notitia* 2 part 3, p. 398; V.C.H. *Lancashire* 7, pp. 242-51.

[30] Worrall, pp. 130-3; 'Lancashire Registers 2 The Fylde', pp. 421-514; V.C.H. *Lancashire* 7, pp. 213-9.

[31] Bossy, *Northumbria;* Bossy, *Rural.*

[32] Lancashire Record Office, Lonsdale Comperta books, Claughton township memoranda book 1701-1804 2895/418 RS 80 & 83; *Marriage Bonds of Lancashire* (Parish Register Society, 40), Melling. Analysis of these documents and 1767 returns was carried out by Mr D. Noble.

[33] St. R.O. DD 2670/ME/429/119.

[34] A.P. Jenkins ed., *Correspondence of Thomas Secker* (Oxfordshire Record Society 57, 1991), pp. 97-8.

[35] L.J.R.O. B/V5/1751; B/V5/1771; Worrall 2, pp. 92-4.

[36] Worrall 2, pp. 92-4.

[37] Statham, p. 124. Statham, who grew up in the area, believed the ruined chapel to be the one built in the reign of James II.

[38] B.A.A. C 382y; L.J.R.O. B/V5/1751; B/V/5/ 1771; Der. R.O., Churchwardens' accounts, Hathersage microfilm XM1/42; Constables accounts microfilm XM1/43; L.J.R.O. Probate B/C/11; Hathersage parish registers; Return of Papists 1705; Return of papists, 1767, K56.

[39] Aveling, *North*, p. 391; Worrall 2, p. 58. I am grateful to Dr. Sheils for permission to use the information on which this section is based ahead of its publication in a forthcoming article.

[40] Penelope Corfield, *The impact of English Towns 1700 - 1800 (1982)*, p. 68. Corfield gives the urban population (in towns of more than 2,500) as 18.7% in 1700, 22.6% in 1750, and over 30% in 1801.

[41] E.A. Wrigley, 'A Simple Model of London's Importance in Changing English Society and Economy 1650-1750', *Past and Present* 37 (1967), pp. 44-70.

[42] Corfield, *The impact of English Towns 1700 - 1800*, p. 7; E.A. Wrigley, *People Cities and Wealth* (1987), pp. 159-170; D.J. Johnson, *Southwark and the City* (1969); R. Finlay, *London: the Making of the Metropolis* (1986).

[43] Cecil Roth, *The Jews in London* (1937) pp. 2 - 25.

[44] Worrall, 2 p. 132-141 - analysis by Mrs Pat Andrews; Lesourd, pp. 173-179; Julia Bellord, *Some Notes on the original returns of Papists in the Diocese of London and of St George's Southwark in the Diocese of Winchester* (forthcoming); original

returns in Lambeth Palace Library, transcribed by Miss Julia Bellord: a name index, in addition to a copy of the transcription, has been deposited in the Lambeth Palace Library and in W.A.A.; Bossy, *Catholics*, pp. 310-2.

[45] John H. Whyte, 'The Vicars Apostolics' Returns of 1773', *Recusant History* 9, no. 4 (1967), pp. 205-14; Geoffrey Holt, 'A Note on Some Eighteenth-Century Statistics', *Recusant History* 10, no. 1 (January 1969), p. 3; Father Thaddeus [Hermans], *The Franciscans in England* (1898), pp. 2-3; J. Harting, *Catholic London Missions* (1950); T.G. Holt, 'The Embassy Chapels in Eighteenth Century London', *London Recusant* 2, no. 1 (January 1972), pp. 19-35; D. Newton, *Catholic London* (1951); E. Walsh, 'The Spanish Chapel in the Eighteenth Century', *London Recusant* 2, no. 2 (1972), pp. 77-85.

[46] Photocopy of the notebook of Richard Challoner made available by the kindness of Mr M. Gandy; General Register of the Secular Clergy, W.A.A. D.1.: in the period 1739-1770 11 priests record baptisms; the families registering baptisms come from 13 Church of England parishes.

[47] Aveling gives 642. John West, *Town Records* (1983), p. 330; Worrall 2, pp. 38-41; Aveling, *York*, pp. 108-59.

[48] West, *Town Records*, p. 330; H.O.L. Main Papers 1706 Return of Papists; C.R. Huddlestone, *Durham Recusants' estates 1717-1778* (Surtees Society 173, 1962); Worrall 2, pp. 17-9, 31-2; Geoffrey Holt, 'The Jesuits in the City of Durham 1700-1827', *N.C.H.*4 (1967), pp. 11-20; D. Shorney, *Protestant Nonconformity and Roman Catholics: Guide to Sources in the Public Record Office* (P.R.O. Reader's Guide 13, 1996).

[49] Worrall 2, p. 110; Geoffrey Holt, 'The Residence of St George: Jesuits in Warwickshire and Worcestershire in Penal Times', *Worcs. Rec.* 20 (December 1972), pp. 45-79; H.W.R.O. 2875(ii), original returns; F.A. Crisp, *The Catholic Registers of the City of Worcester* (privately printed, 1887); West, *Town Records*, p. 322; Lilian Lascelles, 'Dr. Thomas Attwood', *Worcs. Rec.* 7 (June 1966), pp. 5-13; V.C.H. *Worcestershire* 2, pp. 276; 4, pp. 394, 408-10.

[50] Worrall 2, pp. 154-5.

[51] Worrall 2, pp. 125-7; West, p. 322; *The Catholic Church in Norwich* (anonymous typescript, n.d., copy at Douai Abbey); Joy Rowe, 'The 1767 Census of Papists in the Diocese of Norwich' in David Chadd ed., *Religious Dissent in East Anglia* (1996), pp. 187-235.

[52] V.C.H. *Staffordshire* 6, p. 250; M. W. Greenslade, 'The 1767 Return of Staffordshire Papists', *Staffordshire C.H.* 17 (1977), pp. 4, 26-27; J. Gillow, *St Thomas Priory* (n.d. *c.* 1890), p. 96; Clark, *Population*, p. 135.

[53] W.A.A. OB4/116; Peter Phillips, 'A Catholic Community: Shrewsbury 1750-1850', *Recusant History* 20, no. 2 (October 1990), pp. 239-61.

[54] Worrall 1, pp. 124-30; Lancaster Record Office enrolled wills Q.DD; Freeman's Roll Lancaster 87 & 90; Anglican Registers Boyd's marriage index, p. 18; Lancs. marriage bonds RS 81, 87, 88 (1729-34); K. Docton, *Transcript of Lancaster Window Tax* (1958); *Lancashire Registers* 2; Bernard Foley, *Some Other People of the Penal Times* (Lancaster, 1991), p. 113. Bulk, Caton, Dolphinlea, Fulwood, Highfield, Myerscough, Quernmore, Scale Hall, Scorton and Thurnham were all old Mass centres in the parish of Lancaster, but outside the city. The research for this section was carried out by Mr D. Noble.

[55] Worrall 1, pp. 172-3; West, p. 320; Winifred Sturman, *Catholicism in Chester* (1975), pp. 22-5.

[56] Worrall 2, p. 1; Ann Forster, 'It Takes All Sorts', *N.C.H.* 9 (Spring 1979), pp. 97-9; Ushaw, W.V. Smith's extracts from the Eyre MSS.

[57] Worrall 2, p. 71; B. Bennett, *The Catholic Church in Lincoln* (privately printed, 1982), pp. 13-7; J. Kimberley, *The Return of Catholics to Leicester 1746-1946* (n.d., copy at Douai Abbey).

[58] Worrall 2, p. 87; West, p. 320; J. Kirk, 'The History of Catholic Missions in Staffordshire: Facsimile', *Staffordshire Catholic History* 14 (1974), p. 320; M. W. Greenslade, 'The 1767 Return of Staffordshire Papists', *Staffordshire Catholic*

History 17 (1977), p. 27; Clark, *Population*, pp. 133, 183; V.C.H. *Staffordshire* 14 (1990), pp. 155, 222-3; M. W. Greenslade, 'The Papists of Lichfield', in Philip Morgan ed., *Staffordshire Studies* (Keele, 1987), pp. 131-3.

[59] Worrall 2, p. 142; West, p. 312.

[60] Worrall 1, pp. 101, 105; 2, pp. 84-6; Chillington Registers : see Fig. 11, p. 279 above.

[61] Worrall 2, pp. 81-2; *Staffordshire Catholic History* 20 (1981), pp. 7, 17, 19.

[62] Worrall 2, pp. 64-5; Clark, *Population*, p. 115. Analysis by Mr M. Price.

[63] Worrall 2, p. 146; Clark, *Population*, p. 155; 'Catholic Mission Registers of Cowdray House 1874-1822', (C.R.S. 1, 1904), pp. 269-320.

[64] Worrall 2, pp. 97-8; L.J.R.O. K56. Henry (Thomas) Dixon, O.F.M. (Bellenger, *Priests*, DIXO 05) was born *c.* 1729 and sent on the mission in 1756. See also R. Pemberton, *Solihull and its Church* (1905), p. 34; 'Historical Sketches of Oxfordshire and Warwickshire Missions', *Midland Catholic History* 2 (1992), p. 26.

[65] Worrall 2, pp. 67-8; *Miscellanea 13* (C.R.S. 26, 1926) - Catholic registers of Stonecroft, Hexham and Cockshaw, 1721-1821; Clark, *Population*, p. 113.

[66] Worrall 1, pp. 178; 2, pp. 9, 83, 104, 114, 162, 175, 260.

[67] W.J. Nicholson, 'Catholics in Morpeth in the Eighteenth Century', *N.C.H.* 8 (Autumn 1978), pp. 11-9; Joy Rowe, *Catholic Bury St Edmunds* (2nd ed., 1980).

[68] Worrall 1, pp. 9-22; *Liverpool Registers*: analysis of registers and return by C. Bennett.

[69] Worrall 2, pp. 10-3; W.V. Smith, 'Catholic Tyneside', *N.C.H.* 10 (1980), p. 15; J. Lenders ed., 'Catholic Registers of the Secular Mission in Newcastle-upon-Tyne, which became St Andrew's, from 1765', *Miscellanea* (C.R.S. 35, 1936) pp. 198-324; Surtees Society 50 (1867), pp. 175-6, 237-45.

[70] Worrall 2, pp. 168-9; J.S. Hansom ed., 'Catholic Registers of St Joseph's Chapel, Trenchard Street, Bristol, 1777-1808' (C.R.S. 3, 1906), pp. 181-330; B. Little, 'Catholic Bristol', *South West Catholic History* 5 (1987), pp. 45-7; R. Mortimer, *Early Bristol Quakerism: the Society of Friends in the City 1654-1700* (Historical Association, Bristol Branch, 1967).

[71] Worrall 2, p. 61,153-4, 178; J.W. Wardell, 'The Recusants of the Friarage, Yarm, Yorkshire', *Recusant History* 8, no. 3 (1965), pp. 158-66.

[72] Worrall 2, pp. 153-4; 'Register of Brockhampton (Havant) 1733-1855' (C.R.S. 44, 1949), p. 145; V.C.H. *Hampshire*, p. 174. Analysis by Dr. S. Watts.

[73] Worrall 2, pp. 172-3; J. Anthony Williams ed., *Post-Reformation Catholicism in Bath* 2 volumes (C.R.S. 65 & 66, 1975/6); West, p. 310.

[74] Worrall 2, pp. 180-1; P. Hook, 'Catholic Registers of Holywell, Flintshire, 1698-1829' (C.R.S. 3, 1906); H. Foley, 4 & 5; V.C.H. Hampshire 3, p. 174; Statham.

[75] Lesourd 1, p. 10; Bossy, *Catholics*, p. 198.

[76] Lesourd, Table 14, pp. 118, 123.

[77] Worrall 1, pp. 29-41: the figure includes some wives not included in the incumbent's count; M.E. Baynes, 'Recusancy in St Helens before 1649', *N.W.C.H.* (1971), pp. 1-28; V.C.H. *Lancashire* 3, p. 376; for population, see Visitation Return, Appendix 1.

[78] Worrall 2, p. 118; Robert Hole, 'Devonshire Catholics 1676-1688', *Southern History* 16 (1994), pp. 85-99.

[79] Worrall 1. pp. 71-4, 81-5, 93-101; 2, p. 175;J. Walton, 'Proto-industrialisation and the First Industrial Revolution: the Case of Lancashire' in P. Hudson ed., *Regions and Industries* (1989), pp. 41-69.

[80] Worrall 1, pp. 137-44; Leo Warren, *Through Twenty Preston Guilds* (privately printed, Wigan, 1991), pp. 18-9; V.C.H. *Lancashire* 6, p. 249.

[81] Worrall 1, pp. 54-65, 144-7; Ches. R.O. ED/A/4702/3; *Chetham Society* 18, pp. 16-8; V.C.H. *Lancashire* 6, p. 57. Analysis of return by Mr M. Fairclough.

[82] Worrall 1, pp. 71-4; 'Registers of Brindle 1721-1840', *Lancashire Registers 4* (C.R.S. 23, 1922), pp. 1-305; V.C.H. *Lancashire* 1, p. 75.

[83] Worrall 1, p. 95; E.J. Smith, 'Introduction to the Samlesbury Register 1732-1834', *Lancashire Registers 4,* pp. 306-81; V.C.H. *Lancashire* 6, p. 30.

[84] Worrall 1, pp. 62-3; John A. Hilton, 'A Catholic Congregation in the Age of the Revolution, St Benedict's, Hindley', *N.W.C. H.* 17 (1990), pp. 23-6.

[85] Worrall 1, pp. 88-91; Gastrel, *Notitia Cestriensis*; G.P. Connolly, *Catholics in Manchester and Salford 1770-1850* (Ph.D. University of Manchester, 1980), pp. 1-15; V.C.H. *Lancashire* 4, p. 175; R.E. Finnegan & G. Bradley, *Catholicism in Leeds* (Leeds Diocesan Archives, 1994); J.P. Earwaker, *The Court Leet Records of the Manor of Manchester* (1884); Bellenger, *Priests*, p. 70.

[86] Worrall 2, p. 96; L.J.R.O. K56; J. Martin, *The Rise in Population in Eighteenth Century Warwickshire* (Dugdale Society Occasional Papers 23, 1976), p. 12; West, p. 314; S. Pinches, *Catholics in Warwickshire in the Eighteenth Century* (unpublished paper, B.Ed., Warwick University, 1992).

[87] Leo Gooch, 'Papists and Profits: The Catholics of Durham and Industrial Development', *Durham County Local History Society Bulletin* 42 (1989), pp. 41-66; P. Hudson ed., *Regions and Industries* (1989), pp. 103-32.

[88] Worrall 2, pp. 89-90; B.A.A. A468; A652; A461; St. R.O. D590/634 account book of the building of the house and chapel, p. 35; Marie B. Rowlands, 'The Building of a Public Masshouse in Wolverhampton, 1723-34', *Staffs. C.H.* 1 (1961), pp. 23-31; Bossy, *Catholics*, pp. 300-2.

[89] William Hutton, *An History of Birmingham* (1783), p. 128; Judith F. Champ, 'The Franciscan Mission in Birmingham', *Recusant History* 21 (1992), pp. 40-50; Bossy, *Catholics*, p. 310.

[90] Worrall 2, pp. 48-9; Denis Evinson, *The Lord's House* (1991), p. 30; Statham; David Hey, *The Fiery Blades of Hallamshire* (Sheffield, 1991).' Toys' in this context are small metalware products for ornament and use.

[91] Worrall 1, pp. 22-5; Gateshead R.O. Cotesworth Mss BC/1/20; Michael Flinn, *Men of Iron* (1970).

[92] Worrall 2, p. 82; B.A.A. A468; A652; A468; Percy Adams, *Notes upon Some North Staffordshire Families* (privately printed, 1930).

[93] Lesourd, p. 123.

[94] Aveling, *Handle*, pp. 295-7.

[95] Lesourd, Table 15, part 3, p. 121; E.A. Wrigley, *People, Cities and Wealth*, pp. 161-3; Jonathan Barry & Christopher Brooks, *The Middling Sort of People: Culture, Society and Politics in England 1550-1800* (1994), p. 3; Worrall 1, pp. 35-64.

[96] Lesourd, pp. 125-6; W.V.C. Smith, 'Recusants in Northumberland and Durham 1650-1790', *N.C.H.* 23 (Spring 1986), pp. 15-26; M.D.R. Leys, *Catholics in England* (1961), pp. 183-5, 193-6.

[97] Lesourd, Table 3, p. 99.

[98] Worrall, passim.

[99] L. Gooch, *The Last Recusants of England: The Catholic Revival in England* (1991), p. 2; C. Butler, *Historical Memoirs of the English, Irish and Scottish Catholics since the Reformation,* 4 volumes (1819-1821); J.P. Chinnici, *The English Catholic Enlightenment* (Shepherdstown, U.S.A., 1980), pp. 43-75.

APPENDIX 1: THE VISITATION OF 1778: ANSWERS RELATING TO NUMBERS OF HOUSEHOLDS AND NUMBERS OF PAPISTS: LANCASHIRE

Parish	Chapelry	General	Papists
Ashton under Lyne	Moseley	600 families	1 family
Aughton		158 houses	94 papists
Bispham		140 houses	1 papist
Blackburn	Balderstone	85 houses	85 papists
Blackburn	Harewood	300 houses	6 families
Blackburn	Langho	109 houses	10 families
Blackburn	Salmesbury	222 houses	337 papists
Blackburn	Walton le Dale	343 families	158 families
Bolton	Blackrod	245 families	10 families
Bolton	Bradshaw		35 papists
Bolton le Sands		190 families	6 families
Brindle	Holme	150 houses	6 or 7 papists
Brindle		129 houses	280 papists
Childwall	Garston	96 houses	127 papists
Chipping		210 houses	230 papists
Claughton		20 families	16 papists
Cockerham	Shireshead	10 houses	1 family
Cockerham		312 houses	18 families
Croston	Becconsall	60 houses	6 papists
Croston	Chorley	300 houses	412 papists
Croston	Tarleton	141 houses	1 papist
Croston			677 papists
Dean	Farnworth	165 houses	1 papist
Dean	Heaton	88 families	4 papists
Dean	Over Heaton	93 houses	1 papist
Dean	West Houghton	450 houses	2 families
Dean		723 houses	6 papists
Eccles		1,654 houses	12 papists
Eccleston	Douglas	319 houses	347 papists
Eccleston		1,769	402 papists
Garstang	Wyresdale	159 houses	9 families
Garstang		750 families	200 families
Halsall	Maghall	70 houses	17 papists
Halsall	Melling	60 houses	41 papists
Halsall			80 papists
Halton	Aughton	27 houses	1 papist
Halton		70 houses	40 papists
Hoole		80/90 families	1 papist
Huyton		258 houses	14 families 59 persons
Kirkham	Goosnargh	326 families	116

Parish	Chapelry	General	Papists
Kirkham	Hambleton	60 houses	7 papists
Kirkham		1,610 families	276 families
Lancaster	Admarsh	40 houses	18
Lancaster	Caton	80 houses	6 families
Lancaster	Ellel	115 houses	12 families
Lancaster	Gressingham	41 houses	4 papists
Lancaster	Littledale	20 houses	3 families
Lancaster	Overton	90 families	4 families
Lancaster	Poulton Barr	64 houses	1 papist
Lancaster	Stalmine	185 houses	3 families
Leigh	Astley	156 houses	4 papists
Leigh	Atherton	544 houses	12 papists
Leigh		2,495 houses	100 papists
Leyland	Euxton	123 houses	402 papists
Leyland	Heapy	not given	some
Leyland			100 families
Liverpool	Toxteth	74 houses	1 family
Liverpool	Town	7,500 houses	700-800 papists
Lytham		187 families	423 papists
Manchester	Blakeley	406 houses	2
Manchester	Salford	866 houses	some
Manchester	Stretford	220 houses	12 papists
Manchester		6,950 houses	Many, principally poor Irish
Melling	Hornby	283 houses	83 papists
Melling		60 houses	41 papists
North Meols		36 houses	4 papists
Oldham	Ringley	260 houses	36
Oldham	Shaw	336 houses	1
Oldham		1,200 houses	10
Ormskirk	Bickerstaffe	120 houses	40 papists
Ormskirk	Burcough	144 houses	229 papists
Ormskirk	Lathom	200 houses	88 papists
Ormskirk	Scarisbrick	160 houses	800 papists
Ormskirk	Skelmersdale	60 houses	10 papists
Ormskirk		570 houses	188 papists
Penwortham		450 houses	few
Prescot	Eccleston	270 houses	402 papists
Prescot	Franworth	495 houses	59 families
Prescot	Rainford	159 houses	56 papists
Prescot	Sankey	115 houses	1 papist
Prescot	St. Helens	590 houses	800 papists
Prescot		1,060 houses	828 papists
Preston	Broughton	120 houses	381 papists
Preston	Grimsargh	29 houses	110 papists
Preston		1,000 houses	1,000 + papists
Prestwich		3,500	8 or 10 papists

Parish	Chapelry	General	Papists
Radcliffe			1 papist
Ribchester	Longridge	127 houses	197 papists
Ribchester		360 families	90 families
Sefton	Gt. Crosby	70 houses	207 papists
Sefton			many
St Michael on Wyre	Copp	100 houses	26 papists
St Michael on Wyre	Woolplumpton	341 houses	271 papists
St Michael on Wyre		450 families	52 families
Standich	Coppull	134 houses	41 papists
Tatham	Tatham Fell	81 houses	1 papist
Walton on the Hill	Croxteth		numerous
Walton on the Hill	Formby	228 houses	408 papists
Walton on the Hill	Kirkby	235 houses	18 families
Walton on the Hill	Simonswood		numerous
Walton on the Hill	West Derby	198 houses	100 papists
Walton on the Hill		235 houses	80 papists
Warrington	Burtonwood	80 houses	4 families
Warrington	Hollinfare	116 houses	6 families
Warrington	Poolton	73 families	23 papists
Warrington	Woolston	74 families	138 papists
Warrington		1,800 families	63 papists
Warton		60 houses	30-40 papists
Whalley	Altham	354 houses	16 families
Whalley	Burnley	850 families	some
Whalley	Churchkirk	310 families	10 families
Whalley	Clitheroe	290 families	7 papists
Whalley	Colne	?	7 papists
Whalley	Holme	150 houses	6 or 7 papists
Whalley		3/400 houses	few
Whalley	Whitewell	90 houses	85 papists
Wigan	Orrell	188 families	80 papists
Wigan			1,194
Winwick		1,228 houses	700 papists

Source: Chester Record Office EDV/7/1 MF448. Only parishes and chapelries reporting papists are included in this table.

Appendix 2: Sex Structures of West Sussex Mission Congregations in 1767

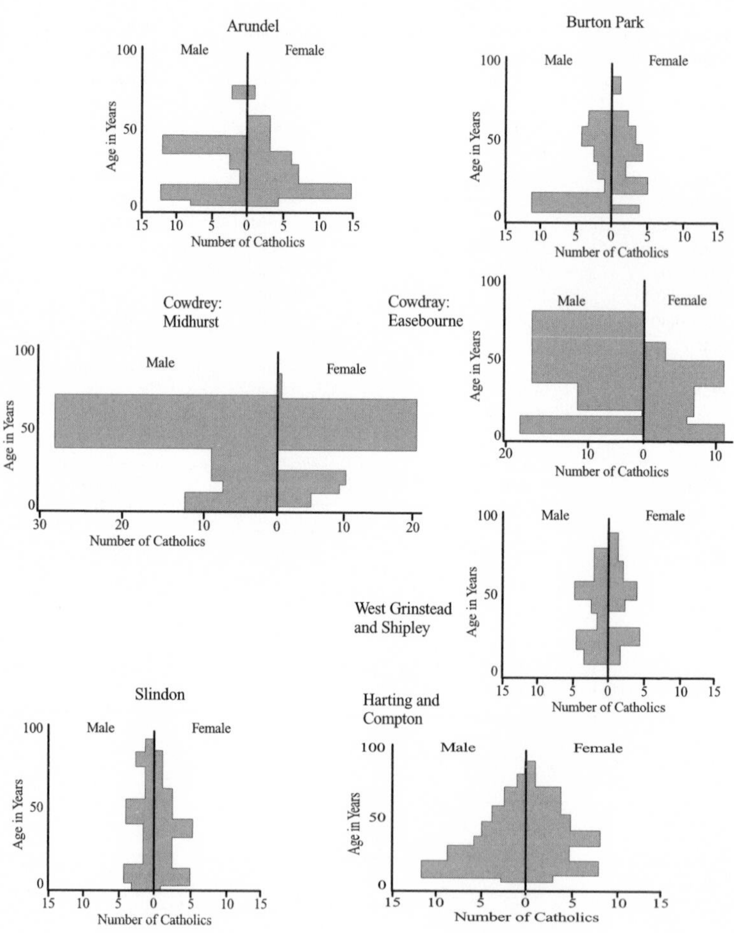

Index

INDEX

Compiled by M.W. Greenslade